T0329828

Foundations of Political Economy

Foundations of Political Economy

Some Early Tudor Views on
State and Society

NEAL WOOD

University of California Press

BERKELEY   LOS ANGELES   LONDON

University of California Press
Berkeley and Los Angeles, California

University of California Press
London, England

Library of Congress Cataloging-in-Publication Data

Wood, Neal.
    Foundations of political economy: some early Tudor views on state and society/Neal Wood.
        p.   cm.
    Includes bibliographical references and index.
    ISBN 0-520-08145-5
    1. Economics—Great Britain—History—To 1800.   2. Political science—Great Britain—History.   I. Title.
    HB81.W66   1994   93-5991
    338.942—dc20   CIP

Printed in the United States of America

The paper used in this publication meets the minimum requirements of ANSI/NISO Z39.48-1992 (R 1997) (*Permanence of Paper*). ∞

FOR ELLEN ONCE AGAIN

Contents

Preface

This book is an attempt to assess the social and political ideas of some generally less well-known and often underestimated English thinkers of the early sixteenth century in order to show how and why they were fashioning an economic conception of the state which became a foundation of later theorizing about politics and economics. This gradually emerging notion seems to have been in response to the beginnings of modern state formation in England and to mounting economic and social troubles. Today when postmodernism appears to have become the dominant intellectual vogue, my preoccupation with the importance of material conditions in shaping social and political ideas—a position spelled out in chapter 2—may strike some as idiosyncratic and others as decidedly old-fashioned, a relic of the Enlightenment project. Nevertheless, my labors—owing so much to the discerning scholarship of J. W. Allen, Arthur B. Ferguson, and Whitney R. D. Jones and to the stimulus of Robert Brenner's brilliant interpretation of early modern economic history—will not have been entirely misspent if they succeed in arousing interest in several neglected figures and shedding fresh light on their thought.

While working on this book I have published three related essays: "Cicero and the Political Thought of the Early English Renaissance," *Modern Language Quarterly* 51 (June 1990): 185–207; "Tabula Rasa, Social Environmentalism, and the 'English Paradigm,'" *Journal of the History of Ideas* 53 (1992): 647–668; "Foundations of Political Economy: The New Moral Philosophy of Sir Thomas Smith," in *Political Thought and the Tudor Commonwealth: Deep Structure, Discourse and Disguise,* ed. Paul A. Fideler and T. F. Mayer (London and New York: Routledge, 1992), chap. 6. The first was originally a paper given in October 1989 at a public symposium on Cicero and his influence organized at the University of Washington, Seattle, by Stephen Jaeger, whom I wish to thank for editing my paper for press and for his kind hospitality as well as the other participants and members of the audience for their useful remarks. The Smith piece and chapter 9 of this book differ in structure and to some extent in content, although there is inevitable duplication. I owe much to the enlightened editorship of Paul Fideler and Tom Mayer and to their inspiration of holding a conference of the contributors to the volume in May 1990 at the Folger Shakespeare Library, Washington, D.C. Our exchange of views energized my own thinking. I particularly want to thank Joe Slavin for his probing reflections and Tom Mayer for his rewarding efforts on Thomas Starkey and his thought-provoking treatment of Thomas More. Nor should I fail to mention Ted Winslow and the members of the political economy seminar of York University's department of economics, who gave me the first opportunity in March 1990 to air some of my views on Smith. I also appreciate the constructive criticism from members of the audience at my public lecture in December 1991, "The Antidemocratic Nature of More's *Utopia*," sponsored by York University.

Authors are always deeply grateful to the many individuals who make it possible for their books to be written and published but who are in no way responsible for their final form or substance. First and foremost is my enormous debt to Ellen Meiksins Wood, to whom this book is dedicated, for her steadfast support from start to finish, her critical reading of various drafts, and ever-helpful and incisive comments. Others who read one or another of various drafts and whose suggestions were of considerable value are David McNally, Cary J. Nederman, and the two anonymous readers of the University of California Press. Louis Lefeber gave me the benefit of his sage counsel on an early version of the Smith chapter. Joanne Boucher made me aware of some points about More that I would otherwise have missed. David Wood performed some of the many irksome research tasks in 1989–1990. Without the superb manuscript editing of Amanda Clark Frost of the University of California Press this book would be far more imperfect than it is. I am greatly obligated to York University for a sabbatical leave in 1987–1988, which enabled me to complete the research for the book and to write most of a rough draft, and for a Minor Research Grant and Professional Expense Allowance. Thanks are also extended to the cooperative and helpful staffs of York University Library, the Metropolitan Toronto Reference Library, and The London Library. Without the cheerfulness, patience, and skill of three typists, the book would never have gone to press: Mrs. Florence Knight of Toronto, Terry Jordan of Hampstead, London, and Marie-Anne Lee of Glendon College, Toronto. Finally, I am perpetually indebted to the undergraduate and graduate students with whom over many years I have discussed some of these ideas, often modifying them as a consequence.

1 Introduction

The Reformers

This study propounds a novel thesis involving a partial reconstruction of the prehistory of modern political economy. The English science of political economy, possibly to become Britain's outstanding contribution to social theory, did not suddenly spring from a void in the late seventeenth-century writings of Petty, Locke, and others. A decisive factor accounting for their pioneering reflections was obviously the vexing social and economic problems of the age. Besides the material situation, however, certain developments long before had yielded some fertile ideas and a style of thinking that may help explain the later mode of social discourse. Because the seventeenth century is generally accepted as the watershed of English history, the social and political thought of the previous period receives relatively little attention. But from the standpoint of the emergence of political economy, the early sixteenth century, *not* the seventeenth, probably marked the beginning of the great divide. The intellectual foundations of political economy, as I will argue, were laid in early Tudor times. For it was then that a number of reform-minded individuals from Fortescue to Thomas Smith, in response to grievous social and economic ills, began to fashion an economic conception of the state crucial for subsequent social and political speculation in England.

These publicists—Fortescue, Dudley, More, Starkey, Brinklow, Crowley, Latimer, Becon, Lever, Thomas Smith—were neither philosophers nor giants among the outstanding intellects of England.[1] Yet they were unusually talented and learned statesmen, literati, propagandists, and preachers, not to be neglected or lightly dismissed, who, aside from Fortescue and More, have received too little notice. To say that they were not social theorists in any systematic sense or political theorists, insofar as they showed little interest in the problem of obligation is perhaps to

1

overlook their true significance in the history of social and political thought. Apart from their temporal contiguity and common nationality, they were joined together by an acute dissatisfaction with the social and economic circumstances of their time and a genuine desire for moderate reform of their society through state action which led some of them to stretch and perhaps even break the bonds of traditionalism. If several of their ideas anticipated the future, nowhere is this clearer than in the conceptions of the state expressed by Thomas Starkey and Sir Thomas Smith.[2] The writings of them all, however, reveal in varying degrees a movement toward an economic conception of the state which reached fruition in the secular and utilitarian position of Smith. In a word, the reformers began to weld politics to economics in such a way that the state was eventually conceived primarily as a mechanism through which diverse economic interests could be promoted and protected and their conflicts reconciled, all for the material well-being and security of the individuals constituting society. Whether their efforts represented the first signs of a novel and all-important paradigmatic shift in social and political discourse may be open to question. What can be said with some degree of assurance, nonetheless, is that their way of thinking about the state, fusing politics and economics into a kind of primitive "political economy," foreshadows two related modes of theorizing which left an indelible stamp on the British world of ideas. One is to be found in the distinctive and influential science of political economy from Malynes and Petty to Adam Smith and Ricardo, the other in the major political theorists from Hobbes, Harrington, and Locke to the utilitarians. Both modes, linked by a common perception of the state, merged in the thought of John Stuart Mill. My focus, therefore, is on the notion of the state in the early Tudor reformers and the identification of the ideas that rendered that notion "economic."

The economic conception of the state is not our reformers' only claim to novelty. For at the core of their distinctive view of the state was a particular way of looking at the social context. These thinkers seem to have been among the first Europeans to engage extensively in the realistic empirical observation of social and economic conditions, to collect and record a wealth of factual information, often in statistical form (prices, wages, rents), and to offer causal analyses of the phenomena, a procedure reflecting a growing appreciation of social process and change. Seldom if ever before had there been such concentrated activity to catalog and assess the reality of everyday life. Seldom before in England had there been such an intellectual outpouring of concern about economic troubles, not to be duplicated again until the early decades of the next century in the controversy over the balance of trade featuring Malynes, Misselden, and Mun.[3] And seldom before was there such concerted and persistent expression of compassion for the suffering of the poor by so many able writers, mainly from the ranks of the privileged few. Their stance of moral protest and their call for reform also places them among the first of the moderns to conceive of legislation as a powerful, positive instrument for enlightened social change.

Two historical factors help to explain the reformers' unique style of thinking, especially their gradual shaping of an economic conception of the state. First was the Tudor effort, beginning with Henry VII and continuing throughout the century, to construct a modern state by unifying, centralizing, and bureaucratizing their regime. This was a lengthy and arduous process in which Henry VIII (and Thomas Cromwell) and Elizabeth were important actors. The other factor, operating within this slowly changing institutional structure, was the social and economic conditions brought about in part by the emergent capitalism of the time, visible largely in the form of capitalist agriculture (principally large-scale grazing operations), the rise of the rural woolen industry, and the development of a single metropolitan market centering on London. Indeed, the reformers might be called the pioneer observers, if unwitting ones, not only of the forging of a modern state but also of the social results of early capitalist enterprise.[4] Obviously the troubles so painstakingly assessed and passionately denounced cannot be attributed solely to the workings of infant capitalism. England was still a traditional society subject to all the difficulties of such entities. Nonetheless, some of what the reformers witnessed was produced by incipient capitalism.

The writings of the reformers were marked by probing analysis and critical protest and they often recommended state measures to remedy the economic and social defects so revealed. Sir John Fortescue (1395?–1479?), the distinguished interpreter of the English constitution and founder of comparative jurisprudence, is included here as a forerunner of the reformers and because of the influence on English thought and practice of his two classics: *De laudibus legum Anglie* and *The Governance of England*. The first was not printed until 1546 and the second not until 1714, but both circulated in manuscript well before publication. The reformers' discourse was in effect launched by Sir Edmund Dudley (1462–1510), who, languishing in the Tower just before his execution, wrote the remarkable little book, *The Tree of Commonwealth* (1510), not to be printed until 1859 although there were a number of early manuscript copies. More's Latin *Utopia* was first issued in 1516 in Louvain, eventually appearing in 1551 in the English translation of Ralphe Robynson, an old friend and employee of William Cecil's. The work of Thomas Starkey (ca. 1499–1538), *A Dialogue between Pole and Lupset*, completed in the early thirties, was probably unknown even in manuscript to his contemporaries and was not published until 1870. The literature of reform reached its climax in the period from the early forties to the early fifties with the output of the "Commonwealthmen," commencing with *The Complaint of Roderyck Mors* (1542) and *The Lamentacyon of a Christen against the Cytye of London* (1542) by Henry Brinklow (d. 1546). Then came the verse and prose of Robert Crowley (1518?–1588), a London printer before entering the church, and the sermons and writings of Hugh Latimer (ca. 1485–1555), bishop of Worcester (1535–1539), Thomas Becon (1512–1567), a protégé of Archbishop Cranmer, and Thomas Lever (1521–1577), master of St. John's College, Cambridge. Possibly the most significant intellectual achievement of these years was that of a writer sometimes associated with the Commonwealthmen, Sir Thomas Smith (1513–1577), classicist, Regius Professor of Civil Law in Cambridge, vice-chancellor, provost of Eton, member of parliament, civil servant, and diplomat. His authorship of *A Discourse of the Commonweal of This Realm of England* (1549), published anonymously in 1581, although previously attributed to John Hales, is now commonly accepted by scholars.[5] While Elizabeth's ambassador in Paris in the mid-sixties, Smith also composed a classic treatment of the constitution, *De republica Anglorum*, printed posthumously in 1583.

The reformers were far from being radicals or revolutionaries in any ordinary sense. Even More, with his daring vision of a communist society, was in many ways in *Utopia* a traditionalist, distrustful of democracy, and an advocate of order, patriarchy, hierarchy, and elitism.[6] In general, the reformers shared the ideal of social harmony and tranquillity, emphasizing such values even more than other European humanists. Solutions to the burgeoning social and economic problems were their aim, but within the established regime and status quo. From their perspective social order was and should be inegalitarian, dependent on a hierarchy of ranks and stations from the lowest to the highest, each with its differential duties and privileges. Every member of society of whatever rank should industriously pursue his vocation and strive in friendship and cooperation with fellow citizens to subordinate particular advantage to the promotion of the common interest. Private wealth must always give priority to common wealth. Aristotle's notion of distributive justice based on proportionate equality and the rejection of numerical equality with its democratic and leveling implications was the operative precept of most of the reformers. The crucial problem became the identification and analysis of the social and economic troubles threatening the unity and concord of the Tudor commonwealth and the prescription of the most effective means of resolution of conflict and restoration of the state's prosperity and strength. The preachers—Latimer, Becon, Lever—were more concerned with spiritual revival and moral regeneration than with proposing concrete social and economic policies, but the other critics appear to have been somewhat less anxious about the souls of their countrymen and more interested in how government could best respond to the grim social realities. The reformers were loyal supporters of the existing social structure and government under law by the crown in parliament. They welcomed the adoption of rational public policies to advance the solidarity and welfare of a truly harmonious community by eliminating poverty, idleness, and waste and by harnessing all human resources for dignified and purposeful self-fulfillment and the realization of England's immense potential. Foremost among their fears was the prospect that increasing delinquency, crime, popular unrest, and insurrection—which they related to the decline of the material well-being of the common people—threatened their cherished ideal of social and political harmony and, if allowed to continue because of lack of decisive action, would destroy the state itself.

The decline in the quality of life and the rise of divisive social conflict, observed and condemned by the reformers, commenced in a relatively short time after Fortescue glowingly reported on the rich fertility of rural England, a veritable Eden that could be productive with little labor.[7] He pointed with pride and satisfaction to the "plentiful crops of corn" and the salubrious lives of English husbandmen, who unlike subjected French peasants were neither overburdened nor exhausted by their work. The subsequent change in English prosperity is testified to by More's acrimony over the greed of landlords and in his memorable line about sheep devouring peasants, the human victims of enclosure by wealthy, land-hungry graziers.[8] Two decades later Starkey protested that it was no longer possible for people to live "accordyng to the dygnyte of the nature of man," although both he and his friend Richard Morison admitted that ordinary Englishmen were materially better off than their Continental counterparts.[9] The theme of the avarice and luxury of the rich minority contrasted with the penury and unemployment of the great majority reached a climax of stinging rebuke in the sermons of the Protestant divines in the reign of Edward VI. The youthful monarch himself expressed his consternation, writing at the age of thirteen that "as gentlemen and servingmen ought to be provided for, so ought not they neither have too much as they have in France, where the peasantry is of no value, neither

yet meddle in other occupations."[10] Enclosure, engrossment and peasant dispossession, depopulation of town and country, runaway price and
rent inflation, the lag in wages, dishonest business practices, the decay of
schools and universities, soaring crime and seditious outbreaks were all
grist for the reformers' mill. Their gloom, protest, and insistence on
change appeared to be amply justified by social conditions, even if they
were often inaccurately described or exaggerated. The Commonwealthmen, at least, seem to have yearned for a return to the good times of a
golden age in the past, possibly the first years of the reign of Henry VII.[11]

Before beginning a detailed consideration of the social and political
thought of the reformers two preliminary tasks remain. First, I will outline the nature of the conditions in which the reformers lived and worked,
highlighting characteristics that may have shaped their thinking. Second,
since my central argument is that their response to those conditions was
the construction of an economic conception of the state, I will assess the
meaning of that conception and its historical novelty.

2 Early Sixteenth-Century England

The ideas of social and political thinkers in every age both reflect and comment on the concrete activities and arrangements of the period. A cautious assessment of such ideas as reflection and commentary helps us to bring the world of practice into sharper focus. Of course, we must make allowance for the way a specific thinker's ideas, like all historical documents, provide access to the contemporary historical situation. The ideas may be less a mirror than a distortion of the circumstances to which they respond, encapsulating the writer's personal interests and prejudices. Reflection and commentary is also mediated by numerous received concepts that form an integral part of the unconscious mind-set of a thinker, an ideational screen through which he or she perceives segments of social and political reality. We must therefore examine past social and political thought in its historical context and consider the influence of inherited notions that may have been held selectively or possibly modified by the thinker. Rigorous analysis cannot afford to neglect either context: historical practice or mediating ideas.

The realm of practice is primary in a most significant way. This historical context furnishes a thinker with the unmediated stuff of his theorizing and with the range of problems and questions to be addressed, those arising out of the urgent practical exigencies affecting the daily activities of a people. The queries raised and solutions proposed by the thinker are in reaction to the serious troubles of individuals whose lives are substantially molded by the political, social, and economic framework within which they participate as actors. Fashioning the stuff of practice, endowing it with order and meaning, initially depends on the thinker's immediate life experience, not in any psychological sense but in a very matter-of-fact, down-to-earth way, for he or she participates from birth to death in an intricate web of human relationships. After all, a thinker is not a neutral observer, contrary to what may be claimed, but an actor on the historical scene. Response to the swirl of practical activity is in the first instance direct, unmediated, and elemental, even visceral. As witness and participant, a thinker knows and experiences, as the case may be, security, comfort, affluence, poverty, hunger, hardship, well-being, joy, fear, anxiety, anger, loneliness, hardship, and despair. All result from the material conditions of the real world. Wealth and luxury, penury and starvation are not mere mental states. The particular response of a thinker is conditioned by living and acting in the immediate historical arena, a specific location in social space with particular advantages and disadvantages. From this perspective Aristotle is not a Cleanthes, nor Montesquieu or Hume a Rousseau or Babeuf. Each reacts differently, depending on his mode of life. Such direct, unmediated experience begins to mold the thinker's view of the world, sensitizing him to a certain range of problems. Only then does this direct, unmediated experience commence to be partially refracted through the mediating prism of inherited concepts and notions.

The received ideational realm plays a secondary role by giving ultimate form to the unwrought perceptions derived from practice and to the final definition of perceived problems, helping to formulate the questions to be probed, their relationships and relative weight, and serving to justify and authorize a particular understanding of reality and the recommendations for refurbishing it. But I emphasize that the prime impetus of the thinker's creativity and the direction taken by his historical reflection and commentary derives not so much from the mediation of received ideas as from his experience in the world of practice. This historical experience generates, shapes, and guides the theorizing response.

It has become increasingly fashionable among historians of social and political thought to assign greater importance to the received ideational realm than to the given material sphere, often to the neglect of the latter. At the core of their argument is the precept that social and political reality is largely structured by our ideas; in this way they are apparently dismissing a realism that stresses the materialistic in favor of a methodology informed by philosophical idealism and grounded in linguistic reductionism.[1] Ideas are ideas, or so the reasoning seems to be, with an autonomy and purity not to be sullied by reference to material circumstances. How strange it is that in this way the cart should pull the horse, so to speak, since the very substance of social and political thought is the maintenance or modification of the material circumstances so summarily discarded.

What I offer here instead is not only the priority of the material world in terms of the direct experience of the thinker, partly mediated by received concepts, but also something of an interplay between the development of the ideas and the concrete historical context, between theory and practice, thought and action. Hence the complex task of the student of ideas is to penetrate and reveal this interaction and to explain the nature of the relationship. Above all, an examination of social and political ideas within the context of practice should not relegate the material factors to the status of mere background for the better illumination of ideas. The historical context should not be conceived simply as a finely wrought setting for the more effective display of the ideas. Rather, to change the metaphor, the world of social and political practice is the very foundation on which the edifice of those ideas about that practice should be erected.

We must therefore make the effort to establish the connection between the social and political thought of the reformers and what was happening in early Tudor England. Important as the mediating function of received ideas may be, much work has already been done in this area by historians, often with the result that insufficient attention has been paid to the world of practice.[2] In arguing then that the reformers were increasingly concerned with the state and contributed in varying degrees to its economic conceptualization, I will say more about how their thinking reflects and comments on the material circumstances in England than on their indebtedness to the treasury of received ideas. What developments in England might have energized their mode of thinking? What was there about the English state and social and economic conditions that perhaps accounted for the direction of their thought? How did their social and political ideas reflect and comment on the development of the English state and the emergence of capitalism in English society? Our enquiry must therefore start with a bird's-eye view of the Tudor state, the economic and social problems engendered at least in part by incipient capitalism, the civil unrest and conflict, and finally the cultural milieu and the received ideas that may have sensitized the reformers to the issues and helped fashion their responses.

The English State

Sixteenth-century England was a turbulent state, from "the fearful period of blood-soaked, arbitrary tyranny," Lawrence Stone's description of the thirties under Henry VIII, through the Marian counter-reformation, to the Elizabethan age and the defeat of the Armada.[3] It was a century of five monarchs beginning with Henry VII (1485–1509), who founded the Tudor dynasty with his victory on Bosworth field, thus ending the thirty years of intermittent feudal struggles and dynastic conflict between Yorkists and Lancastrians known as the Wars of the Roses. He was succeeded by Henry VIII (1509–1547), who in the rupture with Rome over the divorce of his queen, Catherine of Aragon, and his marriage to Anne Boleyn launched the English Reformation. While failing to institute a Renaissance despotism, Henry achieved royal power never since equaled in England. Then followed the young, humanistically educated Edward VI (1547–1553), whose efforts at social regeneration, because of his minority, were unsuccessfully conducted under the regencies of Somerset and Northumberland. Next came Mary (1553–1558), unswervingly committed to Catholicism in the ill-fated attempt to undo the Reformation; and finally, Elizabeth (1558–1603), determined to preserve and strengthen the religious legacy of her father and to consolidate her kingdom.

The sixteenth century was perhaps even more unruly and disorderly than its predecessor. An increasing crime rate, perennial local disorders, some major regional revolts, and severe economic difficulties plagued the state. Despite these pressing problems, the Tudor sovereigns by their political adroitness, artful maneuvering behind the scenes, and calculated use of both new and conventional instruments of government centralized and unified their kingdom and suppressed threats of civil disorder. Testimony to their political skill is their success in achieving their goals, contrary to Continental practice, without a standing army, a massive state bureaucracy, or exorbitant taxation, and their clever manipulation of parliament to secure approval of their measures. The most significant event of the century with far-reaching repercussions was, of course, Henry VIII's breach with the Catholic church. Through his "administrative genius," Thomas Cromwell, and the archbishop of Canterbury, Thomas Cranmer, Henry established and headed the independent Church of England, a foundation to be sustained and strengthened by Elizabeth.[4]

One of the most striking political features of this period in English history was the emergence of a modern state and the unprecedented rise in the power, wealth, and prestige of the crown.[5] Institutionalized rule of increasing centralization and unity and a single system of law and law enforcement were gradually but significantly replacing the personalized rule and administrative, institutional, and legal fragmentation so characteristic of the feudal state. The process of modern state formation in England was a long one and certainly not completed by the end of the Tudor dynasty. The immediate administrative consequence of the religious reformation started by Henry VIII and Cromwell was the elimination of the church as an independent locus of power and its subjection to control by the state. The dissolution of the monasteries, moreover, proved to be a fount of riches and patronage for the crown, further enabling it to integrate the kingdom.

Another course of governmental centralization was proceeding through-out the century. Henry VII personally directed affairs of state through the royal household, as medieval monarchs had done since time imme-morial. By dextrous management of a variety of dispersed feudal bodies, including a large council, he was able to tighten his grip on state business and win the cooperation of the great magnates of the realm. By Eliza-beth's reign, however, the royal household was no longer the hub of governmental power. The queen set the broad lines of policy but left the day-to-day implementation to her privy council, a relatively small circle of trusted officials which served as a collective executive board (in fre-quent consultation with parliament) whose activities were guided by the principal secretary of state with the assistance of a small bureaucracy. Within the competence of the privy council were important matters of state—finance, law enforcement, defense, local government, trade, social policy—that had been decentralized in the reigns of Henry VII and previ-ous feudal kings. Of course, this change did not begin with Elizabeth but with the administrative remodeling inaugurated by Thomas Cromwell. Through his efforts a fraction of officials from the royal council assumed the administrative duties previously performed by the king's household. This in essence is Geoffrey Elton's challenging thesis of the "Tudor rev-olution in government," the shift of rule from the royal household to management by a small council and the beginnings of bureaucratic ad-ministration. Cromwell, nevertheless, failed to completely centralize and rationalize the royal carapace of power and in fact tended to multiply financial and legal functions in separate units. His endeavors can there-fore best be understood as a transition between Henry VII's personalized household and fragmented rule and Elizabeth's more centralized and uni-fied direction by means of the privy council, which brought under its aegis the formerly dispersed administrative offices.

Hand in hand with bureaucratic innovation were other changes con-tributing to the centralization of power and the unification of English state and government. First, from the fifteenth century the legal profes-sion had been reforming the common law, particularly as regards proce-dures, rendering it a more effective instrument of state control which was only rarely at odds with the crown. Second, except in matters of taxation and requests for subsidies, Henry VIII and Elizabeth were both careful to forge close links with parliament. These Tudors took no major steps, in-cluding the break with Rome and the assertion of the religious supremacy of the crown, without parliamentary approval. Third, with the dissolution of the monasteries and the sale of their lands, Henry VIII had at his dis-posal a rich source of patronage that enabled him to cultivate the nobility and gentry and win their support and loyalty, hence that of parliament, a policy astutely promoted by Elizabeth. Fourth, in response to mounting economic troubles and related social dislocation, the idea developed that the state might assume a positive role in improving the lot of the populace, thereby enhancing the strength of the kingdom. To this end and inspired by the growing threats of civil disorder, parliament under Henry VIII and Elizabeth passed numerous statutes, often based on the work of royal commissions. Such legislation dealt with problems like enclosure and conditions of labor and the poor, thus sowing the seeds of the welfare state.

Several factors connected with these developments were crucial to the creation of a unitary state under the supreme authority of the crown. One was the system of local government assiduously strengthened and overseen from the center. Law enforcement in the provinces was largely in the hands of justices of the peace, members of the local gentry familiar with local conditions who were appointed for life by the crown. Their numbers were increased and their conduct was progressively subjected to the surveillance of the center. The power of the crown was also tightened by Elizabeth in 1585 over the lords lieutenant and their deputies in the provinces, who were responsible for military musters in times of national emergency and for arming and training subjects. The crown took care to ensure that lords lieutenant were reliable and dedicated officials, members of the council or prominent local dignitaries, and the monarch acted to standardize and regulate their activities.

Not least of the measures helping to consolidate the state were the administrative steps taken for the outlying reaches of the kingdom: Wales, the North, and Ireland. Although English management of these regions traditionally had been decentralized, the Tudors made concerted and partially successful attempts to impose greater unity and more efficient direction. By the acts of 1536 and 1543 Wales was united and placed under a revamped Commission in the Marches of Wales. English common law replaced Welsh law, the territory was subjected to parliamentary taxation, allocated parliamentary representation, and J.P.s were charged with law enforcement. Similar councils and arrangements were introduced in the area north of the River Trent in 1537 and also briefly by Cromwell in 1539–1540 in the Southwest to include Devon, Cornwall, Somerset, and Dorset. While at Elizabeth's death Ireland had been pacified, if not subjected, comparable councils in Connaught and Munster were established in 1569 and 1571. All these councils became administrative boards through which the privy council exercised its executive powers in the provinces. A certain degree of administrative autonomy still existed in the duchies of

Lancaster and Cornwall and in the palatinates of Durham, Chester, and Lancaster, but the common law was supreme under supervision from the center.

If by 1600 the Tudors had gone a long way toward constructing a centralized unitary polity with a single law and language, their own fortunes were inextricably bound to the state they were shaping. By century's end the monarchy was richer and enjoyed more power and prestige than ever before. Attending to foreign affairs, the Tudors increased the number of ships in the royal navy. Still minuscule in comparison with fleets of some foreign powers, the English navy now constituted a small but formidable and ably commanded force. With the help of privateers and bolstered by the construction of permanent dockyards, the building of coastal fortifications, the resuscitation of strategic garrisons, and the rise of a domestic arms industry it was capable of resisting and turning back the Spanish threat of invasion. There was still no standing army, but Elizabeth in 1558 was able to regularize the musters and institutionalize some military training under the lords lieutenant. In sum, English sea and land capabilities could not be discounted by potential predators. The Tudor sovereigns also had accumulated a bountiful treasury. Besides revenues from taxation and subsidies passed by a normally pliable parliament, the crown was the beneficiary of the sale of monastic lands, which served not only to fill the royal purse but also to be used through patronage to cement connections between court and country, crown and parliament. The difference between Elizabeth's income, for example, and that of her richest subjects substantially widened. The growing funds of the Tudors enabled them to disport themselves with brilliant spectacle—no doubt modest by foreign standards—dazzling the public. Never before had the status of the crown been higher. The pageantry at the seat of power attracted a faithful retinue of courtiers who further linked court to country, as did the pomp, color, and panoply of frequent royal progresses throughout the realm.

By the accession of James I to the throne in 1603, England was a political edifice of far greater cohesion, strength, and purposeful governmental control than when Henry VII gained the crown. The English had become much more aware of themselves as a single people with a single law and language and a unique culture. Through circumspect policies the Tudors had gone a long way in constructing a fledgling modern state, an institutional totality, to a marked degree unified under centralized governmental supervision, so different from the personalized rule of the feudal monarchs who preceded them.[6] The not infrequent application of the term *state* (in the institutional sense) to the English monarchy at the close of the sixteenth century—never so used at its beginning—symbolized what had actually happened. The conventional wisdom that social and political theory lags behind practice is possibly borne out by intimations of the centralization and unification of the state already appearing at an early phase of the process in the reformers' changing vocabulary and new conceptualization of the state.

Emergent Capitalism

Economic and social troubles posed serious problems for the emerging Tudor state during the first half of the sixteenth century, particularly in the agrarian, manufacturing, and commercial sectors. Contrary to the belief of the reformers and their contemporaries, population was increasing rather than declining and as a consequence threatening to outstrip subsistence, leading to inflation and wreaking havoc with the day-to-day lives of the English. Spiraling food prices and rents and the decline of real wages coupled with continuing enclosure and engrossment contributed to social dislocation and rural hardship, the small farmer in particular being replaced by larger landholders. The impoverishment and homelessness of many countrymen and their families spawned vagabondage and criminality, a matter of concern for the local authorities and upper classes. Whether these problems were ultimately a product of incipient capitalist agriculture or the greed of old-fashioned landholders is impossible to say. Nevertheless, the culpability of new agrarian capitalists (beginning to appear in areas like the South and East) for many of the rural woes should not be slighted. Unquestionably, rising capitalist agriculture aggravated an already perilous situation. But rural capitalism, whatever the extent of its responsibility for social dislocation, poverty, unemployment, and crime, was not solely confined to agriculture. The expansion of the textile industry into the countryside may have furnished succor for hard-pressed cottagers dispossessed of their living, but this development in turn deprived some towns of their age-old cloth manufacture, thus resulting in urban poverty and unemployment. These new productive efforts in the countryside generated a further manifestation of capitalism, the growth of a complex network of merchants and traders joined in a nationwide metropolitan market whose center was London, which was rapidly becoming the major entrepot for consumption and domestic and foreign distribution.

The population increase of Tudor England is today associated by historians with many of the social and economic woes of the century. About 6 million in 1300, in the next century and a half the total number of English people was reduced by plague and famine to approximately one-third of that figure. In the late fifteenth century this demographic drop began to taper off. By the time of the publication of *Utopia* in 1516, the population of the country as a whole seems to have been slowly on the upswing, an increase so gradual as to escape the notice of observant contemporaries. Between the twenties and early forties the annual rate of growth was very slow, the population perhaps increasing from about 2.3 to over 2.7 million people. Then, from the mid-forties to the late fifties, before the influenza epidemic of the last years of the latter decade, demographic expansion accelerated and the population reached over 3 million. By the end of the century the total was in the neighborhood of 4 million. So between the time of Fortescue and Shakespeare, the English population nearly doubled, although it remained still about one-third short of the medieval peak. The London of Dudley and More was probably about 60,000 souls; by 1600 the population of the city approached 200,000, having doubled in the previous quarter century. No other urban center in England rivaled London's population of 60,000 in 1500, the nearest being Norwich with around 12,000, York and Bristol with about 10,000 each, and Exeter and Salisbury with less than 8,000. London remained a metropolis of size, wealth, influence, and power unsurpassed in England.

The gradual but constant demographic increase in Tudor England appears initially to have outstripped agricultural capacity. A consequence was the gradual rise in prices from about the time of the publication of *Utopia*; the phenomenon began to be noticeable in the twenties, became worrisome in the thirties, and from about 1540 accelerated, continuing into the next century. Inflation, now described as the "price revolution," proved to be an economic problem of immense proportions. By 1540 the cost of food was 50 percent over what it had been in 1500, and in the following decade food prices rose by a further 200 percent, a rate of increase that quite understandably perturbed the Commonwealthmen and the government of Edward VI. The price of grain and the wholesale value of woolen cloth at least tripled from 1500 to 1550. Rents generally lagged behind inflated food and clothing prices, although some landlords were apparently doubling them in the early thirties; by 1550 many rents had increased a further one-third.

Population growth and limited land resources are today widely blamed for increasing rural poverty and dislocation in specific regions of Tudor England. Market pressures stiffened the competitive drive for available land. The effect of enclosure on small landholders has probably been exaggerated, but it was far from a negligible factor. Related developments such as engrossment, raising entry fines for customary tenants, many of whom had no rights of renewal, and rack-renting in general all helped to create a class of landless peasants, a rural proletariat. Its numbers, ever swelling for these reasons and natural demographic increase, are estimated by one historian to have been as high as 25 percent of the rural population in the thirties and rising throughout the century.[7] Much of the land in some locales was already enclosed before 1500, for example, in Kent, Essex, portions of Suffolk, and the Southeast. A new wave of enclosure, commencing in the second half of the fifteenth century and continuing throughout the sixteenth century, seems to have originated in the efforts of hard-pressed landlords—confronting the depopulation and decay of the countryside which since late medieval times had led to the fall in the number of rent-paying tenants—to profit from the rise in wool prices.

The most grievous rural depopulation had already occurred before 1500 and was slowly ending by 1520. By consolidating strips of land in an open-field system into a single holding (that is, by engrossment) and then enclosing it, converting arable into pasture, and by claiming common and waste land for his own and using it in the same way, the shrewd and enterprising farmer could raise vast herds of sheep to meet the increasing demand for wool and thereby remedy his deteriorating financial position. Successful large-scale graziers were often capitalists, employing wage labor, cutting costs, producing for the market, and investing profits in the expansion of their operations. The number of fledgling agrarian capitalists should not be overestimated, however, for some of the initiative in enclosure and engrossment came from traditional, hidebound landlords and farmers attempting to make a quick profit while the market price of wool remained high. Much of the enclosure for grazing, for instance, in the Southeast and East Anglia, took place in order to furnish a convenient supply of wool for the nearby villages to which the textile industry was relocating from many of the towns. The sale of monastery lands, confiscated between 1536 and 1540 and providing a lucrative income for Henry VIII, proved a windfall for some enclosing and engrossing farmers. Since the end of the previous century the new enclosures in the east Midlands especially, but also in Yorkshire, Lincolnshire, East Anglia, and the Home Counties, probably affected no more than 2 percent of the total acreage as compared to 25 percent in the age of the Stuarts. Nonetheless the effects were serious enough, because of the decline of tillage and social dislocation, for the government from the 1480s onward to try to curb enclosure and attendant abuses by a series of acts and proclamations. Beginning in 1517 and becoming common in the reigns of Edward and Elizabeth, royal commissions investigated all these agrarian problems. These actions probably did little more than deter some of the worst practices.

As time progressed, enterprising agrarian capitalists used enclosure and engrossment not solely for conversion to pasture for grazing but also to implement newly developed techniques in farming the arable, such as convertible ("up and down") husbandry and floating water meadows. Working a revolution in agriculture during the next two centuries, the new methods slowly increased crop production and profits of capitalist farmers. Enclosure and engrossment required more closely regulated field utilization than was possible by the antiquated open-field system or the small holding because of the need for manuring, the raising of nitrogenous legumes, crop rotation, and the periodic alternation of tillage and pasture. Not all enclosure therefore was intended to withdraw land from cultivation for grazing; some aimed to improve crop yields, but the distinction was rarely made by anxious contemporaries who not unnaturally viewed enclosure as a single, unmitigated evil disrupting traditional rural life, placing the premium on sheep over human beings.

Now we begin to understand the nature of rural social conditions so vehemently criticized by the reformers. There can be little doubt that enclosure, engrossment, rack-renting, and natural population increase during the century contributed to the eventual destruction of the English peasant and his customary way of life. The small husbandman could no longer survive on holdings of less than ten to fifteen acres once the open-field system began to disappear and he was increasingly deprived of use rights to common and waste lands. Nor in the long run did the sturdy self-sufficient farmer with twenty-five acres fare much better. Whereas in 1500 small farmers of this classic kind held about half of the land, the proportion gradually fell over the next century and a half to about one-third. The fundamental pattern of holdings changed to larger and fewer farms of sixty or a hundred acres or more, and by the late sixteenth century even the estates of gentleman landlords tended toward a mean between the vast acreage held by the nobility and the diminishing holdings of the traditional gentry struggling for survival in the agricultural revolution. Land, no longer the time-hallowed foundation of "merry England," was increasingly perceived and treated as a commodity to exploit for profit and to buy and sell in the market. The unique triadic structure typical of the social relations of capitalist agrarian production appeared in sections of the South and East: landlords living on rents, leaseholding capitalist tenant farmers subsisting on profits from selling commodities in the market, and agricultural laborers struggling on wages paid by tenant employers. Even by the end of the century, however, less than half of the total rural and urban work force was dependent on wages, and full-time laborers were for long to constitute a minority.

The number of peasants dispossessed of their means of livelihood by enclosure, engrossment, rack-renting, and outright eviction—a situation exacerbated by the slow but continual demographic growth—cannot be calculated on the basis of the scanty evidence. Abandoned farmhouses and deserted villages resulting from enclosures since the late fifteenth century indicated depopulation, although contemporary reports of the countless number of homeless, impoverished, and unemployed should be treated with caution. These dispossessed, however, clearly existed in sufficient numbers to be of grave concern to the propertied classes. The country as a whole during the century suffered a deterioration in real living standards, but the decline was probably under 50 percent. Impoverishment was becoming more severe, although not perhaps by Continental standards, and the number of people living below the poverty line was increasing. The gap between rich and poor ever widened, as did the regional discrepancy in wealth between Southeast and North. Well before mid-century there were clear signs of urban decay in towns like Coventry, Norwich, York, Lincoln, Stamford, Leicester, and Nottingham, where the textile industry was in decline. The lot of the "impotent poor"—the elderly, infirm, and orphaned who traditionally were expected to fend for themselves—was by the time of Edward relieved in a small way by the Poor Law of 1531 and private charity. Some of the dispossessed peasants remained as wage laborers in the countryside, eking out a bare living by spinning and weaving in their cottages. Many young farm people in the later fifteenth century had migrated to the forest regions but eventually they returned because of overcrowding to seek employment, along with some of their elders who had remained behind on the arable, in towns, in London, in particular. An erratic textile market in the forties and fifties only compounded the difficulties of those engaged in the rural manufacture of cloth, some of whom had originally left the towns of the thriving textile industry in the East Anglian and Southeastern countryside. Highways and roads were sometimes clogged with the unemployed, both voluntary and involuntary, "vagabonds," as they were labeled, roaming from village to village and country to town, occasionally begging in groups, a matter of some worry to the local, settled population. Amid these hardships, a select few in urban and rural areas lived sumptuously. Crime seemed to have increased, much of it, as might be surmised, in the nature of theft. The convicted were in the main not professionals but people driven to steal in order to survive. Civil litigation during the century increased tenfold, from 2,000 to 22,000 court cases, a very large number of them concerned with indebtedness. In sum, the human costs paid by the lower classes and some of the formerly privileged were certainly enormous, if not catastrophic, amply justifying the ire of the reformers.

Capitalism originated in the rise of the English rural textile industry as well as in the gradual transformation of agrarian practice. In medieval Europe England was the great underdeveloped supplier of raw materials for manufacture on the Continent. First tin and lead had been the chief commodities sent across the Channel, and then in the twelfth century raw wool became the leading export, reaching a peak in the mid-fourteenth century. Over the next hundred years woolen textiles in the form of unfinished "white cloth" replaced wool as the major export, trade in the latter declining and virtually disappearing. Textile manufacture for export and home use by the age of Fortescue was England's premier industry and continued to be so for two centuries, eclipsing shipbuilding, metallurgy, mining, and tanning. Skilled artisans in most English towns in the fifteenth century manufactured cloth. The industry of the small urban workshop, however, was being replaced by the capitalist organization of production in the countryside. From the fourteenth century the cloth industry had been gradually shifting from town to country—to Wiltshire, Somerset, Gloucestershire, East Anglia, Devon, and the West Riding of Yorkshire—so as to avoid urban guild restrictions and take advantage of cheap rural labor and abundant water power for the new fulling mills. In these long-enclosed counties, moreover, a bountiful supply of wool was either actually or potentially available, the relocation of the industry stimulating the expansion of local grazing. The new rural clothing industry was organized by entrepreneurs, capitalist clothiers who at first bought the raw wool from local producers—they later turned to other regions for their supplies—and contracted with villagers for its spinning and weaving, collecting and marketing the cloth for export to the Lowlands for finishing and dyeing or for sale at home. When, after the middle of the sixteenth century, agricultural improvement made possible the production of different kinds of wool, the London Staplers, who had enjoyed a monopoly on the export of raw wool, now responded to the shrinking foreign market by assuming the function of buying, sorting, and blending the commodity drawn from all parts of the country and selling it to the clothiers.

Fortescue never referred to the unrivaled place of textile manufacture but he did praise the great enclosed fields with their countless sheep, even mentioning the low labor costs of grazing as against tillage.[8] Before he died something like 60,000 bolts of cloth were produced annually for export, increasing nearly two and a half times by the reign of Edward, a figure that does not include the expanding home market, which probably accounted for a sizable percentage of the total output. In about the same time span cloth export from London tripled. The company of Merchant Adventurers monopolized and developed foreign textile trade through Antwerp, where Thomas More, an ambitious London lawyer on a mission to negotiate a trade treaty, wrote book 2 of *Utopia* in 1515. London's huge share (84 percent) of the total cloth exports by 1540 meant that the outports of Southampton, Bristol, Exeter, and Hull were being squeezed out of the trade and suffering as a result. Even more serious was the decline of once flourishing towns because of the shift of the textile industry to the country. Coventry is usually cited as an example of a borough so afflicted, but numerous other towns deteriorated, including Leicester, Nottingham, Lincoln, York, and Norwich. But not all towns were so badly hit. Shrewsbury and Worcester continued to be thriving textile centers known for the fine quality of their products. Nevertheless, critics like Starkey and Smith observed and decried growing urban pauperism, unemployment, depopulation, deserted buildings, and physical dilapidation.

English commercial capitalism appears to have been shaped by the nature of rural capitalist production, the dynamic, driving force behind mercantile and financial activity.[9] The whole complex process of trade relations, of buying and selling in the market, entailing the transfer of commodities of agriculture and rural manufacture to the consumer at home and abroad—wholesaling, transport, credit arrangements, banking, brokerage, and retailing—seems in no small part to have resulted from rural capitalist agriculture and textile manufacture. At the opening of the early modern period England was without the customary banking facilities—merchant banks, money exchanges, public banks—for so long commonplace on the Continent, although when necessary the services of London branches of foreign banking houses were available. By the mid-sixteenth century there had occurred without parallel elsewhere the beginning of a metropolitan marketing system centering on London which came to set prices and dominate local and regional markets.

London was rapidly becoming not only the major center of consumption but also the chief point of distribution for the nation as well as the emporium for foreign and domestic trade. The nucleus of an expanding national and international market, London received and distributed commodities for ultimate inland and overseas sales, owing its development to an important extent to the emergence of rural capitalist production—food, wool, and textiles—and in turn accelerating that production over the years and helping to create a countrywide division of labor. By 1642 the metropolitan market in textiles, foodstuffs (including corn and cheese), livestock, wool, ironware, coal, and land was well established, to which adequate transportation facilities, better than sometimes supposed, were indispensable. Provincial wholesaling merchants began to sell commodities on credit to London factors working on commission. A complex system of nationwide mutual credit arrangements soon evolved through written bills acknowledging debts and bills of exchange or orders to pay, the last a forerunner of the modern check. At the end of the sixteenth century some factors, merchants, scriveners, and goldsmiths specialized in banking, performing the services of receiving deposits, making loans, paying and charging interest, and transmitting periodic statements of account to their patrons. As early as 1650 goldsmith-bankers issued their own banknotes. These nationwide business, credit, and banking arrangements were generated by the developing early Tudor metropolitan market that in turn seems to have arisen in response to the stimulus of emergent rural capitalism.

England then, the first country to give birth to capitalism, was to take another three centuries to mature into a modern industrial society. By the mid-sixteenth century English capitalism appeared to be in a thriving condition. But fledgling capitalism seems to have provoked many of the problems confronting the English before the end of Edward VI's brief reign. More important from our standpoint was the reformers' resulting outrage because of the deep-cutting economic and social stresses and strains, whatever the precise nature of the sources. Critics called for reform and turned to the evolving state, slowly emerging as an institutionalized whole, more centralized, unified, and powerful than ever before, as a potential instrument of remedial change and renewal. And what could be more auspicious at such a time and place in world history than for the reformers in fashioning their conception of the state to lay the foundations of political economy.

Specter of Rebellion

Early Tudor writers, including our reformers, were haunted by the specter of sedition and popular rebellion. Often perceiving a relationship between economic decline and the threat and existence of crime and social conflict, they had reason for anxiety.[10] In the century since Jack Cade's Kentish force of discontented gentry and peasants captured London in May 1450, the realm had experienced numerous local rural and urban disturbances and several major uprisings. Despite the efforts of the early Tudor monarchs, their kingdom was far from peaceful. Some of the outbreaks were grave enough to arouse the fear in government and in the ruling classes that without preventive measures worse might follow. Economic griefs stemming from rural change no doubt aggravated much of the social turmoil. In some cases, however, these economic ills were not the only or even the chief causes of discontent. There seems to have been little correlation between bad harvest years and food scarcity and the most serious troubles. Religious and economic factors, moreover, were so intertwined as to render explanation of some of the disturbances exceedingly complex.

Rural protest in the fifteenth century often took the form of tenant rent strikes, whereas thoughout the Tudor age antienclosure riots took their place, becoming relatively common in the thirties and forties and afterward. These protests usually consisted of leveling the enclosing hedges and were often perpetrated by small groups of countrymen who opposed agrarian innovations introduced by outsiders and who were instigated by local gentry in their mutual quarrels and by municipalities wishing to maintain the rural status quo in their immediate vicinity. Violence against property rather than persons prevailed. Over half the riots in the time of the reformers probably took place in the east Midlands, the southern counties, and East Anglia. In 1548 and in the few following years the rioters, sympathizing with the great uprisings of the time, were more antiaristocratic than their predecessors. Local tax protests also erupted in 1515 in Yorkshire and in the mid-twenties in Suffolk. Disorder, however, was not limited to the countryside. London was relatively quiet throughout the period except for the Evil May Day rioting of 1517 in which Thomas More had a role in bolstering municipal authority. Elsewhere considerable industrial unrest in hard times broke out among the weavers in Coventry, Wisbech, Taunton, and other textile towns. Protestant preachers by their fiery sermons incited the populace in some places to take to the streets, as, for example, with Latimer's visit to Bristol.

More extensive and serious than this rural and urban turbulence were violent regional upheavals, beginning with the Yorkshire uprising of 1489 against royal officials over war taxation. Then followed the Cornish revolt of 1497 in opposition to taxation for the King's Scottish war. Commanded by Michael Joseph, a blacksmith from the Lizard, the rebels marched cross-country to present their complaints in London, where 10,000 were defeated by a royal force of 25,000 at Blackheath. The 1536 "Pilgrimage of Grace," a term for several related revolts of that year, began in early October in Lincolnshire with a march of some 10,000 on Lincoln, spreading to Yorkshire and adjacent countries and then to the Northwest. This uprising was called by one historian "the archetypal protest movement of the century," and another underscores its serious-ness: "The crown was scarcely in greater peril in 1588 or 1642."[11] Anx-ious over the threat and in a propagandistic effort to combat it, Cromwell persuaded Richard Morison to write *A Remedy for Sedition* (1536) and Starkey to pen *An Exhortion to Christian Unity* (1536). The conflict of 1536, originating in the lower orders but soon joined by some of the gen-try, was incited by the interference of royal officials in local affairs, partic-ularly in matters of religion. While objections to enclosure and high entry fines played a part, more significant in this first year of the inde-pendence of the Church of England were the closure of the monasteries, termination of holy days, and confiscation of the treasures of parish churches by governmental functionaries. The situation was further com-plicated by friction among members of the northern nobility and by the possibility of a Catholic invasion from the Continent with the new Cardinal Reginald Pole as a front man. At one time the rebels under Rob-ert Aske succeeded in mustering a well-disciplined army of 30,000 men. After renewed troubles in Yorkshire and the siege of Carlisle by a peasant force in February 1537, Henry VIII acted with bloody resolution. Aske and other rebel leaders were executed and by June peace was restored. Yorkshire was also the site of later conflict, a conspiracy of the clergy in 1541.

Cornwall, fifty years after the remarkable advance on London by "Black Michael," was once more torn by dissension in 1547. Commoners, including some gentry, demonstrated over intervention in local church matters. Riotous opposition turned into full-scale revolt between June and mid-August 1549 when an insurrectionary army of some 6,000 men advanced through Devon and threatened Plymouth and Exeter. Local government in the two counties was in disarray, but the Western rebel-lion was suppressed at the cost of some 4,000 rebel lives. While religious issues were paramount, a poll tax on sheep, assessments on textiles, and a food shortage were far from negligible elements in the confrontation.

The last of the really extensive and violent protests of the century, also in the summer of 1549, took place in East Anglia.[12] The leader was Rob-ert Kett, a substantial Norfolk farmer. The uprising, to become known as Kett's rebellion, spread from his county into Suffolk. The East Anglian insurrection differed from previous conflicts in that economic problems were predominant: enclosure, use-rights of the commons, and inflated prices and rents. Spearheaded by small farmers and leaseholders, who lacked support from the great landholders, the outbreak started with the destruction of enclosures in Kett's Norfolk village of Attleborough in June and culminated in August with the encampment of 16,000 rebels outside Norwich, while other contingents menaced Bury St. Edmund's and Ipswich. After the loss of 3,000 of his followers, Kett was captured and hanged.

The exceptional threat of the insurrections of 1549 can be better appreciated if we use figures given their late twentieth-century equivalent proportionate to the British population. Thus Kett's losses are as if 60,000 were slaughtered in present-day East Anglia, and the size of the Western rebel force would be over 100,000 combatants. To these two major revolts of 1549, moreover, must be added the violent antienclosure uprisings from May to July in Somerset, Wiltshire, Kent, Sussex, Essex, Cambridgeshire, Hertfordshire, Northamptonshire, Buckinghamshire, and Yorkshire. John Guy's assessment is that the troubles of 1549 "were the closest thing Tudor England saw to a class war."[13] To convince Kett's Norfolk rebels of their transgressions and the nature of their civil duty, the dedicated Lutheran humanist Sir John Cheke penned *The Hurt of Sedition* (1549). It is also not surprising, given the gravity of the situation, that Eton's provost, Sir Thomas Smith, on involuntary leave from governmental service, felt compelled in the late summer of the year to draft his penetrating analysis of the deteriorating national economy, which he linked to the widespread disorders. He was not alone in his anxiety over the portent of such popular conflagrations for the unity and strength of the realm or in his connection of the disturbances with declining social and economic conditions, as the public utterances of the Commonwealthmen, among others, bear witness. Whatever the shortcomings of the Tudors, by mid-century they had managed by sword and pen to hold their state together, but at dreadful human cost and suffering.

The Cultural Milieu

The social and political thought of the reformers was clearly not the response of tabulae rasae to contemporary change. They brought to their scrutiny of English society attitudes and ideas from a variety of intellectual sources. The English Reformation and English culture in general were enormously stimulated by the Renaissance, and close links developed between Lutheranism and the new learning.[14] These religious and secular changes in turn owed much to the invention of printing and the increasing educational level of the upper classes. The new learning deserves mention because after Thomas More, the pivotal figure of the early English Reniassance, most of our reformers were Lutherans with a humanistic outlook. Italian humanism began to penetrate the kingdom in the late fourteenth and early fifteenth centuries, reflected, for instance, in the scholarly inclinations and patronage of Henry V's brother, Humphrey, duke of Gloucester, and in the growing interest in the refinement of Latin usage and the imitation of classical models. Except for private instruction, however, the formal teaching of Greek was not available at Oxford or Cambridge until the end of the fifteenth century or later. During the period several visits by the renowned Desiderius Erasmus of Rotterdam contributed to the advancement of English humanism and inspired the London circle of William Grocyn, John Colet, William Lily, Thomas Linacre, and Thomas More. Colet founded St. Paul's School in 1509 to promote the new learning, and in 1517 Corpus Christi, Oxford, was the first college established for this express purpose. Erasmus was undoubtedly the stellar figure of the northern European Renaissance and his association with the English humanists proved to be of inestimable value in his own development. He composed his masterpiece, *The Praise of Folly* (1509), in More's London home at his host's urging. Erasmus spent his last three years in England, ending in 1519, at Queen's College, Cambridge, preparing his famous Greek text and Latin translation of the New Testament.

In the twenties Cambridge became a vigorous center of humanistic studies, and Lutheranism increasingly attracted pupils and teachers alike. Some humanists like More and Reginald Pole, to be archbishop of Canterbury under Mary, were repelled by Lutheranism, while others gravitated to it. The Lutheran precept that belief must rest on the Holy Word required accessibility of the Bible to all, necessitating both its translation into the vernacular and literacy of the laity. Among the chief intellectual factors drawing many humanists to Lutheranism were their passion for learning and education, their critical attitude toward conventional wisdom or received opinion, and their interest in the authenticity and reliable translations of literary texts. Both William Tyndale, whose English version of the New Testament appeared abroad in 1526, and Miles Coverdale, translator of the Bible into the vernacular in 1539, had been students in the exciting Cambridge environment of humanism and Lutheranism, as had Cranmer and Nicholas Ridley, the future bishop of London burned at the stake with Cranmer during Mary's reign, together with one of our reformers, another Cantabrigian, Hugh Latimer, to be bishop of Worcester. Most of the other reformers of a later generation were Cambridge men. In addition, there were Bishop John Ponet; Roger Ascham, Latinist and author of *the Schoolmaster*; Sir John Cheke, the first Regius Professor of Greek and tutor of Edward VI; and William Cecil, to be Lord Burghley, principal secretary and lord treasurer to Elizabeth.

Renaissance learning shaped secular as well as religious thought. Reference to two authors will suffice to illustrate this point. Sir Thomas Elyot, a literary associate of More's, dedicated his humanistic encomium to monarchy and guide to the education of the ruling classes, *The Boke Named the Governour* (1531), to Henry VIII. This work was followed by his popular handbook *The Castel of Health* (1536) and a Latin-English lexicon, *The Dictionary* (1538). A less well-known humanistic scholar was Thomas Lupset, friend of More, Starkey, and Reginald Pole. Starkey's *Dialogue* (1536) purported to be a conversation between Pole and Lupset. In the posthumous *A Treatise of Charitie* (1533) and *An Exhortation to Young Men* (1534), Lupset emerges as one of the first writers of modern English prose, possibly a better one than More.[15] Lupset was also the instigator, if not the actual translator, of Gentian Hervet's widely read rendition of Xenophon's classic on household management, *Oeconomia*, published in 1532 by the royal printer Thomas Berthelet, who published most of the previously mentioned books. These and other authors turned to the great thinkers of classical antiquity—especially Plato, Aristotle, and Cicero—for instruction and precept.

The influence of the ancients is obvious in the social and political thought of the reformers, particularly in More, Starkey, and Smith. More is the example par excellence. Although his debt in *Utopia* to Cicero was enormous, he seems to have looked to Plato's *Republic* for the communism of his ideal state and he may have discovered in the *Laws* a model for Utopian governmental structure.[16] The ideas of Cicero clearly imprinted Starkey's *Dialogue*.[17] Smith followed Cicero on several crucial matters in the *Discourse* and quite consciously set about writing *De republica Anglorum* in the manner of Aristotle's descriptive analysis of an ancient constitution.[18] Reading the ancients may well have imbued the reformers with an acute sense of *humanitas*, with the notion of the common good as the public welfare and economic well-being as a prerequisite to that end. Possibly study of the classics was also partially responsible for Starkey's and Smith's conception of the state, their tendency to view it largely from an economic standpoint, and their perception of law as a positive means of social control and reform. In this connection the reformers may also have absorbed the important lesson of the ancients that humans are in large measure shaped by their social institutions and legal arrangements. Advocacy of the mixed constitution and the rule of law, a persistent fear of tyranny, a deep distrust of democracy, and a commitment to distributive justice, proportionate equality, and social hierarchy may have been reinforced by the classics. Finally, long exposure to the ancients perhaps instilled a keen appreciation of differing cultures and values, an awareness of historical change, and the methodology of the comparative approach in furthering social and political analysis.

But classical antiquity was not the only inspiration of these Renaissance authors. Starkey, his friend Richard Morison, another of Cromwell's propagandists and Edward's ambassador to Charles V, and Smith had resided in Italy and were familiar with its humanistic literature, not least the works of Machiavelli. Morison cited both the *Discourses* and *Florentine History* in *A Remedy for Sedition* (1536), and Smith's library contained these books as well as *The Prince*.[19] The reformers may have applied the realism of Machiavelli and other Italian commentators to their analysis of English society and economy.[20]

The printed word facilitated the surge of scholarship in the service of God and society. William Caxton established the first English printing press in Westminister in 1476, adopting Gutenburg's invention of movable type from a quarter century earlier.[21] Other printers soon followed, helping to produce a larger and more articulate reading audience. By 1500, in addition to foreign works, over three hundred English books had been published, and by the 1520s volumes by humanists and religious reformers could readily be purchased by the well-to-do, although they remained too dear for the ordinary buyer. Between 1525 and 1547 some eight hundred religious works alone—largely of a Protestant nature—appeared in English. About ten thousand separate editions were printed during the century, accounting for perhaps 5 percent to 7 percent of the total European output. The interaction between the increasing availability of printed books and a slowly expanding literacy rate is obvious. Certainly the number of people able to read and write had risen since medieval times, but the numbers should not be exaggerated: possibly 10 percent among poor country men, higher for urban craftsmen, and as high as 40 percent for yeoman farmers. While the universities under Henry VIII and Edward were in some ways rejuvenated, the number of schools, teachers, and pupils throughout the realm did not noticeably increase. The traditional school curriculum, nevertheless, was widely discarded, and the many teachers of humanistic inclination found their efforts buttressed by printed textbooks reflecting the new learning. Gentlemen, merchants, and substantial farmers and craftsmen were becoming readers, sometimes avid ones, and discussants of the new ideas. To these classes it was becoming more and more evident that advancement and profit rested upon education.

Given the influence of the new learning and Lutheran ideas, the intellectual improvement of the upper classes, the Reformation launched by

Henry, and the mounting economic troubles, it is not surprising that Tudor England was an arena of vigorous public debate and controversy, a fact alone distinguishing it from the preceding era. The difference was not solely a result of the increasing numbers of books and readers but was also a product of the seriousness and determination of both authors and audience. A new and growing sense of civic responsibility and social awareness emerged. Most of early Tudor literature displays abiding political concerns.[22] Social abuses and abusers, at least in the eyes of the beholders, were often denounced with a stridency and invective rarely equaled at any time, even by our own most outspoken pundits. This was the age in which the protest pamphlet and tract came to the fore. The English political pamphlet literature seems to have commenced well before the Caxton press with the grievances of the Kentishmen—the articles of Kent—led by Jack Cade in the rebellion in 1450.[23] Thereafter Fortescue, in exile in Scotland in 1461–1463 with his Lancastrian sovereign Henry VI, defended the latter's right to the English throne against the claims of the Yorkist Edward IV in three pamphlets. Along with other tracts by various authors, these works were disseminated south of the border in a propaganda project "by which was sowen amongs the peple matier of grete noyse and infayme."[24] The *Somnium vigilantis* of about the same time, probably wrongly ascribed to Fortescue, also cast aspersions on Yorkist claims.[25]

The intellectual and religious ferment of the sixteenth century, promoted by printing and the social and political turmoil, multiplied these literary efforts and ushered in the first unprecedented period of pamphleteering and public discussion.[26] Thomas Cromwell and his coterie of humanists, including Starkey and Morison, carried on a program in the thirties to shape public opinion, arguing the case of Henry VIII against Rome and for law and order. There followed an ever greater outpouring of pamphleteering and debate during the reign of Edward VI, helped by the easing of some of the restrictions on freedom of expression and printing under Henry. By this time most recognized that England was undergoing an economic crisis. The exchange of ideas was facilitated through more open discussion, the publication of tracts, and the biting diatribes of the Protestant preachers, which reached a high point in the famous Paul's Cross sermons. A new attitude, gaining momentum since the thirties, took hold of the literate classes: that of the articulate citizen moved by a sense of responsibility to express views on the ills of the country and to suggest remedies. Citizens began to feel the duty to promote the common good by participating in the discussion and resolution of public problems. Thus was born a powerful, persistent, and honored tradition. Among the most concerned citizens of the late forties and early fifties were the Commonwealthmen and Sir Thomas Smith, who continued to emphasize the economic role of the state, a characteristic of the thought of their predecessors, Fortescue, Dudley, More, and Starkey. During this era of state formation when serious social ills plagued the body politic, the reformers from More to Smith brought to their pleas for renewal something of the spirit and substance of the new learning plus a Christian solicitude for the weak and unfortunate.

3 Toward an Economic Conception of the State

The reformers responded to their changing political and social environment by fashioning a rudimentary conception of the state giving emphasis to its economic role and functions. Their conceptual efforts can be viewed as the beginning of what was to be much more richly developed in the next century. "Economics," as understood by the reformers in a nontechnical sense, dealt with problems of material prosperity, that is, the management of material resources (production and distribution of the necessities of life) through a social division of labor involving property, property relations, and class differentiation. Traditionally, *economic* (derived from the Greek *oeconomia*) had to do with household management and organization, private income and expenditure and its proper goals. In the early modern era the nation began to be viewed as the household writ large, and economics was increasingly conceived of in terms of public income and expenditure. I use *economic* broadly in the following discussion to include questions of property, finance, taxation, productivity, consumption, farming, enclosure, manufacture, trade, exports and imports, labor, unemployment, poverty, prices, inflation, wages, acquisition, usury, and other such topics.

Practical politics has always been closely linked with economics. The state at any moment in history is embedded in a given system of economic relations and exists to protect that system from internal and external foes. Politicians have usually been acutely aware that their power is rooted in the interests of some citizens over others, that an orderly and stable political society requires the economic well-being of citizens, that the existing state rests on certain economic arrangements, and that such arrangements must be conserved or changed, as the case may be. Social and political thinkers, like politicians, have generally perceived the close ties between politics and economics, some stressing it more than others.

Yet until the modern era thinkers and politicians have often expressed the foremost purpose of politics and the state as ethical or religious, the advancement of the morally good life, however defined. While the economic health of the state (as well as its security) was deemed a necessary condition for the virtuous life, economics was not given preeminence or priority. But from the sixteenth century onward the idea that the primary aim of the state (as well as its security) is economic has increasingly displaced the previously held conception of the state's ethical ends. The first step in this momentous inversion of the ethical and the economic functions and ends of the state appears to have been taken by the English reformers. As a product of their evolving perspective, the state came to be thought of fundamentally as an economic engine driving society.

One might naturally question the legitimacy of applying the terms *economic* and *economy* to premodern and protomodern life, long before the economy had achieved a degree of autonomy, when it remained submerged in society and moral relationships, when *economic* was confined to the household and "economic" behavior was widely motivated by noneconomic factors.[1] Is the application of such a modern expression to the distant past anachronistic? I suggest that even if our conception of the economic differs from a previous understanding and is tied to a different moral and social outlook and to different social arrangements, this difference of definition should not preclude our use of the modern term in the analysis of other than recent formations and behavior. After all, in addition to *economic,* many distinctively modern concepts—like class, capitalism, state, society, sociology, technology, sexism, feminism—need not be anachronistic if handled with care; in fact they can be of considerable value in advancing our knowledge and appreciation of cultures far removed from our own. We need only note the numerous economic histories and treatments of economic thought extending back to classical antiquity, among them M. I. Finley's brilliant *The Ancient Economy* (1973); and the ancients themselves—Xenophon in *Ways and Means* and the pseudo-Aristotelian *Oeconomica*—did not hesitate to discuss in some detail matters we would term economic. It seems quite appropriate then to resort to *economic, economics,* and *economy* in examining protomodern historical phenomena as long as we remain cognizant of their temporal and cultural distance from ourselves.

Signs of a Change

During the fifteenth century the beginnings of a conceptual shift can be detected from the medieval notion of monarchical rule to a theory of the state as an entity. This change constitutes a move from a personalized to an abstract, holistic, and institutional way of viewing political arrangements. The signs of change, some of which appeared in Fortescue, are reflected in vocabulary: the use of *respublica* and "body politic" to refer to England, of the "weale publique of the Realm of England," and of "estate," as in "estate of the realm," to signify the condition or state of the kingdom.[2] Shortly after the French began to employ *l'état*, Starkey and Ponet became the first major English thinkers to use the word *state* in the political sense, and along with Smith they anticipated some of the characteristics of the modern conception of the state to be constructed by Bodin and later English and Continental theorists.[3] Clearly distinguishable from the medieval entity, the state in their hands was depersonalized and conceived abstractly as a constitutional structure of power that could be institutionalized in different ways. The state so conceptualized consisted of citizens, a people, or a society organized by means of government and law into a corporative whole with a life or personality of its own; the state thus becomes a sovereign power acting in certain respects like an individual. These writers distinguished the state, on the one hand, from its citizens or from society, and on the other hand, from its government. Theoretically, at least, a state could exist without its citizens, and governments might change in personnel and form without affecting the existence of the state. Government, moreover, was no longer individualized and personalized into a congeries of separate offices and officeholders but was in abstraction a collectivity acting for the state and by its authority. Although "state" does not appear in the works of Smith, he seemed to have in mind something similar to the modern conception in his use and definition of "common wealth" and in his references to *respublica* and *politeia*.[4] Smith also employed, probably for the first time, the significant term "civil society," to be more widely used than "state" in seventeenth-century England. "Government" and "administration" frequently occur in Smith's *De republica Anglorum*, sometimes in approximately the modern sense. There government or rule in general, for Smith the essence of the state, is endowed with sovereign power, having "the supreme and highest authoritie of commaundement," and the king in parliament is called "the most high and absolute power of the realme of Englande."[5] From these formulations it is only a step to Bodin's identification of the state and its nature with the locus of sovereignty.

Even if the other reformers had no conception of the state in the protomodern sense of Starkey, Ponet, and Smith, they all possessed some idea of the state, however vague, and were united by the economic emphasis given it. Indeed, this emerging economic conception of the state is the most conspicuous feature of their social and political thought. They shared, some more than others, a unique way of discussing the state, focusing on economic problems and their resolution, not unexpectedly in light of the deplorable material decline of their nation. Perhaps it is not too bold to suggest that Starkey, Ponet, and Smith arrived at their proto-modern notion of the state within the framework of the growing centralization and unification of the Tudor monarchy and in reaction to the social and economic troubles produced in part by the rural capitalism of the period. Their perception of these basic political and social changes was undoubtedly forwarded and conditioned by concepts absorbed from their humanistic studies. To the reformers the resolution of the concrete material problems of the day required a strong, unified state that would take dynamic, enlightened action yet remain limited in its power. We must now attempt to find answers to several questions raised by the suggestion that the reformers shared an economic conception of the state. What are the defining characteristics of that conception? Has it any claim to novelty in the history of social and political thought? Can it be distinguished from the perception and discussion of the state by previous thinkers or Continental contemporaries? Does the approach of the reformers indicate a new direction or paradigmatic change in political discourse?

I begin with an acknowledgment. Possibly the first historian to note this characteristic of the Early Tudor writers was J. W. Allen, who half a century ago observed:

> What, perhaps, strikes one most in reading the *Dialogue* [of Starkey], as in reading Crowley and More, is that society is regarded mainly as an association for economic purposes. All the stress is laid upon the question of how to get rid of waste and idleness and selfish greed and competition, how to abolish poverty and secure for all a competence suitable to the dignity of human nature. Nothing is more distinctive of English thought in the sixteenth century than the tendency to think in terms of economics. This is evidenced by a large number of writers who express little or nothing that can be called political thought. In reading Starkey's *Dialogue* or even the *Utopia*, one gets the impression that even love, even religion, are thought of as serving, mainly, an economic purpose.[6]

My study essentially tries to follow in detail and with some qualification Allen's perceptive generalization. His reference to "society" instead of "state" is unfortunate in view of the previous remarks. The reformers had an idea of "society," although with the exception of Smith they rarely used the word, preferring some such term as "commynalty." Looming much larger in their considerations is the state or commonwealth, however conceived and imprecise the meaning. I can therefore hardly agree with Allen that the reformers were not engaged in political thought or with Christopher Morris, who makes a similar judgment: "In one sense sixteenth-century Englishmen had no political theory whatsoever, for they had no theory of what we call the State. The theories they had were theories of Society."[7] Contrary to the opinion of Allen and Morris, political thought (or theory) in a broad sense can be said to describe the reflections of the reformers, unless that mode of discourse is confined to formal theorizing, system building, and the question of political obligation and civil obedience or unless politics is rendered autonomous, divorcing it from sociological and economic factors. If such reasons account for the verdict of Allen and Morris, then much of what is customarily called political thought (or theory) is simply a misnomer. It is inconceivable that many of the ideas of More, Starkey, and Smith can thus be excluded from the category of political thinking or theorizing. Perhaps the novelty of their approach with its stress on social and economic matters, so different from the preoccupations of previous thinkers, led both commentators astray. Nevertheless, the virtue of Allen's statement, despite these difficulties, is its fascinating suggestion that the reformers represented something new in the history of ideas.

Nature of the Economic Emphasis

The conjunction of several related traits in the writings of the reformers reveals their economic conception of the state. First and foremost, with little precedent, is the wealth of economic detail in their description and diagnosis of the conditions of English society. This fondness for collecting economic data seems to reflect the reformers' implicit assumption, the germ of an exceedingly important idea, that an economic infrastructure is the foundation of the state, shaping its very nature.[8] The idea is later developed in James Harrington's theory of the "balance," which is fundamental to his own and William Petty's conceptions of "political anatomy." Never really spelling out this assumption, the reformers perhaps came closest to doing so in their constant reminder that the self-interest of the ruler depends on the enhancement of the interests of his subjects, his private wealth on the common wealth. The very term *commonwealth*, so much taken for granted in the reformer's vocabulary and designating "state" as well as "common interest," seems to imply that a viable political order rests on the collective wealth of the people, their economic health and dedication to the common welfare. For the reformers the strength, stability, and durability of the state is determined to a significant degree by the quality of economic relations among citizens. An impoverished and enfeebled people will produce a weak and impotent state, whereas an economically flourishing and cooperative population is the basis for a vigorous and powerful state. Second, in connection with their analysis of the economic situation in England, the reformers minutely examined the state's social composition in terms of the various groupings constituting the whole, although they employed the traditional rubrics of order and rank. Third, they stressed the economic purpose of the state, and the traditional superior ethical and religious ends tended to be underplayed, if not sometimes excluded. Finally, their recommendations for remedial governmental policy essentially concerned reform of the economy.

All these elements, albeit with differing emphases, reached fruition in Sir Thomas Smith's *Discourse* and *De republica Anglorum*, where they were combined most forcefully and obviously as a single body of thought detailing a secular and utilitarian theory of the state. By postulating that the state is primarily an economic mechanism, Smith launched a new mode of social and political discourse that constituted an elementary science of political economy. When we compare Smith's ideas to past and future endeavors in the world of ideas, we cannot underestimate the significance of his intellectual achievement, for it represents the climax of tendencies perceptible in early sixteenth-century English political thought.

Little comparable to the reformers' assessment of social and economic conditions—in detail, extent, heuristic intent, or sympathy for the victims—existed in prior social and political thought or in their contemporary world. In contrast, the traditional economic concerns of scholasticism seem narrow and formalistic.[9] Among the reformers' famous Continental contemporaries one searches in vain for equivalent descriptions and evaluations of social and economic matters. There is no counterpart in the works of Machiavelli and Guicciardini or in Claude de Seyssel's *The Monarchy of France* (1515), Philippe de Commynes' *Memoires* (1524, 1528), Erasmus's *The Education of a Christian Prince* (1516), and Juan Luis Vives's *On Education* (1531).[10] Before the second half of the sixteenth century in France social and economic details are mainly found in cahiers, laws, and edicts.[11]

The reformers' examination of the material ills of England exhibits a realism uncommon in medieval Europe in their utilization of a wealth of empirical information—severely limited in its validity because of the imprecision and scantiness of the available sources—about prices, wages, rents, and agrarian, manufacturing, and business practices.[12] It was almost as if the reformers had taken the approach of Machiavelli and other Italian humanists of kindred spirit from the sphere of *realpolitik*, from a realistic obsession with political leadership and the conduct of foreign affairs, transferring and adapting it to an evaluation of the problems of everyday life, to the bread and butter concerns of the ordinary Englishman.[13] The reformers, however, did not collect such data for its own sake but for the purpose of discovering the causes of the depressing scene they witnessed and as the basis for recommending changes in governmental policy. This realism and empiricism with its penchant for gathering statistics, coupled with searching causal analysis of social and economic problems, was obviously new to the tradition of political theory, which in the past and in the future displayed a philosophical bias. Nonetheless, despite the lack of much in the way of formal or systematic philosophical underpinning, the thought of the reformers was still political thought, even if motivated more by an acute sensitivity to the correction of social and economic ills by rational public policy than by high-level theorizing and the quest for first principles. The intellectual style of the reformers resembled nothing so much as the birth pangs of modern social science, which in the following century would take the form of the political arithmetic and early political economy of Graunt and Petty and their contemporaries.

This empirical realism and passion for statistics directed toward causal analysis and enlightened public policy was not without precedent or parallel in England. *Domesday Book* in a way symbolized and heralded what was to become centuries later a typical approach to social matters. Before the middle of the fifteenth century a slowly growing pamphlet literature had begun to appear, one that attempted to catalog the material resources of the kingdom (in comparison with other countries) and to evaluate its strengths and weaknesses in order to contribute to sound and prudent governmental action. Such were *The Libel of English Policy*, probably written between 1436 and 1438 by the clerk of the king's council; *The Comodytes of England* of about mid-century, often but probably wrongly attributed to Fortescue; and the tracts in the 1530s of the hard-bitten London businessman, Clement Armstrong.[14] After the Poor Law of 1531, moreover, censuses and listings of the poor compiled by various municipalities so proliferated that by 1601 a handbook had been issued on the procedures to be followed in such catalogs.[15] Nor should the compilations of facts and figures of royal commissions in the first half of the sixteenth century be overlooked, an early notable example being Wolsey's enquiry of 1517—the year following publication of More's *Utopia*—which enumerated buildings razed, lands converted to pasture, and parklands enclosed. Wolsey's muster of 1522 also gathered information, evidently with taxation as the object, on 10 percent of the adult male population, the richest as well as the poorest.[16] The reformers, however, did not simply employ their empirical information and causal analyses in a neutral, detached fashion for the sake of identifying social and economic abuses. Theirs was a voice of heartfelt and often bitter protest against the injustices revealed by their investigations. Seldom before had there been such a concerted endeavor by so many remarkable intellects to discuss and decry economic and social injustices and to assign blame for them in such a moralizing outburst of scathing denunciation, always, however, in a spirit of devoted loyalty to the existing regime.

Poverty, idleness, and waste were among the most urgent problems raised in the reformers' diagnosis of the social and economic condition of England.[17] Previous secular and religious commentators thought of poverty as *systemic,* given the nature of man and social life, a necessary and irreversible feature of all states. Although economic extremes were ideally to be avoided, the poverty of the many and comparative wealth of the few, like the political subjection of the majority to the domination of the minority, were considered part of the inescapable and unalterable essence of human society. The reformers believed in Original Sin, some emphasizing the notion more than others, and in poverty as the divinely ordained way of the world. At the same time, however, they firmly rejected the position that the community could only be expected to relieve the worst hardship and suffering of the most unfortunate. A material environment, they argued, could be achieved by governmental action so that all could lead comfortable lives, according to their rank and station, free from economic insecurity and consonant with human dignity. The present miserable lot of so many people in contrast to their former relative prosperity was in the reformers' eyes a distressing social aberration, for which a naturalistic explanation could be discovered and which might be corrected by the informed management of state and society at all levels. One cannot imagine previous observers of the social and political scene from Plato to Machiavelli writing with such genuine moral indignation or sensitivity to social process and anxiety over the decline in the economic well-being of ordinary people.

In their worries over the problem of the poor, the reformers were the first social and political thinkers of consequence to dwell on the gravity of idleness and waste. These questions had seldom before been recognized, much less addressed. Voluntary and involuntary unemployment, in the opinion of the reformers, resulted from the decay of town and country because of the decline of industry and the devastation wrought by enclosure, engrossment, and rack-renting. The increasing number of deserving poor without jobs meant a fall in productive output, scarcity, and inflation in a treadmill of economic woes. Masterless men without work or home, vagabonds and beggars roaming the highways seeking refuge in the forests or an anonymous existence in London were a frightening prospect to those responsible for the maintenance of law and order. Beier judges vagrancy "one of the most pressing social problems of the age."[18] More's *Utopia* contained the first extensive and serious examination of the subject. The reformers blamed riotous behavior and since 1536 more serious disorders and open insurrection on the declining material circumstances of the common people and they raised the fearsome specter of some future cataclysm of revolt that could destroy the foundations of the state. The reformers therefore articulated the challenging idea that an inadequate social environment led to crime and violence. Delinquency might ultimately be explained by Original Sin, but a prosperous, secure, and harmonious social environment could relieve the strain on man's defective nature. The environmental shortcomings promoting antisocial conduct were poverty and unemployment. Once these were eliminated a major source of the disorder and social turmoil afflicting England would be eradicated. Idleness, however, was not solely a disease of the multitude, for the reformers never hesitated to criticize a segment of the propertied classes for their parasitic greed, exploitation of the labor of others, and indulgent, leisured lives of splendor pursued without socially useful mental or physical effort.

The Tudor theorists made an essential distinction between socially useful and nonuseful labor, between mental or physical work that contributed to well-being and prosperity (that is, the common interest) and endeavor directed solely to the short-term satisfaction of narrow self-interest and sensual gratification.[19] Manpower of every sort was to be harnessed and fully employed for the sake of the common interest, and profligate waste of human resources was to be discouraged. The reformers urged that every incentive be given to socially useful labor so defined, to industry and hard work, initiative and enterprise. Long before the rise of seventeenth-century Puritanism, these Tudor reformers, Catholic and Lutheran alike, expressed the work ethic.

An increasing sensitivity to waste emerged as the reformers prescribed full utilization of human resources for socially constructive purposes. This recommendation included attention to a hitherto disregarded resource: time. The new awareness of time may have resulted from a keener appreciation of the process of social change, brought about by the writers' recognition of the good old days in contrast to the impoverished present, and from the relatively recent introduction of the mechanical clock.[20] Whatever the reason for this growing sensitivity to time, the attitude implied by More and some of the others was that each minute of the working day must be made to count in fruitful labor; Smith even took the daring step of likening a portion of the economy to a clockwork mechanism. Only if all were mobilized for such socially useful and strenuous labor would England be a thriving and vigorous nation.

Along with the detailed analysis of social and economic conditions of England, the reformers treated its social composition. They commented extensively on the existing material conditions, proper functions, and responsibilities of the different socioeconomic strata. This interest was not without precedent in social and political thought, but the detail of discussion and the reformers' willingness to assign blame for the troubles were new. The reformers gave minute attention, perhaps even more than previous observers, including Aristotle, to various socioeconomic groups and their interrelations. Traditional social categories were employed: nobility, clergy, and commons, the last consisting of gentry, landlords, officials, merchants, lawyers, physicians, tradesmen, artisans, yeomen, husbandmen, cottagers, laborers, beggars, and vagabonds. The positions of the groups and subgroups were frequently described, together with an evaluation of their economic role from the standpoint of the common interest; the abuses of the privileged were also itemized. Unlike medieval commentators, the reformers seemed to conceive of the major groups less as corporative wholes than as collections of individuals joined by similar economic interests, each group seeking its own advantage to the detriment of the others. Conflicts within the groups and between them were examined. The question for the reformers was how to weld these disparate and competing group interests into a single common interest, how best to encourage cooperative labor and harmonize the diverse and contentious elements for the health and vigor of the state.

The reformers seldom refrained from apportioning responsibility among the various segments of the population for England's social and economic straits. On this score they differed in some measure from their predecessors in the history of social and political thought, who in the main were reluctant to criticize the propertied classes (as were the Continental humanists of the sixteenth century), to which they usually belonged or served, and who were frequently without intimate experience of the life and work of the ordinary person. In contrast, a number of the reformers were farmers' sons with firsthand knowledge of physical toil. Thus, for the first time a collective voice of explicit and bitter criticism took aim against portions of the dominant classes for their part in the impoverishment and the exploitation of the majority. Chief among the culprits singled out by the reformers were some of the nobility and higher clergy, gentry, landlords, and great merchants motivated by avarice and hubris with slight compassion for the lowly or consideration for the common interest, those living in splendor at the expense of the common people living in degradation and deprivation. Among the acolytes of these purse-proud grandees, the reformers stigmatized greedy lawyers, doctors, and tradesmen, and priests with insatiable appetites for the accumulation of livings to the neglect of their pastoral duties. Individuals of every rank were censured for shady business practices. Also condemned were corrupt and ineffectual public officials who shared in the covetousness of the great, deficient in both will and knowledge to institute telling measures of social and economic amelioration. From the powerful challenge of More to the seething denunciations of the Commonwealthmen and the more moderate comments of Smith, the complaints were succinct, unequivocal, and virtually unanimous.

All these formal statements of the reformers underscored the economic purpose of the state. The chief end of the state for most thinkers from the time of the ancient Greeks had been the creation of virtuous human beings, the shaping of human souls according to a moral and religious standard of the good. Among the greats before the reformers only Cicero, St. Augustine, Marsiglio of Padua, and Machiavelli conceived of the state primarily in secular, nonmoral terms: a vehicle for the maintenance of order and the preservation of life and property. Many of the classic social and political theorists after Plato, however, despite their predominantly ethical or religious notion of the state and argument from natural law, stressed the importance of the economic well-being of society for this objective. St. Thomas and the scholastics, following the precepts of Aristotle, certainly held that the economic welfare of the people was a necessary if not sufficient condition for a life of Christian virtue, that terrestrial happiness was a prerequisite to celestial beatitude, that the prince had a special duty to secure the prosperity of his subjects.

In keeping with the medieval outlook, the reformers agreed that the state should combine the moral goal of the defense and advancement of the Christian faith with the secular aims of protection from foreign attack, conservation of justice and maintenance of law and order, and promotion of material welfare. The preservation of private property, of course, figured as an essential feature of these latter objectives. Special consideration was given to the state's economic purpose. Even the preachers of mid-century, naturally most concerned with the state's religious and moral role, dwelt on social and economic questions. Latimer and the others were an influence on the thirteen-year-old Protestant sovereign, Edward VI, who in a precocious discourse of April 1551 divided the governance of the kingdom into ecclesiastical and temporal regimens, defining the latter as "well ordering, enriching, and defending the whole body politic of the commonwealth." Most of his short treatise focused on social and economic matters.[21] While Fortescue briefly acknowledged the ethical purpose of the state, he showed a keen appreciation of the social and economic context in his major treatment of jurisprudence and the constitution.[22] The same was true of Dudley, who also viewed Christianity as an indispensable means of social control, one that underwrote the unity and harmony of the state. Believing that government should dutifully support the ideological function of the church, he insisted on the strictly spiritual role of the church. More, in his discussion of the place of religion in Utopia in sustaining the domination of the governing elite, was in basic agreement with Dudley, but he spent far more space on the economic ordering of the ideal commonwealth. Likewise More shared the opinion of Fortescue and Starkey that the state should be dedicated to fostering a social environment in which citizens could achieve happiness, to which end morality was fundamental. For all three thinkers, however, economic security and well-being were absolutely necessary for such felicity, and they devoted much of their intellectual effort to showing how these aims could be realized through the material ordering of the state. For More the happiness of the citizens meant a preponderance of pleasure over pain, each individual seeking natural and legitimate pleasures, guided in his quest by an intellectual political elite. But in Fortescue and Starkey, in contrast to More, there is the hint that citizens themselves are the best judges of the pleasures conducive to their own happiness; hence they can also judge the governmental policies most appropriate for the attainment of such pleasures, policies designed to improve the social and economic situation. This movement toward utilitarianism and material improvement accelerated rapidly in Smith's secularized conception of the state in which the basic goal was the common interest, defined largely in economic terms. Smith's state was in part an economic mechanism directed by law and government, operating for the welfare of the people according to their desires—by no means on a parity—registered in parliament. Smith then conceptually began to transform the state into a *political economy*, a machine of economic ends to be achieved by political means. Little precedent for this outlook can be found in the history of social and political theory, and we find little echo in Continental thought.

A final defining characteristic of the reformers' economic conception of the state was their insistence that the improvement of the realm required the intervention of government. The resulting legislation would implement an enlightened public policy derived from the realistic study and intelligent evaluation of social and economic conditions. While loyally upholding the established order, the critics deplored its short-sighted actions—lacking any foundation in prudent, realistic policies—for simply multiplying the troubles. In medieval thought good government depended on good counsel. Before officially acting the responsible prince was expected to seek sound and sage advice from wise men of moral rectitude. This prevailing view was gradually transformed in early sixteenth-century England into the notion that government must premise its conduct of affairs on "constructive policy," to use Ferguson's apt expression.[23] The need for good counsel always remained, but good policies might have to change, to adapt to new circumstances. Several preconditions were necessary for the appearance of this new attitude based on flexible policy. Perhaps the prime mover was the serious alteration in the material affairs of the realm, namely, the mounting economic crisis from about the time of the publication of More's *Utopia* in 1516, with increasing impoverishment and social dislocation, and a growing spirit of self-seeking individualism, developments owing much to emergent rural capitalism. Some action was urgently needed to restore the body politic to its former health and vigor, or such was the reformers' conservative call for regeneration and recovery of the halcyon days of yore (only Smith did not appear to yearn for the past). They perhaps brought to their preoccupation with imminent social and economic disaster something of the spirit of Machiavelli and the Italian humanists. Men were not simply hapless victims destined to turn passively with every movement of the wheel of fortune. Instead, they could boldly seize the initiative and act decisively to control a large part of their lives.

The prerequisite of such a novel attitude was also a growing consciousness of historical change and ever-fluctuating social process. Perhaps this awareness resulted from the comparison of past and present or from the study of differing cultures and peoples in past and present provoked by travel and reading the classics of the ancient world. Obviously, the realization had dawned that a rational explanation could be sought and discovered for the difficulties besetting the state, that natural causes of an empirical type could be identified on the basis of which effective remedies could be devised. No longer had mankind to accept helplessly every material trial and tribulation as the inexorable and inscrutable ordination of Divine Providence.

But the realistic determination of the human causes of human problems alone was insufficient to account for the shift from the medieval concept of counsel to the idea of constructive policy held by some Tudor intellectuals and practitioners. A novel understanding of law and legislation was also necessary to challenge the common medieval outlook. The view in the Middle Ages was that all law, both customary and promulgated, was something to be found or discovered, the result of an intellectual instead of a volitional process. To be legitimate law had to be the embodiment of some higher principle of divine or natural justice. In the early sixteenth century the notion that law could be made, that it could be devised by an exercise of human will, began to be discernible. New laws could be fashioned, existing laws changed and annulled, and custom abrogated.[24] Soon thinkers recognized also that a statute need not be simply negative in the sense of prohibiting and restraining. The realization dawned on informed and concerned citizens, not least some of the reformers, that law could be employed positively and creatively as a powerful instrument of social change, providing of course that it embodied rational governmental policies. In sum, the human environment could be shaped to meet the needs of human beings by those or on the advice of those who realistically understood the nature of the social process and the principles of social causation. Some men of affairs and intellectuals of the time, influenced by the new learning, may have been encouraged in thinking in this way by their reading of Plato and Aristotle in particular.

The reformers recognized that the crucial problem of the Tudor state—and for that matter any state—was its own preservation and security: the containment of social conflict, the maintenance of law and order, and thus the strengthening of central authority. In this era of growing centralization of the state and increasing economic and social disruption, the ideas of the reformers could be distinguished from those of their predecessors and of their Continental contemporaries by the profound insight that the vital questions of state security and social stability were at root economic in nature. Politics then, from their vantage point, became fundamentally a question of economics. Serious political and social problems were in their hands reduced to economic problems. In essence, the Tudor reformers were on the verge of performing the remarkable feat of transmuting politics into political economy. The cure for the ills of the Tudor state was a rational economic program of policies and measures to be instituted by a benevolent and prudent government.

4 Forerunner of the Reformers

Sir John Fortescue

The name and significance of Sir John Fortescue (ca. 1394–ca. 1476), one of the greats of English legal culture, are unfortunately seldom recognized outside a small circle of specialists.[1] He was the first to expound the nature of the English constitution and its relationship to the common law and he is credited with founding comparative jurisprudence. Some of his institutional recommendations, the source of most of our knowledge of the early jury and legal profession, may also have influenced governmental centralization under the Tudors. His ideas seem to have become known first through the circulation of manuscript copies of his works in the late fifteenth century. The *De natura legis naturae*, earliest of his three principal books, is the most distinguished exposition of fifteenth-century English philosophy of natural law.[2] His last work, *The Governance of England*, did not appear in type until 1714, but the famous *De laudibus legum Anglie* was published in the original Latin by Edwarde Whitechurche in 1546; twenty reprintings followed. The first English translation of *De laudibus*, by Robert Mulcaster in 1567, went through many editions before the end of the century. John Selden, pioneer of legal history and intimate of Thomas Hobbes, issued an important critical edition in English in 1616, as did Edward Waterhouse in 1663. There can be little doubt about the immense impact of Fortescue on constitutional and legal theory and practice. John Rastell, brother-in-law and religious adversary of Thomas More, in *Liber Assissarum* (1513) relied on *De laudibus*, and some of the legal philosophy of Christopher St. German was but a gloss on it. More seems to have been familiar with Fortescue's views, as were Thomas Smith and Francis Bacon. Sir Walter Raleigh describes *De laudibus* as "that notable bulwark of our laws." In the bitter constitutional struggles of the seventeenth century Fortescue was an honored authority exploited by contestants for their own partisan purposes, studied by Coke and Hale, read by Filmer, Hobbes, Locke, and Somers.[3]

Although Fortescue was a crucial connecting link between medieval and early modern English political ideas, historians of political thought have paid him scant attention in recent years. Such apparent lack of interest is puzzling because some of his ideas lie at the heart of early modern English political theory: a firm opposition to absolutism and tyranny, a dread of popular unrest and democracy, a dedication to the supremacy of law, a theory of parliamentary or mixed monarchy, an insistence on natural law as a limit on political action, and a vague notion of consent or reciprocal obligation between government and governed. Critical as these concerns are from the standpoint of historical political theory, my intention is to elucidate Fortescue's conception of the state and his relation of society and economy to government and law.

John Fortescue was born about 1394—but possibly ten years earlier—in Devon, the second son of Sir John Fortescue, one of Henry V's stalwarts at Agincourt whose ancestor had crossed to England with William the Conqueror. Before 1420 young John began the study of law at Lincoln's Inn, later serving it in various official capacities. He practiced law on the western circuit, gained a reputation for being a property trustee, served as justice of the peace in several counties and on a number of royal commissions, was returned eight times to the Commons by the voters of Tavistock, and was appointed sergeant-at-law and eventually a king's sergeant. On 20 January 1442 Henry VI named him chief justice of King's Bench, a post he held for nineteen years; and subsequently he was knighted. His tenure ended in 1461 when the Yorkist claimant Edward IV forced the reigning Lancastrian monarch Henry VI to flee to Scotland. Fortescue was embroiled in the conflict for the rest of his life. A loyal Lancastrian, he followed his royal master into exile in Scotland, where he was appointed lord chancellor and in the years 1461–1463 composed *De natura* and three tracts defending Henry's title to the throne. When the asylum given by the Scots to the refugee court ended in 1463, the venerable lord chancellor accompanied Queen Margaret and the young Prince of Wales Edward to France, while the king, returning to England, was shortly captured and imprisoned. In France, where the royal party remained for seven years in the castle of Koeur at St. Mihiel in Bar, Fortescue wrote *De laudibus*, probably between 1468 and 1471. Following the restoration of Henry VI in the fall of 1470, the exiles traveled to England on 14 April 1471, the very day that in the continuing struggle the monarch was captured at Barnet, to be held and soon killed in the Tower. Fortescue was taken the following month in the Battle of Tewkesbury, but he was pardoned in October and apparently appointed to Edward IV's council. The *Governance* may have been written for the Yorkist sovereign in the years before the author's death (ca. 1476) in his manor at Ebrington, Gloucestershire. A prosperous landed gentleman and experienced politician, Fortescue proved himself a courageous and determined servant of the crown and a skillful and tough-minded advocate and judge, deeply versed in the law of the realm, knowledgeable in Roman law, and with more than a passing acquaintance with the learning of his age.

My discussion of Fortescue's thought concentrates on *De laudibus,* supplemented by reference to *De natura* and the *Governance.* The background to the composition of *De laudibus,* a short work in Latin of thirty thousand words or less in fifty-four chapters, is expressed by the author in the opening pages: "Not long ago, a savage and most detestable civil war raged in the kingdom of England. . . . "[4] The book is a dialogue between the young Prince of Wales Edward and "a certain aged knight, chancellor of the said king of England, who was also in exile there as a result of the same disaster. . . . "[5] Fortescue urged his royal pupil to study the laws of the kingdom, not in order to acquire a detailed technical knowledge but to understand their general character. The respective remarks of pupil and teacher are confined to separate alternating chapters, the prince asking questions and summarizing points previously made. The arguments unfold in lengthy statements by the chancellor. Comparing the English common law with the civil or Roman law of Continental countries, especially France, Fortescue concludes that the English constitution and law are superior, founded as they were on customs of the greatest antiquity. Various subjects receive attention. Fortescue treats the sources of human law in the law of nature, in customs, and in statutes and examines English civil and criminal law with respect to procedure and substance, comparing the English laws with Roman law and Continental institutions. Fortescue explains the nature of the English constitution in terms of the notion of mixed or parliamentary monarchy, which he contrasts with the regal absolutism of France. He also describes the use of the jury in English civil and criminal procedure, making comparisons with Continental arrangements, and he details the organization and educational requirements of the English legal profession. Perhaps the most fascinating feature of the book, from our perspective, is Fortescue's detailed attempt to situate the constitution and law of England and France in their differing social and economic contexts.

Fortescue displayed a strong sense of realism, as Arthur Ferguson has commented.[6] His major works focus on concrete practical problems using a method that is comparative, causal, empirical, and in a limited fashion even historical. Nevertheless, Fortescue's reliance on experience and observation is tempered by the typical medieval technique of making deductions from certain principles gleaned from authoritative sources. In *De laudibus* he quotes or cites seventeen different books and authors, including the Bible (fifty-two quotations), the corpus of Roman and canon law, French and English chronicles, Aristotle, St. Augustine, and St. Thomas Aquinas.[7] His references to classical sources seem to have been taken from no more than a dozen commonly used anthologies of the period rather than from the original works. His comparative and evaluative method he derives from Aristotle's axiom in the *Rhetoric,* "Opposites juxtaposed are more apparent," which he uses to assemble and contrast considerable empirical detail about England and France.[8] Not content merely to compare and contrast English and French law and institutions, Fortescue believed that he had discovered the cause of the differing arrangements in their interaction with their respective social environments. As we might expect, the meagerness of his sources severely restricted his historical grasp. Comparing ancient states in light of contemporary European developments, however, he displayed a sensitivity to the maturation of Western political life. By examining history in *De natura,* he proposed to identify kings whose rule conformed to the precepts of natural law, a procedure justified by the biblical axiom, "By their fruits ye shall know them," adding that "experience increases not a little our confidence in arguments."[9] This pragmatic test for the ultimate evaluation of the merits of a constitutional system was of some importance to Fortescue, as we shall see. Later in *De natura* he declared that the nature of mixed monarchy not only could be found in the writings of St. Thomas but was also "taught by experience and ancient history."[10] Presumably borrowing from Aristotle, in a remarkable statement in *De laudibus* he urged Prince Edward to study law: "Whilst you are young and your mind is as it were a clean slate [tabula rasa], impress on it those things, lest in future it be impressed more pleasurably with images of lesser worth."[11] The notion of tabula rasa was to become the hallmark of English empiricism, with its implications for a doctrine of social environmentalism which so shaped the thought of some of the Tudor reformers and thereafter of John Locke.

In examining Fortescue's ideas we do well to keep in mind the broad social and political contours of his outlook. He was decidedly a conservative with an unshakable faith in a hierarchical society, an unswerving devotion to monarchical government and law, and a deep distrust of popular rule. He believed that natural human inequality—distinctions of sex, age, and intellect—was reinforced in political society by differences in family, property, and office arising from convention; such distinctions were then institutionalized in a hierarchy of dominant and subordinate strata.[12] Social order, the very antithesis of any kind of parity, thus rested squarely

on these natural and conventional disparities. Besides his belief in the efficacy of social hierarchy, Fortescue was profoundly committed to kingship and law. Regal absolutism might be the preferred ideal, but he was
ever fearful of its potential for tyranny, so in practice he approved limits
on royal power, as in the case of England's mixed monarchy. King as well
as people were to be subject to the law, one they made together in conformity with the moral principles of the law of nature. Although Fortescue
only mentioned republics and democracy in passing, he apparently found
the latter highly suspect, no doubt thinking the leveling and egalitarian
elements likely to degenerate into mob rule and despotism, making democracy one of the worst types of government for its diametrical opposition to social order. Even English mixed monarchy, he argued, should be
freed as much as possible from popular control by increasing the financial
independence of the crown. So tyranny from below, implicit in democracy and a result of democratization, was to be avoided as much as tyranny from above, which might be the consequence of unchecked regal
absolutism.

Vocabulary of Politics

While Fortescue conceived of political rule in a highly personalized way,
largely as kingship, his terminology and treatment of the ends of government sometimes suggests a more institutionalized and holistic approach
to the state. In *De laudibus* the most frequent political words are the traditional *dominium, regnum, regimen*; in the *Governance* we encounter
dominion, reaume, or *realme, kingdome*. Richer in its political terms than
the other two works, *De natura* employs *res publica* (or state),[13] *civitas*
both for city and state,[14] and *societas* (or society)[15] in addition to the language of *De laudibus*. Also of interest is the use of *gubernatio* (government)[16] and especially and more frequently *administratio* or a variant[17]
for government, rule, or management, for example, *administratio rei
publicae* (government of the state). There is thus an intimation in *De
natura* of a differentiation of state from both government and society. In
this regard chapter 13 of *De laudibus*, an explanation and defense of
mixed monarchy, is important. The chapter begins with a definition of a
people (*populus*) from St. Augustine's *City of God*: "A people is a body of
men united by agreement on law or justice and by a community of interest."[18] Fortescue appears to mistake this for Augustine's own definition of
a people, failing to realize that the bishop of Hippo was actually quoting
Cicero (in *De re publica*) in order to take issue with him. Perhaps Fortescue did not recognize the true author of the quotation because he took
it out of context, so to speak, from some contemporary anthology. Writ-

ing half a millennium before Augustine, Cicero was defining the state or *res publica* as the "thing" (*res*) or "property" of the people, *res populi*. *Populus* in this case denoted not any mere collection of persons but a union of many in respect to justice (*ius*) and the common interest (*utilitas*). This in effect was Cicero's definition of *res publica* which Augustine disputed, and we know that the Roman statesman distinguished government from state and, less precisely, society from state.

Fortescue's next move in chapter 13 should not be overlooked. He clearly identified Cicero's state or *res publica* (although believing it to be Augustine's own notion of *populus*) with the body politic.[19] The reference is to the mixed monarchy in which Fortescue likened the intentions of the people to the source of life; the people are the "heart," supplying the various bodily parts with blood, the king is the "head," directing the body.[20] People and king are integral components of the greater whole, the body politic. Consequently, Fortescue actually equated the body politic with Cicero's state. This interpretation can be confirmed in the *Governance*, where Fortescue uses body politic as the equivalent of realm or kingdom.[21] In other words, through the very words and figures of speech he chose, Fortescue may have been hesitantly trying to convey the nature of the state in an abstract, corporative, and institutional way.[22]

Fortescue's use of *dominium* (or *dominion* in the *Governance*) followed an important convention of discourse. Whatever the precise sources of his concepts of *dominium politicum*, *dominium regale*, and *dominium politicum et regale*, he was apparently adhering, broadly speaking, to the traditional notion of *dominium*.[23] In classical Latin *dominium* meant property ownership and the rights of ownership; during the Middle Ages the term acquired the broader designation of rule, a rule that reflected the fusion and confusion of property right with public authority so characteristic of feudal social relations. From the early thirteenth century a distinction had been made between *dominium utile*, the usufruct (landed holding) possessed by a vassal, and *dominium directum*—which involved no actual possession—the power held by a lord.[24] In other words, *dominium directum* signified overlordship, and it appears that Fortescue was extending this medieval usage to rule over the realm. A king, for example, was not in any real sense the owner of all landed property under his jurisdiction, but he was the judge of whether it was being used justly or unjustly. *Dominium*, as Fortescue employed it, was synonymous with *regnum* and realm, *res publica* and *civitas*, the body politic. By the term he denoted the political direction or command of a people, their form of government, and more vaguely and imprecisely their state. *De natura* refers to a number of different kinds of government after the natural dominion of the age of innocence ended with the fall: political, despotic, regal, and mixed government (the last called *dominium politicum et regale*).[25] Mentioned without discussion are other forms of *dominium* existing at different times and places: aristocracy, oligarchy, and democracy. *Dominium* of every kind entails a recognition of the differences in "dignity," in human value or worth; rule by means of law, natural or positive; and in the post-lapsarian form, the power of punishment of governors over governed. Inequality, law, and coercive power then were the chief features of Fortescue's "state."

Since political dominion and regal dominion and the mixture of the two are important in *De laudibus* and the *Governance*, Fortescue's views on their historical origins and nature are apposite.[26] In political dominion, the most ancient of the three forms of state, found in Cain's City of Enoch and republican Rome, government by a plurality meant government under laws originating with the people. Regal dominion or absolute monarchy began for Fortescue with Ninus, son of Belus, but was also manifested at times in ancient Israel and imperial Rome as well as in contemporary France. The regal ruler governed by hereditary right through laws he himself made without having to consult the people; he was subject only to natural law. The mixed regal and political dominion characterized at times ancient Israel and imperial Rome in addition to many other ancient kingdoms, such as Egypt, Ethiopia, and Arabia and finally Scotland and England of Fortescue's day. Under English mixed monarchy, on which Fortescue focused, the king ruled by hereditary right but was subject to the law of the realm. All legislation required the consent of both king and people and must conform to natural law; judges could not be commanded to render judgments against the law. Neither regal nor mixed monarchy, in Fortescue's opinion, was superior to the other. Both were equal in the sight of God, and the power of each was the same, although the authority of regal monarchy was inferior to that of the mixture because of the difference in origins. Fortescue evidently did not object in principle to royal absolutism. Provided that the king was of upright character and wisdom, took counsel with his subjects, acted prudently and adhered to the law of nature, his rule was ideally the best because it was in the image of the divine governor. The problem with absolute regal government, however, was that it might easily fall to a king neither moral nor wise, thus degenerating into tyranny, the worst form of rule. Recognizing the dangerous potential of regal absolutism and the universal weakness of human nature, Fortescue recommended limits on the royal power (as in England) since the king of a mixed monarchy "hath not a loose rein for it, like the other," the regal king who lacks a "bridle."[27]

Fortescue's brief account of the historical origins of regal and mixed monarchies, intertwined with his descriptions but logically separated from them, is further testimony that his theory of dominion approached an institutional conception of the state. While each type of monarchy originated under natural law, regal monarchy was historically by far the older. It arose when men, overcome by greed, ambition, and arrogance, conquered and subjected their neighbors through conquest. Nimrod, Noah's grandson and mighty hunter (Genesis 10:1–10), the first to establish such a kingdom, governed tyranically, enslaving the conquered, who submitted in return for protection. In fact, Fortescue termed his dominion "despotic," not "regal." The first true regal monarch was Ninus, king of Assyria and founder of Nineveh (according to Greek mythology) and supposedly son of Belus (Belos or Bel), the god of the wind of ancient Mesopotamian religion. So on the basis of reading the Bible, St. Augustine, and other such sources, Fortescue offered all too briefly a force theory of the origins of the state, a view to be repeated at greater length a century later by Jean Bodin, who also referred to Nimrod.[28] Regal monarchy was followed, according to Fortescue, at a later time in historical development by mixed dominion, early examples of which he described in *De natura* and in his other two books. Fortescue referred briefly to its origin in England, instituted by the Trojan refugee Brutus in the distant past, a legend popularized by Geoffrey of Monmouth.[29] In contrast to regal monarchy, the mixed variety began not in force but in consent. Fortescue's explanation fell short of the idea in the early modern sense of a contract or covenant founding political society.[30] Nevertheless, from his standpoint, the mixture resulted from some kind of understanding or settlement by which rulers and ruled submitted to mutually agreeable laws aimed at the security of lives and possessions.

Fortescue initially explained the legislative process of the English mixed monarchy in *De natura*: "For in the kingdom of England the kings make not laws, nor impose subsidies on their subjects, without the consent of the Three Estates of the Realm," adding that this form of government might be called "political," "regulated by the administration of many."[31] The notion of the English mixture appeared first in chapter 9 of *De laudibus* and was fully expounded in chapter 13. A summary of the treatment in *De laudibus* also appeared in the first three chapters of the *Governance*, where in chapter 3 Fortescue referred not to *dominion*, as he did in the previous two chapters, but to *jus regale* and *jus politicum, jus* in this context denoting jurisdiction or right. The most complete description of mixed legislation appears in chapter 9 of *De laudibus*:

> For the king of England is not able to change the laws of his kingdom at pleasure, for he rules his people with a government not only regal but also political. If he were to preside over them with a power entirely regal, he would be able to change the laws of his realm, and also impose on them tallages and other burdens without consulting them; this is the sort of dominion which the civil laws indicate when they state that *What pleased the prince has the force of law.* But the case is far otherwise with the king ruling his people politically, because he is not able himself to change the laws without the assent of his subjects nor to burden an unwilling people with strange imposts, so that, ruled by the laws that they themselves desire, they freely enjoy their properties, and are despoiled neither by their own king nor any other. The people, forsooth, rejoice in the same way under a king ruling entirely regally, provided he does not degenerate into a tyrant.[32]

France epitomized regal absolutism that had become tyrannical, whereas England was the ideal of mixed monarchy. In the former a virtually enslaved citizenry existed, whereas in the latter there ruled a powerful king with free, contented, and loyal subjects. Quoting in *Governance* from the gospel of St. Matthew, "By their fruits so shall you know them," Fortescue dwelled there and especially in *De laudibus* on the economic consequences of the two different types of monarchy: widespread impoverishment and discord in France, a flourishing, prosperous people in England.[33]

Fortescue's conception of *dominium politicum et regale* was possibly a move in the direction of modern constitutionalism. He did not, however, seem to be advocating a source of power and authority independent of the crown, one functioning in a positive way to limit and control the royal prerogative.[34] This is the essence of the theory and practice of modern constitutional monarchy: the ultimate check exercised by citizens on the policies and actions of the crown. Certainly, as Fortescue saw it, the king in a mixed monarchy was under the law of the land like any other citizen. Nonetheless, the king was supreme within the regal sphere, absolute in the exercise of his prerogative powers, subject only to divine and natural law. In the political sphere he was limited by the will of his subjects, expressed in parliament, for example, in matters of taxation. Each sphere, the regal and political, had powers of its own immune to interference by the other. If Fortescue was not breaking new ground with this view, he was in fact describing quite accurately the current English constitutional practice of the crown in parliament rather than anticipating the constitutionalism of John Locke.[35]

Purpose of the State

If Fortescue has gone beyond the typically medieval personalized notion of governing and seems to be on the threshold of conceiving of the state institutionally and corporatively, in what sense can that conception be said to possess an economic dimension? Clearly accepting the medieval convention that the king's major duty was fighting and judging for the good of his subjects,[36] Fortescue appeared at the same time to have something more in mind as to the proper ends of the state. A suitable place to begin is with the comments in *De laudibus*, which echoed the earlier *De natura*, about the *summum bonum* for which all mankind should strive. "Happiness or blessedness (*felicitas sive beatitudo*)" should be the supreme goal of human desire, a matter, Fortescue tells us, on which all philosophers of the past—peripatetics, stoics, epicureans—have agreed, as they have that virtue is requisite to human happiness, in spite of their differences on the meaning of virtue.[37] In *De natura*, guided by the teachings of St. Thomas and Aristotle, he wrote that the object of human law, and by inference of the state, is the creation of virtuous and thus happy human beings.[38] His ideal, of course, was Christian virtue, the sine qua non of genuine happiness in the here and now, but temporal morality and earthly felicity were merely preparatory to ultimate beatitude, to be found only in heaven and dependent on divine grace. The state's major aim then was to fashion and maintain a social environment most conducive to the quest for true virtue and happiness; its means for doing so were the laws, "rules by which perfect justice is manifested."[39] The justice of law is neither commutative nor distributive but "Perfect Virtue," so whoever enjoys justice "is made happy by the law." Not the least of the essentials for temporal Christian virtue, true happiness, and the possibility of eventual celestial beatitude is an adequate material life—comfortable and secure—for all according to their station. Economic well-being alone is insufficient for Christian virtue and happiness, but it is a necessary precondition.

With this preliminary recognition and acceptance of the standard medieval position, Fortescue turned next in *De laudibus* to the material conditions of happiness that should be fostered by the state. The emphasis throughout is on the state's role in the protection of the lives and properties of citizens and its promotion of their economic well-being. By way of St. Augustine, as we have seen, Fortescue endorsed Cicero's definition of *populus*, in actuality the latter's conception of *res publica* or state: a union in agreement about justice and the common interest.[40] Stressing the "interest" (*utilitas* or *commodum*) of the people, Fortescue identified common interest with the desires of the citizens, that which with the king they consented to in parliament.[41] In practice, this meant that the English king could not legitimately "change the laws without the assent of his subjects nor to burden an unwilling people with strange imposts, so that ruled by laws that they themselves desire, they freely (*libere*) enjoy their properties, and are despoiled neither by their own king nor any other."[42] A political king "is obliged to protect the law, the subjects, and their bodies and goods."[43] English laws have adapted to the "interest (*utilitas*) of the kingdom" and "are made not only by the prince's will, but also by the whole realm, so they cannot be injurious to the people nor fail to secure their advantage (*vel non eorum commodum procurare*)."[44] The English monarch cannot "by himself or by his ministers, impose tallages, subsidies, or any other burdens whatever on his subjects, nor change their laws, nor make new ones; without the concession or assent of his whole realm expressed in his parliament."[45]

One of the prominent features of these statements is Fortescue's preoccupation with the protection of property. Of considerable interest is his idea in *De natura*, which diverges from the Augustinian and patristic notion that property (and property differentials) was coeval with the foundation of the state and human law and thus like the state was a divinely inspired human convention for penalizing and remedying sinful man, a means of disciplining and ordering fallen man. Fortescue, whose position seems close to but not identical with the Thomistic view, agreed that before the fall in the state of innocence all things had been held in common.[46] At the same time, however, he believed in the natural rather than the conventional character of private property. Between prelapsarian communism and the appearance of the first state a lengthy time ensued, he declared, using St. Augustine's calculation of over three and a half millennia, during which time fallen man without government or positive law was ruled by the law of nature.[47] The distinction—and he could not have been clearer about it—between *meum* and *tuum*, between what is mine and what is thine, that is, the institution of private property, appeared in this postlapsarian but prepolitical age under the aegis of natural law. The changeless and universal law of nature ruled both the state of innocence and the state of sin, in the one authorizing communism and in the other the acquisition of private property.[48] The law of nature itself did not alter, but the human condition did. So private property was certainly "natural," but natural in the sense that it corresponded to man's fallen nature, not to his unsullied natural being before the fall.[49] Private property therefore began with Adam and with Cain and Abel after the fall: "property in things, especially in things acquired by the sweat of the brow, first accrued to man by the law of nature alone, seeing that there was then no other human law; and consequently buyings, sellings, lettings, hirings and the like, took their origin from the law of nature."[50] Fortescue never wrote of a natural right of property, although he implied it, and obviously in this precivil condition each individual had the natural moral obligation under the law of nature to respect the property of others.

What is more, in this discussion of property and the state's obligation to protect it, Fortescue formulated a primitive labor theory of property. People are entitled, he suggested, under the law of nature to what they acquire by their own efforts:

> . . . afterwards, when they forsook their state of innocence, presently the Lord said to the human race, "In the sweat of thy brow thou shalt eat bread;" in which words was granted to man a property in the things which he should acquire by his labour. . . . For since the bread which a man gained by his labour was his own, and no man could eat bread without the sweat of his own brow, every man who toiled not was prohibited from eating the bread which by his own sweat another man had acquired; wherefore property in the bread so gained accrued only to the man who had toiled for it, and every other man was deprived of any share in it; and in this way property capable of descent first took its rise. For our ancestors taught us to understand under the name of "bread," not only what is eaten and drunk, but everything whereby man is sustained; and by the word "sweat," every industry of man. And because property so acquired ensues as a compensation for the sweat by which the body of the acquirer is enfeebled, the reason of the law of nature hath united it to its acquirer, so that the property gained might compensate the damage resulting from his loss of bodily wholeness; and thus the property takes the place of man's bodily integrity, which he has lost, and coheres as an accident to the toiler, and so thenceforth accompanies his blood. And yet property is not an accident natural to man, but accrues to him by the rules of the law of nature, and, after the likeness of a natural accident, is united to him, not by the ties of the laws of nature, as nature had been originally instituted, but as nature now exists, stript of her liberty and pristine powers in accordance with the requirements of man's defects.[51]

This interesting and somewhat obscure declaration requires comment, partly by way of exegesis. Private property is apparently compensation for the purposeful labor—very broadly construed—expended in acquiring it; this conclusion follows the principle of distributive justice (not mentioned in this connection by Fortescue) "to each his due," which means in theory that more goes to those who labor more (and more expertly) and proportionately less to others. In practice, however, any evaluation of the quantity and quality of labor begins not with the labor itself but with its fruits, the property accumulated. By definition the accumulators of the most property are presumed to have labored more (and more capably) than those with less property. Labor thus becomes a function of acquisitive ability instead of the converse. Acquisitive success invariably determines the assessment of the labor, the one customarily prejudging the other. Fortescue fused his labor theory of property with a personality theory in order to justify and rationalize descent and inheritance of possessions. A portion of one's very being, one's persona, is transferred to and embedded in the object acquired by labor. An individual's property so acquired embodies his personality, becomes a part of his self and thus a part of the patrimony to be transmitted through inheritance, just as a portion of his persona is reproduced in his children. Finally, although Fortescue did not explicitly say so, presumably once the state is established, in order for it to act legitimately under natural law, its positive law must institutionalize and protect by its coercive power each citizen's natural entitlement to his private property.

Fortescue's stance is therefore clear enough. The protection of private property and the freedom to acquire and exchange it under law, if not the main purpose of the state, is absolutely critical to its survival and welfare. The king must secure the lives and possessions of his subjects and make no law, amend or suspend no law, impose neither taxes nor levies without their consent. Any attempt to raise funds from his subjects without their approval is an infringement on their entitlement by the law of nature to private property, a threat to their natural liberty. Statutes must reflect the common interest, what the citizens through parliament desire and only what they desire, and essential to that desire making up the common interest is freedom of person and property. In the course of his comments Fortescue stipulated that the liberty of a people is the freedom to live under laws that they themselves desire,[52] with the proviso that all human laws must accord with the divine and natural law.[53] Any law in an absolute monarchy, like that of France, which is simply an expression of the king's will replaces the liberty of citizens by their servitude under a tyrannical regime. In *De natura* Fortescue leaves no doubt as to the high value he placed on liberty: "What can be more irksome than to be robbed of liberty? or more repugnant than to be deprived of one's own will, and subjected to the will of another?"[54] The theme is repeated in *De laudibus*:

"A law is also adjudged cruel, if it increases servitude (*servitutem*) and diminishes freedom (*libertatem*)."[55]

Fortescue's discussion of how the liberties of Englishmen were protected and furthered under their parliamentary monarchy plainly shows that he believed that no citizen would be deliberately impoverished by a good government and that every individual would be given every incentive to prosper, thus contributing to the economic well-being of the whole. Thus the conditions under which each subject would be able to maximize his material advantage without jeopardizing the comparable endeavors of his fellow citizens were vital to the common interest. Fortescue, moreover, insisted that the self-interest of the ruler was identical with the protection and encouragement of the pursuit of self-interest by his subjects.[56] It would be the interest of the sovereign to govern prudently in such a manner, for he would thus have far more freedom and power than a greedy absolute monarch. Both kinds of ruler might in principle have equal power, but the exercise of regal dominion would lack the authority, the support, and the loyalty of the citizens and prove far more difficult in practice. A regal king, said Fortescue, in threatening the lives and possessions of his people, grinding them down with arbitrary taxes and subsidies for his own egotistical ends, was "impotence itself."[57] Ultimately the wealth, freedom, and power of a monarch and the deference accorded him depended on thriving and materially prosperous subjects who in the unhampered pursuit of their individual happiness loyally backed their ruler in his various enterprises and willingly supplied him with funds and manpower required for the security of the realm. As did Aristotle before him and Machiavelli and Hobbes after him, Fortescue appealed to the egoism of the ruler, arguing that his worldly desires would only be realized in proportion to his commitment to advancing the enlightened selfishness of his subjects. Tyranny, always unthinking and irrational, could only lead to self-destruction of the sovereign and his state.

Economic Consequences of English and French Government

The economic dimension of Fortescue's thought on the state achieved a high point in his unprecedented comparison of material circumstances in France and England in *De laudibus*. The impoverishment and abject misery of the one and the economic prosperity and happy contentment of the other were in large part a result of their differing constitutional systems: the French *regnum regale* and the English *regnum politicum et regale*. The major assumption of the comparative analysis is the prime economic goal of the state. If a thriving economy is desired, then the mixed form of government must be preferred to absolutism. The criterion determining the choice of one constitutional type over the other is its capability of producing the most desirable material advantage. Fortescue's emphasis on economics—the economic ends of the state we have seen; the economic conditions and composition of the state and the economic policies of government will be discussed below—seems to be a novel aspect of his thought, perhaps a harbinger of much of future English speculation about the state, perhaps even the germ of political economy.

Fortescue's perception of the contrasting material situation in France and England may be faulted for its detail and for the reasons given for the differences. His contemporaries nevertheless appear to agree with him in their admiration of English prosperity in comparison with the economic stagnation of France and other Continental states. Tudor commentators in the next century, living in times of acute material hardship and social dislocation, looked back nostalgically to the last decades of the fifteenth century as a kind of golden age. An anonymous pamphlet, *The Comodytes of England*, probably incorrectly ascribed to Fortescue, proclaimed that "the comune people of thys londe are the beste fedde, and also the best cledde of any natyon crystyn and hethen."[58] An Italian visitor to England about 1500 remarked that "the riches of England are greater than those of any country of Europe" and that "every one who makes a tour in the island will soon become aware of this wealth."[59] The reasons offered for the economic prosperity were the fertility of the soil, the sale of tin abroad, the high productivity of the woolen industry and flourishing foreign trade in woolens, and the prohibition on export of gold and silver. Especially impressive to the Italian was the great wealth of London, which had attracted many artisans from overseas.[60] Fortescue's economic comparisons seem then to have been not too wide of the mark.

The *De laudibus* examination of France and England begins with the statement that on the basis of "experience" the author intends to explore the consequences of regal government in the one and mixed government in the other.[61] There follows a description of the autocratic impositions of the French crown on the people, chief of which was the quartering of troops without consent or compensation.[62] Not one small town was free from being "plundered by this abominable extortion once or twice a year." Other royal assessments are cited, the infamous *gabelle*, or salt tax, and the *taille*, which with similar repressive measures, despite the abundance of commodities produced in villages and towns, had the result that

> the people live in no little misery. They drink water daily, and they taste no other liquor unless at solemn feasts. They wear frocks or

tabards of canvas like sackcloth. They do not use woolens, except of the cheapest sort, and that only in their shirts under their frocks, and wear no hose, unless to the knees, exposing the rest of their shins. Their women are bare-footed except on feast days; the men and women eat no flesh, except bacon lard, with which they fatten their pottage in the smallest quantity. They do not taste other meats, roast or boiled, except occasionally the offal and heads of animals killed for the nobles and merchants. On the contrary, the men-at-arms eat their poultry, so that they are left with scarcely their eggs for themselves to eat as a rare delicacy. And if anyone grows in wealth at any time, and is reputed rich among the others, he is at once assessed for the king's subsidy more than his neighbours, so that forthwith he is levelled to their poverty.[63]

The financial exactions of French absolutism and its high-handed judicial procedures, Fortescue notes, condemned the vast majority of the people to penury and virtual enslavement, in contrast to the nobility who, free from oppression, lived in splendor.

In the next chapter Fortescue invokes Aristotle—"Opposites placed in juxtaposition are more manifest"—to validate the comparison of England and France.[64] Fortescue then turns to the economic effects of parliamentary monarchy in England, where the king did not rule tyrannically and his subjects flourished. All taxes, subsidies, and laws required the consent of the whole kingdom voiced in parliament. Englishmen lived in abundance and contentment, a far cry from the wretchedness of the French:

Hence every inhabitant of that realm uses at his own pleasure the fruits which his land yields, the increase of his flock, and all the emoluments which he gains, whether by his own industry or that of others, from land and sea, hindered by the injuries and rapine of none without obtaining at least due amends. Hence the inhabitants of the land are rich, abounding in gold and silver and all the necessaries of life. They do not drink water, except those who sometimes abstain from other drinks by way of devotional or penitential zeal. They eat every kind of flesh and fish in abundance, with which their land is not meanly stocked. They are clothed with good woolens throughout their garments; they have abundant bedding, woolen like the rest of their furnishings, in all their houses, and are rich in all agricultural goods and agricultural equipment, and in all that is requisite for a quiet and happy life, according to their estate. They are not brought to trial except before the ordinary judges, where they are treated justly according to the law of the land. Nor are they examined or impleaded in respect of their chattels, or possessions, nor arrested for crime of whatever magnitude and enormity, except according to the laws of the land and before the aforesaid judges. These are the fruits which the political and regal government (*regimen politicum et regale*) yields.[65]

From the last sentence it is obvious that for Fortescue a constitutional system was to be evaluated by its practical results. The best qualified judges, he seems to have been saying, are those living under a system of law and subject to its full weight. For the people the acid test, or so Fortescue suggested, was economic. From their standpoint, was the law conducive to their economic welfare or did it render them destitute? Did the constitution of the state foster an environment of freedom and personal security, serving to safeguard life and property, so that the individual could reap the full material rewards of his calling? Fortescue upheld a pragmatic criterion for the ultimate assessment of the worth of a constitution, just as Bacon later was to do for science. The term used by both was *fruits*, with its manifold connotations. The value of a constitution, no less than of a science, was to be estimated on the basis of the material benefits it conferred. The biblical imagery of St. Matthew, "By their fruits shall you know them," quoted by Fortescue in the *Governance* comes to mind.[66] Labor in field and workshop accounts for a variety of goods and commodities, just as Fortescue said: "How rich in fruits are the villages and towns of the kingdom of France."[67] The people who lived and labored under the law were best placed to appreciate its good or to feel its cruel oppression. The citizen was essentially a consumer of law, Fortescue implied, a suggestion reminiscent of Aristotle's "shoe-pinching" argument for democracy: the best judge of the fit of a shoe was the wearer, not the maker.[68] Needless to say, Fortescue, who believed that parliament contained directly or indirectly all citizens, was not a democrat.

Another illustration of Fortescue's economic turn of mind and the close connection he made between legal arrangements and the socioeconomic context is found in his treatment of the jury in England and its absence in civil law nations. Much of twelve chapters (chapters 20–32) is allotted to a comparison of judicial procedure under common law and civil law (with France in mind). A jury of twelve men was required in England to resolve "the issue of a plea," whereas under civil law the testimony of only two witnesses called by the judge was sufficient.[69] The explanation for the difference, according to Fortescue, lay in the unique character of English state and society, so different from that in civil law countries. The law "by which truth is sought in England is not common to other nations, for they cannot like England, make adequate and similar juries."[70]

This fact Fortescue did not attribute to any defect in the laws elsewhere but solely to "the fertility of England."[71] His contention is perplexing because he also referred to the fertility and abundance of goods in France. Perhaps he meant to say that where regal monarchies like France had degenerated into tyrannies, the people gained no benefit from the richness of their country. English mixed monarchy, in contrast, favored the use and exploitation of the kingdom's wealth by all citizens proportionate to their station, allowing each to acquire a fair share of the commodities produced.

But the question still remains: Why did England alone possess the jury? Fortescue resolved the problem first by his description of the nature of the English jury and second by his related explanation of English agrarian conditions, comparing them to those in civil law countries, France being the prime example. He characterizes jury members in the following ways: "twelve good and lawful men of the neighbourhood"; with "lands or rents for the term of his life to the value of at least forty shillings a year"; with "sufficient possessions over and above moveables to maintain their status"; "neighbours, able to live of their own, sound in repute and fair-minded"; "honest men worthy of credit"; "twelve trustworthy men of the neighbourhood in which the fact in question occurred, knowing the circumstances and also the habits of the witnesses, especially if they are neighbours and cannot but know if they are worthy of credence."[72] In addition to being "neighbours" who knew the accused (at least four of the twelve had to be from the hundred in which the vill was located where the alleged infringement of the law was said to have occurred), jurymen could not be related or hostile to him.[73] In other words, jurymen had to be economically independent persons of substance, at least forty-shilling freeholders (yeomen) who qualified for the franchise.[74] This excluded the propertyless and those with minimal property and all who at least in part were economically dependent for wages and keep on others: servants, laborers, cottagers, and smallholders. If the defendant was one of these poor or a yeoman, the juryman had to be his peer, that is, one of nongentlemanly status like a yeoman or well-to-do free tenant possessing land of his own who was accustomed to manual labor. Gentlemanly defendants could not be judged by the likes of these but only by others of gentlemanly status.[75] The reason for the property qualification in the first case was to safeguard against the bribery or corruption of the juror or prejudice in favor of the defendant because of economic dependancy on him. Fortescue also thought that an individual who relied on tillage for a livelihood, in contrast to a grazier, was less rational, suffering from a "rusticity of mind," a "rustic ignorance," which would disqualify him from discovering the truth, thus rendering him inadequate for jury service.[76]

Fortescue's opinion was that a jury of twelve such substantial yeomen or middling men of landed property could be formed without difficulty in any English locality, while abroad it would have been impossible to do so. The reason for the difference was the general economic prosperity of the English countryside and the rural poverty and backwardness of the Continent. Rural England in Fortescue's glowing words was a veritable Eden, productive and bounteous:

> England is indeed so fertile that, compared area to area, it surpasses almost all other lands in the abundance of its produce; it is productive of its own accord, scarcely aided by man's labour. For its fields, plains, and groves abound in vegetation with such richness that they often yield more fruits to their owners uncultivated than ploughed lands, though these are very fertile in crops and corn. Moreover, in that land, pastures are enclosed with ditches and hedges planted over with trees, by which the flocks and herds are protected from the wind and the sun's heat; most of them are irrigated, so that the animals, shut in their pens, do not need watching by day or by night. For in that land there are neither wolves, bears, nor lions, so the sheep lie by night in the fields without guard in their cotes and folds, whereby their lands are fertilised. Hence, the men of that land are not very much burdened with the sweat of labour, so that they live with more spirit, as the ancient fathers did, who preferred to tend flocks than to distract their peace of mind with the cares of agriculture. For this reason the men of the land are more apt and disposed to investigate causes which require searching examination than men who, immersed in agricultural work, have contracted a rusticity of mind from familiarity with the soil.[77]

Because of this remarkable fertility and productivity, not even the smallest settlement lacked potential jurymen: knights, esquires, substantial householders or franklins, numerous free tenants and yeomen.[78] Juries, Fortescue pointed out, could easily be called because many yeomen had incomes of over a hundred pounds per year and knights and esquires, required for the trial of their peers, were worth over three times as much. In other countries—Fortescue was thinking of France—so few well-to-do people lived in the same neighborhood that an individual eligible for jury service could scarcely be found:

> For, outside cities and walled towns it is rare for any except nobles to be found who are possessors of fields or other immoveables.

There, again, the nobles do not have an abundance of pastures, and it is not compatible with their status to cultivate vineyards or to put hands to a plough, though the substance of their possessions consists in vineyards and arable, except only meadows adjoining large rivers and woods, the pasture is commonly to their tenants and neighbours.[79]

Where then, Fortescue asked, could one discover outside England "twelve honest men of the neighbourhood" to sit on a jury?[80] Qualified men with firsthand knowledge of a dispute simply did not exist, so that a jury would have to be composed of persons from other areas, scattered over the countryside or from the poor of the neighborhood, neither alternative being acceptable.

These two quotations detailing English and French rural conditions, apart from attempting an explanation of the different kinds of judicial arrangements in England and abroad, are of considerable interest because they contribute to an understanding of Fortescue's conception of the state, exemplifying as they do his empirical approach and economic concerns. He unhesitatingly defended enclosure for the pasturage of livestock. Grazing on enclosed land was responsible for rural prosperity, he thought, the pastures being held by individuals, not in common by poor husbandmen, the normal arrangement outside England (no doubt he was thinking of France).[81] English grazing, he informs us, was far more extensive than tillage, although the arable was productive, while abroad tillage was more widespread than grazing.[82]

Fortescue's emphasis on enclosure and grazing, together with his remarks about the free tenant (*tenente*) and yeoman (*valettus*), deserves further comment because he was observing a fundamental structural change slowly taking place in the agrarian sector, a change without parallel elsewhere. From his intimate acquaintance with the countryside in Devon, Somerset, Wiltshire, and Gloucestershire, where he had substantial holdings, much of it in livestock and mixed corn and livestock farmland, Fortescue seems to have been keenly aware of enclosure and of what is now identified as the beginnings of capitalist agriculture there and eastward in Sussex and Kent. By his time most of this land had already been enclosed and some of it, for example, in Gloucestershire and Somerset, was being irrigated by floating water meadows. The archetypal capitalist farmers of the time were graziers with enormous herds. These pioneers of early capitalist enterprise were usually free tenants, copyholders, and yeomen (tenants as well as freeholders in their own right), soon to be followed by the gentry. The working, nongentlemanly capitalist farmers were among the first and most ruthless enclosers of common and waste land, engrossing their scattered holdings in the common fields and leasing arable and pasture from the gentry, all chiefly for the purpose of grazing their livestock. Wool was the foundation of the wealth of the nation, and the high profits from relatively low-cost grazing operations were an irresistible attraction for acquisitive farmers. At least part of the economic troubles and social dislocation arising in the latter half of the century and increasing in the age of More, Starkey, and Smith can be attributed to the endeavors of capitalist graziers.

Political Economy of Kingship

Fortescue's last work, *The Governance of England*, also reveals his economic emphasis. Written in English in twenty short chapters, the book comes to about half the length of *De laudibus*. Its purpose was quite different from that of the earlier volume, for this work was a compilation of advice probably composed for Edward IV sometime after Fortescue received the ruler's favor and became a member of the royal council. Except for the first three chapters summarizing the author's idea of mixed monarchy from *De laudibus*, the tome consists of a series of memoranda setting forth policies—mainly of a financial and economic nature—to be observed by the king in order to maintain and enhance his power and authority. Parliament receives surprisingly little attention. In fact, had Fortescue's recommendations for the financial independence of the crown and the strengthening of the council been implemented, the existing powers of parliament would have withered away and the nature of the constitution would have been radically altered.[83] While the *Governance* did not deal in Machiavellian fashion with the methods of exercising royal power, what did perhaps distinguish Fortescue's thought from previous medieval writers was the idea that well-conceived policy could be an effective tool for positive reform.[84] Furthermore, these policy recommendations were almost entirely economic in nature, on this score putting Fortescue far in advance of Machiavelli.

That the *Governance* can be called a rudimentary handbook on the political economy of kingship is plain from a short chapter-by-chapter synopsis of the contents. Chapter 4 begins by asserting that the revenues of the French king far surpass those of the English monarchy, because the former rules tyrannically to the detriment of his subjects, depriving them of their due, with the result that "the myght of reaume is nerehand destroyed. . . ."[85] The English sovereign, in Fortescue's view, should never resort to the unjust and self-defeating measures of the French crown, even though his revenues must be increased. If unpopularity is to be avoided and royal authority bolstered, the English king (chapter 5) cannot live on the basis of borrowing and credit, nor should he adopt the artful and high-handed means of the French, as Fortescue put it, "exquysite meanes of geytinge of good."[86] Royal coffers must be filled, but not by alienating any more of the royal domaine, that is, by further sales of crown land. Fortescue then makes a distinction (chapters 6–8) between two kinds of royal expenses: "ordinary charges" and "extraordinary charges."[87] The first are fixed. They can be calculated in advance and budgeted on the basis of past experience. The second are unpredictable and cannot be estimated prior to the fact. The king must have sufficient fixed yearly revenue to cover the ordinary charges: regular household expenses and wardrobe, salaries of officers of state, upkeep of courts and councils, maintaining the marches and Calais and the navy, and the cost of royal works. Beyond the revenue necessary to meet the ordinary charges, the crown should have a large permanent source of income for extraordinary outlays required by diplomatic missions, rewards and gifts, special commissions and visitations, new buildings and clothing, and foreign attack. The king's income for such contingencies (chapter 9) should simply exceed that of the greatest lord of his realm, otherwise the latter will aspire to be king. In order to acquire sufficient funds (chapter 10), the crown should become a powerful landlord with vast holdings and many lucrative rent-paying tenants, never relying on typical French measures like the salt tax. For this purpose lands alienated by the crown in the past to reward subjects (chapters 11, 14, 19) must be regained by an act of resumption made with the assent of parliament, thus providing the source for a steady royal income from rents. The landed endowment of the king through the proposed act of resumption will offer a degree of financial independence from parliament and become "a newe ffundacion of is Crowne . . . [The king] shall be thereby the grettest ffounder off the world. Ffor thereas other kynges have ffounded byshopriches, abbeys, and other houses off relegyon, the kyng shall then have ffounded an holl reaume, and endowed it with gretter possescions, and better then ever was any reaume in christendome."[88] The endowment or new foundation will enhance the power of the king and every citizen will prosper. As a consequence, the English state "shalbe a collage, in which shul syng and pray for euermore al the men of Ingland spirituel and temporel."[89] Besides these topics Fortescue treated the problems of poverty and insurrection (chapters 12–13) and the reorganization and functions of the royal council (chapters 15–16) in addition to offering a miscellany of advice about royal offices (chapter 17), pensions (chapter 18), and patents and gifts (chapter 20).

The problem of usurpation of power from below and the means of reducing the threat of popular uprisings, a topic receiving no attention in *De laudibus* is analyzed in chapters 12 and 13 in the *Governance*. Fortescue seemed particularly sensitive to the matter because the Lancastrian monarchs were plagued by popular unrest, a threat that reached epidemic proportions in the next century. His handling of the subject, in fact, anticipated the Tudor reformers' serious concern. He immediately rejected a current view that the best method of limiting the possibility of rebellion by the commons was through keeping them poor, as in France.[90] Thereby, so it was claimed, the people were so impoverished as to be unable to equip themselves with weapons and armor for revolt. Fortescue's first response was that a similar policy in England would render useless the indispensable fighting force of archers drawn from the yeomanry on which the might of the kingdom and its internal security so depended, for they would no longer be able to afford bows and arrows.[91] He then argued that the existing poor already were the chief participants in English uprisings. His conclusion was that "it semyth that poverte hath been the holl cause of all suche rysynges."[92] If the commons were impoverished, he warned that the result could well be a civil disaster like the Hussite Wars (1419–1436) in Bohemia where the people united against the nobility and shared collectively all the appropriated possessions. The explanation for the failure of the French people to revolt, poor and wretched as they were, was their lack of "heart and courage," so characteristic of the English commons.[93] This resort to a notion of national character in accounting for the differences was, of course, at odds with Fortescue's basic economic explanation in *De laudibus*. This contradiction appears to be the only one of its kind and perhaps involved only a momentary outburst of English chauvinism rather than a fundamental inconsistency. A wealthy citizen body would not rise up against constituted authority, Fortescue insisted. Widespread poverty, furthermore, was a breeding ground for criminal activity, thus constituting another threat to law and order.[94] This causal relationship, he contended, was demonstrated by the lower incidence of executions for crimes in prosperous England than in impoverished France.[95] Despite somewhat naive use of evidence, Fortescue at least perceived an empirical connection between poverty and crime, an idea to be more fully expounded by the Tudor reformers.

Fortescue was convinced then that the surest remedy for civil unrest and crime was for the crown to strive to make the common people economically secure in person and possessions.[96] Indeed, the office of the king, the royal honor, and the Christian faith obliged the monarch to do so. Where the commons prospered, as under English mixed monarchy, moreover, requests for subsidies for the common interest and defense of the realm received the support of the parliament and were willingly granted to the crown. In France, in contrast, the absolute monarch could not ask the impoverished commons for funds and dared not seek financial relief from the nobility for fear they would combine with the people against him. At first glance, some of these concerns seem to contradict the portrayal of England in *De laudibus* as fertile and thriving. If the English commons were in such an enviable material position, why should every precaution have to be taken against the possibility of civil disturbance? Fortescue seemed to be cautioning that the wealth of the English (in contrast to French poverty) should not be taken for granted or allowed to deteriorate, that there was still room for improvement. From his own self-interest, if nothing more, the king must be ever vigilant about the economic welfare of his subjects.

Directly related to this recommendation that the furtherance of economic prosperity of the commons would establish social harmony, reduce crime, and increase royal power and authority as well was Fortescue's advice on the reorganization of the royal council (chapters 15–16), recommendations that apparently influenced the early Tudor monarchs. His intention was to reshape the council, often merely a conclave of great magnates bent on their own advantage, into a genuine advisory body of the king's own men who would serve him and his interests. Fortescue proposed that the council be a moderately paid and perpetual body of twenty-four wise and loyal members, evenly divided between clerical and secular personages, all to be chosen by the king and at his discretion periodically increased in number. Members would have no other duties and receive rewards and gifts only from the king, who would appoint one of them to be presiding officer. The chancellor, treasurer, and lord privy seal might attend by choice or invitation. When the chancellor was present, he would be in the chair. A register book was to be kept containing rules of procedure and a record of decisions. The council's main functions would be to deliberate on important state business, to advise the king on policy, amending laws, making public appointments, and granting rewards, and to draft legislation to be presented in parliament.

First among the council's policies listed by Fortescue were those of an economic nature aimed at promoting the material interests of the realm.[97] Every attempt was to be made to curtail the drain of money from the kingdom and to ensure the flow of bullion into it—a key policy of later mercantilist doctrine—and to recover any plate, jewels, and money that had recently been allowed to be taken abroad. Fortescue recommended efforts to import cheap foreign goods and sell agricultural commodities in foreign markets at the highest prices. Although the details are vague,

Fortescue apparently was thinking of government regulation designed to maintain a favorable balance of trade by encouraging the export of farm products at high prices and restricting imports so that in overseas commerce monetary gains would exceed losses. He also prescribed care in maintaining and expanding the navy but made no reference to manufacturing or mining. Fortescue underscored that his recommended policies would be of "the grettest profyte and encrease, that euer come to this lande."[98] Finally, he warned that the English should learn from the example of ancient Rome. When the role and activities of the senate so decayed under the emperors that it ceased to be the great council of state, the fortunes and powers of the ruler waned. If the English king would keep the Roman example in mind and follow the suggestions of Fortescue, "his lande shall not only be ryche and welthy, as were the Romans, but also is hyghnes shalbe myghty, and off poiar to subdue his ennemyes, and all other that he shall liste to reygne uppon."[99]

Without engaging in the argument about Fortescue's status as the last great English medieval legal and political theorist or the first of the moderns, I can nonetheless point out how some elements of his thought in more developed form became central to the outlook of our Tudor reformers. Clearly Fortescue was a reformer, but not in the sense that they were. His relatively prosperous age, unmarked by the severe conditions of the poor during the early Tudor era, naturally failed to elicit from him cries of moral anguish and protest so characteristic of the reformers. Yet he recognized widespread and debilitating poverty to have been the fundamental cause of civil unrest, insurrection, and crime, warning rulers that their own self-interest depended on advancing their subjects' interests. In his estimation, therefore, the successful government should concentrate on furthering the common interest, defined mainly as the security of the lives and possessions of subjects and the increase of their economic welfare, to be best achieved by the cooperation of king and people in parliament. On the one hand, Fortescue appears to have been a legal positivist, believing that law could be used creatively to shape and improve social circumstances.[100] On the other hand, however, he subscribed to the traditional medieval view that law was the discovery and application of divinely ordained ethical principles. While he may have been on the threshold of conceptualizing the state in institutional terms, he tended to personalize rule in the conventional medieval fashion. However he may have conceived of the state, his primary focus was nonetheless on its economic purposes; this is the only conclusion to be drawn from his pragmatic evaluation of the superiority of English over French polities and from his recommendations for strengthening regal power. No more a radical or a democrat than our Tudor reformers, Fortescue was a conservative who wished to restore peace and harmony and reinvigorate a traditional society of rank and hierarchy. Given the political anarchy of his times, he was preoccupied with the question of responsible government and the prevention of tyranny, so he saw the mixed constitution as equally the best remedy against arbitrary rule from above or popular revolt from below. On this score Fortescue and the reformers seem to have been in firm accord.

5 First of the Reformers

Sir Edmund Dudley

Sir Edmund Dudley (ca. 1462–1510) may not have been a profound thinker or systematic political analyst, but there is good reason to label him the first of the Tudor reformers. His reputation in the world of ideas has probably suffered as much from his position sandwiched between the imposing intellects of Fortescue and More as from the prolixity of his single, slender unpublished book. To give Dudley his due, he did not enjoy the luxury of ample leisure to marshal and expound his views in the secure comfort of his study. Rather, he was a shrewd and competent man of action whose imprisonment and imminent execution drove him to put pen to paper, perhaps in a last desperate bid to save himself. All this said, he was by no means an insignificant figure in the annals of English government or in the history of political thought. His little volume, *The Tree of Commonwealth* (1510), of which four manuscript copies survive from the sixteenth and seventeenth centuries (it was not printed until 1859), can be called the first major Tudor work in political theory.[1] Not a comprehensive treatise, it is a manual addressed to the new sovereign, Henry VIII, which, because of the author's concern about the problem of civil disorder, deals primarily with the ideal of a prudent monarch's administration, his proper functions and moral responsibilities, and the means of rendering his subjects peaceful and loyal. Dudley does little to advance Fortescue's incipient conception of the state, except to continue its economic tendencies, but his treatment exhibits some perceptive sociological analysis. The distinguishing features of the work are its pronounced anticlericalism, its early exposition of the doctrine of the divine right of kings, and its humanistic attention to the education of the nobility and the patronage of scholars by the church.

Son of John Dudley and grandson of the well-known Lancastrian, John, Lord Dudley, Edmund was born about 1462 in Atherington, Sussex;

he attended Winchester and briefly Oxford, where his uncle, William Dudley, bishop of Durham, was chancellor in 1483. Edmund turned to the study and practice of law in Gray's Inn and was appointed Double Reader in 1496, the same year he was made undersheriff of London. He acquired a name as a lawyer specializing in property cases. Sergeant-at-law in 1503, the following year he was selected speaker of the House of Commons— Henry VII's seventh and last speaker—and a legal counselor to the king. Two years later he was made chairman of a royal council on legal and judicial matters and became active in the work of Star Chamber. During his career he managed to amass a fortune from landed holdings in thirteen counties, from commercial ventures, and from labors for the crown, with goods alone valued at £5,000. Dudley was unquestionably a devoted, talented, and enterprising if tough and ruthless public servant.

Dudley not only gained the hostility of the City by intervening in its internal controversies and prosecuting merchants for customs and export violations but he also incurred the enmity of the landed classes by loyally executing the king's policy of asserting royal property rights and enforcing payment of feudal dues. Henry VIII, who succeeded his father on 22 April 1509, was so angered by reports of the activities of Dudley and another official, Richard Empson, that the next day he ordered their arrest and imprisonment. One contemporary account refers to the "unreasonable and extort doing" of both officials, which "noble men grudged, mean men kicked, poor men lamented, preachers openly at St. Paul's Cross and other places exclaimed, rebuked and detested."[2] The new monarch, in order to placate some of his leading subjects over the unpopular measures of his father, thus began his reign by making scapegoats of Dudley and Empson. Why he selected them and not others is unclear. Perhaps it was because they were without powerful connections.[3] Dudley was tried for treason, convicted, confined to the Tower, and executed some sixteen months after his arrest. In the first few weeks after the trial, evidently before composing *The Tree of Commonwealth*, he wrote a petition listing over eighty instances of financial victimization by the crown in which restitution should have been made.[4] On the way to the block on Tower Hill, he spoke briefly to Thomas More, who was also to lose his head a quarter of a century afterward by command of the same sovereign.[5] Fate seems to have been cruel to the Dudleys, for Edmund's son John (1502–1553), the duke of Northumberland who replaced Somerset in the government of Edward VI, was executed, as was the grandson, Robert (ca. 1532–1588), earl of Leicester, paramour to Queen Elizabeth.

Dudley composed *The Tree of Commonwealth* as he languished in the Tower, awaiting some sign of mercy from his new sovereign. Perhaps the author hoped that this literary effort for the edification of the young, inexperienced Henry VIII would gain him a reprieve. Dudley described the king in the opening pages as "the Prince that shall revive the comon wealth within this his realme (the which long tyme hath been in sore decay)," saying that his purpose in writing "is that all things well orderyd may so contynew and encrease to the Better."[6] He intended "to write a rememberance, (albeit perchaunce both rude and vnlernyed)," and he later referred to "this symple and rude treatise . . . mad by a person most ignorant and being also in worldly vexation and troblid with the sorroful and bytter rememberans of death."[7] Dudley produced this memorandum for the prince just as several years later another faithful public servant, Niccolò Machiavelli, relieved of office, imprisoned, tortured, and exiled, drafted the much more famous *Il Principe* to win the attention of a noble patron. Less brilliantly written and less startling in its pronouncements, Dudley's endeavor is nevertheless not completely overshadowed by Machiavelli's classic, and in some ways it is just as rewarding. Never as daring or provocative as Machiavelli, Dudley adhered in substance to the moralistic mirror-of-princes' tradition. He may not have dealt with the mechanics of political power and statecraft or dwelled on the conduct of foreign relations and war as Machiavelli did, but within his purview he was no less realistic. In his recommendations for governmental administration and his appreciation of the economic basis of kingly rule and the relationship of royal power to the major social groups of the realm, his claim to a realistic understanding of politics is unmatched by Machiavelli. One can think of no better agenda for Tudor centralization and rationalization and for the foundation of a national church than this short manual, which also heralded the approach and some of the concerns of the later reformers.

Dudley's book might well have been entitled *The Prince*, for he was primarily interested in the role of the monarch, the conservation and increase of his power by means of rational administrative measures, and the prudent handling of the social groups on which royal power was based. His emphasis on the power of the king, its centralization, and the elimination of competing loci of power seemingly arose from his fear of civil disorder and rebellion. Of the three possible sources of trouble—clergy, nobility and people—the latter were the most serious threat for the obvious reason that the commons, supported and led by contingents of the other orders, possessed the manpower necessary for insurrection.[8] Dudley had good cause to be anxious about the danger of social upheaval given the signs of economic deterioration, the Jacquerie or bloody peasant revolt in

France, and the Yorkshire and Cornish uprisings of 1489 and 1497. He cited the Jacquerie because of the attack on the nobility and danger to the regime.[9] He lamented the Cornish revolt led by the blacksmith of the Lizard, Michael Joseph, for being another "lewde enterprise": "I pray god save this realme from any suche captein hereafter."[10] Consequently, Dudley underscored as vital factors in the maintenance of regal power and peace in the realm a healthy economy and a sound education for the nobility, subjects given little or no treatment by Machiavelli. Dudley's perspective, unlike Machiavelli's, was institutional and administrative, with attention paid to sociological, economic, and educational matters. With only one brief exception he failed to discuss parliament, its relationship to the crown, or the rights of citizens; the concept of mixed monarchy is not mentioned.[11]

Dudley understood Christianity, on which the English state was founded, as the fundamental unifying force in society, the prime means of harmonizing the actions of the citizenry and controlling those of the ruler. Well before the doctrine of the divine right of kings was current, he asserted the idea that the prince was God's regent on earth, divinely ordained to rule both the temporal and spiritual spheres, and obligated to God alone to reign for the good of his people.[12] Since the prince wielded both swords, as God's earthly vicar he exercised primacy over the church. The church, which existed to assist the king in spiritual matters, was therefore enjoined to leave the temporal sphere to the monarch, neither interfering nor sharing in the affairs of state. While the king had the task of distinguishing the temporal from the spiritual, Dudley would probably have accorded the church the right to determine its own doctrine and to manage ecclesiastical affairs through its own courts.[13] Just as all subjects including the clergy were obliged by divine commandment to obey the king, so the monarch was duty-bound to God, the only check on the exercise of his power apart from prudence and self-interest. Dudley's anticlericalism and his views on the church-state relationship are Machiavellian before Machiavelli as well as reminiscent of Marsiglio of Padua's conclusion and Hobbes's future position. From the standpoint of practice, Dudley's attitude pointed to the more extensive powers over the church granted to Henry VIII by the Act of Supremacy.

If Dudley's religious perspective violated convention, his outlook on society was conservative and traditional, upholding the time-hallowed concept of the great chain of being:

> But let vs all consyder y^t god hath sett an order by grace bytwene hym self and Angell, and betwene Angell and Angell; and by reason

between Angell and man, and betwene man and man, man and beest; which order, from the highest pointe to the lowest, god willyth vs fyrmely to kepe without any enterprise to the contrary.[14]

Each subject of the state from the most exalted to the most humble was to occupy a divinely ordained rank within a hierarchical social order and to have the traditional rights and duties corresponding to his position. Government existed to preserve and invigorate the hierarchy, to see that all ranks were filled, that justice was accorded to each member, that everyone performed his duties, and that no one was without the benefits appropriate to his status. For the majority, the poor commoners, this meant that each deserved gainful employment suitable to his rank and that no one should suffer discomfort or distress from lack of food, shelter, or clothing. Such was the time-honored social ideal that Dudley as well as Fortescue shared with the later reformers. Dudley concluded his advice book, stating that:

> It hath ben declarid what reward, aswell worldly as hevenly, our sovereigne lord and every one of his subiectes, that is to say, every person in his degre, shalhaue for doing ther dewties to kepe vp this tree of comonwealth within this realme of England, in maner and forme before rehersyd and declarid.[15]

Meaning of "Tree of Commonwealth"

Dudley's traditionalism is fully illustrated by his laborious and detailed use of the elaborate tree of commonwealth metaphor throughout the work. The tedious imagery is enough to discourage all but the most persevering reader. One historian calls the work, not without justice, a "complicated and wearisome allegory," and another, speaks of this "medieval allegory carried almost to the length of parody."[16] If, however, we are to fathom what Dudley was saying, the handicap of the ornate metaphor must be overcome. He introduced it as follows:

> The comon wealth of this realme or of the subeictes or Inhabitauntes thereof may be resemblid to a faier and mighte tree growing in a faier feild or pasture, vnder the couerte or shade whereof all beastes, both fatt and leane, are protectyd and comfortyd from heate and cold as the tyme requireth. In like maner all the subiectes of that realme wher this tree of comon wealth doth seuerly growe are ther by holpen and relyved from the highest degree to the lowest. But for a troth this tree will never long stand and growe uprighte in this realme, or in any other, withowt diverse strong rootes, and fastened sewer in the grounde.[17]

The roots sustaining the tree and holding it in the ground are five in number, the "principall and cheif" being "love of god" and the others justice, truth, concord, and peace. The prince is the "ground" out of which grows the main root, the love of God; apparently the four other lesser roots also sprout there. The root of justice—Dudley concentrates on the administration of justice—depends on the king himself "for the whole auctoritie therof is hym by god, to mynister by hym self or by his deputies to his subiectes."[18] To a great extent the root of truth or trust rests on the example set by the king to the citizenry, in the first instance in his relations with the nobility:

Then how glad shall euery noble man be of the company of an other, and one will trust and love an other. What frendship and confydens shall then be betwene men and men from the highest degre to the lowest. How kyndly and how loveingly will merchaunts and craftysmen of the realme by and sell together and exchaunge and bargain one thing for an other. How diligently and busyly will the artificers and husbondmen occupie ther Labor and Busynes, and how well content man will be, from the highest degre to the lowest, to encrease ther howshold seruantes and laborers, whereby all idle people and vagaboundes shalbe sett a worke. And ouer this, how glad shall all strangers and people of outward nacions be to deale and medle with the comodities of this realme.[19]

Concord, the fourth root, begins with the king and with the spiritual and temporal lords. The prince must take special care to see that his nobles are not in conflict with one another, and he must work to remove all causes of friction between the temporality and spirituality. The root of concord should be well secured in the commons, for they are the great majority of all subjects and should not be oppressed by their superiors. Nobles should therefore be charitable toward the less fortunate and be "the helpers and relevers of poore tenantes, and also be the manteynors and supporters of all poore folkes in godes causes and matters."[20] To these ends the prince should not only run an efficient and honest administration, but he should also take steps to safeguard and improve the welfare and material well-being of the commoners. Above all he must prevent the idleness of every subject, for idleness is a fundamental cause of disunity and rebellion: "the verie mother of all vice in man and whoman, both noble and vnnoble, and the Lyneall of pouertie and myserie, and the deadly ennymie to this tree of comon welth."[21] Equally reliant on the prince is the fifth root, peace, which depends on his skill in the conduct of foreign relations. On this score Dudley stresses the necessity of peace for a flourishing export trade, on which depends the wealth of the kingdom and the contentment of citizens. Wars threaten the tree of commonwealth in that

> the comodities of this noble realme are so noble and with that so plentuous y^t thei can not be spent or all imploied within the same, But necessarily ther must be entercourse bytwene this realm and outward parties for the vtterance therof, and speciallie for the wull, clothe, tynne, leade, Fell and hide, besides other diuerse comodities y^t do greate ease to the subiectes.[22]

The metaphor becomes too intricate in the second half of the book to reproduce, except for a brief summary. If the five roots are healthy and vigorous, a different fruit corresponding to each is produced by the tree. Love of God yields the fruit of the "honour of God"; justice, the fruit of "honorable dignitie"; truth, "worldly prosperite"; concord, "tranquylite"; peace, "good example."[23] As one might guess since it grows from the principal root, the fruit of the honor of God is the most excellent, preserving the other fruits, the necessary and sufficient condition for the availability of the rest. The honor of God benefits everyone in the realm, as do in a lesser way the other four fruits. Each of the latter in addition has a special beneficiary, respectively: the prince, nobility, commons, and clergy. Each fruit will be served, to rich and poor alike, with a sauce, the "dreede [dread] of god."[24] Before being sauced and eaten, the four lesser fruits must be pared and the parings carefully distributed among the special beneficiaries of the fruit in question. The parings of the four lesser fruits—rooted in justice, truth, concord, and peace—are "compassion or pity," "trew defence," "trew exercise," "encrease of vertue and conning."[25] To cite the most obvious example, the prince who dispenses justice with the dread of God must when the occasion demands temper strict justice with the "paring" of compassion or pity. To continue with Dudley's elaborate conceit, each of the four lesser fruits has a different poisonous core that must be removed and not eaten: "unreasonable elacion," "vain delectacion," "lewde enterprise," and "subtyll glorie."[26] If the poisonous cores, however, are combined with the principal fruit, the honor of God, they are altered and rendered harmless, in each case becoming: "vertuous elacion," "trew exaltacion," "noble enterprise," "parfytt glory." Apparently, if the prince loses his dread of God in the dispensing of justice through his deputies and courts and fails to benefit from the paring of the fruit of justice, compassion, or pity, by thus eating the poisonous core of the fruit, he will be overcome by an unreasonable elation. He will display an overbearing hubris in his exercise of power and authority, an egoism that may well degenerate into tyranny. Or the commons, no longer mindful of God and his commandments, may forfeit the peace and harmony that result from eating the fruit of concord by consuming its poisonous core of lewd enterprise. Instead of honoring God and enlisting in some noble cause, they will foment rebellion.

Dudley's imagery is confusing and obscure, but it reveals his values and priorities. First, the metaphor exposes the great importance he attaches to Christianity as an instrument of social and political control. Christian belief is the bedrock of unity and harmony in the state, but only if the prince supervises the church and if the clergy refrain from holding public office, confining themselves to spiritual duties. Second, the metaphor expresses the absolutely crucial role assigned by Dudley to the prince in secular as well as spiritual matters. He is the fountain of justice, the arbiter of all internal conflicts, the source of civil order, the supreme example of conduct for his subjects, and the promoter of economic prosperity. Almost in the Hobbesian sense, the prince is the energizer and manager of the whole system. Without his wise and prudent rule according to the divinely ordained duties of his office, the social and political edifice will collapse. The metaphor further suggests Dudley's sensitivity to the social structure of the realm and his belief that princely power depends on harmony within and between the social groups composing the whole. No less than Aristotle, Dudley was aware of the sociology of politics, and if civil disorder was to be avoided, the bonds of community had to be tightened. Both Aristotle, and Dudley perhaps even more so, realized that the best remedy for social conflict and rebellion was economic abundance and well-being. Impoverishment and idleness were for Dudley prime sources of "lewd enterprise" among the commons, the incubator of revolt, and therefore had to be corrected by positive policies if the state was to survive. Thus, in Dudley's estimation, one of the state's foremost objectives was economic—the creation of wealth shared proportionately by all.

Dudley's allegory, of course, raises the critical problem of the meaning of "commonwealth" and more generally the nature of his political vocabulary. Does the term denote state or, as Brodie has suggested, society?[27] Dudley's opening description of the tree of commonwealth provides some help: "a faier and mighte tree growing in a faier feild or pasture, vnder the coverte or shade whereof all beastes. . . . are protectyd and comfortyd."[28] Then he says: "All the subiectes of that realme wher this tree of comon welth doth severly growe are ther by holpen and relyved from the highest degree to the lowest."[29] The pasture in which the animals are grazing is clearly the "realme" or state, a political society under law and government. He refers to the "subiectes" of the realm, subjects ordered by degree in an organized political society of ranks and stations. Like Fortescue, "realm" not "state" is used here and elsewhere in the text. Occasionally "countrie" and even less frequently "nacion" and "kingdom" are employed.³⁰ Fortescue's "body politic" never appears, nor any Latin terms for state. That realm or state is not identified by Dudley with commonwealth is obvious from scattered remarks: "for the comon wealth of the realm," "this tree will never long stand or growe upright in this realme," "this tree of comen wealth in his realme," "this tree of comon wealthe in a Christian realme," "this tree of comenwealth within this realme of England."³¹ The reference to Henry VIII at the beginning of the book further illustrates Dudley's distinction between commonwealth and state, for had he equated them the words would make little sense: "he is the Prince that shall revive the tree of comon wealth within this his realm."³²

That Dudley did not identify the two concepts also seems confirmed by the later development of the metaphor. The soil in which the roots of the tree of commonwealth are fixed and grow is the conduct of the prince. He is responsible in the main for the health of the five roots—love of God, justice, trust, concord, peace—and the five corresponding fruits. The existence of the prince, the head of state and in Dudley's opinion the prime mover and director of its activity, assumes the existence of the state or realm in which the tree either flourishes or not according to the success of the sovereign's policies and their implementation. When Dudley lamented that "this tree of comen wealth is welnie vtterly fayllid and deade" among Englishmen, he did not mean that the realm was breathing its last, only that commonwealth as distinct from state was in serious decline.³³ If by "commonwealth" Dudley intended to signify either state or society or both, the word is conspicuous by its absence in his only two lists of the various types of human association: "realme, Citie, company, fellowship" and "realme, Citie, towne or fellowship."³⁴ "Realm" (the state) appears in each, not "commonwealth," and by "company" and "fellowship" he appeared to be thinking of the plethora of formal and informal social groupings. So it seems safe to assume that "commonwealth" stands for neither state nor society in Dudley's glossary, nor does it denote "government." He never employed "government" or the favorites of Fortescue. Indeed, Dudley had no word for government in the abstract and collective sense; he wrote only of specific offices, officeholders, and councils.³⁵

What then did Dudley mean by "commonwealth," if he was not thinking of state, society, government, or any combination of them? Fortescue referred in Latin to the common utility or interest (*utilitas*) or advantage (*commodum*). Dudley did not do so in English simply because he apparently identified "commonwealth" with the common good, public welfare, or common interest. He may have been among the first to use the term in this fashion; it does not occur in Fortescue's *Governance*, thirty-five years earlier. The usage of "common weal" as state dates back to the fourteenth century, as common good or interest, only to the late fifteenth century, but "common wealth" in both senses dates only from the late fifteenth and early sixteenth centuries. Dudley's formulation "comenwealth within this realme of England" and its variations conform to the earliest examples of "common weal," meaning common good or interest, as given in the *Oxford English Dictionary*: 1469, "comyn weal of the realme of Ingelonde"; 1526, "commune wele of the hole body."[36] The evidence leaves little doubt as to Dudley's meaning.[37]

The elaborately embellished metaphor of the tree of commonwealth was Dudley's attempt to define the common good or interest of the English state. Of what then, as he perceived it, did the common interest consist? Rooted in the love of God, justice, trust, concord, and peace, the common interest entailed first the preservation and strengthening of the Christian faith by the prince, assisted by church and clergy, in order to unify and harmonize relations between and within ranks in society. The common interest also comprehended the honest and efficient administration of justice by the royal magistrates so as to uphold the king's power, authority and dignity and guarantee a social environment of law and order. Next, the common good required an enlightened and prosperous nobility, at peace with itself and other elements of the population, with a genuine sense of responsibility to lesser orders. Finally, and not least, the common interest depended on a contented, industrious, and fully employed commons engaged in productive husbandry and the arts, whose abundant commodities would fully supply the material needs of the kingdom as well as ensure a favorable balance of trade, thus further increasing the wealth and enhancing the economic well-being of the nation. A state governed to advance the common interest so defined would be free of internal disorder, strong and secure in its relations with other sovereign powers, and at peace with its neighbors.

An important feature of Dudley's notion of the common interest was his perception of the realm as a plurality of social groups, each with interests in competition and conflict with the interests of the others. Hence the basic political problem of the realm was the reconciliation of these divergent interests, the welding together of groups into a cooperative whole with the aim of reducing the possibility of unrest and rebellion. Dudley furnished his readers with a guide for understanding the sociology of the common interest and for policies informed by that understanding. He continued somewhat more explicitly and systematically the approach adopted by Fortescue which was to become the model for conceptualizing political practice and of recommending governmental policy developed and refined by later reformers. At base the outlook assumed that a fundamental purpose of the state was economic, the satisfaction of the material needs of citizens of every rank. Any other course spelled certain disaster. Consequently, mastery of affairs of state rested on measures designed to ensure the production of wealth, thus maximizing the common interest. In a literal sense, commonwealth depended on each citizen's contributing in a different way but sharing in prosperity proportionately by rank and order. All receive something, some more than others, according to the value placed on their contribution by those who receive most. The political solution to the ever-present threat of civil unrest and to the goal of preserving the state from external foes increasingly comes to be understood in economic terms.

Political Sociology of the Common Interest

In order to analyze Dudley's political sociology of the common interest,[38] I begin with brief attention to the king's administration of justice, so vital to the operation of the whole state. Then we will be able to consider in detail Dudley's attitude toward the church and clergy, indispensable support to the monarch in his pursuit of social tranquillity and cooperation in the realm, and his reflections on the nobility and his deep concern for the commons. For in his view the latter provided the labor necessary for production and the creation of national wealth; moreover, because of their numbers and inferior status, they were always a source of anxiety over internal discord. Once the clergy were tamed and removed from an active role in the political arena, rendered dutiful and subservient collaborators of the prince, special care would have to be taken for the quality and conduct of the nobility. The control of the commons, however, was for Dudley the most worrisome problem for the head of state.

According to Dudley, justice originates with the king, whose authority is derived from God.[39] The administration of justice must be solely in his hands, although he cannot, of course, personally apply and enforce the law. For this purpose the monarch must choose intelligent and virtuous judges and officials, individuals of learning and conscience. The king nevertheless bears ultimate responsibility for their actions. His chancellor will appoint able county officers who will deal impartially with all subjects and who will not use their position for the promotion of powerful local interests. Upright sheriffs immune to bribery and the favors of local magnates must also be selected. All officeholders must be honest, fair, efficient, and beholden to no one save the king himself. An officer of state should never fear to act impartially, even when the matter in hand affects him personally or when he thinks the king has a special stake in the issue. Dudley insisted that officials be independent and autonomous of any social group, so that a narrow interest would not be substituted for the common interest; nor would they surrender to the pressures of any great men of the realm. This required first of all that the clergy not be given temporal office, for to do so in Dudley's opinion would destroy both office and church. While a public servant might well be a member of the nobility, he was to act only on the merits of a case, never out of friendship or to the advantage of another notable, even one of superior rank. No special pleading by interested parties could be allowed to deflect officers from the true course of justice. King and deputies should always be zealous in their protection of subjects from the oppression of "greate men and their superiors" and in their defense of the poor against their betters.[40] In all that is done in the name of the crown by officials, the king should staunchly support them. Since perjury is one of the foremost obstacles to justice, Dudley thought the law against it needed strengthening—here he made his only reference to parliament. The king, acting within the law, must never seem to punish any subject by personal command or without due process "but to draw them or entreate them by dew order of his lawes."[41] Always appearing exemplary in his conduct, he should show himself a dignified and honorable figure for the edification and imitation of his subjects.

Dudley's attitude toward the place of religion in the state is obvious from his conviction that the prince, not the clergy and church, is the guardian of the principal root, the love of God, and the soil from which it grows.[42] The prince not the church is the assistant of God with the duty of disciplining all who disobey the divine creator. Clerics must therefore dedicate themselves to spiritual affairs and eschew temporal matters and governmental office.[43] Their energies belong in pastoral duties, caring for the souls of their flock, not in amassing riches, for example, through the current fashion of accumulating benefices.[44] Dudley warned the clergy in particular against glorifying themselves and allowing a vainglorious estimate of their own dignity and importance to blind them.[45] Rather, he urged them to display humility and loving regard in the diligent and soul-searching pursuit of their pastoral calling. The prince then must keep the clergy under close surveillance to ensure the conscientious performance of their appropriate functions and to remove any causes of friction between them and the temporality.[46] All leading posts in the church should be made by the prince on the basis of ability, intelligence, and in particular virtue.[47] Subordinate offices in the church should be filled with regard to talent, not family connections, ambition, or royal favor. Besides the spiritual health of the laity, Dudley charged the church with the responsibility of improving the universities, so important for the education of clergy, nobles, and commoners.[48] Respected centers of learning in the past, the universities had declined from their former high standards. The vitality and ability of the clergy depended on the reform of the universities, for where today, Dudley asked, are the accomplished theologians and scholars of yore? Within the universities the church was urged to do all it could to encourage promising scholars and to attract them to clerical life, offering every opportunity for advancement once they had taken holy orders. The church was to promote able young clerics and scholars, awarding benefices to such clergymen, not to those largely interested in multiplying church revenues. Dudley, in sum, proposed church reforms designed not only to consolidate and increase the power and authority of the monarch but also to make sure that the clergy contributed positively and creatively to the prosperous unity of the kingdom.

Dudley saw in the landed nobility a potent source of trouble for the crown. Yet at the same time he fully recognized their indispensable role in the social hierarchy. They furnished the nation's leadership in peace and war and controlled much of the resources on which the economic well-being of the majority rested. Thus the prince's treatment of the nobility involved a delicate balancing act. Because the prince depends on the nobles to a significant degree, by his conduct he must convince the nobility of his good faith and by his policies establish an atmosphere of mutual confidence and trust.[49] Nonetheless he must also distance his government from them, asserting and retaining his independence from the dignitaries of the realm and their followers and family allies. He cannot allow them to do as they please, either by aspiring to usurp his power or undermine his authority or by participating in a free-for-all among themselves. In particular, the ruler must not permit the nobles to oppress the commons, the greatest number of whom owe their livelihood and loyalty to peers and gentry of the realm.[50] The prince is obliged to see that the nobility partake of the fruit of the root of trust—worldly prosperity—which he has nourished for their specific benefit, but he cannot allow their wealth and power to divide and ruin the kingdom.

Despite their seeking and enjoying worldly prosperity, the nobility, Dudley argues, can be contained and rendered a force for social stability by the prudent, impartial, honest, and efficient administration of the crown and also by one of the chief instruments of the royal effort to realize the common interest, the clergy. Dudley implied that the clergy were equipped to help the prince control the nobility in two ways: through the quality of education in the universities and through the dutiful performance of the clerical pastoral role. An enlightened and prudent nobility, Dudley seems to suggest, one that was honorable and virtuous, content with their possessions without lust for more, was to some extent dependent on the caliber of the universities. "For veryly I feare me," as things now stand, "the noble men and gentlemen of England be the worst brought vp for the most parte of any realme of christendom, And therefore the children of poore men and poore folke are promotyd to the promocion and auctorite yt thee children of noble Blood should have yf thei were mete therfore."[51] If the universities were reformed and more sons of the nobility attended and were properly instructed, or such seems to have been the implication of Dudley's remarks, they would be able to assume governmental posts hitherto occupied by educated persons of lower station. Two centuries later John Locke made much the same point in *An Essay Concerning Human Understanding* (1690), admonishing his gentlemanly audience that they would find the "Credit, Respect, Power, and Authority" owed to their rank and wealth "carried away from them, by Men of lower Condition who surpass them in Knowledge."[52]

One of the perils of the fruit of worldly prosperity to which the nobility were vulnerable was the poisonous core of "vaine delectation," which might prove irresistible, once tasted.[53] Dudley worried that the nobility might be dissatisfied with their power and wealth, and he intimated that however enlightened they might be by a suitable education something more was needed to keep them on the straight and narrow during the full course of their lives. A reformed clergy liberated from worldly interests for a life dedicated to pastoral guidance could be just the corrective required to curb the upsurge of hubris and vainglory among prospering aristocrats. He emphasized that "vaine delectation" was an obsession with worldly prosperity culminating in uncontrollable appetites, insatiable greed, and overweening pride. The result could only be self-destruction, the alienation of man from his true self and from God: "And thus doth vngracious delectation involve and so wrapp our vnderstanding and memorie yᵗ nether we know, nor wyll not know, god, our neighebor or our selves."[54] Such an aberration was epitomized by historical figures like Nebuchadnezzar, Nero, and Solomon, who, little better than animals, ceased to be truly human. If tempted, we should be reminded that each and every one of us is but "a vile carcass" in death, that "nakid ave cam and nakid we shall depart."[55] Because of satanic lust and pride "men have forgotten from whens thei cam and what thei be." Dudley summarized these somber reflections:

> Loke when our glorious garmentes be don off, and we nakyd, what differens is then betwene us and the poor laborers. Peraduenture a more foole and shamefull karcase. Also loke whether our naturall mother brought us not into this world with like sorrowes and paines, and the symple bodie all nakyd, as the child of povertie and myserie.[56]

These egalitarian expressions did not raise the banner of social leveling. On the contrary, Dudley remained thoroughly committed in theory and practice to an inegalitarian, hierarchical social order. But he wished it to function properly, with those of superior rank assuming their rightful obligations instead of being misled by a false appraisal of their own value. The enthusiastic commonwealth preachers voiced a similar attitude less than forty years later, with the same sentiments of fundamental human parity at birth and death. Like Dudley they were loyal, antidemocratic defenders of the status quo. Hobbes too spoke out against the vainglorious minority, who from his perspective were the few rotten apples in the social barrel that affected all the others, rendering a war of all against all a grim reality and necessitating an absolute sovereign power to end self-destructive anarchy. There seemed to be little doubt on Dudley's part— not, however, expressed in so many words—that Christian faith fostered and propagated by the reformed universities and clergy was the most effective antidote for such a sickness of soul, not only among the nobility but even in the prince and commons as well. Hence faith remained the surest medicine against disorder and rebellion, which might usher in the tyranny of one, the few, or the many. Yet Dudley as well as Hobbes invested the key to civil order in a powerful sovereign.

A discussion of Dudley's views about the commons in his rudimentary political sociology must begin with his stress on the fruit of tranquillity (growing from the root of concord) as of special benefit to the people. Concord should be deeply implanted in them since they constituted a major proportion of the population.[57] Dudley named them—merchants, craftsmen, artificers, franklins, graziers, tillers—and described their lot: "Theis folke may not grudge nor murmure to lyve in labor and pain, and the most parte of there tyme with the swete of ther face."[58] Tranquillity was thus absolutely essential for useful labor in trade, manufacture, and farming so typical of the life of these commoners who were least able to help themselves:

And for them it is so necessarie yt, if thei lack it, farewell the greatest parte of bying and selling emongest them, Farewell the conning
of Craftesmen, farewell the [tra]vaile of the artificers, farewell the
good trew service of laborers and servants, farewell the good trew
diligence of Tylth and Husbandrie, and, in effect, farewell all the
honestie and trew diligens emongist the comynaltie.[59]

It was also important that some commoners, the well-off merchants and
substantial farmers, partake of the fruit of worldly prosperity springing
from the root of trust. Vital to all business transactions of the commoners
was the keeping of promises and the honoring of contracts, which only
prevail in an environment of mutual trust and confidence.[60] Likewise international peace remained a prerequisite for the enterprising activity of
the commons in the export and import of commodities.

The prince, of course, played a leading role in the promotion of trade
Dudley noted thriving foreign trade and commerce as basic factors in
the wealth of the nation and the contentment of the commons.[61] Friendly
international relations were necessary if the English were to remain prosperous and to become more so from the export of such surplus of goods
as wool, woolen cloth, tin, lead, hides, and timber. In regard to overseas
trade Dudley was concerned by the decline in the quality of some English
commodities like wool and woolen cloth, which were no longer so highly
esteemed or eagerly sought after as they once had been by foreign buy-
ers. The responsibility for the fall in reputation Dudley attributed to producers whose wool was no longer of its accustomed fineness and especially to merchants and traders who connived to make exported goods
appear better than they actually were. Dudley hoped that the negligence
of producers and the dishonesty of exporters would be corrected so that
other countries would not capture foreign markets traditionally held by
the English.

The prince, of course, played a leading role in the promotion of trade
by maintaining peace and avoiding war through salutary alliances and
treaties and through policies that encouraged and developed foreign trade,
productivity, and high standards for goods.[62] Such actions were to his distinct advantage, Dudley hastened to point out. By enriching the realm the
prince would enrich himself through the increase in duties and imposts.
On such matters regarding the economy of the state Dudley never hesitated to link the self-interest of the sovereign to the common interest,
just as Fortescue had done before him.[63] A rich and powerful head of state
was always reliant on a rich and powerful nation, which in turn rested
largely on a prosperous and industrious commons: "His welth and prosperite standith in the welth of his trew subiectes."[64]

Dudley was generous in his advice on the norms that should govern the behavior of the common people. His recommendations aimed at sustaining the social hierarchy, preserving the solidarity and peace of the state with a minimum of civil disorder, and improving its economic conditions. Commoners, he cautioned, should be satisfied with their status, obey their superiors, and not covet riches. Rents and payments should be made when due and services responsibly performed. The people were warned against taverns, gambling, and wearing clothes unsuitable to their station.[65]

Dudley stressed the importance of thrift, perseverance, and industry in the labor of the commons and condemned slothfulness and idleness, the source of all vice and of discord and rebellion.[66] But he warned that the concord that may bless the commons must not be taken advantage of and allowed to degenerate into "tranquilitee in ease and pleasure."[67] If dire social consequences are to be avoided, idleness must be discouraged from youth onward:

> Sett your children which be yong betymes to some trew labor or busynes, and y^t as soune as thei have any discrecion to do any thing. And let not ther men or servantes savor or delyte in the perillous paring of idlenes, for if thei have a felicite therein in there youth it is a greate marvell if ever thei fall to be good labourers or artificers, but will rather serve a gentleman, and y^t in the worst maner. For a trew conclusion, the more parte of the men childeren grow to be beggers, theves, or bothe. . . .[68]

Because idleness and poverty breed crime and disorder, the parings of the fruit of tranquillity—"trew exercise" or "timely exercise"—should be distributed throughout the people so as to encourage the labor ethic and discipline so indispensable to a flourishing and healthy realm:

> To none other but to ther owne childeren and seruantes, for the good lyfe of all the commynaltie in substance standith in trew labor and lawfull busynes, and it is behovefull for them to exercise the same both erly and late, and not to slugg in there beddes, but to be therat full trewly in the morning; and then most conueniently is there best spede or iorney.[69]

Long before the rise of Calvinism, Dudley advised in the name of the common interest what was to become a persistent theme in the writings of the later reformers: work, diligence, self-control, and thrift for all, especially for the nongentlemanly working classes without whose labors the state could not exist.

Dudley differentiated between two groups of the common people. In addition to the majority for whom these warnings were largely intended, there was a small elite, or as he put it the "cheif of theis folke," the sub-stantial merchants and wealthy graziers and farmers.[70] Among the mer-chants he probably included the clothiers and among the graziers and farmers the well-to-do tenants and yeomen, all of whom were pioneer-ing early capitalist enterprise in parts of the countryside, among which his own county of Sussex was prominent. Dudley was perturbed because these prospering businessmen and husbandmen were beginning to im-pinge on the interests and prerogatives of the nobility, for instance, in the accumulation of landed property. Moreover, in their pursuit of riches, status, and power they exploited and oppressed the less fortunate of the common people. Possibly he feared that these self-made men might dis-place members of the gentry fallen on hard times, a development already starting to occur, and thus corrupt the lesser nobility. (Wealthy men of trade who invested their capital in landed property and thriving graziers and farmers a generation or so later were to acquire gentlemanly rank and become lords of manors.) While this tiny upwardly mobile elite of new men were, like the nobility, Dudley thought, attracted by the fruit of worldly prosperity, by contrast "to the multitude of the comens it is nei-ther profitable nor necessarie, for the fruite of suer [sure] tranquilite is sufficient for them."[71] He urged the former not to envy their superiors' riches but to be satisfied with reasonable profits and to remain honest in all business transactions, never yielding to the temptation of usury or re-sorting to fraudulent practices in buying and selling.[72] Dudley was possi-bly the earliest English theorist to identify and express concern over this rising class of acquisitive individualists, a relatively new but growing phe-nomenon, already noted in a more limited way by Fortescue and to re-ceive increasing attention from the later reformers.

Dudley was interested in the common people not solely because they were the mainstay of the economy but also because of their insurrec-tionary potential. In addition to these measures and the improvement of their material circumstances as remedy for the constant threat of their unrest, he advised obedience to superiors, contentment with their status, and the faithful performance of customary duties. From the standpoint of his allegory, conflict and rebellion were ever-present dangers because the fruit of tranquillity, so beneficial to the people in the fulfillment of their callings, also contained the poisonous core of "lewde enterprise." Un-less prudent governmental policies were followed, the poison would be ingested by the commoners to their own detriment and the possible destruction of the state.[73] Lewd enterprise, Dudley pronounced, always sends two advance "messingers" to spread its toxin in preparation for its own disruptive appearance. The first messenger, "discontentacion and murmurr," incites the populace with feelings of displeasure at doing their duty and obeying superiors.[74] The second messenger, "arrogancy," transforms popular discontent into false pride, a spreading malignancy causing the poor to doubt the superiority of their gentlemanly masters.[75] Infected by a rising spirit of egalitarianism, the poor would come to see themselves as equals of gentlemen and radically question distinctions in rank and degree. Arrogance thus culminates in lewd enterprise, in a rebellious attitude growing among the people, soon changing into open insurrection when promises of support are received from some of the clergy and nobility and elements of the affluent merchants and farmers. Dudley seemed to believe that the revolutionary threat from below came from an oppressed peasantry. He offered two object lessons to potential rebels, both peasant uprisings ending in disaster for the participants and greater oppression than before: the Jacquerie in mid-fourteenth-century France and the Cornish rebellion of 1497.[76] The poisonous core of lewd enterprise was therefore to be avoided at all costs. When combined, however, with the fruit of the honor of God, it could be transmuted into "noble enterprise," which the commons might wish to savour: " . . . yet cast not away this enterprise of your core for it may fortune to be to you a cheif Frind. Therfor kepe hym close within you vnto the tyme ye may lawfully vse hym."[77] The meaning of this cryptic message is not clarified. Perhaps Dudley had in mind the future possibility of some great military enterprise for the defense of the realm in which the commons would be called on to take part in heroic combat.

Although like the reformers Dudley was socially conservative, believing in a harmonious hierarchy of rank and order, he clearly differed from them in his preoccupation with securing and strengthening royal power, his anticlericalism, and his failure to discuss parliament or refer to the mixed constitution as a safeguard against tyranny. Moreover, he made no contribution to the development of an institutionalized conception of the state. Yet he could be called the first of the reformers in that on some important points he set the agenda for their reflections. His emphasis on the economic purpose of government—its promotion of the common interest by prudent and rational action, taking into consideration the major social groups of clergy, nobility, and commons—also characterized the thought of the reformers. Like some of them he perceived religion and educational reform to be the basis of the responsible and enlightened leadership of the ruling classes. Nevertheless, much of his concern was directed to the ways and means of improving the material conditions of the people. On this question his argument, in line with Fortescue's and premised on an overriding desire to conserve monarchical power, was twofold. First, the ruler's self-interest and the advancement of the common interest are identical. A wealthy people means a wealthy and secure prince. Second, inspired by an incipient social environmentalism, Dudley contended that an economically prosperous commons appreciably reduced the threat of civil disorder and insurrection and decreased the rate of criminal behavior. To these ends, therefore, government should strive to assure a thriving foreign trade by maintaining peaceful relations with foreign powers and by setting high standards for all goods to be exported. Agricultural and manufacturing productivity must also be stimulated by the cultivation of thrift, industry, and labor discipline among the commoners and the discouragement of idleness. At the same time, however, Dudley displayed pronounced anxiety over what he saw among some of the nobility and affluent commoners as the rise of acquisitive individualism, which endangered the harmonious cooperation of the social whole. These are some of the themes so richly and eloquently articulated by the subsequent reformers, beginning with Sir Thomas More.

6   The Enlightened Conservative

Sir Thomas More

So much has been written about Thomas More (1478–1538) and so many scholars have variously interpreted his masterpiece, *Utopia* (1516), that it may seem presumptuous to add to the huge body of commentary.[1] Within the scope of this study, however, some points of interest about the political ideas of *Utopia* still need to be raised, for instance, More's conception of the state, the book's reflection of English social and economic conditions, and the social and political structure of the commonwealth of Utopia. My analysis of this last topic seeks to demonstrate that More's ideal polity is not democratic in any conventional sense. Despite the indisputable radical characteristics of Utopia, More was essentially conservative in outlook, like his predecessors Fortescue and Dudley and his Tudor reforming successors.

More was born on 7 February 1478 in the parish of St. Lawrence Jewry in the City of London, some sixteen years after Dudley and about the time of Fortescue's death. Grandson of a prosperous London baker, More was the son of John More, a lawyer who became a justice of King's Bench, and Agnes Graunger, daughter of another lawyer, Sir Thomas Graunger, sheriff of London in 1503 and a high court justice. Young Thomas attended St. Anthony's School and served as a page to Cardinal John Morton (who figures in book 1 of *Utopia*), archbishop of Canterbury and Henry VII's lord chancellor. After less than two years at Oxford, More entered Lincoln's Inn in 1496 and was a barrister from about 1502. Already an accomplished Latinist, he studied Greek with William Grocyn and met Erasmus, who became an intimate friend and dedicated *The Praise of Folly* to him. More was one of the most eminent of the early English humanists, a versifier, translator, and author of an incomplete and controversial historical biography of Richard III, the first of its kind in English, written about 1513 and published posthumously. Invited about

1501 by Grocyn to give a series of public lectures on *The City of God* in his parish church of St. Lawrence Jewry, More proved to be a popular expositor of the historical and philosophical views of St. Augustine. More also closely studied Plato, reading the major works in the original, including the *Republic* and the *Laws*. He married the daughter of a wealthy Essex landholder, Jane Colt, who bore him four children but died after seven years of marriage. The law practice flourished, and More was elected to the parliament of 1504 and appointed undersheriff of London. His annual income before the age of forty was possibly as high as four hundred pounds, enhanced by a second marriage to the widow of an affluent City merchant. The Mores were an extended family—in contrast to normal English practice—with the children of both of More's wives and the children's spouses and offspring living in the single household under the benign supervision of Thomas, an unusual domestic arrangement universalized in the description of Utopian society. *Utopia*, first published in 1516, was a moderate European literary success during his lifetime. In 1517 More was one of the City notables who tried to pacify London apprentices who were rioting against resident foreign artisans; he was later asked by Wolsey to investigate the disturbances, known as Evil May Day.

Eager to advance his career and mindful that political rule must benefit from wise counsel even if the Platonic ideal of the philosopher-king was unrealizable, More entered governmental service. In 1517 he became a member of the royal council under the lord chancellor Cardinal Thomas Wolsey, and in 1521 he was knighted and created undertreasurer of the exchequer. Somewhat later the More establishment moved to a thirty-four-acre estate in Chelsea where he built a stylish Tudor mansion with a separate chapel, a residence that was not beneath the visits of the royal sovereign himself. The new home became a congenial meeting place of a circle of humanist friends and acquaintances: John Rastell, More's brother-in-law and future religious adversary, the dramatist John Heywood, and possibly Lupset, Pole, Starkey, and Elyot.[2] Appointed royal secretary and speaker of the House of Commons, More helped negotiate the Peace of Cambrai (1529) with the Holy Roman Emperor. When Wolsey fell from favor, he was replaced as lord chancellor by More, who held the office from 1529 to 1532.

The 1525 war of the southern German Lutheran peasants against their lords and masters, an uprising vehemently denounced by Luther himself, brought in its wake wholesale slaughter and pillage. The bloody episode—along with the persisting threat of Lollardy—haunted the English crown, church, and men of property, More not least among them. Concluding that Lutheranism was directly responsible for the turmoil and menaced the peace of the Tudor realm, More was zealous in his official capacity and as an ardent publicist in denouncing and extirpating the Lutheran heresy in England. "He proved relentless," Guy writes, "in the work of apprehending and questioning suspects, on several occasions actually detaining men at his Chelsea house."[3] There in the porter's lodge was a set of stocks for the purpose.[4] During his chancellorship half a dozen heretics were burned at the stake, and More was personally active in five of the cases.

More's tenure in government was severely complicated by Henry's divorce and marriage to Anne Boleyn, events that More strenuously opposed and that were to eventuate in his downfall. In fact, he was an energetic supporter of the Aragonese faction, working on behalf of Catherine against Anne. More declined to attend the coronation ceremony for the new queen, resigned, was committed to the Tower, and eventually tried for refusing to take the oath to the Act of Supremacy by which Henry became head of the English church. He was convicted and executed on 6 July 1535. In the twentieth century More was canonized by the Roman Catholic church.

Except for the sentiments expressed in *Utopia*, More did little in his fifty-seven years to suggest that he was an outspoken champion of the poor or an advocate of democratic principles, and we cannot expect him to have done so. He was a propertied man of means, a dutiful servant of the crown, and a defender of the hierarchical status quo, with the greatest respect for authority; moreover, he was a convinced exponent of law and order who could be ruthless and fanatical in the extermination of religious dissent. But even though I contend that throughout his career More was in many ways a traditionalist and a conservative, he was not close-minded, inflexible, or unenlightened. Nor do I agree with William Morris that on the basis of *Utopia* More can be seen "as the last of the old rather than as the first of the new."[5] Since the brilliant analysis of Hexter, there can be no question of the modernity of *Utopia*, of More's "humanist realism" in the radical Utopian project of communism, egalitarianism, and social environmentalism.[6] More, indeed, was doing something quite new, presaging the mode of social thought of the Enlightenment. In the composition of *Utopia* he was a philosophe before the time of the philosophes, an advance guard of the Age of Reason.

But what was the relationship between More the enlightened conservative in his private and public life and More the radical author of *Utopia*? How were the socially conservative attitudes and beliefs of the London lawyer, humanist, and statesman during the early English Renaissance reflected in his portrayal of the ideal commonwealth? Acknowledging a disjunction between the conservative person and the radical book tends to confirm the thesis that *Utopia* is a masterful joke, a dazzling satire, an "idyll" not an "ideal."[7] But if More genuinely intended *Utopia* to be a serious work in social and political theory, then it is virtually inconceivable that there was no close relationship between its apparent radical posture and the conservative perspective of the author. One obvious link that few would deny was between his own extended London household and the patriarchal arrangements permeating *Utopian* society. Utopia is customarily criticized for its monotonous routine and drab conformity, so different from More's own life, except perhaps for his self-discipline, methodical ways, and obsession with time. *Utopia*, however, no less than More the person, places a high premium on social order and respect for authority. Social cooperation and harmony are central features of the ideal, just as they were among More's own values. One could therefore maintain that in certain respects a congruence can be established between the cherished principles of the person and those of the book. The conservative strands of the book, if anything, magnify the conservative elements of More's own social outlook.

The fit between the two, however, works in some cases and not in others. The most prominent and at the same time most radical traits of Utopian society—communism and egalitarianism—can by no stretch of the imagination be said to mark the views of More the person. Did More the author mean them to be taken literally, to be actually implemented in European society, a question directed to the whole nature of his enterprise in *Utopia*? The universal abolition of private property and its collectivization in Utopia constitute an undoubted rupture with what can be understood of his personal values. But there may be room for second thoughts about Utopian egalitarianism. Was it as radical as it seems? Moreover, is Utopia a democracy, as many assert? If it is, then here is a further instance of the disparity between author and person. If, however, Utopia is neither as egalitarian nor as democratic as many assume, are we justified in arguing that its conspicuous radicalism conceals a conservative infrastructure and that the distance between author and person was not so great after all? These are some of the questions to be seriously considered in an exploration of More's conception of the state in *Utopia*. The answers I propose are the primary reason for my labeling the political thought of that great work "enlightened conservatism."

A member of an English mission to renegotiate wool and cloth treaties in Flanders in 1515, More took advantage of several months of leisure to write book 2, the major portion of *Utopia*. Book 1 was evidently composed on his return to London. Written in Latin and first printed in

Louvain in 1516, the work had appeared in four editions by 1519 and in German translation in 1524. Only with the first English translation of 1551 by Ralphe Robynson did the work really become a best-seller, passing through numerous editions between then and now.[8] The title of the third Latin edition (Basel, March 1518), the last that More may have seen before publication, is *De optimo reipvblicae statv deque nova insula Vtopie* . . . , perhaps best rendered for twentieth-century readers as *On the Best Form of State: The New Island of Utopia*. Each of the two parts of the work is headed by the title *De optimo reipvblicae statv*. The book purported to be a conversation between the author, Peter Giles, the town clerk of Antwerp introduced to More by Erasmus, and the fictitious Portuguese traveler, Raphael Hythlodaeus. Their discussion took place in the garden of Giles's house. Book 1 uses the question of crime to castigate a deficient social environment. In the process More delivered a scathing and detailed denunciation of contemporary European conditions. He seems to have been thinking fundamentally of the situation in England. In marked contrast to this bleak portrait of poverty and misery, unbridled greed, and the domination of the many by the few, book 2 consists of Hythlodaeus's supposedly true account of a happy, prosperous, and unexploited people living in the collectivistic and egalitarian society of Utopia, an island republic of the New World. The message of the work on the face of it appears clear enough. If the contemporary European problems delineated in book 1 are to be resolved, then society and government must be reconstructed along the lines of Utopia. Hythlodaeus completes his picture of Utopia with the statement: "Now I have described to you, as exactly as I could, the structure of that commonwealth which I judge not merely the best but the only one which can rightly claim the name of a commonwealth."[9] More insisted that he was not presenting an ideal state on paper, thinking perhaps of Plato in the *Republic*, but depicting an actual state, Utopia, visited and lived in by Hythlodaeus.[10] Utopia, Hythlodaeus concludes, is an immortal commonwealth, one that will last forever, not subject to social change, free from the civil discord afflicting all other existing states. So quite unambiguously More was describing in *Utopia* the nature of the ideal state.[11]

What was More's purpose? Did he think that European society could really be reconstructed in the image of Utopia? According to Logan, More was responding to what he considered the false optimism of the northern humanists who believed that enlightenment and moral renewal of the ruling classes through humanistic education and counsel would lead to social and political amelioration.[12] More felt that the deterioration of European society had gone too far for such an indirect approach, for reshaping the consciousness of those responsible for the deterioration. The problem required direct attack through reform of European institutions and social and political arrangements.[13] The key to any truly remedial change was thus institutional, not educational.

More may also have been challenging the humanists' inconsistency in their profession of the ideal of *vera nobilitas*, or true nobility, at least as Quentin Skinner has recently interpreted *Utopia*, a view not necessarily at odds with Logan's.[14] Following Cicero's *De officiis*, the humanists identified true nobility with virtue instead of with birth and wealth. At the same time, perceiving the dangerous democratic implications of their doctrine, they nevertheless held that the locus of virtue was among members of the ruling classes, consequently defending private property, inheritance, and social hierarchy. More threw down the gauntlet in his portrayal of Utopians as a virtuous people in a commonwealth where virtue was widely appreciated and rewarded. Egalitarianism and the abolition of money and private property were absolutely necessary social conditions of their virtue and hence their true nobility. So the very kind of society rejected by the humanists was for More the sole one in which true nobility could be universally realized. He argued in effect that if the humanists really meant to equate true nobility with virtue and to see it prevail, then they had no choice but to prefer Utopia over the existing society of demeaning acquisitiveness, of property and degree. For More's Utopia was the very opposite of the contemporary social order (depicted in book 1 of *Utopia*) with its "nobility, magnificence, splendour, and majesty" commonly thought to be "the true glories and ornaments of the commonwealth."[15] Contrary to ordinary humanist opinion, then, European society was without true virtue and true nobility, the marks of the only authentic commonwealth, which of course was Utopia.

Whatever his intentions, More seemed to be convinced that any notion of wiping clean the canvas of European society and beginning afresh was out of the question. Like Plato in the *Republic*, he probably did not take his scheme for the ideal state in the literal sense of a blueprint for the remaking of existing society in England or elsewhere in Europe. He concluded *Utopia* with the sentence: ". . . there are very many features of the Utopian commonwealth which it is easier for me to wish for in our countries than to have any hope of seeing realised."[16] That he had just commented on Hythlodaeus's report of Utopia, "I cannot agree with all that he said," including "their common life and subsistence—without any exchange of money," poses the question of More's attitude toward communism and egalitarianism.[17] Certainly the character More in the dialogue raises serious objections to communism, and nothing in More's actual life or other writings suggested any sympathy for it.[18] But if his rejection of communism is granted, how is *Utopia*, the apotheosis of communism, to be read and used? And if the work was not a joke or satirical conceit but the sincere expression of an authentic social ideal, what possible role could it play in the institutional reforms that More thought were so desperately necessary to counter the maladies of Europe?

Instead of being a revolutionary manifesto for the collectivistic reconstruction of European society, perhaps *Utopia* was intended to offer an ideal type or theoretical model, a normative device like Plato's Kallipolis or Hobbes's Leviathan.[19] Perhaps More thought that his social ideal would serve at least two fundamental and related purposes. The Utopian model was apparently designed to inform the reader in the most forcible and realistic manner possible of the sickness of European society. *Utopia* proceeds both explicitly and implicitly to compare and contrast the dire conditions of Europeans and their corrupt institutions with the idyllic life of the Utopians, in a way reminiscent of Plato's juxtaposition of Athens with Kallipolis. In contrast to the virtuous, happy, harmonious, and prosperous condition of the Utopians, Europeans were subjected, impoverished, and divided by their self-seeking and close-minded ruling classes. Utopia is a just state profoundly different from the unjust states prevailing in Europe. Contemporary states like England with their inhumane and inequitable practices and institutions were doomed to perpetual disorder and even disintegration—stark contrast to the order, stability, and permanence of Utopia.

But More's comparison and contrast, however historically significant it may be, for it was the first detailed social criticism since classical antiquity, was not intended as an end in itself. Once Europeans had been made to confront the gross injustices of their own society (in contrast to what might possibly have been), *Utopia* offered a model for change and improvement. While the Utopian model could not be replicated in Europe to replace what existed, it could be a valuable guide and standard for constructive policies aimed at the correction and reform of contemporary conditions.[20]

The Utopian model may have been intended to suggest a program for remedial action. The system of private property did not have to be transformed into radical collectivism. Nor was the egalitarianism of the Utopians, the uniformity of their lives, and the lack of privacy to be duplicated. What could be done instead, on the basis of wise counsel and prudent governmental action, informed by the principles and norms of the Utopian ideal type, was to remove some of the worst abuses of the system of private property, to close the gap between rich and poor, to curtail monopoly and questionable business practices, to raise the living standards of the people, to alleviate their unemployment by encouraging agriculture and manufacture, and to improve the education of all classes.[21] On the political front the sale of offices might be prohibited, public appointments made on the basis of merit, and restraints placed not only on the absolute power of government but also on the encroachment of the masses in affairs of state.

The object of these and similar reforms would be the promotion of the welfare and happiness of citizens according to the spirit, if not the letter of Utopia. By using Utopia as norm and preceptor, not as a mold for reproduction, such salutary measures could correct without social upheaval some of the most glaring injustices of contemporary European states, thereby revitalizing and preserving a traditional way of life. No matter how much he praised the society of the islanders, the open-minded More apparently did not believe that the doctrine of *Utopia* was the last word, the definitive expression, of the social ideal.[22] The subject was still open to further discussion and the exchange of ideas, perhaps even to revision and amendment. At the end of the dialogue, leading Hythlodaeus away to supper, the character More remarks: "I first said, nevertheless, that there would be another chance to think about these matters more deeply and to talk them over with him more fully. If only this were some day possible!"[23]

Idea of the State in *Utopia*

Little has been written about More's conception of the state in *Utopia*. Adhering to convention, More used *res publica* in the generic sense of the state or commonwealth throughout, more frequently than Fortescue in *De natura*, and *dominium* does not appear. He never employed the body politic metaphor. Of course, in his specific references to the Utopian republic, it is only natural that he should rely on *res publica*, as he did on *regnum* in regard to European kingdoms. Both republics and kingdoms, and all polities for that matter, however, he subsumed under the general category *res publica*. *Civitas* is used not to denote Utopia but to describe the fifty-four confederate city-states composing Utopia, the capital city of each of these member states (although he uses *urbs* more frequently), or states other than *Utopia*.[24] It is interesting that More did not employ *regimen*, a favorite of Fortescue's, or any other abstract, collective term for government. More preferred naming specific categories of officials: *consilarius*, advisor or councillor; *iudex*, judge; *magistratus*, magistrate; *consilium*, the ruler's council.[25] A king and the governor of a Utopian city-state are both *princeps*.[26] More did not distinguish society from state, never employing *societas* or any other comparable word. Unlike Fortescue, he used *usus*, not *utilitas*, with *publicus* or *res publica* for common interest; he also paired *salus* with *publicus*, *res* with *communis*, and *commodum* (like Fortescue) with *publicus* and with *suis* to distinguish common from private interest.[27]

More's conception of both common interest and state was primarily economic, developing on this score what Fortescue and Dudley had begun. I hasten to add, however, that More made little or no contribution to economic theory or practice in any technical sense. He had no notion of the economy separate from other social relationships in the state, nor did he deal systematically with the way in which the economic potential of the state could best be utilized for the satisfaction of human wants. His specific economic prescriptions in *Utopia* are somewhat vague and are devoid of any illuminating economic ideas. Yet in spite of these deficiencies and much that is naive and simplistic in his approach, his conception of the state remains fundamentally economic. Fully aware that England and Europe had great potential wealth, he asked in effect why the majority of laboring poor received no benefit. Why were the idle few living at the expense of the many? Throughout *Utopia*, almost to the exclusion of all else, he focused on questions of labor, productivity, idleness, poverty, and unemployment. He stressed the economic aims of the state, social structure, existing social conditions, and he made recommendations for change. He identified human needs, defined mainly as economic, and the way they could best be realized through reordering the state. More was never the mouthpiece of the European ruling classes. He took them severely to task for their shortsighted greed and parasitism, and he was compassionate about the economic plight of the underprivileged. In both actions and words he was an ardent defender of law and order, but there is an obvious connection between that priority and his sympathy for the poor and condemnation of the rich in *Utopia*. For he recognized that civil strife and rebellion occurred in circumstances of poverty, economic decline, and social disintegration and that law and order required their amelioration. Whatever else it might be, *Utopia* was a persuasive and ingenious project to demonstrate how civil order must be rooted in the economic health of the state. More perceived the problems of state and the problems of the economy as inseparable.

The immediate cause of European economic troubles, and hence the basis of the ever-present conflict and disorder, according to *Utopia*, was avarice and greed, which More argued arose in all living beings out of "fear of want."[28] Only in man, however, did More also identify pride as a source of greed. Even when the basic human desires for existence had been satisfied, pride drove the individual to desire more than his fellows and to strive to surpass them in the attainment of worldly goods. Pride, More declared, is the "one single monster, the chief and progenitor of all plagues"which

> measures prosperity not by her own advantages but by others' disadvantages. Pride would not consent to be made even a goddess if no poor wretches were left for her to domineer over and scoff at, if her good fortune might not dazzle by comparison with their miseries, if the display of her riches did not torment and intensify their poverty. This serpent from hell entwines itself around the hearts of men and acts like the suckfish in preventing and hindering them from entering on a better way of life.[29]

More was adhering to St. Augustine's stress on Adam's defection from God and fall from grace through pride. Another Augustinian, Thomas Hobbes, was in general agreement with More, also attributing social divisiveness and conflict to pride. Here, however, the similarity between More and Hobbes ended. Hobbes proposed an absolute sovereign for the containment of "the children of pride," to prevent their self-destruction and preserve the state, the crucible of civilized life. More, in contrast, thought that while pride cannot be completely eliminated, it must be appreciably reduced for men to live happily in a stable and enduring commonwealth.[30]

Pride and its manifestation in avarice and greed, *Utopia* insisted, could only be lessened by the complete abolition of private property and money. To the degree that private property and monetary exchange exist in society, pride, avarice, and greed will disrupt human relations. Money and lust for its accumulation—all resulting from pride—are responsible for delinquency and crime, conflict, poverty, anxiety, and unhappiness among men.[31] Private property and property differentials—the foundations of monetary avarice and greed—must therefore be abolished if men are to be truly happy and live satisfying, contented lives.[32] Communism for More was the cure for social ills and the "principal foundation of the whole of the structure" of Utopia. By recommending such a solution, he was certainly putting forward an economic conception of the state. Political and social problems of the most far-reaching kind could only be remedied by the economic reorganization of the state on collectivistic principles and the elimination of money as a medium of exchange.

The abolition of private property and money for the curtailment of pride, however, had to be accompanied by another radical change in social relations. Social parity was the rule in Utopia because the "general welfare (*salutem publicam*)" depended on "equality (*aequalitas*) in all respects."[33] The poor did not exist. No one possessed anything, yet all were rich.[34] All were equally free from worry, want, and insecurity. Each worked according to his ability and very few were exempted from physical labor. No social group or individual of whatever office was able to dominate and exploit others. More characterized the equality (*aequalitas*) of Utopians as a profound and universal fairness (*aequitas*).[35] Justice (*iustitia*) rested on a basic equality in the distribution of honors, offices, and rewards, in all the goods of life allocated to citizens, an equality engendering a unique fairness in human relations.

In these stipulations More rejected the idea of distributive justice founded on proportionate equality. First conceptualized by Plato and further developed by Aristotle, such a system had long been employed to justify economic, social, and political inequities in the state.[36] The division of the state into a ruling, wealthy, leisured minority and a subjected, poor, laboring majority was explained and rationalized by the principle of proportionate equality based on human inequality, either innate or socially acquired, or a mixture of both. Those of good birth and property, engaged in mental rather than physical labor, were defined as making the most valuable contribution to the community; they were thereby entitled to a larger share in its goods than the propertyless members of humble origins, dependent for their livelihood on the drudgery of physical toil. These latter functioned solely for the welfare of the former, to obey and to serve. An arrangement of this kind, More protested, was the depth of injustice, to the advantage of those "who are either idle or mere parasites and purveyors of empty pleasures" and to the disadvantage and neglect of "farmers, colliers, common laborers, carters, and carpenters without whom there would be no commonwealth."[37] Actual states were not at all true commonwealths, for they existed only to increase the wealth of the dominant, idle few by the exploitation of the laboring majority. All contemporary states, Hythlodaeus affirms unhesitatingly, are "nothing else than a kind of conspiracy of the rich, who are aiming at their own interests under the name and title of the commonwealth."

A genuine commonwealth or *res publica* like Utopia, as a public thing, must be truly public or common, incorporating a justice that is equal and fair. Criticizing the so-called justice of the states of his age, More wrote:

> . . . among which [states], upon my soul, I cannot discover the slightest trace of justice and fairness. What brand of justice is it that any nobleman whatsoever or goldsmith-banker or money-lender or, in fact, anyone else from among those who either do not work at all or whose work is of a kind not very essential to the commonwealth, should attain a life of luxury and grandeur on the basis of

his idleness or his nonessential work? In the meantime the common laborer, the carter, the carpenter, and the farmer perform work so hard and continuous that beasts of burden could scarcely endure it and work so essential that no commonwealth could last even one year without it. Yet they earn such scanty fare and lead such a miserable life that the condition of beasts of burden might seem far preferable. The latter do not have to work so incessantly nor is their food much worse (in fact, sweeter to their taste) nor do they entertain any fear for the future. The workmen, on the other hand, not only have to toil and suffer without return or profit in the present but agonize over the thought of an indigent old age. Their daily wage is too scanty to suffice even for the day: much less is there an excess and surplus that daily can be laid by for their needs in old age.[38]

More insisted that the rule of true equality and fairness must replace the regime in which cash value was the measure of all things. In the latter, he noted, "It is scarcely possible for a commonwealth to have justice or prosperity—unless you think justice exists where all the best things flow into the hands of the worst citizens or prosperity prevails where all is divided among very few—and even they are not altogether well off, while the rest are downright wretched."[39]

Clearly More rejected by implication the standard of proportionate equality for the apportionment of the community's goods. Instead he proposed distributive justice resting on the precept of arithmetical equality. Aristotle had discussed distributive justice according to both norms. Proportionate equality he described as the measure of distributive justice in aristocracies and oligarchies, whereas arithmetical equality was axiomatic for the distribution of goods, regardless of birth, wealth, office, or honors, in democracies, the best example being ancient Athens with its popular ideal of *isonomia* (equality before the law). Obviously More's call for social and economic parity in Utopia went far beyond the actual practical arrangements of any historical state. Notwithstanding his advocacy of such revolutionary egalitarianism, the structure and institutions of the government of Utopia appear to compromise his demand for social equality.

In addition to his belief that permanent civil peace and harmony could only be attained by transformation of the social infrastructure of the commonwealth through radical material equality, More's novel economic conception of the state is also visible in other ways. Unlike previous political thinkers, More emphasized productivity almost to the point of obsession. Nothing comparable to his detailed treatment of economic behavior and organization had appeared before. While Dudley showed an awareness of the importance of labor discipline, his comments were only made in passing. But More required that idleness be banished from Utopia in order to maximize production. With some exceptions all citizens were expected to engage in useful physical labor on the essential economic tasks of the commonwealth.

More made the crucial distinction, perhaps for the first time, between socially useful and socially useless work: labor required for goods and services contributing to the well-being of the community was useful, that concerned solely with the production of frivolous commodities and unnecessary luxury items was useless.[40] The latter goods, of course, were not permitted in Utopia. On the basis of demonstrable intellectual ability, a handful of citizens were encouraged to specialize in beneficial mental labor, but no one was allowed to live in idleness and luxury, parasitic on the work of others. Idleness was the paramount sin of Utopia and the effective use of each citizen's time was absolutely fundamental. Everyone was expected to make the best of each working day in productive activity and self-improvement. To ensure that all were thus employed and not wasting time in idle and unnecessary pursuits was "the chief and almost the only function" of the two hundred lesser magistrates, the syphogrants, each elected annually by every thirty families in each of the fifty-four constituent city-states (*civitates*) of the Utopian confederation.[41]

In contrast to nonessential labor, narrow pursuit of self-interest, and idleness, which constituted much of the accepted way of life in other states, Utopians were supposed to devote themselves energetically and industriously to the prosperity of all. Utopian productivity was consequently so high, especially in cattle and grain, that besides being able to maintain surpluses for two years in advance, ample supplies were available for export. Vast amounts of gold and silver were thus accumulated, to be used for the import of goods that could not be produced at home.[42] More subscribed to what was to become the mercantilistic ideal of the self-sufficient state with large surpluses for export and a favorable balance of trade, thereby drawing in enormous amounts of treasure for future overseas purchases. These economic arrangements ultimately depended on a disciplined, highly productive work force.

The fundamental principal animating More's economic conception of the state emerges from his summary of the moral philosophy of the Utopians—a section often discounted by commentators—where the best life of the individual is explained.[43] Logan praises the passage for being "the cornerstone of the Utopian edifice."[44] Since happiness (*felicitas*) or well-being is sought by each person, the foremost purpose of the state is to create a social environment most conducive to the felicity of the individual citizens. Happiness for Utopians is expressed in terms of pleasure (*voluptas*). At the heart of their notion of happiness is virtue (*virtus*), which means a life according to nature, following the dictates of natural reason. Apart from loving and honoring the Supreme Being, a natural life of reason—the virtuous life—consists of maximizing pleasure and aiding others to do likewise. Pleasure and the avoidance of pain are central to a life of virtue which conforms to nature and is guided by reason. Justice in the broadest sense is the condition in which the pleasure of each depends on the attainment of pleasure by everyone. An unjust life characterizes the individual who seeks his own pleasure at the expense of the pleasure of others.

Pleasures are bodily and mental, corresponding to man's animal and rational makeup. More differentiated qualitatively between the pleasures of each kind, between true and false bodily and mental pleasures. True pleasures he describes as natural, false pleasures as unnatural. True pleasures neither violate the moral dictates of natural reason nor result in the loss of a greater pleasure or in pain. The quest for false pleasure, arising, for example, from pride and mere sensual gratification, predominates in countries where people are engaged in the acquisition of honor, rank and status, wealth and possessions, and in such pastimes as gambling and hunting. These false and vain pleasures typify the sumptuous lives of luxury and leisure of a few in contemporary Europe at the cost of the suffering and misery of the many. In contrast, true pleasure, the only source of genuine and lasting happiness, arises out of a compassionate and humane fellowship of all members of a community. Of the true pleasures those of the mind, "the first and foremost of all pleasures," have to do with intelligence and contemplation of truth directed toward a morally virtuous life, the foundation of authentic happiness.[45] More thus began his disquisition on moral philosophy by asserting that the end of the state is human happiness, which he defined in terms of virtue and the virtuous life, to be attained by cultivating the pleasures of the mind.

How does this analysis of virtue relate to More's economic conception of the state? The answer is found in his comments on the true pleasures of the body. Happiness does not rest solely on the mental pleasures. In the last analysis true mental pleasure and a morally virtuous life depend on the true bodily pleasures. A necessary requirement for mental pleasure and a morally virtuous life is the satisfaction of bodily needs by means of ample provision of food, shelter, and clothing for the prevention of the bodily pains of hunger, thirst, cold, and damp. According to More, we should eat, drink, clothe, and shelter ourselves for the sake of bodily health. Any failure to protect and maintain our health by not tending properly to our bodily needs will deprive us of true bodily pleasure, which in turn will imperil our mental pleasure, thus diminishing our happiness. In fact, happiness is a synthesis of mental well-being and bodily health, the latter a condition of the former. So important is bodily health to the mental pleasures and thus to happiness, explained More, that "almost all the Utopians regard it as great and as practically the foundation and basis of all pleasures." "Health is above all things conducive to pleasure," More emphasized, announcing that Utopians "give the palm to health."[46]

In sum, society must therefore be collectivistic and egalitarian so that the health of all is guaranteed. As Logan explains: "Since health is the most important pleasure (being a condition of all others), the first contributory goal, and that of highest priority, must be to secure (insofar as it can be secured) the health of all."[47] Once private property and money and all their deleterious consequences are replaced by the rule of arithmetical equality in the distribution of the material necessities of life and in medical care, then the health of all will have been secured and the people can concentrate their energies on the mental pleasures, live virtuous lives, and enjoy lasting happiness. The state in *Utopia* was thus first and foremost an economic mechanism for the universal attainment of this highest earthly bliss. More ended his description of Utopian practical morality by announcing that "there is nowhere a more excellent people nor a happier commonwealth," continuing with some lines on their happy, contented lives.[48]

English Economic and Social Problems

Opposed to this secure and cooperative Utopian community is More's portrayal in book 1 of conditions in Europe, particularly in England, the focus of the discussion.[49] His examination of the poverty and subjection of the English, plagued by unemployment, social dislocation, and conflict, further exemplifies his economic conception of the state. More's voice, the first in the history of social and political thought to be raised in such extensive protest and criticism of the troubles afflicting the common people, sets the agenda for the later Tudor reformers. The basis for Hythlodaeus's discourse on England was the problem of crime and punishment of criminals. The dialogue casts doubt on the efficacy of severe punishment as a deterrent for relatively minor crimes. The blame for crime is the faulty social environment in which a majority of unemployed and impoverished are exploited by an idle few living in luxury; as a result the poor are often forced to turn to criminal activity for the sake of survival. Referring to the Cornish rebellion of 1497 (also cited by Dudley), More warned that unless the appalling conditions were corrected, England would not only experience an increase in crime but also might be threatened by sedition.[50] Because More was writing at the beginning of a long period of increasing economic crisis and perceived in it the potential for social upheaval, the Cornish uprising was an omen of what might happen in the future if the economy further deteriorated. His anxiety over the danger of civil conflict echoes the worries of Fortescue and Dudley.

Just as More saw agriculture as fundamental to Utopia, so in book 1 he focused on the problems of the English countryside, the chief source in his opinion of social difficulties. He commenced by pointing an accusing finger at those who exercised power: "the great number of noblemen who not only live idle themselves like drones on the labor of others . . . but who also carry about with them a huge crowd of idle attendents who never learned a trade for a livelihood."[51] Once the servants of the wealthy lose their employment, they become idle vagabonds and troublemakers, often criminals because of their lack of qualifications for available jobs. In addition to the nobility and wealthy farmers, others guilty of avarice and idleness share the blame for the sorry state of affairs: merchants (including bankers and goldsmiths), officials, priests, and lawyers.[52] Agricultural abuses, emphasized by the later reformers, are noted: rack-renting, engrossing, monopoly (or "oligopoly"); middlemen who buy up calves and lambs for fattening prior to marketing; forestallers and regraters hoarding supplies of grain for a rise in prices.[53] Most of More's ire, however, he vented on enclosure, which he deemed the worst offense of well-to-do landholders, accounting for rural poverty, unemployment, and crime.

More introduced the subject of enclosure in an oft-quoted passage about sheep, "which are usually so tame and so cheaply fed, [but] begin now, according to report, to be so greedy and wild that they devour human beings themselves and devastate and depopulate fields, houses, and towns."[54] In areas known for fine and expensive wool, gentlemen and even abbots greedy for profit enclose arable for conversion into pasture, destroying houses and settlements in their acquisition of land for grazing, "leaving only the church to pen the sheep in. And, as if enough of your land were not wasted on ranges and preserves of game, those good fellows turn all human habitations and all cultivated land into a wilderness."[55] Thousands of acres were thus enclosed for the maintenance of sheep. Tenants farming the arable were evicted, and small freeholders were dispossessed, either compelled to sell their lands or deprived of them by force or fraud. Dispossessed peasants, unsuccessful in their search for agricultural employment because the land was no longer tilled, became vagabonds and beggars. Their former holdings, converted to pasture, were cared for by a single shepherd. Enclosure and the mass dispossession of the peasantry also accounted for spiraling food and wool prices. More incorrectly believed that inflation was a result of a persistent sheep disease, but he also blamed monopoly (or "oligopoly," as he put it), herd ownership falling into the hands of a few, who thereby were able to set prices.[56] Poor cottagers, who had formerly made cloth at home, could no longer afford to buy wool and were forced to join the ranks of the unemployed and impoverished landless cultivators, swelling the numbers of idle who resorted to begging and criminality. In the meantime, the greedy few responsible for the plight of these unfortunates lived with their retainers and hangers-on in "wanton luxury," lavishly spending their ill-gotten gains on extravagant dress and food, frequenting taverns and brothels.

In the course of his diatribe against enclosure and self-seeking enclosers, More identified, at least implicitly, an important characteristic of the structure of the social relations of property. He complained bitterly about the enclosing landlords—presumably both gentlemen and affluent freeholders and tenants—who dispossessed their poorer tenants (*coloni*):

> By hook or by crook the poor wretches [the tenants] are compelled to leave their homes—men and women, husbands and wives, orphans and widows, parents with little children, and a household not rich but numerous, since farm work requires many hands (*ut multis opus habet manibus res rustica*). Away they must go, I say, from the only homes familiar and known to them, and they find no shelter to go to.[57]

Somewhat later he said that "the high price of food is causing everyone to get rid of as many of his household (*familia*) as possible, and what, I ask, have they to do but beg, or—a course more readily embraced by men of mettle—to become robbers."[58] These two passages offer a glimpse of circumstances in parts of rural England. First, the Latin *familia* is properly translated "household" instead of "family," the latter unlike the former customarily denoting blood relationship. A farming household in this sense included family and servants and laborers. Second, the dispossessed peasants' households so described by More were certainly those of poor husbandmen but possibly even those of more affluent farmers squeezed out by enclosing landlords. A yeoman, for example, might be as prosperous as a lesser gentleman and hold as much or more land, or he might be of middling or low income, just scraping by on his freehold and any acreage he might be leasing. Whatever his income, the yeoman was a freeholder and also usually a tenant, as indicated by Sir Thomas Smith's definition fifty years later that yeomen were "fermors to gentlemen," that is, tenants renting land owned by gentlemen.[59] Consequently, in a period of rack-renting, engrossment, and enclosure by acquisitive land-lords, the poorer yeomen were especially vulnerable to dispossession be-cause of the cutthroat competitive pressures of the market. Hugh Lati-mer's father was a Leicestershire yeoman who fought for the king against the Cornishmen at Blackheath in 1497; he might still have been alive when More wrote *Utopia*.[60] Latimer recollected that his father paid £3 to £4 rent per annum. At a rate of 5 pence to 6 pence per acre at the begin-ning of the sixteenth century, the elder Latimer, apart from his freehold, must have farmed a relatively large holding of considerably more than a hundred acres. So perhaps it is not unreasonable to surmise that besides very poor smallholders, tenants like Latimer and even more substan-tial ones with two hundred acres or more were for a variety of reasons the victims of rapacious landlords and market forces. Third, the English household included more than the nuclear family of parents and children, suggested by More's words describing a household as "not rich but nu-merous, since farm work requires many hands."[61] The "many hands" would be members of the nuclear family in poor households and in more prosperous ones day laborers and male and female servants in husbandry, both categories receiving wages.[62] Laslett estimates that between 1574 and 1821 in a sample of one hundred English settlements about 47 per-cent of the households of husbandmen and 78 percent of those of yeomen included servants. The respective percentages were no doubt lower at the beginning of the sixteenth century.[63] Still, as More's second passage sug-gests, in hard times the number of hands was reduced, a comment more likely referring to servants than to members of the nuclear family. We know that the elder Latimer kept a hundred sheep and tilled enough acre-age to employ half a dozen men. It is quite conceivable then that farmers like him as well as the far more numerous poor smallholders were in More's mind. Some of the first group and countless more of the second were being dispossessed.

While Fortescue described extensive grazing operations and praised them,[64] More condemned the very conditions so admired by his prede-cessor. More's somewhat nebulous references may be among the first bits of literary evidence for the existence of the characteristic structure of capitalist agriculture, gradually arising in England and nowhere else in Europe. Imprecise as these two passages are, More seemed to be on the verge of identifying the well-known triad, consisting of the landlord whose income was from rents from his tenants, the capitalist tenant farmer living off the profits of his commodities sold in the market, and laborers depending on wages paid by the tenants out of their profits.[65] Possibly More was observing and deploring some of the immediate social results of capitalist agriculture. Part of the social problems of the countryside could be traced to the acquisitive, entrepreneurial activities of the great capitalist graziers, many of whom were tenants, and to the ineffectual efforts of lesser capitalist tenants and more traditional smallholders to compete with them. Big capitalists were eliminating little capitalists in the cutthroat contest for farming profits. More's economic conception of the state was in this way a product of the concrete social and economic changes that were reshaping much of rural England and would continue to do so over the course of the next three centuries.

A sign that the conservative More did not seriously advocate radical reconstruction of England according to the Utopian blueprint was his recommendation for broad policies to counter the agrarian problems highlighted.[66] His approach was reformist, not revolutionary. He proposed that graziers and enclosers who destroyed farms and villages should either restore them or hand them over to those willing to do so. Activities of forestallers and monopolists were to be curtailed so that prices would not be artificially increased. Farming the arable was to be encouraged and cloth-making by cottagers reinstated. He recommended that all steps be taken to reduce unemployment and put the idle to work. Through Hythlodaeus, More issued an eloquent admonition to Henry VIII and to all kings, appealing to their self-interest by stressing the threat of civil disorder unless they ruled for the common interest of their subjects.[67] In what was substantially a repetition of the case made by Fortescue and Dudley, More passionately defended giving priority to the economic ends of the state by identifying the interest of government with that of the people.

Structure of the Utopian State

More's conservatism—manifested, for example, in his commitment to law and order and his distrust of social change—should not be overlooked in *Utopia* because of the work's overt radicalism. Some of the social and governmental arrangements of Utopia seem to reflect his conservatism and opposition to democracy. Yet Utopia has customarily been held to be a democratic state by those who have thought carefully about the subject. So Karl Kautsky called Utopia "an entirely democratic community."[68] Russell Ames declared "the core of the book . . . republican, bourgeois, and democratic."[69] The question is never really confronted by George Logan, who apparently like most other commentators takes Utopian democracy for granted. Edward Surtz's judgment is that "insofar as all offices are elective and therefore all citizens have a share in the rule, Utopia is a democracy." He adds that "Utopia is a representative democracy with free elections,"[70] that More's "ideal is democratic, representative government," and he refers at least twice to Utopia as "More's democracy."[71] The problem with these verdicts is that they seem to be made on the basis of wishful thinking instead of close scrutiny of the textual evidence. No one appears to confront the question: if More actually intended the Utopian state to be democratic, why did he not say so, and say it clearly and emphatically? If Utopia was meant by More to be a democracy, he never described it so, for example, using *popularis* in conjunction with either *res publica* or *civitas*, the customary Latin designations for democracy. Despite the egalitarian collectivism of the Utopian state, certain of its important characteristics—slavery, patriarchalism, the inferior status of women, the form of government, rule by a small intellectual elite—are not at all democratic. In short, Utopia, radical as it seems, cannot be termed a democracy in any acceptable sense.

The Utopian state (*res publica*) is an island confederation of fifty-four city-states (*civitates*), each with a population of about 100,000 to 150,000 adults, or a total adult population of approximately 8 million.[72] A uniform and unchangeable constitution drafted by Utopus, the founder and lawgiver, is the fundamental law of the confederation. The component city-states are identical in most ways: physically, socially, economically, politically, and culturally. A national or confederate senate of 162 members, "three old and experienced citizens" from each of the fifty-four city-states, meets once a year in the capital city-state of Amaurotum.[73] More does not specify how the national senators are chosen, nor does he say whether they are officials in their respective city-states. He gives no details about the nature of central government, beyond explaining that its main functions are to "discuss matters of common concern," to conduct foreign relations, and to adjust and balance economic scarcities among the member units.[74] This is sufficient institutional background for a detailed assessment of the antidemocratic features of Utopian society and government, beginning with slavery.

Unlike the ancient Greeks and Romans, we today consider the institution of slavery in Utopia incompatible with democracy. Slavery is one of the several serious blemishes on the egalitarian society envisioned by More. At a time when slavery was already extinct in England and France and only sixty years before Jean Bodin complained bitterly that the admission of slaves to his country would be "most pernicious and dangerous," their existence in More's just society is surprising, even shocking.[75] We are never told the number of slaves, but they were apparently not a negligible factor, although we cannot label Utopia a "slave society" in the accepted sense.[76] Slaves (*servi*), acquired from various sources, could be prisoners of war captured by Utopians (not by their mercenaries) in battle, citizens found guilty of major crimes like adultery or the overzealous expression of religious views, foreign criminals sold to Utopians, and "impoverished drudges" of other countries who volunteered for slavery in Utopia where they would be well treated and allowed to leave whenever they wished.[77] Women as well as men could be enslaved. Slavery was not hereditary, and all slaves were public property, evidently used only in public service. For good behavior a slave might have his sentence remitted or lightened by the chief magistrate of a city-state or by popular vote.[78] Enslavement was the Utopian substitute for capital punishment. Otherwise the criminal's labor would have been lost to the community. Capital punishment was reserved for a slave who rebelled or for anyone who took up a matter of common interest outside the appropriate public forum.[79]

Utopian slavery is aptly characterized by Surtz as "hard labor for life."[80] Slaves were expected to perform the menial, hard, or filthy tasks shunned by free citizens. Jobs assigned to slaves included work of an unspecified kind in rural communal households (two per household), wagoneering for internal travel, butchery and hunting, and heavy, dirty labor in the common dining halls.[81] Slaves were evidently not employed in the principal Utopian trades: textiles, masonry, metal working, carpentry, and clothing.[82] The question remains as to the extent of slave labor for public works, quarrying, mining, forestry, and the like. We are told that during slack periods in their normal occupations, free citizens repaired roads and harvested crops.[83] Another labor force of Utopians, the "Buthrescae," religious ascetics dedicated to hard work, "not so very few in number," engaged in arduous public and private service, behaving "as servants and as more than slaves."[84] They performed much of the back-breaking toil traditionally assigned to slaves, such as building and quarrying, but it is not clear that their labor in these occupations replaced the work of slaves. Apparently, therefore, Utopian slavery was instituted in part for penal purposes to replace capital punishment for serious crimes, not for the sake of a large labor force to relieve citizens of their labors and to provide them with leisure.[85] For this reason Utopian slavery might possibly be excused, but the enslavement of war captives, the purchase of foreign criminals, and the acceptance of volunteer slaves from abroad remain a distasteful and inhumane state of affairs in conflict with the Utopian ideals of equality and justice. And the exclusion of slaves of all categories from the mental pleasures deemed so essential to the highest Utopian goal of moral virtue means that slaves were considered incapable of becoming fully human.[86] Their existence and treatment violate Utopia's very reason for being.

Another undemocratic feature of Utopia is its universal patriarchalism, which strongly affected the status of women and the arrangements of government.[87] Each of the fifty-four member city-states consisted of six thousand urban households and an unspecified number of rural households.[88] Urban households constituted the primary social units of the state edifice. Rural and urban households were much larger in size than those in More's England. The rural household, composed of not less than forty men and women and two slaves, was more of a transient commune for the service of a two-year agricultural apprenticeship required of all young men and women than a kinship group or family in the normal sense. Twenty of its members returned each year to the city after their term was over. The urban household of ten to sixteen members was a genuine family. Male children and their wives and offspring remained in the household, whereas female children joined the family of their husbands. The Utopian urban household was therefore an extended family, in direct contrast to the normal English nuclear family.[89] English nuclear families, smaller the lower they were on the social scale, seemed on the average to be at least half the size of the Utopian extended family. As conceived by More, the Utopian extended family may have reflected his own ménage in London, but it decidedly broke with current English practice.

The undisputed head of the Utopian household was the patriarchal father. Members of the rural household lived under a "master and mistress, serious in mind and ripe in years," and the urban family remained "subject to the oldest parent unless he has become a dotard with old age."[90] More probably meant the oldest father. This interpretation is confirmed by his later statements that Utopian public officials were called "fathers" and that most minor delinquencies could be handled within the family without recourse to law: "Husbands correct their wives, and parents their children."[91] Wives played a dutiful and subservient role in the patriarchal household: obeying and serving their husbands, bearing and raising children, performing customary domestic chores in addition to making family clothing and plying one of the lighter trades like working wool or flax. The common meals shared by every thirty households were dominated by the elderly males, who were always served first with the choicest portions.[92] A household functioned as both the basic social and economic unit, the male child usually learning the craft of his father, although he might be "transferred by adoption" to another household for the acquisition of a different skill. The family was also the fundamental military unit. More explained that wives "are placed alongside their husbands on the battle front. Each man is surrounded by his own children and relations by marriage and blood so that those may be closest and lend one another mutual assistance whom nature most impels to help one another."[93] Thus Utopia "is like a single family," added More, and the Utopians "live together in affection and good will. No official is haughty or formidable. They are called fathers and show that character. Honor is paid them willingly, as it should be, and not exacted from the reluctant."[94]

The inferior status of women, a function of this patriarchalism, clearly raises the question of whether Utopia can be called democratic. At first glance Utopian society seems enlightened in its treatment of women. They as well as males could become students.[95] They served as soldiers, accompanying their husbands on military campaigns. Their testimony was considered in proceedings for divorce.[96] They were eligible to be priests, one of the most honorable posts in the republic, although their appointment was rare and restricted to elderly widows.[97] When, however, we consider Utopian patriarchalism, these emancipatory characteristics are counterbalanced by male prerogatives. Women are never explicitly granted or denied the right of suffrage in More's account, but the patriarchal ethos and the designation of officials as "fathers" strongly implies that women could not hold public office and casts doubt on whether they could be full voting members of the community.[98] Within the patriarchal household women were clearly subservient to men. The husband was the judge and corrector of his wife's conduct, her duty being to obey and to serve him. No servant problem occurred in Utopia, we are informed, because the domestic responsibilities of every household were assumed by the women, and the same was true of the common dining halls, where the females of each household took turns in preparing meals.[99] The lot of the Utopian woman seems even more onerous than that of her English counterpart. Since there were no creches or nurseries, wives shouldered the full task of raising and caring for their children in addition to making the clothing for all members of the household.[100] Beyond these household obligations, women had other heavy burdens not shared by contemporary English females. Besides soldiering, women (like men) served a two-year agricultural apprenticeship, worked in the fields at harvest time, and learned a trade. For committing serious legal offenses, women along with men were punished by enslavement. Utopia was clearly dominated by males, and females, apparently lacking political rights, represented the crucial source of labor for the household economy.

The nature of political institutions in Utopia is difficult to describe. From what More says about governmental structure, however, it would be rash to conclude that the republic is a democracy. The basic unit of government was a group of thirty families who annually "chose" an official or lesser magistrate, the "syphogrant," or in the new Utopian language, "phylarch."[101] More's term phylarch, derived from the Greek *phylarchos* or Latin *phylarchus*, head of a tribe, suggests that the thirty families were a "tribal" or kinship group of some kind.[102] More failed to elucidate this matter, but the phylarchy of thirty families was obviously a neighborhood association holding its common meals in a dining hall that was also the residence of the elected official, the phylarch or syphogrant.[103] He appears to have always been male, for More refers to the "syphogrant and his wife" who preside over the common meals. Most likely he was the head of one of the thirty households of the syphograncy, but we are not informed how he was chosen. Did the patriarchal heads of the thirty households elect the syphogrant from among their eligible senior members, or was he selected by all adult males (most probably not females) of the families? Presumably younger adult males who were household heads were not elected to the post, since its basic function was to watch over the labor process, and it would hardly have been appropriate for relatively young and inexperienced citizens to be assigned the responsibility. That syphogrants were elected by the thirty heads of households from among their oldest and most qualified males seems to be the arrangement most compatible with the patriarchal values and the nature of the system as a whole. If this is what More intended, needless to say such an election procedure is obviously undemocratic.

Other characteristics of Utopian government also seem to fall short of democracy. Over each ten syphogrants and their three hundred households, More reports, "is set" a "tranibor" or "protophylarch," yielding a total of twenty tranibors for the six thousand urban households of each city-state.[104] These twenty, "elected annually but not changed without good reason," were in effect chosen for life. Drawn only from the small intellectual elite of "literati," they constituted the supreme governing body, the senate (*senatus*) of each of the city-states. More gives no precise information about the selection of tranibors. We are told of a popular assembly (*comitia publica*) but nothing about its composition and functions.[105] A popular assembly consisting of more than the six thousand heads of households would be so gigantic and unwieldy as to be impracticable and certainly inconsistent with the dominant Utopian patriarchalism. The two hundred syphogrants of the city-state also formed an assembly (*comitia*) with the major duty of selecting new members of the literati and electing by secret ballot a lifetime governor or chief magistrate (*princeps*) of the city-state from four candidates chosen by the people (probably by the popular assembly), one candidate from each quarter of the city. More does not explain the process of election, except to say that all candidates, like the tranibors, had to belong to the literati. The senate of twenty tranibors convened daily with the governor and two different syphogrants (for each meeting) to consider common business, settle disputes between citizens, and pass decrees. Matters of common interest could only be raised in the senate and popular assembly. In either case the issue was presented to the assembly of syphogrants, who consulted with their constituent families and reported their conclusions to the senate of tranibors.

The question of Utopian democracy is also raised by the character of its judicial system, about which More said little. Huge popular juries were an important component of ancient Athenian democracy, and even in monarchical England juries of "twelve honest men of the neighbourhood" were the norm so praised by Fortescue.[106] In Utopia, however, juries of any kind apparently played no part in judicial procedures. Most delinquencies were settled within the household by the patriarchal father. Serious crimes, usually involving citizens of different households, seem to have been judged by the senate of tranibors, acting as a court, the only judicial institution mentioned by More.[107] Utopian laws were few in number and intelligible to every citizen. Because the legal profession had been abolished, noted More, "each man is expert in law," pleading his own case.[108] Except for adultery, most violations of the law did not carry fixed penalties, which were imposed by the senate in each case. There seem to have been only two capital offenses.[109] The sentence of slavery for adultery and other serious crimes, on the good behavior of the criminal, could be remitted or lightened by either the governor or the people.

So in addition to the absence of popular juries and the presence of a relatively small slave force, if we also conclude that Utopia was a society dominated by males (elderly patriarchs, in particular), the final picture is by no means democratic. Even without the assumption of a patriarchy, even if contrary to the scanty textual evidence we were able to see Utopian women as political equals of men, the conclusion would have to be the same. Sargent's evaluation of Utopia is apposite; he called it "authoritarian, hierarchical and patriarchal" but nevertheless "a society which was economically equal and more egalitarian in some other social institutions than the society in which he lived."[110]

Overall, the Utopian system was identical for all fifty-four city-states. W. E. Campbell, referring to the governor of the city-state, is not far wrong in terming the system "an elective monarchy."[111] To which description the important fact should be added that the "monarch" and members of his council were chosen for life from an extremely small elite. The only reasonable judgment to be made here is that ultimate power in a Utopian city-state was shared by the narrow aristocracy of the literati—intellectual, not hereditary, in its composition—with the six thousand patriarchal heads of households.

Meritocratic Rule under a Mixed Constitution

In each Utopian city-state only about five hundred people of both sexes out of a total adult population of over one hundred thousand were exempt (other than the sick and infirm) from manual labor.[112] Of these the two hundred syphogrants were legally exempt but continued to work in order to set a good example. The remaining three hundred of all ages and both sexes, a tiny fraction of the citizenry, were allowed to devote their lives, as long as they continued to show ability and dedication, to knowledge and learning. Any craftsman by study and by demonstrated talent might be admitted to the group.[113] Of this elite, the "literati," More wrote: "There are not many in each city who are relieved from all tasks and assigned to scholarship alone, that is to say, the individuals in whom they have detected an outstanding personality, a first-rate intelligence, and an inclination of mind toward learning."[114] On the recommendation of the priests, who themselves formed part of the literati and were charged with the supervision of the educational system, the assembly of syphogrants (by secret vote) selected new young talent who held their positions as long as they lived up to their promise. From the standpoint of the exercise of political power in Utopia the literati were an absolutely crucial body. A minority of the syphogrants may have belonged to the literati. Moreover, the tranibors and governor of each city-state, however exactly they were elected, together with all confederate ambassadors, were chosen from a slate of the intellectuals. The national senate, made up of three members (one probably the governor) from each city-state, evidently was also made up of the literati from the city-states. Since many of the literati were too young for public office or were females (see below) and because of the patriarchal emphasis on age and experience, the choice of these officers was appreciably narrowed to a group of possibly no more than fifty.

The leading role played by the literati in Utopian government raises several questions. What role did women play? More provided no answer. Given the nature of Utopian patriarchalism and the inferior status of women, it seems highly probable that female intellectuals specialized in scholarly and professional work (in addition to family responsibilities) and did not hold public office as tranibors, governors, or ambassadors. The priesthood is one exception, for elderly widows were eligible, but their choice seems to have been a rarity. More, of course, rejected the principle of heredity for Utopia, but an impartial observer might wonder about the extent to which the literati could in time become a self-perpetuating elite. A household headed by a member of the literati and quite naturally given over to intellectual endeavors, for example, would have been an atmosphere more conducive to the cultivation of knowledge and learning than that in an ordinary craftsman's dwelling, even allowing for the high interest of all Utopians in mental activity. Hence, aside from the matter of inherited traits, the former household might have been a more fertile source of recruitment for promising young intellects. To what degree, moreover, were members of the literati not holding high public posts given preference by other citizens in the selection for lesser office?

Possibly the most significant question posed by the literati and their monopoly of high governmental office has to do with the egalitarianism of the island republic. In Utopia arithmetical equality reigned, but was not this parity contradicted by the hierarchical distinctions in eligibility for political office? On this score the postulate of proportionate equality clearly seems to have operated in the distribution of offices and rewards, although based on intellectual merit instead of birth and wealth. Utopian society can perhaps best be characterized in terms of a mixture of the principles of arithmetical and proportionate equality, the one relating primarily to the realm of economics, the other to politics. Yet such a picture is complicated by Utopian patriarchy with its maleness and age premium. Intellect was unquestionably highly esteemed by Utopians, but male intellect coupled with old age reigned supreme. Consequently, Utopia is not a completely egalitarian society any more than it is a democratic polity. Its hierarchy gives precedence to male citizens combining mental superiority and maturity of years.

The exclusive, governing meritocracy of elderly males, so distant from the conventional meaning of democracy, along with the abolition of private property and economic egalitarianism, is the end product of the very foundation of Utopian society, namely, the system of public education. More's treatment of this subject is also brief. The educational level of Utopians was exceptionally high, for they valued mental pleasures as "the first and foremost of all pleasures."[115] A great proportion of ordinary people spent their leisure in study and learning, voluntarily attending public lectures before daybreak. Common dinners and suppers always began with a reading, followed by conversation on a topic set by the elders which was "neither sombre nor dull."[116] Utopian hunger for intellectual enlightenment was fostered by a universal system of public instruction that was the responsibility of the priests. More provides a sign of their critical importance to the state when he states, "To no other office in Utopia is more honor given. . . . "[117] If a priest committed a crime, he was subject to no tribunal, only to God and his own conscience. Priests had the power to exclude any Utopian from divine service, "almost no punishment . . . more dreaded."[118] The thirteen priests of each city-state were popularly elected by secret ballot from the literati and ordained by the members of their assigned parishes. Priests apparently held office for life. In addition to religious duties, they acted as censors of morals and oversaw public instruction. More comments on their educational functions:

> They take the greatest pains from the very first to instill into children's minds, while still tender and pliable, good opinions which are also useful for the preservation of the commonwealth. When once they are firmly implanted in children, they accompany them all through their adult lives and are of great help in watching over the condition of the commonwealth. The latter never decays except through vices which arise from wrong attitudes.[119]

Fortescue too urged that the mind of the child, tabula rasa, be imprinted by caring and careful nurture with right opinion.[120] This vital ideological task of shaping Utopian attitudes was performed by the priests. Public instruction was thus employed to curb and mold the "foolish imagination of the common folk," fashioning them into acquiescent material for the rule of the intellectual elite, into loyal citizens who harmoniously cooperated in subordinating their private interests to the public welfare.[121]

In sum, More's ideal state, collectivistic with many egalitarian aspects, nonetheless reveals many conservative and traditional elements: slavery, patriarchalism, subjection of women, elitist rule, and a social hierarchy. Universal education, besides the usual functions, has the social and political aim of ensuring ideological conformity and cultural hegemony and underpinning the power of an intellectual aristocracy. The humanist More in practical affairs was socially and politically a conservative preoccupied with civil order, ever fearful of popular unrest and tyranny from below and above. Throughout his life he gave priority to obedience to the law, uniformity of religious belief, the strengthening of social unity, and the ensurance of stability, all with the goal of preserving the status quo. His Augustinianism apparently imbued him with a brooding pessimism as to the possibility of civil peace because of the anarchic and self-destructive nature of fallen man driven by pride in the form of sexual lust, avarice, and power seeking.[122] This outlook, coupled with More's Platonic conviction that human wisdom must inform and guide political action, that power is a corrupting influence, and that social harmony should be maintained at all costs, may have inspired his project for the immortal commonwealth of Utopia at a time when England was menaced by growing economic troubles and civil strife.[123] That ideal, if incapable of realization, might have been intended to promote principled reforms by existing governments. Conservative as Utopia may be, it is conservatism with a new face, one stressing the political objective of human happiness and requiring the economic well-being of all as a guarantee of social solidarity. This is the challenging lesson of *Utopia*: a perceptive agenda for social reform in the future. The lasting legacy of More's great work may well be its economic conception of the state, a creation of his enlightened conservatism.

If something of More's enlightened conservatism is reflected in the lack of democracy and imperfect egalitarianism of the Utopian commonwealth, how can its fundamental scheme of government best be defined? In a word, the Utopian constitution is a *mixture* in the classic mold. The essence of the traditional doctrine of the mixed constitution is the prevention of both democracy, viewed as tyranny from below, and absolutism, tyranny from above, by a single ruler or a number of notables.[124] Sovereignty is thus diffused by an intricate arrangement of mutually checking offices and institutions which impede the usurpation of power by any particular class, group, or individual and ensure governmental stability and continuity. An important reason for More's writing *Richard III* and *Utopia*, both evocations of the dangers of tyranny, may be, as Thomas Mayer suggests, Henry VIII's occupation of Tournai between 1513 and 1519, during which time he advanced "a complete theory of imperial kingship, partly cast in a new language of sovereignty."[125] Whether *Utopia* was at all a response to the tyrannical potential of Henry's assumption in the period of "all the prerogatives of a *rex imperator*" can never be known with any assurance. What can be said, however, is that More, clearly fearful of the dangers of political absolutism, provided Utopia with a mixed constitution designed to inhibit tyranny and the factionalism and partisan intrigue conducive to its rise. Three passages testify to his intention. The first is found among Hythlodaeus's recommendations in book 1 for possible reform of existing states: "Special legislation might be passed to prevent the monarch from being overmighty and the people overweening. . . . "[126] The second justifies the exclusive power granted to the senate and popular assembly "to take counsel on matters of common interest."[127] The object, More wrote, "is to prevent it from being easy, by a conspiracy between the governor and the tranibors and by tyrannous oppression of the people[,] to change the order of the commonwealth."

More strengthens this effort to block the emergence of the subversive activity of factions and cabals as a prelude to the rise of tyranny by a third provision that anyone "who solicits votes to obtain any office is deprived completely of the hope of holding any office at all."[128] Political power in Utopia was obviously meant by More to be so circumscribed as to minimize the possibility of factionalism and cabals and the closely related threat of tyranny by an "overweening" populace or by "overmighty" dignitaries, thus guaranteeing permanence and order.[129] While sovereignty in Utopia may have been virtually dissolved by More's ingenious arrangements, he appears to have retained a locus of ultimate power (for lubricating the complex machinery of government and resolving possible institutional conflicts) in the meritocratic elite of literati.

More could have turned to a variety of sources for working out his Utopian mixture. He might have given Fortescue's *dominium politicum et regale* republican refinement.[130] In More's own world a significant component of the republican ideal of civic humanism, derived from Cicero, was the notion of the mixed constitution. Contemporary Venice with its institutional mixture was no doubt also a familiar model, as it was later for Thomas Starkey, who unlike More explicitly acknowledged it.[131] Farther afield, More must also have been thoroughly acquainted with the ancient Roman republican mixture, and with that of Sparta through his reading of Plutarch's life of Lycurgus.[132]

Still another possible source may have been Plato's scheme in the *Laws* for the best practicable constitution of Magnesia. Scholarly discussions of the Utopian state sometimes compare and contrast it to Plato's ideal Kallipolis of the *Republic*, but the Magnesian constitution of the *Laws* is usually neglected as a possible guide for More. Perhaps because of Plato's prescription in his last dialogue for a social hierarchy based on differential property ownership, commentators overlook the institutional parallels between Magnesia and Utopia. Apart from important differences in respect to private property, the Magnesian republic with its slavery, patriarchalism, citizens' militia, common meals, rule of law, universal education, and above all the mixed form of government bears some resemblance to Utopia.[133] Students of More should also remember that his beloved St. Augustine's anxiety over *libido dominandi*, the power-seeking propensity in fallen man, is anticipated by Plato's emphatic warnings in the *Laws* about the corrupting effects of power. No less than Acton, Plato believed that all power corrupts and absolute power corrupts absolutely. No individual could resist the temptations of power, and the more power he possessed, the more likely he was to be corrupted and act tyrannically. Hence, one of Plato's foremost purposes in the *Laws*, on the basis of this axiomatic principle, was to contrive for Magnesia an immortal governmental structure immune to the abuse of public office by power-holders, thereby preventing civil strife and social change. Plato, despite his radical blueprint for the architecture of the Magnesian state, like More, displayed a pronounced conservatism.[134]

The problem of the exact pedigree of the Utopian mixed constitution is probably beyond solution and may no doubt be only of antiquarian interest. Nevertheless, a brief summary of the Magnesian project and comparison with More's governmental blueprint may serve to illuminate the nature of the latter and confirm that it is indeed a mixture. Magnesia, Plato informed us, was a mixture of "democracy" and "monarchy," of the principles of liberty and authority, combining popular participation with permanence and order. The mixed government of Magnesia was intricately balanced and checked so as to contain the destructive power-seeking inclination of man, to block the socially disruptive manifestation of pride so dreaded by St. Augustine and More. For Plato each public office in relation to other offices and governmental bodies was designed to circumscribe the actions of the holder in order to prevent his use of power in a willful and arbitrary manner. Magnesian government was organized to render virtually impossible the rise to power of a single absolute ruler or a small faction as well as the many-headed hydra of the people. Democratic institutions in Magnesia were essentially electoral and judicial rather than deliberative and policymaking. Genuine deliberation and decision-making was confined to the "monarchical" component, a complex of offices and councils dominated by a minority of wealthy (by Magnesian standards), elderly, and enlightened citizens who with the priests and some promising youths composed an extragovernmental group, the Nocturnal Council, so-called because of its meetings before dawn for theological and philosophical discussion.

The parallel between the Magnesian and Utopian mixtures is by no means exact, but the general congruence is interesting. Utopian government in each of the city-states consisted of two levels, in Plato's language, "democratic" and "monarchical." The "democratic" level consisted of the two hundred neighborhood associations of thirty households; the assembly of their chairmen, the two hundred syphogrants; and an undefined popular assembly. The role of the two assemblies was largely electoral and occasionally consultative. The "monarchical" level consisted of the senate of twenty tranibors and the governor, all elected for life, who were assigned deliberative, policymaking, and judicial tasks and the direction of affairs of state. Utopian democracy was compromised by the all-pervasive patriarchalism and by the selection for life of all senior magistrates and priests from a small group of intellectuals, the literati. These magistrates and priests formed the real locus of power in the Utopian state, acting as a beneficent ruling class of enlightened and experienced statesmen, not, however, completely free from "popular" control. More, like Plato, apparently saw the two levels as mutually balancing. For More the vigilant patriarchal heads of households and the two assemblies constituted a "democratic" check on the exercise of power by the ruling elite, while the elite in turn functioned as a salutary limit on the people. The social and political architecture of Utopia itself may have been inspired by an intellectual mixture composed of elements derived from two of More's possible literary sources, the collectivism and wisdom of the guardians in Plato's *Republic* and the institutional arrangements in the *Laws*.

Utopia is an ingenious social and political mechanism devised by More for the restraint of fallen man. More was too much of an Augustinian to think that human pride could be eradicated. At best its divisiveness could be appreciably reduced. Crime still existed in Utopia but at a far lower rate than elsewhere. The ideal state of Utopia, not so ideal as to fail to take into consideration the intractable nature of humans, was constructed to thwart the excesses of pride, for an attempt to obliterate pride altogether would have meant the destruction of man. An ever-vigilant patriarchy strictly supervising the extended families and their relations with other households and keeping citizens busy and industrious at their respective labors, plus the liberalization of divorce and the severe penalty of enslavement for adultery all worked to control sexual passions. Avarice and greed for material possessions were countered with Utopian communism, the elimination of private property and monetary exchange. The *mixed constitution* impeded the *libido dominandi*. Both the desire for possessions and for power, and even to some extent sexual lust, would also be kept in abeyance by economic prosperity and security for all, a major goal of the Utopian state. More resolved the Platonic question of the philosopher-king aired so anxiously in book 1—the problem of how to apply wise counsel to affairs of state or to combine human knowledge with political power in the formulation and implementation of public policy—through the recruitment of the ruling elite and educators from an exclusive corps of the most able and highly trained citizens.[135] Universal education working in close association with this intellectual aristocracy would shape the mentality of all Utopians to ensure ideological conformity and suppress dissent, thereby producing loyal and cooperative citizens dedicated to the common interest. Thus an immortal commonwealth would be established and the dangers of disorder and tyranny overcome. More, the enlightened conservative, had imaginatively woven innovative and traditional strands into a coherent intellectual fabric.

If Dudley in *The Tree of Commonwealth* can be said to have begun the early Tudor literature of reform, it was Thomas More six years later in *Utopia* who issued the first manifesto of social protest and call for improvement. In his critical assessment of the grievous social and political problems of England, he blazed a trail to be followed by the later reformers. His critique and his reform program, of course, not the radical collectivism of *Utopia*, anticipate the endeavors of his successors. It was his brand of conservatism, his penchant for law and order, for social harmony and hierarchy, not his outrageous flirtation with communism and egalitarianism, which stamped much of the thought of his successors. His conservatism, like theirs, was enlightened, aiming at a rational, moderate remedy for the appalling situation so scathingly described and denounced. Others to follow might offer more detailed and insightful analyses of social conditions or more practicable recommendations for their resolution. But in an important sense the later reformers did little more than develop some of the ideas in More's masterpiece. First and foremost, they held a similar economic conception of the state, a notion that a basic purpose of government was to promote the material welfare of citizens. Whatever else was essential to human happiness, they agreed with More that it could not flourish in the midst of poverty, homelessness, unemployment, and social dislocation. Both More and his successors, however, pointed out that the dire material circumstances should be alleviated not solely because of charitable fellow-feeling but because of a prudential calculation that the order, stability, and strength of the state depended on the prosperity of all. For the reformers as for More the self-interest of government ultimately rested on the promotion of the common economic interest. Government, therefore, was to use its power, informed by knowledge and wisdom, to act positively and creatively in constructing a social environment most favorable to the happiness of all, regardless of rank and degree. Only in this way, More thought, with the later reformers following suit, would crime, delinquency, and seditious behavior be reduced, and social cooperation be restored and divisive conflict ended.

More and the later reformers all worried over the irresponsible exercise of political power and the threat of tyranny. Fostering the material well-being of the vast laboring majority was their prescription for lessening the possibility of popular subversion and thereby thwarting any democratic and leveling tendencies among the masses. There always remained, nonetheless, the serious question of tyranny from above, particularly since the action necessary for social amelioration required the expansion of governmental power. In resolving this threat More followed the line of reasoning begun by Fortescue and to be continued by Starkey and Thomas Smith. The best prevention of tyranny in the view of all four was the mixed constitution. More, however, differed from the others in that his version of a constitutional mixture was a radical departure from customary theory and practice. Security against tyranny was obviously his goal as well as theirs. But instead of adhering to one of the conventional objectives of the doctrine of the mixed constitution—preservation of the propertied status quo with its property differentials and monopoly of political power—More devised a governmental mechanism with collectivism and meritocracy to safeguard a propertyless status quo. However More may have differed from the others on this matter, these reformers all agreed that English social ills could only be ended by establishing a genuinely cooperative community of citizens through rational governmental efforts at economic renewal.

7   A Life of Dignity in the "True Commyn Wele"

Thomas Starkey

The son of a prosperous and important member of the Cheshire lesser gentry, Thomas Starkey (d. 1538) was probably born sometime after 1498.[1] He may have attended Magdalen College School, Oxford, and he certainly entered Magdalen College, where he received a B.A. in 1516. Elected a fellow in 1518, he remained in Oxford until 1523, then perhaps journeying to Italy with Thomas Lupset. During the next ten years Starkey spent much time on the Continent, where he figured in the humanistic circle of his friend and patron Reginald Pole in Padua, studied civil law there and in Avignon, somewhere along the way earning a theological degree. *A Dialogue between Pole and Lupset* was probably written between 1529 and 1532, to be touched up later with the intention of presentation to Henry VIII. Starkey returned to England for good in December 1534, and became one of Thomas Cromwell's coterie of humanistic advisors, but apparently neither Cromwell nor the king saw the manuscript, which was not published until 1878. At the crown's request, however, Starkey corresponded with Pole in an effort to persuade him to support the king, a project that ended in failure. Starkey's defense of the Reformation settlement, *An Exhortation to the People Instructynge Theym to Unitie and Obedience,* was offered to the king in 1535 and published the following year by the royal printer. In early 1535 Starkey was appointed a royal chaplain and the following year he received the mastership of the collegiate chapel of Corpus Christi, London. He died in Somerset, 25 August 1538.

Whether the *Dialogue*—"one of the most significant works of political thought written in English between Fortescue and Hooker"[2]—accurately represented Starkey's views or those of the two participants, Pole and Lupset, is a problem that need not detain us. Reginald Pole (1500–1558), the principal discussant, also educated at Magdalen, was Henry VIII's distant cousin, but he fell out with the king in 1532 over the divorce.³ Fortunately, Pole was in Italy at the time and prudently remained there. In 1536 he wrote a lengthy critical letter on the Reformation settlement to his royal kinsman in response to questions put to him by Starkey the previous year; the letter was published in Latin in Rome and later in English, with a vituperative personal attack on Henry, as *A Defence of Ecclesiastical Unity*. With the accession of Mary in 1553, Pole became archbishop of Canterbury and one of the queen's trusted aides during the English Counter-Reformation.

Thomas Lupset (ca. 1495–1530), a pupil in Dean Colet's household at St. Paul's, was at Cambridge during the time of Erasmus's residence and assisted him in his editorial work.⁴ A student in Paris between 1517 and 1519, Lupset, who probably knew More through Erasmus, was given the responsibility for the printing of the second Latin edition of *Utopia*.⁵ By the time he was in Corpus Christi College, Oxford, where he received the B.A. about 1520, Lupset has been described as "very probably the most educated man of his years in England."⁶ With his friends Pole and Starkey, Lupset spent many months abroad until his death from consumption in late 1530.⁷ He seemed to be highly favored by the king and his works, including the *Exhortation to Young Men* (1539), were published in the thirties by the royal printer.

Starkey originally composed the *Dialogue* as an "aristocratic reform manifesto," according to Thomas Mayer, to urge Pole to take public office and to assume leadership of a faction of the nobility in the uncertain political atmosphere of the period.⁸ At the time Henry was warmly disposed toward Pole, who had just returned from a highly successful mission in Paris, accompanied by Starkey and Lupset, to obtain favorable opinions on the royal divorce. Pole refused the king's offer of the archbishopric of York, and both Starkey and Lupset were rewarded for their services with benefices. When Pole left England in 1532, Starkey, probably having already completed the *Dialogue* and disenchanted by his patron's negative response to Henry's overtures and his opposition to the divorce, decided to seek royal employment, studying civil law in preparation. Later he may have polished up the manuscript for submission in order to bolster his credentials for a post. Events, however, moved swiftly, and prudence dictated that the manuscript be shown neither to Cromwell nor to his sovereign.

Starkey has been praised for being the "first writer of a humanist dialogue in English."⁹ The untitled manuscript, probably known to very few if any of Starkey's contemporaries, well worked by the author, is obviously unfinished; undivided into chapters and parts, it is at least the length of *Utopia*. The sources of the *Dialogue's* ideas are legion. Starkey clearly appropriated More's analysis of social conditions, and he shows that he had closely studied Cicero and Aristotle as well as the writings of Italian humanists like Gasparo Contarini and Donato Giannotti.[10] The *Dialogue* purports to be an extended conversation of two days' duration, possibly in 1529, between Lupset and his noble friend at one of the Pole family manors in Bisham near Maidenhead. Evidently Starkey meant to divide the book into two parts, the first amounting to about two-thirds of the total, one for each day of the conversation.[11] After lengthy introductory remarks—reminiscent of the last section of book 1 of *Utopia*—in which Lupset convinces his reluctant friend that wise men should be concerned with affairs of state and apply their knowledge to politics, Pole sets the three main topics for subsequent discussion: (1) the nature of the "true Commyn wele," (2) the "dekey of our commyn wele," and (3) the cause of this decay and its remedy.[12] He deals with points one and two in the first part of the *Dialogue*. The second part focuses on the third matter.

The metaphor that predominates in both parts is medical, which is not surprising given Starkey's keen interest in the subject. One of his favorite expressions is the "body politic." The state is likened to an individual writ large, with body and soul comparable to society and government. After the "diseases" of English society and government are identified in part one, their causes are revealed in part two, together with advice on the proper therapeutic measures. Throughout, the ideal of a true commonwealth serves as a standard and guide just as the healthy condition of the individual functions as a model for the physician. Starkey shows a traditional concern with the problem of counsel but he manifests his modernity in his causal analysis, which he based on historical example and experience as the foundation for rational policies of reform to be implemented by positive governmental action. Because he was a man of letters without political experience, his recommendations for reform sometimes fail to display the realistic turn of mind and shrewd insight of his predecessors, all seasoned and skillful actors in the public forum.

Starkey's ideal of the healthy state is fundamentally conservative. He envisioned a cooperative commonwealth of ranks and orders, free from discord, whose members were joined together in the conscientious performance of their respective duties by loving fellowship, rising above selfish aims for the sake of the common interest.[13] Like the works of Starkey's predecessors, the *Dialogue* offers an essentially economic conception of the state, with due attention paid to the various social groups of which it was composed. To even a greater extent than More, Starkey worried about the problem of idleness, believing it to be one of the three major diseases of the body politic. Along with Dudley and More, he saw in education the remedy of many of the ills of the English state. Starkey by no means disregarded the danger of popular insurrection, but he viewed with greater urgency the threat of absolutism, either by the prince or a faction of the aristocracy. Just as More in *Utopia* wished to guarantee the dominance of the ruling class of literati through mixed government, at the same time limiting that class's use of power, so Starkey adapted the same constitutional device to his own aim of bridling the crown and ensuring the responsible action of the nobility in their leading role.

Political Terminology

Starkey's political language is the richest, the most varied, and the most difficult to understand of the writers so far surveyed. Throughout the *Dialogue* he employs the terms "natyon," "cuntrey," "reame," "cyvyl lyfe," "cyvyl ordur," "polytyke body," and "polytyke ordur." Of special interest is his use of "commyn wele," "state," and "commynalty." He was probably the first to employ the word *state* in a way approaching the modern institutional sense, distinguishing it from both government and society. For this usage he deserves recognition not so much for linguistic innovation but for revealing something of importance happening in English political society and in the patterns of political thought. It is therefore worthwhile to examine his political lexicon with reference to the vocabulary of a few of his contemporaries.

Commonwealth or "commyn wele" appears in the *Dialogue* with two different meanings. The first, conforming to conventional usage, designates the common interest, for example: "they schold above al regard the commyn welth & yet every man sekyth hys owne profyt," or "that the common wele ryse of the partycular wele of every one, then every man ought to study to maynteyne the partycular wele to the settyng forward of the commyn."[14] Dudley, as we have already seen, used *commonwealth* exclusively in this sense. This was also a practice of Starkey's contemporaries like Clement Armstrong (ca. 1477–1536) and Christopher St. German (ca. 1460–1540).[15] The latter, however, was apparently thinking of *state* when he translated *res publica* as "public weal" and also "common welth."[16] Sir Thomas Elyot insisted in 1531 that "public weal" was the only correct translation of *res publica*. In his opinion, *publica* of *res publica* referred to *populus*, the whole people regardless of rank or station.[17] The rendering of *res publica* as common weal, in contrast, erroneously implied a sharing, an arithmetical equality he found abhorrent, falsely identifying *res publica* with *res plebeia* or weal of the commons or multitude.[18]

So by the time Starkey was writing the use of *commonwealth* for both common interest and state was probably not exceptional. While he was not the first to employ *commonwealth* in both senses, he may have been among the first to resort to such frequent use of *commonwealth* for *state*, indeed more frequent than for *common interest*. He referred to "platos commyn wele," the ideal state of the *Republic*; to the "destructyon of al commyn welys," apparently meaning states, not common interests; to "the grete dekey fautys & mysordurys . . . of our commyn wele"; and to the sedition, civil war, and discord "that hathe destroyd al commyn wellys," again all states, not common interests.[19] One of the chief purposes of the *Dialogue* was to discover "what ys the veray & true Commyn wele, wherin standyth & when hyt most floryschyth."[20] Pole and Lupset then proceeded to discuss the nature of the "true commyn wele" and to construct definitions of the ideal state which aimed at the common interest.

If Starkey was among the earliest writers to equate *commonwealth* and *state*, he was possibly also the first to employ the word *state* in something like the modern political sense, although he often used "reame," or realm, for the English state.[21] Neither his three predecessors nor his three contemporaries did so. In the *Dialogue* "state" may refer, as was customary with St. German, for example, to status or condition: "the welthe & prosperouse state of every partycular man," "every mannys state," "state of chrystundome," "state of our reame."[22] Related to this meaning was the "state" (the form or order) of the commonwealth: whether it entailed the rule of one, the few, or the many: monarchy, aristocracy, democracy. Venice in this respect is singled out for praise, being "in one ordur & state" for over a thousand years.[23] England he calls a monarchy or "state of pryncys," and the best preventative against tyranny, he suggests, is a "myxte state."[24] From denoting the status of individuals and polities, Starkey used *state* for the defining characteristic of a commonwealth, its form or condition of government. And from *state* in this sense, he seems to have taken the further short but important step of identifying *state* with the institutional totality of the commonwealth:

> . . . the hart thereof ys the kyng prynce & rular of the *state*, whether so ever hyt be one or many, accordyng to the governance of the commynalty & polytyke state, for some be governyd by a prynce alone, some by a conseyl of certayn wyse men & some by the hole pepul togyddur . . . he or they wych have authoryte apon the hole *state* ryghwel may be resemblyd to the hart.[25]

Starkey on the same page again mentions the rulers of the "state," and later in regard to tyranny he stipulates that the laws "must rule and governe the *state* & not the prynce aftur hys owne lyberty & wyl."[26]

These quotations suggest that Starkey was beginning to conceive of *state* and *commonwealth* as synonymous in the institutional sense but distinct from government. He never seems to have employed "government," which was of somewhat later usage, but he did use "governyed," "governour," and "governance."[27] The last term is also found in St. German and Elyot.[28] By *governance*, whose usage dated back to the fourteenth century, Starkey signified both the manner of governing and the office or power of governing. He appeared almost to be giving to *governance* an abstract, collective meaning, thereby suggesting that states do not govern, although they are defined by the nature of their government. The government of a state, as we recognize it, is an abstraction, the rule of a collectivity, comprising individuals and offices, which may change in character and personnel, and in the process of such change the nature of the state may alter. Nonetheless, the state as a structure of power with a corporative, institutional identity continues to exist, albeit with different features.

In the first quotation we should note that Starkey introduced the long-used term "commynalty," conventionally denoting either the "commons" or "multitude" or, of even older lineage, the whole people (regardless of rank) of a state or municipality, a community.[29] Dudley employed "comynaltie" in the first sense of "commons," as did Henry Brinklow in his acerbic *Complaynt of Roderyck Mors* of 1542, where he identified "comynaltye" with "the body of this reame," the commons in contrast to the "head," the nobility.[30] Similarly, Elyot contrasted "commonalty" with *populus*, or people, which consisted of "all the inhabitants of a realm or city, of what estate or condition so ever they be."[31] In contrast, "commonalty," the English equivalent of *plebs*, differed from *people* in that it "signifieth only the multitude, wherein be contained the base and vulgar inhabitants not advanced in any honour of dignity." In the second sense of the whole people, the word occurred in *The Libel of English Policy* (1436–1438), in the opinion that England and Ireland should stand together "as one commonalty."[32] A popular rhyme of 1446 registered the protest of the "Comalte" of Coventry (all the members of the corporation) against the enclosure of the city's common fields by the rich burgesses of the municipal council.[33]

In using "commynalty" in the second way Starkey did something of interest in connection with his conceptual separation of state from government. He equated the word with Elyot's "people" and meant all who composed the state: prince, nobles, clergy, and commons.[34] He also used "multytude" in the inclusive sense to refer to all ranks and orders—as was "pepul"—and not restricted to designating the commons.[35] "Nobility" for Starkey generally included gentry, although sometimes they were distinguished.[36] The "polytyke body" was composed of all the various ranks and orders.[37] Any conflict between them, that is, within the "commynalty," in the sense of community or society, would impair the health of the body politic. Previously, Starkey referred to every "commynalty cyty & cuntrey, as hyt were, a polytyke body," explaining that like an individual a commonwealth was composed of body and soul. The body was the "multytude of pepul," the "citizens" of every "commynalty city or cuntrey."[38] Although Brinklow followed the conventional body-head distinction in regard to the state to differentiate commons from nobility, Starkey applied another dichotomy, that of body and soul. The soul of the "polytyke body" or the state was "cyvyle ordur & polytyke law, admynystryd by offycers & rularys," law and government.[39] The soul permeated the whole of the body giving it life and direction. Yet the individuals who held office and administered the law were physically parts of the body; only in their political capacity were they of the soul, or such seemed to be Starkey's reasoning. The "head" of the "polytyke body" consisted of princes, lords, and bishops; the "hands," of warriors and artisans; the "feet," of farmers.[40] Starkey criticized the parts of the head of the English body politic for pursuing their own narrow ends, disregarding the "welth of the commynalty," that is, the common interest of the entire body: head, hands, and feet.[41] By "commynalty," he seems then often to have meant approximately what we do by *society*, a word he rarely used.[42] A society or "commynalty" organized under law and government to form a state or commonwealth comprised all citizens who enjoyed its benefits and performed their civic duties. Finally, when Starkey wrote of the commoners, the common people as distinct from higher ranks and orders, he used "commyns" and "commyn pepul," not "commynalty."[43]

If the "commynalty" or society composed of individuals of every station was the body of the politic body, the soul of law and government administered by parts of the head rendered the body political, transforming it into a state or commonwealth. A state was therefore a society organized by law and administered by government. Like reason, the essence of the human soul controlling the body, government and law ruled the "multytude of pepul & hole commynalty."[44] In effect a state is a corporative whole with an abstract, collective existence. The state is to be analytically differentiated from both society and government. The state is a society imprinted by "cyvyle ordur" or "polytyk ordur,"[45] provided by government, "a multytude conspyryng togyddur in vertue and honesty."[46] For Starkey, moreover, the state was not simply a convention or human contrivance for the preservation of the common interest but a natural entity, existing for the fulfillment of man's rational being. The state was the means of advancing that rationality, the cooperative endeavor of a society bound together by love and justice for the realization of common interest. One of Starkey's achievements is that he suggested for the first time in England the basic ingredients of the modern notion of the state. No longer was the state conceived of only in terms of individual, personalized rule. From his standpoint, the state was almost an institutional totality, a corporative whole, a constitutional structure of power conceptually differentiated from the society of individuals composing it and from the collectivity of magistrates governing them.

Ideal of the State

Starkey not only made an advance in political vocabulary but developed the economic conception of the state of his predecessors. This is apparent from his definitions of the "true commyn wele" or ideal state, his norm for examining the conditions of the English state and guiding proposals for its reform. Three of these definitions, employing the familiar terms of his political lexicon, follow.

> . . . the gud ordur & pollycy by gud lawys stablyschyd & set, & by hedys & rularys put in effect by the wyche the hole body as by reason ys governyd & rulyd, to the intent that thys multytude of pepul & hole commynalty *so helthy & so welthy havyng convenyent abundaunce of al thyngys necessary for the mayntenance therof*, may wyth dew honowr, reverence & love relygyously worschype god, as fountayn of all gudnes maker & governower of al thys world, every one also dowyng hys duty to other, wyth brotherly love one lovyng one a nother as membrys & partys of one body.[47]

> . . . wych ys no thyng els but the *prosperouse* & most perfayt state of a multytud assemblyd togyddur in any cuntrey cyty or towne governyd vertusely in cyvyle lyfe accordyng to the nature & dygnyte of man.[48]

> . . . we schold have a multytud of pepul convenyent to the place *floryschyng wyth al abundance of exteryor thyngys requyrd to the bodyly welth of man*, the wych lyvyng togyddur in cyvyle lyfe governyd by polytyke order & rule schold conspyre to geddur in amyte & love, every one glad to helpe a nother to hys powar to the intent . . . that the hole myght attayn to that perfectyon wych ys

determyd to the dygnyte of mannys nature by the gudnes of god,
the wych ys the end of al lawys & ordur for thys wych purpos they
be wryt & ordeynd.[49]

These quotations represent the essence of Starkey's political thought.
Through his typical language—"commynalty," "cyuyle life," "polytyke
ordur"—he seemed to be groping to distinguish between state, society,
and government. The state is united by the mutual love and cooperation
of each individual performing his duty. Emphasis is placed on unity and
harmony, on the state as a single whole or body, organized to further the
common interest. Each of the passages also lays stress on economic well-
being, health, prosperity, and plentiful goods: "floryschyng wyth al abundance of exteryor thyngs requyryd to the bodyly welth of man." Starkey
thus continued the approach of his predecessors by giving priority to the
common interest over the interest of any individual or group within the
state, by defining the common interest in economic terms, and by conceiving of it as one of the main aims of the state.

A characteristic of the last two definitions of the ideal commonwealth
is the opinion that the state should be governed "accordyng to the nature
& dygnyte of man."[50] Indeed, the chief purpose of Starkey's state was to
attain through proper laws and good order "that perfectyon wych ys determyd to the dygnyte of mannys nature."[51] At the beginning of the
Dialogue Lupset explained the meaning of human dignity, introducing a
continuing theme of the book.[52] Man, made by God in his image, in acting virtuously and perfecting his mental powers most nearly attains the
nature of his divine creator. Far surpassing all other beings, whom he can
dominate by his wisdom, man is called by ancient philosophers "an
earthly God." Human reason, if properly utilized, is capable of fathoming
the mysteries of terrestial and celestial phenomena. Because of his divinely ordained nature, man can attain the universal virtues of wisdom,
justice, temperance, and courage. In considering the astonishing ingenuity and enterprise of man—the establishment of civil order with its cities,
towns, and laws, the development of the many arts and crafts, and the
cultivation of the earth—one can only conclude that man outstrips all
other creatures in dignity and excellence, just as he in turn is exceeded by
his maker. Man "hath in hym a sparkul of dyvynyte, & ys surely of a ce-
lestyal & dyvyne nature seyng that by memory and wyte also he con-
ceyvyth the nature of al thyng."[53]

According to Starkey, the individual achieves the highest felicity or
happiness in fulfilling the excellence and dignity that is his by nature.[54]
Starkey agreed with Aristotle that man is a union of body and soul and

rejected Plato's view of his being essentially a soul imprisoned by the body. Thus, the realization of human excellence, and consequently the attainment of the greatest happiness, required not only virtue but also most significantly material comfort, the nourishing of the soul *and* the care of the body. Starkey admitted that happiness could be secured by fostering the soul alone but nevertheless concluded that the highest felicity required bodily well-being, for which worldly prosperity was the prime requisite. The highest happiness was associated by Starkey, as it was by More, with "true pleasures" as distinguished from vain pleasures. True pleasure is derived not simply from perfection of the soul, that is, from a full and rich mental life. Bodily health and comfort are also critical, as for More, which means that a person must have more in the way of material benefits than is necessary for mere survival and minimal subsistence. Vain pleasure, in contrast, arises largely from the satisfaction of gross, sensual appetites and as such is demeaning to human excellence and dignity. The state thus existed to enable individuals to be truly happy by realizing their natural excellence and dignity, for which economic well-being was a necessary condition. Although not alone in his stress on Christian virtue as the chief aim of the state, Starkey was unique among the reformers in his language of human dignity, only matched at century's close by Richard Hooker. For Starkey the all-important ideal of man's dignity entailed the imperative of state policy to promote the common interest, fundamental to which is the material welfare of all.

As we might expect from a sincere Christian, however, Starkey's optimism about human dignity produced its contrary, his pessimism about fallen man. Starkey pointed to the "fraylty of man," who, overcome by sensual pleasure, tended to follow the morally reprehensible course in life.[55] Negligent and blinded by self-love and narrow self-interest, individuals invariably disregard the common interest, thus proving incapable of governing themselves well.[56] Since each individual "naturaly ys gyven to folow plesure, quyetnes & ease," he invariably seeks to do what is least difficult and most profitable.[57] The tyranny defiling so many states then is not divine punishment for human sin but partly the result of human negligence and partly the "malyce of man who by nature ys ambycyouse & of al pleasure most desyrouse."[58]

Nevertheless, Starkey apparently blamed much of human evil not so much on the selfishness of pleasure-seeking man as on human error arising from false opinion. In a passage recalling Fortescue's portrait of the human mind at birth as *tabula rasa* and More's less explicit comment in *Utopia*, Starkey, like Fortescue, citing the authority of Aristotle, affirmed that:

> . . . the mynd of man fyrst of hyt selfe ys a clene & pure tabul wher
> ys no thyng payntyd or carvyd, but of hyt selfe apt & indyfferent
> to receyve al maner of pycturys, & image, so mannys mynd hath
> fyrst no knolege of truth nor fyrst hath no maner of wyl wherby
> hyt ys more drawne to gud then to yl, but aftur as opynyon & sure
> persuasyon of gud & of yl growyth in by experyence & lernyng, so
> ever the wyl conformyth & framyth hymselfe to the knolege before
> goten in so much that yf hyt be persuadyd that gud ys yl & yl gud
> then ever the wyl chesyth the yl & levyth the gud, accordyng as
> sche by opynyon ys instructyd.[59]

Men, he repeated elsewhere, are corrupted by false beliefs into thinking
that evil is good and good evil, conducting their lives by such erroneous
understanding.[60] Lupset even went so far as to say that "ignorance" is the
"fountayn of al yl."[61] Ignorance, however, Pole insisted, is no excuse for
iniquity but results instead from man's innate weakness and negligence,
his propensity to imbibe false opinions. Whatever the source of the divisive selfishness of man, Starkey plainly thought the state absolutely necessary for the prevention of anarchy and the destruction of civilized life
constantly threatened by inescapable human egoism. Moreover, the idea
of the external shaping of individual behavior, so much a practical consequence of the conception of tabula rasa, helps explain Starkey's (and
More's) social environmentalism, that is, the attention to educational reforms and the improvement of English conditions by positive governmental action, for example, the reduction of crime by the elimination of
poverty and unemployment.

Starkey's dualistic view of man seemed fundamental to a dualistic conception of the state as an entity having two essential and interrelated
functions, one positive and one negative. The state, on the one hand, has
the positive task of guiding man in the realization of his natural excellence and dignity, to produce conditions for the highest human happiness.
On the other hand, the state has the negative role of controlling human
egoism and checking its socially disruptive potential by the rigorous application of law and governmental power for the preservation of order. To
function positively in the manner described, the state must fashion and
maintain a social environment conducive to the economic well-being and
prosperity of all citizens. If the state neglects to do so, it will fail in its
negative function of policeman, judge, and hangman; and if delinquent in
respect to the negative role, the positive action will be of no avail, actually
bringing about the demise of the body politic. The impoverishment of a
people because of inertia or the shortsighted and misguided policy of government can only spell distress and widespread unhappiness for it is

"manyfest that the lake of necessarys for nuryschyng & clothyng of the body, ys the sure & certayn cause of infynyte myserys & manyfold wretchydnes."[62] Such penury and hardship can only result in civil discord, in "al kynd of mysery, for grete poverty in any cuntrey, hath every couplyd gret mysery sche ys the mother of envy & malyce dyssensyon & debate, & many other myschefys ensuyng the same."[63] Where there is plenty and little poverty, moreover, the number of thieves will be vastly reduced and crime in general will be negligible.[64] But Starkey had more in mind than ordinary crime and its elimination through wise economic policies of government. He warned that "in no cuntrey may be any grettur pestylens or more pernycyouse then cyvyle warre sedycyon & dyscordys among the partys of the polytyke body, thys ys the thyng that hathe destroyd al commyn wellys."[65] Again he emphasized the "pestylens" of civil disunity, admonishing that "thys thyng above al other most cure must be had."[66]

Starkey like More offered a social explanation of civil disorder and crime, as did Armstrong who blamed Evil May Day of 1517 on the numerous London poor, unemployed because of the influx of foreign commodities.[67] The root cause, according to Starkey, of this pestilence of the body politic—the other diseases being underpopulation and idleness— was the absence of justice and equity, bringing impoverishment and all its dire effects. He was thinking primarily of the inequitable distribution of goods among the people. One part had far too much, exemplified in the luxurious lives of a few, and the other part had far too little, the great majority living in poverty. He was insistent that all things should be equitably distributed according to the dignity of all. But he did not intend a just allocation conforming to the principle of arithmetical equality. He visualized citizens united in love, each doing his duty and performing his office according to his "state offyce or degre."[68] Rulers should expect obedience from citizens required by their "state and degre." Proportionate equality was also the rule in regard to material rewards: "ryches & convenyent abaundaunce of al worldy thyngys, mete to the mayntenuance of every mannys state accordyng to hys degre."[69]

Even Starkey's criticism of primogeniture and entail, contrary to expectations, is premised on a version of proportionate equality.[70] While arrangements for inheritance were to be preserved for the nobility, since the English were naturally "somewhat rude & sturdy of mynd" and required great family heads for the maintenance of social peace and solidarity, they were to be abolished among the lesser gentlemen and lower ranks.[71] Perhaps the younger sons of all families, no matter their status, could receive some portion of the inheritance, but, Starkey asserted,

among the lower orders primogeniture and entail stemmed from and reinforced a kind of arrogance that "every Jake wold be a gentylman, &
every gentlyman and knyght or a lord."[72] By this somewhat serpentine
reasoning, Starkey implied that primogeniture and entail (with the exception of the upper nobility) paradoxically encouraged a parity of outlook and promise of higher station in the future that in actuality weakened a true social hierarchy of rank and orders.

Starkey was adamant that a stable, unified state must have a thriving
economy without poverty and unemployment so that all citizens prosper
in proportion to their station and live happy, contented lives befitting
their natural excellence and dignity. Conversely, he cautioned, without
the power and authority of the state to check human egoism, great wealth
and prosperity would divide and ruin the civil order. Economic well-being
for the advancement of human dignity and social order and governmental
restraint of human egoism were axiomatic to Starkey's ideal of the state.

A final trait of Starkey's vision of the true commonwealth is his notion
of the relationship between the interest of the individual and the common
interest. He drew a close analogy between a person's body and soul and
the state's society and government. Just as each individual had a special
"wele" or interest to promote, so the state possessed a common interest.[73]
Because men are naturally egoistic, blinded by self-love and ambition, the
immoderate pursuit of their narrow interests threatens the interest of all.
If, however, it can be shown that a true private interest of the individual
exists, identical for each, characterized by what is necessary for the maintenance of physical well-being, the control of divisive egoism, and the
fulfillment of excellence and dignity, then the sum of these authentic private interests equals the true common interest. The state should therefore encourage citizens to cultivate their genuine interests and realize
their true beings. Three factors fundamental to the legitimate private interest of the individual, and by analogy to the state, relate in each case to
body and soul. Two of the three relate to the body and one to the soul.
The first factor is bodily health, strength, and beauty.[74] Health is the
"ground & foundatyon" of true individual interest, as More also believed. Without health riches are of no avail to the individual, rendering
him incapable of the highest virtue and real happiness. Similarly, bodily
strength and beauty (lack of physical deformity) are necessary to one's
physical and moral welfare. The second requisite of true private interest
is wealth, an abundance of exterior and worldly goods necessary for the
well-being of the individual and proportionate to his rank and station.[75]
Basic to a salutary wealth, besides economic security and material comfort, are children and good friends. From the bodily components of true

private interest, Starkey then turned to the soul and the third factor fundamental to individual interest, moral virtue; he spoke of "natural honesty & vertue of the mynd," honoring God, and openness, equity, and justice in dealings with others.[76] Without virtue, health and riches were deemed useless, for unless properly employed, the bodily components would be used by the individual to destroy himself and others. The attainment of the three—health, wealth, virtue—would lead to true happiness or "felycyte, convenyent to the nature of man, & to hys dygnyte."[77] Although a person might be virtuous, he could not achieve the highest morality and hence the greatest happiness without health and economic well-being.[78] On these matters Starkey's outlook generally coincided with More's.

The idea of the union of body and soul in the true happiness of the individual Starkey then applied to the state.[79] Just as he viewed the soul as the animus of the body, so the life-giving element of the state or "polytyke body" was its soul—law and government. Society and government were to be joined in the state like the union of body and soul in the human being. Starkey assayed the condition of the English state in terms of the three components of private interest, which by his reasoning were the same for the common interest. Since the state is the individual writ large and their genuine interests are identical, the true commonwealth and individual are qualitatively similar. Whether an actual state is an authentic one depends on its embodiment of the true common interest defined as the sum of the real individual interests, or such was the logic of Starkey's enquiry into the English commonwealth. Corresponding to the three components of the true individual interest are the three characteristics of the state that truly serve the common interest. They concern the nature of the population, the economic condition of society, and the quality of law and government, or, according to Starkey's analogy, the health and wealth of the body and the virtue of its soul.

If the body politic is to have health, strength, and beauty, there must be a population of neither too many nor too few, one that is sufficient for socially useful labor in agriculture and crafts but not one that strains the food supply.[80] The people must be healthy and vigorous, strong in the sense that each part performs it functions and duties and each remains in due proportion to the other parts, without, for instance, an excess of artisans or a shortage of farmers. The true state must be wealthy in that an abundance of material goods should be available for the nurture and economic well-being of all members of society, commensurate with their status. Only by the elimination of poverty and widespread economic misery will the chief cause of dissension and rebellion be removed. Unlike his three predecessors, Starkey in the *Dialogue* assumed but never explicitly asserted that the self-interest of rulers depended ultimately on a prosperous citizenry. For him the soul of the body politic, the government acting through law, if it was to function properly and remain secure, always had to aim at the common interest instead of its own selfish ends, avoid tyrannical and irresponsible conduct, induce citizens to live virtuously according to the excellence and dignity of man, promote the prosperity of all, see that each did his duty according to his rank, and ensure that all were united in mutual love and dedication to the good of the whole.[81]

Economic and Social Shortcomings and Their Remedy

On the basis of this model of the ideal state and the true common interest, Starkey turned to an evaluation of conditions in England, much of his analysis based on empirical observation. Lupset feared that the ideal was impossible to realize because "al thyngys be here so fer out of ordur so fer out of frame."[82] To which pessimism Pole replied that it might not be as impossible as his friend imagined, although it was true that things "are fer from that ordur & such state as we have descrybyd for, many & grete fautys ther be reynyng among us here in our cuntrey & commynalty."[83] These faults, he continued, needed to be identified so that "at the last we may peraventure fynd some mean to restore our cuntrey to hyr commyn wele agayne & as nere as may be reformyng hyt to the exampul that we have prescrybyd before."

Lupset then introduced the investigation of English society by a summary of its economic ills:

> For who can be so blynd or obstynate to deny the grete dekey fautys & mysordurys he of our commyn wele other when he lokyth apon our cytes castellys & townys of late days ruynate & fallen down, wyth such pore inhabytans dwellyng therin, or when he lokyth apon the ground, so rude & so wast wych by dylygence of pepul hath byn before tyme occupyd & tyllyd, & myght be yet agayn brought to some bettur profyt & use, or yet, above al when he lokyth un to the manerys of our pepul & ordur of lyvyng, wych ys as ferre dystant from gud & perfayt cyvylyte, as gud from yl, & vyce from vertue & al honesty.[84]

After discussing the three bodily diseases—depopulation, idleness, disunity—endangering the health, beauty, and strength of the English state, Lupset and Pole turned to another of its infirmities, poverty, then concluding the first part of the *Dialogue* with the affliction of its soul, law and government. While Starkey postponed his social pathology and therapy to the second part, I will integrate his remedies into the following account of his primary analysis and then consider his political analysis and recommendations in the succeeding section.

Starkey's comments on population assumed that its increase was evidence of prosperity—a thriving citizenry testified to a true state. Urban and rural areas of contemporary England, in his opinion, were suffering severe depopulation.[85] His portrayal was a grim one—foreshadowed by *Utopia*—of decaying and abandoned buildings in town and country, of deserted villages whose houses and churches had become sheepfolds and stables. Because of the shortage of manpower, arts and crafts had declined and much of the land lay uncultivated. To Lupset's objection that in reality England was overpopulated, the population outstripping resources, and that the basic problem was idleness, Pole responded that the realm had supported far more people in the past and that Continental countries maintained larger populations in much smaller areas. He argued that a country deficient in people lacked the power "to maynteyne the floryschyng state of the polytyke body," citing Egypt, Asia, and Greece as examples where depopulation brought decline and ruin.[86] The solution to England's demographic decline was the encouragement of marriage and procreation by the application of the carrot and stick in governmental policy. Secular priests should be allowed to marry.[87] The nobility should no longer be permitted more servants than could afford to have families.[88] To this end they might be provided with dwellings and a portion of the waste at a nominal rent. Citizens with five or more children should be exempt from military service, and bachelors should be taxed.[89]

Starkey was perturbed by idleness, just as Dudley and More were.[90] He maintained that large numbers of people were of little avail if many of them lacked industry, were idle, or dissipated their energies in frivolous pastimes and socially useless occupations. Nobles employed far too many servants, a point emphasized by More. A swollen clergy accumulated possessions for their own benefit instead of succoring the poor and needy. The upper classes were generally more concerned for their own profits and pleasures than for the good of society.[91] Plowmen and artisans lacked the diligence displayed in foreign lands and were given to gluttony and vain pursuits.[92] A third of the population of every rank acted like "drowne bees in a hyve," Starkey contended, either living in idleness or engaging in occupations of no advantage to the commonwealth.[93] Men were not meant thus to wallow in idleness and pleasure, he asserted, "for man ys borne to be as a governour rular & dylygent tyllar & inhabytant of thys erthe, as some by labur of body to procure thyngys necessary for the mayntenance of mannys lyfe, some by wysdome & pollycy to kepe the rest of the multytude in gud order & cyvylyte."[94] All men, Starkey concluded, whether physical or mental workers, whether servants or plowmen, priests or gentlemen, had to perform tasks according to their rank as befitted "the dygnyte & nature of man."[95]

Starkey, like More, distinguished between useful and useless labor, both physical and mental, that which was of some real benefit to society and that which was not.[96] Thus the question was not simply one of idleness but one of socially useful labor. Many workers produced goods or products whose sole purpose was the satisfaction of sensual appetites and pleasures, making fashionable clothing and ornaments of dress, producing unnecessary food and drink, composing and singing new songs. Since such misguided employment among the lower classes was a product of defective education of youth, Starkey charged the parish priest with the responsibility of training in letters or crafts each child from the age of seven to be a diligent worker in a socially useful calling.[97] Idle people would be banished from towns, and craftsmen would be rewarded for their excellence, a matter to be supervised in the country by local priests and gentlemen. In the cities officers acting like ancient censors—comparable to Utopian syphogrants—would supervise labor discipline, direct the education of youth, and see that people were not engaged in frivolous occupations.[98] Entry to the arts and crafts was to be strictly controlled so that only the fittest were admitted and those who failed to perform satisfactorily were excluded. Starkey recommended reduction of the huge retinues of servants employed by the nobility, thus freeing manpower for the crafts. Abbeys were not to be destroyed but reformed, and youths were to occupy no place in them. Merchants were to import only necessary goods, not luxuries and useless commodities that pandered to pleasure seeking. Export would be limited to what was produced in abundance at home. With youth well educated and idleness so discouraged by these measures, the main cause of theft and beggary would have been removed and the crime rate appreciably lowered. Starkey also agreed with More that thieves, except those guilty of highway robbery with murder and manslaughter, should not be punished by death but sentenced to labor for the benefit of the state.

Starkey likened the disease of the English state to deformity or lack of beauty in the human body and he called the malady disunity.[99] Mutual envy and distrust resulted in lack of agreement and conflict between the various social groupings, setting temporality against spirituality, commons against nobility, and subjects against rulers. Starkey said relatively little about such internal contentions beyond the provision of several remedies. Perhaps the surest cure for dissension was the application of justice and equity so that one part would not have too much and the rest too little.[100] He also urged more equitable distribution of goods among citizens, the allocation, of course, being proportionate. Each person was to perform his function and duty, not interfering with the activities of others; those discontented with their chosen callings would be penalized and all seditious individuals perpetually banished or sentenced to death. No part or group within the state, Starkey finally recommended, could be allowed to grow or decrease in disproportion to the others. Given the needs of the state and the nature of the available manpower, this measure was to prevent social imbalance, the sure road to disorder. In this connection, the contemporary lack of occupational balance would be adjusted: he noted too many priests, lawyers and proctors, servants, and purveyors and makers of useless commodities and too few good clerks and judges, craftsmen, and tillers of the soil.

Starkey's second major concern with the body of the English state was wealth. The economic prosperity of the state and its citizens was crucial to the common interest just as it was to the interest and happiness of the individual.[101] His analysis began by calling attention to the economic deterioration of England, "the grete poverty of thys reame & the grete lake of thyngys necessary & commodyouse to the manyteynyng of a true common wele."[102] Many years ago, Starkey wrote, perhaps thinking of the "golden age" of Fortescue, a point of reference for both Dudley and More, England was the richest country of Christendom.[103] Starkey gloomily stressed the "grete wrechydnes & poverty" and "grete skarsenes & penury," illustrated by the hordes of beggars in a declining population.[104] England's abundant natural resources and wealth were not being fully utilized, he lamented. The English poor were certainly better off than the lower classes elsewhere, but their poverty was far more severe than before and clearly did not indicate a flourishing commonwealth. Numerous beggars and idlers, of course, might result from lack of enterprise and industry. In the main, however, the problem seemed to be a genuine and widespread impoverishment, affecting rich and poor through no fault of their own but arising from the failure of governmental policies. Not without cause did all classes complain of the lack of money, for they were obviously worse off than in the past. Prices were inordinately high, accompanied by a scarcity of necessary commodities: corn, cattle, and foodstuffs. Cities, towns, and castles lay neglected, the buildings allowed to fall into disrepair, becoming filthy and dilapidated, so different from the prosperous urban centers of Flanders and France. English gentlemen, unlike their counterparts abroad, were fleeing the decaying towns and cities to live on their country estates. Commodities important for home consumption—cattle, corn, wool, tin, lead—were being exported at a time when it could least be afforded, and goods were being imported that could have been produced at home; many among the latter were of little social use. At the same time a mere handful of the very wealthy lived luxuriously amidst the squalor of the miserable common folk, erecting stately mansions from imported materials.

Although Starkey complained of the enclosure of arable that led to the ruin of villages and towns, his criticism was not as heartfelt as More's.[105] In fact, Starkey in the words of Pole offered a tempered defense of enclosure. Since England's food supply depended on cattle and sheep—the source of much of the kingdom's wealth—as well as on corn and other crops, enclosure was essential. Without wool to export, the import of much needed merchandise would have become virtually impossible. Lupset intervened with a plea that was accepted by his friend. He urged that the rule of moderation, as in all things, apply to enclosure and the raising of sheep and cattle. The breeding of livestock demanded greater attention than it had hitherto received. Too much rich pasture, resulting from the ambitious enclosure of fertile arable, was not ideal for livestock and resulted in an increase of diseased animals. Lupset recommended leaner pasture on which sheep and cattle could be raised more profitably. Moreover, he noted that inordinately extensive enclosure had led to scarcity of corn and prices beyond the reach of the poor. Because the conversion of arable to pasture had largely been done by a wealthy minority, who had raised rents and entry fines, poor farmers had lost their holdings and the remaining arable was ill cultivated by those who had little incentive for raising crops. Starkey then favored enclosure, providing it was conducted in a rational and limited fashion; he was possibly the first to appraise and defend the practice explicitly and in detail in a work that was not a technical treatise on agriculture.[106] In so doing he struck some sort of mean between the enthusiastic impression of Fortescue and the passionate condemnation of More.

Reform of the grievous condition of the economy depended, according to Starkey, on wise and prudent government policies and their vigorous implementation.[107] He concluded that much of the growing impoverishment could be mitigated by assuring that townsmen were diligent in the performance of their duties and not permitted to waste their time and money in gambling, games, gluttony, and drunken carousal in taverns. "Conservaterys of the commyn wele" in the image of Roman censors (and perhaps of More's syphogrants) were to oversee the behavior of townsmen. Both people and nobility, like the ancient Romans and contemporary Swiss, would be obliged to participate in martial exercises, one means of dissuading them from constant pleasure seeking.[108] Cities and towns were to be kept clean for the sake of public health, buildings refurbished, gentlemen required to build urban abodes and reside in them, and everyone expected to pay annual sums for public works.[109] Exports would be confined to surpluses not needed for the subsistence of the people and imports limited to what was required for that purpose and what could not be produced at home. Only limited amounts of luxury items such as wines, velvets, and silks could be purchased abroad, and the import of frivolous commodities was to be restricted.

This last matter, a decided worry if we are to judge from Starkey's distinction between socially useful and useless labor and his discussion of related subjects, was also a concern of contemporaries like More who feared the far-reaching effect on English society. Clement Armstrong, not the least perceptive of critics, denounced the import of "such quantite of strange merchaundise and artificial fantasies" for contributing to the idleness of the English.[110] Starkey, like Armstrong, believed that the export of raw wool should be prevented in order to stimulate the home textile industry.[111] Other unwrought materials such as tin and lead were not to be exported for the same reason. Customs duties, especially on the import of necessities, would have to be decreased, and exports and imports were to be carried only in English vessels. Starkey's recommendations for the regulation of manufacturing and trade directed to the problem of alleviating unemployment and poverty were in general agreement with Armstrong's proposals, although in less detail.

What little Starkey said about agricultural reform equaled the few stipulations in More and exceeded the discussion in Armstrong. Starkey urged that the statute of enclosure be enforced so that enclosure would be less profligate, tillage encouraged, and land more conscientiously utilized, with delinquencies in this regard to be penalized. High rents were to be lowered and farmers compelled to raise more cattle. Starkey offered something approaching a brief outline that would be skillfully filled out and modified just over a decade later by the penetrating economic mind of Sir Thomas Smith. Whether Smith was familiar with Starkey's suggestions is beside the point, since in their basics they probably represented informed economic discussion of the time.

An examination of Starkey's economic views cannot omit his advice to the king written in 1536 after the Act of Separation. While some might think that the suppression of the monasteries would further impoverish the realm by depriving many of their livelihood, he reflected, the effect could be just the opposite. He was sure Henry appreciated that the wealth of princes depended on the prosperity of their subjects, whose impoverishment bred sedition. Thinking of the crown's new-found riches from the confiscation of monastic properties, Starkey warned that the amassing of wealth by rulers without liberality toward their subjects was highly imprudent behavior. But Henry, so wise in the ways of the world "wyl most lyberally dyspense thys tresure & dyspose thys ryches, to the ayd succur & comfort of your most louyng & obedyent pore subyectys," Starkey assumed, later postulating that "thys ys a sure truthe that the wyll & dede of euery pryuante man for a commyn wele may be alteryd by the supreme authoryte in euery cuntrey & kynd of pollycy."[112] So Starkey, adhering to the logic of his doctrine of tabula rasa, called for constructive governmental action—Elton labels him "a primitive Keynsian"—to use the newly acquired fortune from the monasteries for the improvement of society and the revival of the economy by curtailing underpopulation, poverty, and unemployment.[113] He believed this amelioration could be accomplished first by employing the funds from the sale of monastic properties to relieve the condition of nobles who had fallen on hard times so that they could once more devote themselves to the defense of the country in time of war. Second, the transformation of the monasteries from centers of idleness and vice into schools of learning would advance the education of gentlemanly youth and create a substantially reduced and enlightened clergy.[114] For the lower orders Starkey's third proposal concerned the effective use of confiscated property. He opposed lease of lands to a few great lords and wealthy gentlemen who had no pressing need for them. To do so would "much deface & gretly dymynysch the profyt of your acte & publyke vtylyte," providing no succor for the common people.[115] Instead, in order to increase the population and prosperity of the kingdom, he recommended the division of the new lands into many holdings to be leased by copyhold at moderate rent to young men in service and others of lowly status. Starkey's brief to his royal master obviously fell on deaf ears.

Reform of English Government and Ruling Classes

At least equal to the space allotted in the *Dialogue* to the social and economic defects of the English body politic was that devoted to diagnosis of the malady of the soul—law and government—and the therapeutic proposals. The ultimate responsibility for the "many dyseasys or mysordurys" of the state's body Starkey assigned to the failure of government and those holding the leading offices—the ruling classes: prince, nobility, and clergy.[116] But Starkey apportioned no blame to merchants and greedy farmers, unlike More, who, in turn, neither directly indicted the clergy nor the structure of government.

England, Starkey claimed, had long been ruled "under the state of pryncys" who by their "regal powar & pryncely authoryte" believed that all things pertaining "to the state of our reaume" depended solely on their will.[117] Disputing this view, he insisted that the king should not rightfully be at liberty to do simply as he pleased but should be restrained by a common council of the realm and by parliament and should be subject to the laws and bound by them. These checks would adhere to reason and constitute the king's true liberty. A king above the law doing whatsoever he wills "ys the open gate to al tyranny."[118] In matters of policy Starkey contended that the wisdom of one is not superior to the wisdom of many, no doubt thinking of the king in parliament and the counsel afforded by official bodies of the realm. Starkey hastened to avoid the stigma of treason by protesting his loyalty to the English sovereign, whom he called sage and upright, but he urged that some thought be given to the prevention of tyranny in the future.[119] Only if some permanent guarantee of a beneficent prince were institutionalized would policies be sufficiently enlightened to remedy the manifest defects of the state. Our sights, Starkey noted, do not have to be set as high as Plato's ideal in the *Republic* to perceive the best practicable means of avoiding tyrannical rule and ensuring wise public measures for the cure of the sickness of the body politic.[120] Then through Pole he expounded the argument that tyranny was not God's punishment for human sin.[121] Since tyranny is an evil, its source cannot be divine. Rather the evil of tyranny must be traced to man himself, to his transgressions and negligence. If man alone, not God, is responsible for tyranny, then it is within human power to devise a means of forestalling tyranny. And if human shortcomings in the form of overweening ambition, lust, and negligence can alone be blamed for tyranny, then in effect men have the power to mend their ways and depose a tyrant.[122] This pronouncement, coming as it did at the height of Henry VIII's reign, can indeed be construed as subversive.

For the purpose of preventing the rise of a tyrant in England, Starkey envisaged a monarch elected by parliament in much the same way as Venetians selected the doge in their republic.[123] Since England, however, was a princely state based on a well-entrenched hereditary principle, he proposed a second-best scheme, that of the "myxte state," also evidently framed with Venetian government as a model.[124] The English hereditary royal power would be balanced by countervailing institutions in a system of government in which the laws were the ultimate authority: "they [the laws] must rule & governe the state & not the prynce aftur hys owne lyberty & wyl."[125]

Going well beyond Fortescue's *dominium politicum et regale*, Starkey could perhaps be called the first English theorist to construct a notion of the mixed constitution in the classical mold. His scheme was monarchical, unlike More's Utopian government, which was less explicitly presented as a mixture. Nevertheless, there were some vague similarities between the two constitutional structures. Starkey's proposals are not always easy to follow. The traditional office of constable would be revived as a counterpoise to royal authority.[126] Presumably it would be or become a hereditary position as it had been in the past. The constable would head a permanent council of state appointed by parliament in the first instance and thereafter replacements would be elected by the council. It would act for the whole people, like a "lytle parlyament," sitting in London.[127] In addition to the constable, the council would consist of three hereditary officials—the lord marshal, steward, and chamberlain—together with four chief judges, four citizens of London, and the archbishop of Canterbury and bishop of London. In view of Starkey's stipulation that only nobles (apparently peers and gentry) would be allowed to study law and be admitted to the bar, the council with its four hereditary officials and four judges was heavily weighted in favor of the aristocracy.[128] The council would have four main duties: preserving liberty and preventing tyranny, appointment of the king's council, approval of all matters of war and peace recommended by the king's council, and the convening of parliament. Starkey gave little attention to parliament. It was to meet on matters of great urgency to the realm.[129] Apparently in the mixed polity envisioned by Starkey, with its structural checks on the exercise of power, parliament would serve as one more institutional limit on governmental action. The council of state in effect would constitute a permanent body of guardians of the law and guarantors of the public interest, something like the *nomophylakes* of Plato and Aristotle, watching over the constitution, scrutinizing all policies and activities of government, and if necessary calling parliament. Starkey termed the council "a wonderful stey of the pryncely state and stablyschyng of the true commyn wele."[130]

Royal authority in Starkey's mixture was to be vested in the king and his own private council, the latter chosen by the council of state and composed of ten persons: two doctors each of divinity, civil law, and common law, and four nobles. Obviously this was to be a body completely manned by members of the higher and lower aristocracy. The council would be charged with the day-to-day management of governmental business (not already taken up by the council of state): the conduct of foreign affairs; the removal of the causes of sedition (probably entailing among other matters the formulation and execution of social and economic policies); the appointment (on the basis of merit) of the chief public officials, including bishops; rendering all officials accountable for misconduct; and receiving complaints of law from citizens.

The three pivotal institutions and offices of Starkey's mixed state were thus the king and his council, the constable's council of state, and parliament. Although in some sense each of the three existed to keep an eye on the others, the council of state was clearly dominant and the whole arrangement seemed to assure responsible control by the nobility.[131] A very rough parallel can be detected between Starkey's ideal and More's Utopian mixture with its senate of tranibors under the governor, the assembly of syphogrants, and the popular assembly, the unifying and controlling element being the elite of literati. Starkey's mechanism (as well as More's) was conceived to prevent tyranny and make the aristocracy (however defined) the bastion of ultimate and responsible power, like the famous classical notions of the mixed constitution—Plato's Magnesia, Aristotle's "polity," Polybius's and Cicero's tripartite Roman system— and the Renaissance idealization of Venice and Florence by the humanists Contarini and Giannotti.[132] The common aim was to check any possible source of tyranny, including the self-seeking and irresponsible factionalism of the aristocracy.

Some of Starkey's proposals for local government and legal reform are also of a novel character. A functionary would be chosen for every great city, like the ancient Roman censors, to be "conservaterys" of the common interest.[133] They would supervise the work of lesser magistrates, including urban overseers similar to the Roman *aediles* charged with the care of the ornaments and health of the city. Starkey also recommended the abolition of the common law derived from the Normans, a "barbarouse natyon," and the adoption of Roman law.[134] Laws were to be simplified and improved, eliminating the many savage and tyrannical ones, and written in English and Latin instead of the customary French of the common law. Primogeniture and entail were to be restricted to the nobility and possibly the greater gentry. But younger sons would be eligible for a portion of the inheritance. Fathers, in accord with Roman law, would have the right of disinheritance.[135]

Starkey, like More, criticized lawyers.[136] The avarice of the legal profession was a constant and vexing issue for English social critics. An early comment was that of William Langland in the late fourteenth-century *Piers Ploughman*, who castigated "lawyers who served at the bar, pleading their cases for as much money as they could get. Never once did they open their mouths out of love for our Lord; indeed you could sooner measure the mist on the Malvern Hills, than get a sound out of them without first producing some cash!"[137] Starkey was obsessed by the plethora of lawyers, so many of whom were solely motivated by greed—"thes hungry advocatys & cormerantys of the court"—to prolong legal controversies.[138] He prescribed an effort to rectify this sorry state of affairs by calling to the bar only virtuous and honest men of means.[139] To further this end Starkey suggested confining the study of law to the nobility.[140] (Although he failed to be specific here, he may have also included the gentry.) In sum, Starkey maintained that a critical precondition of his social and economic remedies was the overhaul of government, first by the introduction of an institutional mixture at the center and then by the reform of local government, the legal system, and the legal profession. The aristocracy emerged as the decided beneficiary in these governmental proposals.

Refurbishing the governmental and legal apparatus would be of little consequence, Starkey apparently believed, unless the nobility holding the key civil posts were individuals of the highest intellect and moral probity dedicated to the common interest. Because he took a jaundiced view of the existing ruling classes, he considered their regeneration vital to the welfare of the state.[141] He cited their deficient education as one of the foremost reasons for Tudor troubles.[142] He described the nobles as feeble, idle, vain, self-indulgent hedonists, wasting their income, time, and energy in sumptuous living, being brought up "in huntyng & haukyng dysyng & cardyng etyng & drynkyng & in conclusyon in al vayn plesure pastyme & vanyte."[143] Their every whim gratified by armies of servants in the courtlike atmosphere of princely mansions, the nobility acted as if they had been born into this world fully trained and prepared for the future duties of ruling their inferiors.[144] If their main purpose in life was to uphold justice and conserve the state and its citizens, they would require careful molding from early years through appropriate schooling in moral and intellectual matters.

Starkey was not a lone voice in his worry about the educational shortcomings and decay of the gentlemanly orders. The question was also of the utmost urgency for other humanists. Among our reformers Dudley was the first to criticize the nobility for being "the worst brought vp for the moste parte of any realme of christendom."[145] Thomas More, as bitter as Starkey in condemning the aristocracy and no less forthright in blaming them for the ills of England, constructed a contrasting ideal state where education was treasured by all and rule was by a select few elders of a small intellectual elite. Sir Thomas Elyot was deeply distressed over the negative attitude of his peers to learning, blaming it on pride, avarice, and parental neglect.[146] Lupset's own *Exhortation to Young Men* likewise addressed the problem, urging gentlemanly readers to begin by caring for their souls.[147]

Starkey's brief set of recommendations for the rehabilitation of the nobility focused on the establishment of schools throughout the country for the compulsory education of aristocratic children.[148] He contended that such institutions were essential to civility and successful political rule. Abbeys so important in the past for religious instruction might serve as models for the new schools and even be converted with the aim of educating young gentlemen. The schools were to be headed by wise and virtuous scholars always remembering their responsibility for training the future rulers of the commonwealth. Instruction would concentrate on turning out pupils of virtue by making Christian doctrine the core of the curriculum. The intellects of the gentlemanly youths, however, needed careful nourishment. Youthful bodies required attention as well as their souls; Starkey specified training in the martial arts which would continue in later years in the military exercises participated in by commoners. Starkey was ever aware that the Tudor nobility as a warrior class was so decadent and enfeebled as to be incapable of satisfactorily performing its traditional role.[149] Later in the *Dialogue* he urged the nobility to study civil law and proposed an aristocratic monopoly over the legal profession.[150] Apart from his own study of law in Avignon and Padua, Starkey may have been inspired by Fortescue's advice to the young prince to master not the details but the general principles of the law, cited by St. German in a similar proposal for knights and other nobles.[151] For Starkey the practical consequence of his educational recommendations would be a truly noble nobility. He said nothing about the universities, a brief discussion of which he confined to the question of the reform of the clergy. Qualified graduates of the new schools were no doubt intended to go on to Oxford or Cambridge if they so desired.

As for the reform of that other mainstay of the true commonwealth, the clergy, Starkey considered clergymen indispensable to civil order because they set an example of virtuous Christian living for all to emulate.[152] If Christian teaching was to govern the conduct of individual citizens, religion had to be rooted in well-trained, conscientious, and self-denying clerics. Starkey's suggestions for the reconstitution of the clergy arose from his perception of the inadequacy of the existing church to perform its proper function in the state, beginning with the papacy itself, although he was probably writing before the break with Rome.[153] He criticized the pope for greedily usurping the power of the general council of the church in the appointment of cardinals, for "usurpyng a certayn clokyd tyranny under the pretext of relygyon."[154] Within the existing relationship between Rome and England, Starkey called for greater autonomy of the English church and the limitation of papal power in respect to the appointment of archbishops and bishops, dispensation of laws, right of appeal, first fruits, and the settlement of suits, with the exception of schism. In short, he proposed that the English church maintain its governance in its own hands. He did not go so far as Dudley in advocating that the English church confine its activities to spiritual matters, functioning as little more than the instrument of the secular ruler. But pursuing his own course, Starkey was no less critical than his predecessor of the English clergy. Far too many of their swollen numbers, like the nobility, led idle, pleasure-seeking lives dedicated to amassing worldly possessions.[155] Higher prelates seemed concerned only with eating and drinking, and he branded abbots "idul abbey-lubburys."[156] Priests, poorly educated in monasteries and ordained as young as twenty-five years of age, were ignorant, vain, and vicious creatures, collecting benefices in order to multiply their profits.[157] This scathing attack on the clergy was a familiar protest of the time, one that underscored the materialistic orientation of the church and its abdication of much of its pastoral role.

To counteract these shortcomings of church and clergy Starkey offered a wide variety of measures, some of them challenging.[158] Bishops and priests were to be compelled to reside in their dioceses and parishes and to take more pains in caring for their flocks. The incomes of clerics at all levels would be regulated so as to ensure a much larger allotment of funds for charity, education, and the building of churches. Starkey required that abbots and priors live with their brethren and be subject to triennial elections. Ordination for the priesthood was to be set at the minimum age of thirty and restricted to those of demonstrated virtue. The rule of celibacy would be abolished and the clergy would no longer be exempt from punishment for crimes. In an attempt to reduce crime among the laity, the traditional privilege of sanctuary would be abolished. Starkey endorsed some of Luther's recommendations, admitting that despite his low estimate of the German reformer, not all of his cherished reforms were misguided.[159] Among those he approved were the translation of the Bible and the divine service into the vernacular and the simplification of sacred music.

Above all, Starkey insisted that the education of the clergy was essential for the welfare of the commonwealth, just as he argued for the improvement of the nobility. The most able youths intending to enter the priesthood were to be given every encouragement to attend university, where they would be instructed in both virtue and learning.[160] Neither Fortescue nor More seemed interested in the universities. Dudley, however, saw in their regeneration the key to a revitalized clergy and enlightened nobility.[161] As concerned as Dudley with strengthening the nobility through better education, Starkey confined his recommendations to the establishment of schools for them. He only touched on the question of the universities in connection with clerical reform, although in all likelihood he was mindful of their function of training talented young gentlemen. He charged that the universities had seriously declined in quality, evidently blaming the inadequacy of their curricula for the lack of a genuine moral and intellectual education. Instead of spelling out what could be done by way of reform, however, he recommended a recent book on the subject by the "byschope of Carpentras."[162] The reference is most probably to *De liberis* (1533) by Jacopo Sadoleto (1477–1547), the noted humanist, a politically moderate member of the papal curia and a future cardinal.[163] For the guidance of the clergy, Starkey also praised Erasmus's directions for preachers and urged the translation of his *Instruction of Christian Man* (1514).[164]

Starkey's examination of England's problems and his proposals for their resolution were in some ways the most penetrating and unquestionably the most systematic and comprehensive of those considered so far. More engaged in utopian speculation, Starkey attempted to do the best by way of practical reform within the limits of the English situation. Nevertheless, one cannot help but agree with Ferguson that Starkey's reformed England would have been nearly as regimented as More's utopian ideal.[165] Although much of Starkey's work is marked by a familiar traditionalism, he no less than previous reformers displayed an interest in empirical observation, causal explanation, and a comparative institutional approach as a foundation of his social and political prescriptions. The *Dialogue*, after a fashion, was one of the first full-scale proposals based on acute analysis of contemporary conditions for the renovation of an existing state since Cicero engaged in a roughly parallel enterprise in *De legibus*. Starkey's endeavor, in conclusion, can best be summarized and its significance suggested by reference to several of the interrelated axiomatic ideas of his outlook.

Despite man's essentially selfish and anarchic nature, Starkey saw the human being as divinely created and capable of fulfilling his inherent excellence and dignity. The realization of his Godlike nature was possible because at birth his mind was a blank tablet, amenable to being imprinted by experience during his early years. Consequently, the intellect, outlook, and conduct of the individual—his knowledge and morality—were in the broadest sense the result of his education and the influence of the social environment in which he lived. This doctrine of social environmentalism, shared to an extent by More, was to be rigorously articulated in Locke's philosophy, emerging as a basic assumption of modern British empiricism and much of the thought of the Enlightenment.[166] In Starkey's notional realm this postulate appears to have been responsible for his emphasis on the education of the nobility, clergy, and workers; on the role of Christian belief for a united and harmonious society; on the need for social and economic improvement; and on the positive, constructive function given to government and law. If humans were to some extent malleable raw material to be molded by their environment, then it was within their power to determine their circumstances and to a point their intellect and conduct. From this principle flowed another: the political element is crucial to organizing human beings into a cooperative association conducive to the fulfillment of their divine qualities and the containment of their destructive egoism. Government and law therefore constitute a potent means of imprinting the raw human material with the desirable image, desirable in the sense of that ordained by God and cherished by Christians.

Starkey's idea of the creative role of the political in fashioning man and society involved somewhat tentative and imprecise distinctions between state, government, and society. One of the first to use *state* in something like the modern sense, Starkey meant by it not any society but one structured by government and law to actualize the values of its members. He assumed a Christian polity composed of citizens who believed that men should live in peace and concord, loving one another and worshipping God. Government and law must order society to impede human selfishness from gaining ascendency and to assist citizens in attaining their distinctive excellence and dignity. Christianity is not only the true religion and morality but also a powerful tool of social control for the achievement of solidarity and harmony. So government and church should be mutually supportive, with the lead taken by the political.

Another principle Starkey shared with the early reformers, even with More in practice if it is not always clear in *Utopia*, is the assumption that a Christian polity should embody a social ideal hallowed by tradition, a vision predating Christianity. The ideal was that of a hierarchy of different degrees and stations, arranged by human callings, related as superior to inferior from the most exalted to the most humble, each with its different functions, duties, and privileges. A society of this kind—the natural world in microcosm—reflected the *scala naturae*, the natural order in God's cosmos and its every being from the lowest to the highest. A few in accord with divine ordination were called to command and to defend and many more of subordinate status to obey and to labor, in Langland's words, "the ignorant folk could not speak for themselves, they could only suffer and serve."[167] The natural governors of the true Christian polity were hence the nobility and their clerical coadjutors, together making up the ruling classes, managing all the others.

Another of Starkey's basic beliefs, also shared by the other reformers, is the conclusion that for all members of the true Christian polity, regardless of rank in the social hierarchy, the paramount goal was happiness, which was the primary purpose of their union. The happiness of the citizens, defined morally and materially, was therefore the major aim of the state and the basis of the common interest. While citizens had the supreme end of achieving Christian virtue, its essential condition was the economic well-being of all. Depending on their position in the social hierarchy, some required more economic goods for their happiness than others, but no one, even the lowliest, should lack the necessities of life; each was entitled to material comforts relative to his station. Starkey predicated individual happiness of the highest kind on genuine Christian virtue and the absence of economic hardship and insecurity. An economic conception of the state was at the core of his thought, as it was for his predecessors and successors. Widespread poverty and unemployment and the attendant cost in human life and suffering are hardly the nursery of happiness. Since man at birth is a self-seeking tabula rasa, a defective social environment can only produce defective human beings, degrade man as a creature of dignity and labor, breed idleness, despair, and crime, and end in discord and rebellion, the destruction of the state. To avert such disasters, Starkey urged the ruling nobility to take positive governmental action through rational economic and social policies; he assigned the clergy the role of assisting by their counsel, upholding dutiful civil obedience, performing conscientiously their pastoral functions, monitoring any breaches of justice and equity, and setting an example to all by the purity of their lives.

Finally, Starkey recognized that government was no better than the human beings composing it. Because the dominant nobility—even if adequately educated—were no less prone to greed and ambition than persons of lesser worth, the state apparatus would have to be contrived to check and limit the power holders in order to reduce the possibility of tyrannical and irresponsible rule. A mixed constitution was his answer to the problem, one in which prince and nobility were subject to law and institutionally restrained from the arbitrary exercise of power.

While few if any of Starkey's contemporaries read the *Dialogue* in manuscript, the work reflected some of the most significant intellectual trends of the age. Many of its social and political ideas can be traced to humanist and classical sources, but the impress of *Utopia* is unmistakable. Starkey must have studied the work very carefully and discussed it with Lupset and Pole, who both knew More. Starkey adopts and goes beyond More's analysis of English social conditions. In addition to the many details the two books have in common, they share important themes: social environmentalism and the vital role of education; the emphasis on happiness and the crucial part played in it by health, so dependent on material circumstances; an economic conception of the state; an obsession with tyranny; a dread of democracy; and a notion of the mixed constitution. If the relationship between Plato's Kallipolis of the *Republic* and Magnesia of the *Laws* is that between the ideal and the best practicable state, the connection between the Utopian prescription and Starkey's reforms seems to be approximately the same. The principles of the one inform the practical program of the other.

8   Social Protest and Christian Renewal

The Commonwealthmen

In response to mounting economic difficulties and multiplying civil disorders in the 1530s and 1540s, the Commonwealthmen, a group of Lutheran churchmen and social critics including Crowley, Latimer, Becon, and Lever, vented biting criticism of English social conditions. Despite Starkey's anxiety over the possibility of insurrection, he could not have foreseen when he originally wrote the *Dialogue* that the north was to erupt in rebellion in the autumn of 1536. The Pilgrimage of Grace was the first serious uprising since Black Michael's Cornishmen were put down outside London in 1497. Popular discontent continued after the disturbing events of 1536 and 1537, including an abortive conspiracy in Yorkshire, to break out once more in open revolt in Cornwall in 1547 and 1548 and in the Western Rebellion of Devon in 1549. Troubles during the same period also occurred in Somerset, Wiltshire, Oxfordshire and elsewhere, and in the summer of 1549 Kett's Rebellion erupted in Norfolk and Suffolk. Although this last upsurge of violence seems to have been the only one chiefly motivated by economic concerns, all the conflicts were fueled by inflation, scarcity, unemployment, and social dislocation. The Commonwealthmen displayed anxiety over this civil turmoil and the prospect of more in the future unless the English mended their ways. In 1536 the new bishop of Worcester, Hugh Latimer, whose powerful sermons three years before had ironically incited near-riot in Bristol and Exeter, roundly denounced the Pilgrimage of Grace.[1] No one sympathized more than Latimer with the impoverished and oppressed; nevertheless he viewed the northern revolt as an effort by the selfish and unscrupulous to hoodwink the poor into active disobedience against established authority. He described the uprising as one of the Devil's "most crafty and subtle assaults" in the guise of justice and righteousness.[2] The London mercer Henry Brinklow, like Latimer a champion of the poor, wrote six years afterward that if only all obeyed God and remained faithful to him, rebellion would not be a serious threat.[3]

The Impassioned Pleading of Henry Brinklow

Henry Brinklow (d. 1546) is the most convenient beginning for a discussion of the Commonwealthmen since in some ways he anticipated their ideology and serves to introduce an exploration of its major themes.[4] He was the eldest son of the yeoman Robert Brinklow, a landholder of Kintbury, Berkshire, who died in comfortable circumstances only three years before Henry. From what little is known about Henry, he was apparently a member of the Franciscan order who converted to Lutheranism, becoming a mercer and citizen of London and marrying a certain Marguery (surname unknown). He seems to have done moderately well in the City, living with his family in an establishment employing two servants and bequeathing over a hundred pounds in cash to relatives, friends, and the poor. The instructions of his will suggest strong convictions: "I forbid mourning gowns to be worn for me, nor no multitude of torches and tapers"; the "residue of personalty to Marguery my wife, on condition that she wear no worldly fantastical dissembling black gown for me"; "I will my hole creditt be paide although both my wiffe and my children be lefte very pore."[5] For religious reasons Brinklow was forced to seek asylum abroad; he published the first edition of the *Complaynt of Roderyck Mors* in 1542 in Savoy, followed by three Geneva printings, one probably in 1545 and two about 1550. His other well-known tract, *The Lamentacyon of a Christen against the Cytye of London, made by Roderigo Mors*, first appeared in 1542, subsequently in a Nuremburg printing, and then in an edition of 1548.

The *Complaynt*, over twice the length of the *Lamentacyon*, was a short work of twenty-six chapters, not much longer than Dudley's little treatise.[6] Far from being a systematic analysis, the *Complaynt* was a fervent, sometimes eloquent account of the deteriorating situation in England and an indignant protest and demand for reform, often of a highly impracticable kind. The book opened with reference to the oppression of Brinklow's countrymen: "the many cruel lawes and hevy yockys vpon the showlders of the peple of my natyue contry (specyaly vpon the comons), and agayn consyderyng how lytle the poore be regarded and prouyded for."[7] He concluded on the same note: "The body of this reame, I mean the comynaltye, is so oppressed and over-yocked, as fewe reamys vnder the sonne be, by wicked lawes, cruel tyrannes, which be extorcioners, and oppresors of the common welth. For all men are geven to seke their own pryuate welth only, & the pore are nothing prouyded for."[8] Then came the final words of moral outrage: "At this day the extorcyon and cruelnes of the temporal rulers is so come to pas, that in maner every one of them is become a very Nero. And the yockes of the lawe be so heuy, that no faythful Christen man is able to beare them."[9]

Brinklow addressed his book to parliament with the hope that it would be well enough received that "thyngs nedeful may be redressyd to the glory of thy name, the commodyte of the comon welth, and to the better provysyon for the pore."[10] He trusted that the "litle Worke" would lead to the "instruction" of members of parliament, initiating a "reforma-cyon" for the advancement of the common interest "and for no partycu-lar or pryuate welth to them seluys."[11] Later he affirmed his faith in gov-ernment as the only instrument for his contemplated reforms: " . . . seing there is no pour vpon erth aboue the temporal, to redresse cyuyle mat-ters, comon welthys, and to change wycked lawys and euyl customys."[12] Yet he seemed doubtful about the efficacy of parliament—at least as cur-rently organized—in a reforming role, and his didactic and strident tone could hardly have endeared him to its members, if they ever read the tract.

Although Englishmen, Brinklow began, were bound to obey the laws of their parliament and not to resist by force any that violated God's word, at the same time they were obliged to *disobey* any that did so, even on pain of death.[13] He proceeded in his badgering style. Parliament at each meeting, four times a week, should commence with a sermon of an hour to an hour and a half's duration to be given by a preacher, "some honest, well lerned man," who, instead of flattering his audience, would speak the truth to commons, lords, and king, informing them of their du-ties.[14] Lords and commons should deliberate together, "for it is not ryches or autoryte that bringeth wisdom."[15] Brinklow's skepticism about the in-stitution is confirmed when, after blaming the landlords for the country's economic woes, he says that parliament could be expected to do little to correct the situation since its members belonged to the landlord class and stood to lose most by any genuinely remedial measures.[16] Ultimately, Brinklow seems to have believed that the reform of England depended on the reform of parliament, despite his failure to be explicit on the subject. In other ways, he was more radical than the Commonwealthmen, almost a leveler a century before his time.

The condemnation of the exploitation of the poor in the *Complaynt* focused on rural conditions and their impact on the rest of the country.[17] Brinklow was particularly critical of landlords who acquired former church lands, who were more grasping and tight-fisted even than the former owners. The rack-renting of the new proprietors, "euyn to the cloudys," the raising of entry fines, and the eviction of customary tenants without leases meant that the small husbandman, reduced to little more than the status of the landlord's "slave," first resorted to begging in order to survive and then to theft, for which the penalty was hanging: "so lytle is the lawe of loue regarded, oh cruel tyrannys!"[18] Enclosure also brought about dispossession of the poor and the increase of their burdens. Enclosed parks, forests, and chases—some of the most fertile land in England given over to game for the sport of gentlemen—deprived the poor of necessary corn and grass.[19] Enclosure of arable for sheep by covetous landlords— "Of lordes which are shepardes" is the title of chapter 15—dispossessed peasants of their livelihood and destroyed villages and towns so that "a pore man scarcely [had] an hole to put in hys head for these gret extorcyonars."[20] These developments led to spiraling inflation and increased the cost of living.[21] Prices of food and clothing, indeed of all goods necessary for subsistence, rose steeply in comparison to the past, so much so that even the rich suffered. The rural poor were further victimized by royal purveyance, whereby subjects provided the king's agents with commodities at the old low prices for the use of the royal households.[22] Brinklow did not fail also to blame growing impoverishment and unemployment on greedy rack-renting and enclosing landlords.[23] High rents and conversion of arable to pasture forced up the prices of all agricultural commodities at an exorbitant rate and deprived the small countryman of the very basis of survival and well-being. So critical to the English economy, the wool industry was also sorely affected by the astronomical rents. Compelled to raise prices on woolens to cover inflated costs, merchants were better off before when cloth was selling at one third less, and carders and spinners suffered from the scandalous prices of the necessities of life.[24] No longer could merchants sell cloth abroad because of its high cost, and they were losing the domestic market to imported textiles made of a mixture of foreign and English wool.

Brinklow's remedies for this plague of economic infirmities were innovative and egalitarian, more so than anything envisioned by Starkey or the Commonwealthmen, but far less utopian than More's scheme or in the next century Winstanley's project. Yet the proposals of the *Complaynt* were obviously incapable of realization, given English circumstances. Two ideals seem to have motivated Brinklow's recommendations. He held the view, frequently expressed by the Commonwealthmen, that the earth was God's property, to be cared for by landowning gentlemen. Their function was to serve as "stuardes" or, as we might call them, trustees, accountable to God for the land's use.[25] In addition, Brinklow thought that whereas England in the early sixteenth century contained a few rich and many poor as the way of things, it was highly desirable that there be only a few poor and many who were not wealthy but who were living in comfort.[26] His scattered and fragmentary suggestions for reform, apparently derived from these principles, were four in number. First, the king should lower the rents of his own lands to the level of forty or fifty years ago and compel all landlords to follow suit or forfeit their holdings.[27] Second, the king should rent to the people at modest rates a great portion of his parklands, requiring his lords to do the same.[28] Third, just as each priest should only have one benefice, so each man should have but one farm, manor, or lordship, sufficient for a comfortable living, for example, at an annual value of twenty pounds rent.[29] An individual might be allowed two holdings, provided they did not together exceed twenty pounds in value; even if the combined value was well below this limit, no one would be permitted more than three holdings. Finally, Brinklow was convinced that the confiscated church lands and goods were badly misused by the crown.[30] He suggested a beneficial alternative to the current royal practice. The confiscated lands and goods should be divided into three parts, one to be given to the rural poor, one to the urban poor, and one to the king. A portion of the goods would be used to maintain houses for the ill and impoverished, to provide physicians and surgeons for the urban poor, and to endow certain free schools.

Besides these radical economic proposals, Brinklow recommended any number of other measures, all in the name of the common interest and largely dealing with the church and its doctrine, justice and its administration, and the hardships of men of business. A dedicated and zealous Lutheran, he raised a critical voice against the English church and what he claimed to be its idolatry.[31] Indeed, nearly a third of the *Complaynt* is devoted to religious matters (although the material is not concentrated in one section). Brinklow advocated one benefice per priest and opposed the payment of first fruits to the king, now by law their recipient instead of the pope. His most interesting proposal for religious reform related to heresy. Rejecting the prevailing persecution by the church, he maintained that heresy should be determined by a hearing. If the accused was found guilty, he was to be admonished and, if he continued in his erring ways, banished from the kingdom but never imprisoned or executed.[32] In the sphere of justice Brinklow proposed to rescind the current law by which the family of a convicted traitor, felon, or murderer forfeited their goods and property and were thereby left destitute.[33] Judges would be salaried to prevent them, as he put it, from living like lords by robbing the poor.[34] He criticized the legal profession for profiting from the prolongation of law suits.[35] The inhumane treatment of prisoners came in for comment.[36]

They should be well fed and speedily brought to trial. He proposed various legal changes to relieve the financial plight of men of business. The law should ensure that all creditors—not simply the principal ones according to current practice—of a merchant who had lost his goods through misfortune receive something, with a portion reserved for the maintenance of the debtor.[37] Parliamentary privilege freeing members of payment of their debts while in session should be abrogated.[38] Customs duties on imported goods should not be allowed to increase as they did, thus leading to higher prices, which burdened both merchants and consumers.[39] Finally, Brinklow urged that the king should be readily available to hear the grievances and complaints of his subjects.[40]

The *Lamentacyon* expressed the author's outrage about economic problems in London. As in the *Complaynt*, Brinklow worried about the predicament of the poor in contrast to the wealth of a few:

> . . . London, beyng one of the flowers of the worlde as touchinge worldlye riches, hath so manye, yea innumerable of poore people forced to go from dore to dore, and to syte openly in the stretes a beggynge, and many not able to do for other, but lye in their houses in most greuous paynes, and dye for lacke of ayd of the riche, to the greate shame of the, oh London![41]

The City and its citizens were rebuked for their extravagant outlays and profligate use of riches, while making no effort to alleviate the appalling state of the poor.[42] Londoners, claimed Brinklow, failed to study the New Testament, were idolatrous in their worship, and combined with the bishops against preachers of the true word.[43] They should repent, read God's law, diligently pray, and choose better officials and judges. To combat the evils of the City, Brinklow once more proposed a radical and impractical remedy: the king should distribute the wealth of the City among the poor and other towns in proportion to their size.[44] He offered no explanation for how this was to be accomplished.

Profile of the Commonwealthmen

The accession to the throne in 1547 of young Prince Edward, who was tutored by Sir John Cheke the Lutheran Regius Professor of Greek in Cambridge and brother-in-law of the monarch's principal secretary, Sir William Cecil, seemed the opportunity for the beginning of a genuine religious and social reformation. The insurrectionary outbreaks of 1547–1549 forcefully impressed the government with the urgent need for reform, and during the years before Mary became queen the Commonwealthmen achieved prominence as influential social critics. Lutherans of rural origins like Brinklow, they were not, however, cast in his homespun mold but were of the highest education, graduates and Church of England clerics who had attained positions of responsibility and were respected by those in power. Never a party in any formal sense, they were linked by their shared ideas and ideals. Among the foremost were Robert Crowley (1518?–1588), Hugh Latimer (1485?–1555), Thomas Becon (1512–1567), and Thomas Lever (1521–1577).[45] Crowley stood somewhat apart from the others. He was an Oxonian, only becoming a cleric after a brief period as a crusading publicist. The other three were Cambridge men who entered the church at the outset of their careers.

Crowley, like Pole and Starkey before him, was born in Gloucestershire and attended Magdalen College, Oxford, known for its humanistic studies. Also at Magdalen was John Foxe (1516–1587), author of the much read and cherished *Acts and Monuments* (1563), better known as the *Book of Martyrs*. They became close friends and were fellows of their college. Between 1549 and 1551 Crowley turned to printing in London, living and working in "Ely rentes," Holborn. His press issued some of the earliest Welsh books, but perhaps the most famous publication was his modern rendition—the first of its kind—of William Langland's late fourteenth-century masterpiece of social protest, *Piers Plowman*. Printed in 1550, it went through three impressions that same year. Crowley also published his own short works: the versified *Epigrams*, *Voyce of the Last Trumpet*, and *Way to Wealth*, all in 1550; the next year *The Fable of Philargyrie, the Great Gigant*, and *Pleasure and Payne*; and the undated *An Informacion and Peticion* appeared. These tracts were more sophisticated and crisply executed variations on some of the themes expounded a decade before by Brinklow. Abandoning printing and literary pursuits, Crowley was ordained a priest in 1551, and at the beginning of Mary's reign fled with his wife to Frankfurt, possibly in the company of an associate, John Day, the Protestant publisher of Foxe's *Book of Martyrs*. Returning on Elizabeth's accession, Crowley became vicar of St. Giles, Cripplegate. He was shortly deprived of the living for refusing to wear the surplice and briefly jailed for causing a commotion. From 1559 to 1567 he was archdeacon of Hereford; then in 1563 he was appointed canon of St. Paul's and later vicar of St. Lawrence Jewry. Surviving longer than any of the Commonwealthmen, he died in 1588, the year of the Armada and the birth of Thomas Hobbes. J. J. Scarisbrick described Crowley as "a man of burning compassion from whose pen came pages of remorseless denunciation of greed and covetousness, and who deserves to stand with Langland, More, the Diggers and Marx as one of the great apostles of social justice."[46]

Hugh Latimer was born in Thurcaston near Leicester, the son of a yeoman. He studied at Cambridge, becoming a fellow of Clare Hall in 1510, where he remained for over twenty years, and a university preacher in 1522.[47] In the mid-twenties he was converted to Lutheranism by the humanist Thomas Bilney of Trinity Hall. Bilney was convicted of heresy and burned at the stake in 1531, an execution sanctioned by Sir Thomas More, the lord chancellor.[48] Latimer was suspected of heretical views in the twenties (and later) and prohibited from preaching by the bishop of Ely. Cambridge was turning into a hotbed of religious subversives; the "Germans," who met at the White Horse Inn, included, besides Latimer, the producers of the English Bible, William Tyndale (1495–1536) and Miles Coverdale (1488–1568), and the future author of the *Book of Common Prayer* and archbishop of Canterbury, Thomas Cranmer. In the thirties among the distinguished members of the faculty who fell under the spell of Luther were John Cheke (1514–1557) and Thomas Smith (1513–1577). By the autumn of 1529 Latimer was the leader of the Cambridge religious reformers. His career, like Smith's, was advanced by the Lutheran William Butts of Gonville Hall, physician to Henry VIII. Evidently recommended by Butts, Latimer preached his first sermon before the king at Windsor in 1530, and probably through Butts he received the royal benefice of West Kington, Wiltshire, in 1531. A favorite of Anne Boleyn's, he was appointed one of her chaplains, and although he was tried for his religious convictions in 1532 and acquitted with a royal admonition, he preached weekly before the king. From 1535 to 1539 Latimer was bishop of Worcester, but he resigned after refusing to sign the Six Articles. Barred from preaching, he was imprisoned in 1539 and again in 1546, to be released under the general amnesty after the death of Henry. Although never again to hold high church office, Latimer was appointed court preacher to Edward VI and became famous for his fiery condemnations of conditions in England. Writing at the time of Kett's Norfolk rebellion in October 1548, Sir Anthony Auchar voiced concern to Cecil about the effect of the reforming preachers on civil order, citing "these men called Commonwealths" and singling out "that Commonwealth called Latimer."[49] During much of the time before his death Latimer accepted the hospitality of his old friend Archbishop Cranmer and resided in Lambeth Palace. On the orders of Queen Mary in 1555 Latimer, Cranmer, and another old Cantabrigian, Bishop Nicholas Ridley (1500–1555) of London, were burned at the stake in Oxford, opposite Balliol College. Latimer's last words, as the flames licked about them, were the memorable and often repeated: "Be of good comfort, Master

Ridley, and play the man. We shall this day light such a candle, by God's grace, in England, as I trust shall never be put out."[50]

Thomas Becon, probably born in West Norfolk, presumably studied at St. John's, Cambridge, receiving his B.A. in 1530–1531; he was ordained in 1533 and began his clerical career in Norfolk and Ipswich.[51] At Cambridge he fell under the sway of Latimer, whom he portrayed in *The Jewel of Joy*, dedicated to Lady Elizabeth, the future queen: "a man worthy to be loved and reverenced by all true hearted christian men, not only for the pureness of his life which hath always before the world been innocent and blameless, but also for the sincerity and godliness of his evangelic doctrine."[52] Because of his radical religious views Becon was in trouble with the authorities during Henry's reign and required to make several recantations. He spent much of his time during this period wandering about the countryside, living with friends, forging close links with some of the gentry, and writing and publishing, for which he won great praise. Once Edward came to the throne, Becon served as chaplain in Somerset's household, as a preacher at Canterbury and a chaplain of Cranmer's, who deeply influenced him, and then as rector of St. Stephen's Walbrook in the City. After being committed by Mary to the Tower in 1553, he was released and went first to Strasbourg and then with his family to Marburg, where he lived under the patronage of Philip, landgrave of Hesse. On his return to England in 1559, he was made prebend in Canterbury cathedral and given several benefices, including Christ Church, Newgate. His collected works were published by John Day, the friend of Crowley and Foxe. In the judgment of Becon's biographer, he was a superb "propagandist—a vociferous shouter of slogans and battle-cries who could kindle the enthusiasm which others were able to turn to account."[53]

The youngest of the principal Commonwealthmen, Thomas Lever of Bolton, Lancashire, was like Becon a pupil in St. John's, Cambridge, where he became a fellow. Before the age of thirty he was preaching for Edward VI. He was master of his college from 1551 to 1553, resigning when Mary became queen to lead a group of Oxford and Cambridge students into exile to Strasbourg. After time in Zurich, Geneva, and Wesel, he settled in Aarau, between Basel and Zurich, where he was minister of a congregation of ninety-three souls. Miles Coverdale was a member of this community of exiles. Lever's flock, which emigrated from Wesel, was the most stable of the communities of English believers and, according to Garrett, "provided after 1630 a model for the development of a new type of corporate colonization in New England—which thereafter became distinctively characteristic of the whole Puritan movement westward to the

Pacific from Massachusett's Bay."[54] Returning from Switzerland in 1559, Lever became rector and archdeacon of Coventry and prebend of Durham. Like Crowley, because he refused to wear the surplice and opposed the supremacy, Lever found his advancement in the church blocked by Elizabeth, and he ended his years as master of Sherburne Hospital in Yorkshire.

The reforming sermons and literary labors of the Commonwealthmen terminated at the death of Edward VI and the accession of Mary. Because of their religious convictions and active role in the new Anglican establishment, with the exception of Latimer they shared in the common experience of exile on the Continent. Even Brinklow at an earlier date found it necessary to flee abroad. The English émigrés were a remarkable group, nearly eight hundred men, women, children, servants, a large proportion being gentry, clergy, and theological "students." Some proceeded to France and Italy, but the greatest number settled in Germany and Switzerland, forming their own congregations in the cities that afforded them protection. Besides Crowley, Becon, and Lever, the refugees included Miles Coverdale; John Foxe; John Day; Sir John Cheke; Starkey's old friend and Edward VI's ambassador to the German emperor, Sir Richard Morison; Elizabeth's cousin Francis Knollys; young Francis Walsingham; John Hales of the enclosure commission; Bishop John Ponet; two future bishops of London, John Aylmer and Edwin Sandys; and Sir Anthony Cooke, father-in-law of Sir William Cecil (now serving Mary) with whom Cooke was in constant touch. Their exodus seemed to be well organized and substantially subsidized by London merchants. That they were permitted to leave England was possibly the result of Lord Chancellor Stephen Gardiner's belief that he was thus solving the religious question and of Cecil's desire to secure English Protestantism. Indeed, the inspiration of the emigration appears to have been Cecil's, who was aided by Cranmer.[55] Cooke's household in Strasbourg became a center of propaganda, producing tracts by Becon, Ponet, and others, sometimes singly and sometimes collaboratively, which were smuggled into England by way of Emden. Christina Garrett feels that the settlements were a novel "experiment" in "religious colonization," the forerunner of the Puritan migration to the New World in the next century.[56] Of more immediate practical importance at the time, Garrett also maintains, was the exiles' return in 1588 transformed from "a political faction of disaffected country gentlemen" into a "political party" in order to contest the passage in parliament of the Supremacy bill.[57] Whatever their role in England, it is clear that the Commonwealthmen and kindred spirits played a significant part in the life and activities of the courageous refugees.

Their Social Ideology

The social ideology of the Commonwealthmen appears to have been largely an amalgam of elements of Lutheranism and medieval Christian thought (perhaps of scholastic and even prescholastic origin). The Commonwealthmen were probably indebted to Luther for their stress on brotherly love and moral equality and the harmony that should characterize human relationships. Also of apparently predominant Lutheran inspiration were their scathing attacks on selfishness, greed, and hubris and, conversely, their heartfelt compassion for the victims of egoism, the poor and unfortunate who needed brotherly comfort and solace. The image of Christ as the ever-caring and loving shepherd of his flock was their cherished ideal. At another level Luther may have been the source of their concern for the moral duty of the individual to cleave strenuously to his calling, to labor conscientiously, and to abhor all idleness. Finally, there was a definite Lutheran ring to their notion that each person had an absolute moral obligation to obey all superior authority and to abstain from all resistance no matter the provocation. The only exception was passive disobedience of a command to violate God's law. The society founded on these Lutheran principles, at least as perceived by the Commonwealthmen, would be a caring, humane community united through love in Christ. All would live and work happily and peacefully together, respecting authority and placing the common good above selfish interests. The unfortunate would be affectionately and solicitously succored by their more fortunate brethren. A genuine effort marked by fraternal good will and where necessary personal sacrifice would be made to improve the material circumstances and lift the flagging spirits of those whose lot was only to serve and obey.

Possibly the main feature of medieval Christian derivation in the Commonwealth ideology was the goal of a cooperative polity. The ideal was one of a static, essentially changeless society that once properly ordered should be carefully conserved to prevent any deviation from the norm. By definition the true Christian polity entailed the rejection of all tyranny and the maintenance of every precaution against willful and arbitrary rule. Human beings were normally equal under God, but a Christian polity entailed a social inequality exemplified in a hierarchical community of orders and degrees, according to each person's function in the social division of labor, from the lowest to the highest. The duties and privileges of the citizen were relative to his rank in the social scale, the whole a social replica of Aristotle's *scala naturae*, the medieval great chain of being. Regardless of status, however, all were expected to cooperate and toil in Christian love for the good of others, each performing his allotted task to the best of his ability.

Government of the Christian polity had more than the negative function of upholding law and order. Princes were under a much weightier obligation than merely to be God's "jailers and hangmen," as Luther following St. Augustine would have it. The state should act positively in creating a social environment conducive to the leading of a virtuous life by all Christians. The major purpose of the state was therefore twofold: ultimately to protect and encourage the worship of the true God and promote human conduct according to his law and mediately to fashion and maintain the social conditions that would render the first aim attainable. Security against external foes and the guarantees of peace and order within the state, the traditional defending and judging, were crucial to the final objective, but much more was needed for humans to be authentic Christians. The state should also take a critical lead in eliminating material distress so that individuals could be truly human. In a word, economic considerations were fundamental to this ideal of the state. A strong and vigorous material life in which citizens were freed from want and misery, able to perform with satisfaction their labors and enjoy their fruits, was the key to the richest spiritual life, a necessary if not sufficient condition for Christian virtue and happiness. Such was the moral position suggested by Fortescue and Dudley and more fully developed by More and Starkey. "Terrestial beatitude," in the language of St. Thomas Aquinas, and all it implied from the standpoint of the social and economic well-being of a people was the essential beginning of the Christian's journey to the final destination of "celestial beatitude." The idea of the dual aim of the state, primary and secondary, spiritual and material, seemed to be the theoretical font of the Commonwealth preoccupation with the economic situation in England.

Woven of Lutheran and medieval Christian strands, the social ideology of the Commonwealthmen—especially their emphasis on a loving, caring community and a paternalistic state managing the economic sphere—was hardly revolutionary, characterized as it was by an enlightened conservatism. The Commonwealthmen were at least equal to Brinklow in their passionate outcry against the social injustices of the time; nonetheless, although they were more comprehensive and intellectually polished in their approach, they lacked his radical and innovative ardor. Not for them the leveling of wealth by governmental fiat. Their plea was one of conservation. They called for the moral regeneration of the existing hierarchical order; their nostalgic quest seemed aimed at recapturing England's golden past where plenty had existed for all and no one suffered from involuntary poverty and unemployment. Hugh Latimer's fond memory of a vanished time was not untypical.[58] In an autobiographical recollection in a sermon he cited the case of his father, a Leicestershire yeoman, about the turn of the century. He paid rent of three to four pounds per year, tilled enough arable to employ half a dozen laborers, pastured one hundred sheep and thirty cows, furnished himself with the horse and harness to fight for his king against the rebels on Blackheath in 1497, paid for the schooling of young Hugh, provided a dowry of five pounds for each of his daughters, entertained his neighbors, and gave alms to the poor. Now, Latimer sorrowfully reported, the present tenant paid sixteen pounds or more annual rent "and is not able to do any thing for his prince, for himself, nor for his children, or give a cup of drink to the poor."

The Commonwealthmen (and some of their contemporaries) lamented the passing of the good old days—perhaps not with the poignant minutiae of Latimer—and portrayed in somber colors the economic woes of their country.[59] They attributed the change since the beginning of the century to the rise of unbridled greed and ambition, to a pernicious individualism that was laying waste the kingdom. The lust for private profit and drive for power and status in complete disregard for the public welfare, they charged, was manifest among many lords, gentlemen, landlords, clergy, officials, merchants, lawyers, and physicians. The hapless victims of this unrestrained covetousness were the little men of the soil and the workshop, the great majority of the population. A kind of "populism" permeated the outlook of the Commonwealthmen, as Julian Cornwall observes, the idealization of the small producer and tradesman.[60] Undoubtedly a well-worn sentiment in the sermons and writings of the Commonwealthmen was their deep commiseration for the predicament of modest, struggling husbandmen and artisans increasingly deprived of their livelihood by affluent landlords and merchants.

Unlike Brinklow and Starkey, the Commonwealthmen made few practical recommendations for reforming the conditions they described in such detail and condemned with such bitterness. Their prolific sermons and writings contained the principles to inform and guide the necessary reforms but did not specify explicit governmental policies. More important for the Commonwealthmen than state action to alleviate such dreadful material circumstances was the urgent need for the moral regeneration of the English, those of every order, so that in true Christian brotherhood people of every degree would no longer thirst for riches and power but would instead labor diligently in their callings and be content and happy in their stations, ever obedient to superior authority. This the Commonwealthmen believed was their cardinal mission as clerics: to turn the hearts of their flock to Christ. Once magistrates and public officials were enlightened by the true word, they could take appropriate measures to correct the iniquities resulting from the unprecedented acquisitiveness threatening the eventual destruction of the state. Governmental action without moral renewal would be to no avail. The outlook of the Commonwealthmen exerted a profound influence on Edward VI and some of his advisers. Reform based on Commonwealth precepts was the watchword of the day, reform to be accomplished by the instrument of the state. R. H. Tawney's comment in 1911 on royal policy between 1549 and 1553 is still relevant: "[it] constitutes surely one of the most remarkable attempts to control economic conditions by Government action which has ever been made."[61]

Because the Commonwealthmen were striving for social and economic reform not so much directly through governmental action as indirectly through conversion of their auditors and readers to Christ, it is not surprising that their political vocabulary was neither rich nor innovative. For them even more so than for Starkey, "common wealth" denoted *state* instead of common interest. More frequently than commonwealth, however, *state* was designated by "realm," "country," "England." Crowley wrote of the "weale publyke" and "polytyke body" and referred to "so noble a realme and commone wealth," "bodie of a commenwealth," and "the publique wealth of thys noble realme of Englande."[62] Possibly because he belonged to an older generation, Latimer employed "common wealth" for the state more sparingly than did either Becon or Lever.[63] Becon likened the commonwealth to a body and Lever compared it to a ship.[64] "Pale" in conjunction with commonwealth is found in Lever: "pale of the parke of this commune welth" and "the very pale, wall, and bulwarkes of the commen wealth."[65] His purpose may have been to suggest a community of shared civility as well as territorial limits. He employed "comynaltye" or "communaltye" and other variants for commons or common people,[66] but in one instance "a christen comminaltye wythin Gods house" seemed to have the broader sense of community or society, as it did for Starkey.[67] The use of "state" by the Commonwealthmen in any meaning was exceedingly rare. In Crowley's *Voyce of the Last Trumpet* are the lines: "The ende why all men be create / As men of wisdome do agre / Is to maintaine the publike state / In the contrei where thei shal be."[68] Becon in *The Jewel of Joy* asserts, "The state of England was never so miserable as it is at the present." By "state" both seemed to mean status or condition. "Gouvernance" appeared occasionally, although only individual officials—princes, kings, magistrates—were mentioned, never the abstract or collective "government."[69]

Contrasting with the paucity of political language of the Common-wealthmen is the conceptual richness of expression of their contempo-rary, associate, and sympathizer, John Ponet (1516?–1556), who assaulted the Marian regime in *A Shorte Treatise of Politike Power* (1556), a bril-liant defense of tyrannicide and one of the landmarks of sixteenth-century political thought.[70] Ponet detested the Marian state that had de-prived him of his see, executed his patron Cranmer, and forced him into exile in Strasbourg, where he plunged into the propagandistic activities of his fellow émigrés and completed the little classic in the year of his death. Except for his all-important rejection of their belief in passive obedience, he shared many of the views and the life experience of the Common-wealthmen. Born in Kent, probably of a humble family, he went up to Queen's College, Cambridge, receiving his B.A. in 1532 and remaining as a fellow. A Lutheran cleric and Greek scholar with scientific interests, he was a friend of Cheke, Smith, and Aylmer. Evidently succeeding Becon as chaplain to Cranmer in 1547, he was a close associate of the archbishop and was appointed bishop of Rochester in 1550 and bishop of Winchester in 1551. He was apparently involved in the abortive rebellion of late 1553 and early 1554 led by Sir Thomas Wyatt of Kent to depose the new queen.[71]

That Ponet's book, as the title indicates, was first and foremost a politi-cal work—unlike anything written by the Commonwealthmen—engag-ing in abstract argumentation for the justification of active resistance to a tyrannical ruler may explain why his political language was richer and more interesting than theirs. Although he shared their vocabulary, his continuation of the usage of *state* begun by Starkey is noteworthy, ap-pearing over a dozen times in the volume.[72] By *state* Ponet also meant condition or status.[73] Somewhat more often, however, he used the term in Starkey's sense of an institutional totality, a structure of power. Ponet first employs *state* in connection with laws "necessarie for the maynte-naunce of the state."[74] Then he refers to "diverse kyndes of states or poli-cies," namely, the conventional classification of states by the number who govern: monarchy, aristocracy, and democracy.[75] A combination of these three simple types, Ponet says, is called a "mixte state."[76] More clearly than Starkey, he differentiated *state* from the government as a collectiv-ity, although he used "common wealth" instead of "state" in the first of the two relevant passages: " . . . common wealthes and realmes may live, when the head is cut of, and may put on a newe head, that is, make them a newe governour."[77] The second passage maintains that a good ruler should seek "to see the hole state well governed"; he adds: "An evil per-sone comyng to the gouernement of any state, either by vsurpacion, or by election or by succession, vtterly neglecting the cause why kings, princes and other gouernours in comon wealthes be made (that is, the wealthe of the people) seketh onli or chiefly his owne profit and pleasure."[78] In addition to the frequent expressions "politike power" and "ciuil power,"[79] Ponet also used the *corpus politicum* of Fortescue in Starkey's version of "politike body," seemingly assuming the latter's body-soul dualism: "Kinges, Princes and other gouernours, albeit they are the headdes of a politike body, yet they are not the hole body. And though they be the chief membres, yet they are but membres: nother are the people ordained for them, but they are ordained for the people."[80] Ponet used neither "society" nor "commynalty" to refer to the community, although he may possibly have implied as much by "people."[81] His political terminology perhaps represented only a slight advance over Starkey's, but together they suggest that we are on the threshold of the distinctively modern conceptualization of the state.

The Commonwealthmen adhered to the medieval Christian notion of the state's dual purpose, spiritual and material. While they stressed the spiritual function of the state, its economic objectives were by no means belittled. So Latimer contended that the "king's honour" rested on the realization of two aims: first, that "his subjects be led to the true religion," and second, that "the commonwealth be advanced; that the dearth of these foresaid things [the economic necessities of life] be provided for, and the commodities of this realm so employed, as it may be to the setting of his subjects on work, and keeping them from idleness."[82] Later he contended that no one labored more than the king who defended and promoted the faith, upheld justice, harmonized the estates, and "provide[d] for the poor; to see victuals good cheap."[83] Becon's position on the calling and duty of magistrates was similar. They should "procure, above all things, the wealth of the poor commonalty" and "employ all their endeavours to avance, beautify, enrich, and make wealthy their realm and country."[84] In addition to preserving and strengthening Christian belief, Becon's prince was obligated to defend his subjects, render them justice, and protect their goods.[85] A magistrate must "rule with the temporal sword" in order "to defend the widow and fatherless, to conserve the commonwealth" and "to seek the quietness and commodity of his subjects, even as a father seeketh the health and profit of his natural son."[86]

Ponet's political thought displays an increasing emphasis on the state's secular and economic goals. Arguing that the state, whose source was God, was thus ordained to "mayntene iustice," at the same time Ponet affirmed that the civil power was not concerned with the soul of man, only with his body "and those things that belong vnto this temporall life of man."[87] In confining the aim of the state to the care of the bodies of its citizens, Ponet seemed to take a significant step in the direction of secularizing its conception. Without reference to the spiritual purpose of the state, he stressed in a number of passages that the state's object was the "wealthe and benefit" of the people.[88] For example, he wrote: "As a good phisician earnestly seketh the healthe of his pacient and a Shipmaister the wealthe and sauegarde of those he hathe in his ship, so dothe a good gouernor seke the wealthe of those he ruleth."[89] Nonetheless, Ponet was not unequivocal, for he reverted occasionally to the dualistic formulation.[90] We can only conclude, however, that for him the state existed fundamentally, if not exclusively, to ensure the security and economic well-being of its citizens. It was his stress on the secular function of the state that was important in future theorizing.

To be sure, Ponet did not go so far as some of his more earthbound contemporaries—early analysts of the economy—in playing down the moral end of the state. Clement Armstrong bluntly claimed in the mid-thirties that "a right order of a comon weale may be said in England to have vitall [victuals] as plentiful as in old tyme."[91] And the anonymous author of the 1548 tract *Policies to Reduce This Realme of England vnto a Prosperus Wealthe and Estate* put Armstrong's thought no less directly, if more comprehensively, in a remark that Ponet might have applauded: " . . . the Floreshing estate of a realm . . . consisteth cheifly in being stronge against theirvasion of eneymies, not molested with cyvile warres *the people being wealthie,* and not oppressid with famyn nor penury of victuelles."[92] A decade after Ponet's death Sir Thomas Smith, in drafting his *De republica Anglorum* in Toulouse, succinctly defined the purpose of the association of citizens in the state—omitting any mention of its moral value or spiritual aims—as "the conservation of themselves in peace as in warre."[93] In abbreviated form this was how Hobbes, Harrington, Locke, and the pioneer political economists conceived of the state in the next century. By this time the state was more clearly defined and conceptualized in secular terms, its traditionally held moral objectives so receding from view as to virtually disappear, to be replaced by a concentration on economic matters.

Catalog of Grievances

Hardly ever in English history has more devastating and caustic criticism of social conditions been voiced than in the time of the Commonwealth-men. The complaints—familiar to readers of Dudley, More, and Starkey—were even more sweeping and detailed than theirs, a climax to the social protest of the previous decades. The language of social criticism in any age has rarely been so scathing and comprehensive in its blame, all the more surprising since the Commonwealthmen, far from being mere rabble-rousers, were respected persons of standing, moderation, and intellect. Not until the nineteenth century, not even in the pronouncements of the seventeenth-century Levellers or the English radicals of 1789, was the discourse of protest so sharp and uncompromising. Perhaps only Edmund Burke rivaled the rhetorical power of these conscience-stricken clerics, and no doubt if acquainted with their writings he would have relished their conservative ideal of a cooperative Christian polity and their nostalgia for the past.

Their critical comment ranged from perceptive generalizations about the changes in English society to the enumeration of specific economic abuses jeopardizing the livelihood and welfare of the ordinary citizen and the unity and harmony of the state itself. What Crowley's doggerel said of the City of London might well have symbolized the attitude of the Commonwealthmen toward the entire social situation:

> And this is a Citye in name, but, in dede,
> It is a packe of people that seeke after meede [profit or gain];
> For officers and al do seke their owne gaine,
> But for the wealth of the commons not one taketh paine.
> An hell with out order,
> I maye it well call,
> Where euerye man is for him self,
> And no manne for all.[94]

Becon further delineated the Hobbesian den of anarchic egoism to which English society was reduced, moralizing: "The pride of these our days is Lucifer-like, the covetousness is unsatiable, the whoredom is monstrous, the unmercifulness is butcher-like, the malice is immortal . . . "[95] He continued in this disenchanted vein: "Every christian heart, beholding this most ungodly state of the world, cannot but lament and bewail the abominations used in these our days."[96] The practical author of *Policies to Reduce This Realme of England* brought down to earth the cruel lot of the people who no longer lived in a community but in Crowley's "packe" and in "Lucifer-like" times of covetousness: "Moste parte of the persons and people lyve in extreme pouertie. victuall being alwaies at so heighe price tht . . . a great nombre of the people shalbe in dainger of famyn."[97]

The nature of the social criticism and attitudes of the Commonwealthmen becomes clear if we consider their analysis of economic and social conditions, their identification of those chiefly responsible for the difficulties, their fear of sedition, and their emphasis on labor and calling. Like previous Tudor critics, the Commonwealthmen, for whom burgeoning impoverishment and unemployment were ominous signs of the disintegration of English society, drew a connection between idleness and penury on the one hand and beggary, vagabondage, crime, and insurrection on the other. Civil disorder was the high price being paid for the increasing prosperity of the greedy few at the expense of endless deprivations of the many. Inflated prices and rents, shady business practices, usury, and an unquenchable thirst for land filled the coffers of the landlords, merchants, and a growing breed of middleman and broker, exacerbating the desperate struggle for survival in the lower ranks.

The Commonwealthmen deplored the exorbitant cost of food, clothing, and the necessities of life, a swollen cost that, according to William Forrest's estimate in 1548, was a fourfold rise from the recent past.[98] Crowley and Latimer were worried by the high cost of coal in London, which they blamed on the avarice of upwardly mobile colliers who had managed to corner the market and acquire a voice in local government.[99] The soaring prices of food and clothing were attributed to increasing land rents and questionable procedures. Enclosure of commons and engrossment by wealthy landlords and graziers deprived countless poor husbandmen of their livelihood and dwellings, forcing them off the land, as did disreputable business methods such as rack-renting, lease mongering, forestalling and regrating, and usury.

In contrast to the plight of dispossessed smallholders stood the splendid homes of the rich. Becon castigated those "who greatly delight in building gorgeous houses and sumptuous mansions."[100] Lever echoed this criticism, comparing the palatial mansions of the wealthy with the hovels of the poor and decrying the lack of any accommodation whatsoever for the most unfortunate.[101] He noted that not only did rural housing of the poor suffer from the greed of the rich but also "whole towns are become desolate and like unto a wilderness, no man dwelling there, except it be a shepherd and his dog." Small country towns of a hundred households, Becon affirmed, were reduced to thirty, and where there had once been fifty, now only ten were occupied.[102]

The decay of grammar schools and universities—a subject dear to Lever—also testified to the general deterioration of the quality of English life. He lamented the schools starved of funds from private and public patronage and deplored "the pullyng downe of gramer scholes, the deuylishe drownynge of youthe in ignoraunce, the vtter decaye of the vniuersities, and mooste vncharitable spoyle or prouysion, that was made for the pore."[103] Poor pupils, Lever complained, were no longer able to continue their studies in Cambridge. Of the previous two hundred divinity students there, not a single one remained, and many grammar schools had been abandoned.[104]

Indictments of enclosers and engrossers abounded. The author of *Policies to Reduce This Realme of Englande* was not far from the mark in his pronouncement: "Is ther not exclamacion made almoste in euery notable Sermonde against the insaciable Shippasturers?"[105] Angered by the profligate enclosers, Crowley charged: "Your greedye gut could neuer stynt / Tyll all the good and fruitful grounde / Were hedged in whyth in your mounde."[106] The Commonwealthmen were bitter about the failure of parliament and various royal commissions to stem the tide of enclosure during the reigns of Henry and Edward.[107] In Lever's view enclosure of commons was the greatest burden to which the people were subjected.[108] Labeling enclosing graziers "greedy wolves" and "cumberous cormorants," Becon protested that they oppressed the poor "by devouring their common pastures with their sheep." The dire result was

> that the poor people are not able to keep a cow for the comfort of them of their poor family, but are like to starve and perish for hunger if there be not provision made shortly! What sheep-ground scapeth these caterpillars of the commonweal? How swarm they with abundance of flocks of sheep! and yet when was wool ever so dear, or mutton of so great price?[109]

"Caterpillars of the commonweal" was an expression Becon applied not only to sheep but also to enclosing gentlemen, landlords, and graziers.[110] Their hunger for land led them to "devour the people as it were a morsel of bread. If any piece of ground delight their eye, they must needs have it, either by hook or by crook." Driven by an enormous appetite, the affluent coupled field to field, pasture to pasture, house to house, manor to manor.[111] Surveyors were employed to identify every inch of their properties so that the rents of already overburdened tenants could be increased to make, in Crowley's words, "the vttermost peny of al their groundes."[112] Latimer's conclusion about surveying landlords was that "the commons be utterly undone by them."

In their questioning of enclosure and engrossing the Commonwealthmen asked what was sufficient for the life of the modest husbandman. Intimately acquainted with rural conditions, Latimer calculated that the ordinary plowman needed some sheep to fertilize his cornfields, swine for bacon (the "venison of the poor"), a horse to draw his plow and transport his produce to market, and cows for the milk and cheese on which he must live and pay rents.[113] Pasture was absolutely essential for his livestock. As things stood, however, enclosure of the commons deprived the husbandman of the grazing land on which the whole operation depended and thus threatened his very existence. In Becon's opinion, which in condensed form roughly paralleled the autobiographical passage of Latimer's paraphrased earlier (see p. 167), after paying the rent the smallholder needed sufficient profit from selling his commodities for the nourishment of himself and family, for bringing up his children in "good arts," for hospitality, for bearing the "charges of the commonweal," and for charitable outlays.[114] With enclosure, engrossing, and rocketing rents, a sufficient living by these standards for numerous smallholders was no longer possible.

Apart from their criticism of enclosing and engrossing, the Commonwealthmen enumerated the most pernicious of the practices wreaking havoc on the lives of the poor: rack-renting, lease mongering, forestalling and regrating, and usury. Rack-renters—landlords who on the expiry of the tenant's lease boosted the entry fine and rent beyond a reasonable amount—were severely rebuked.[115] For Latimer and Becon such behavior was theft and the gain a gift from the Devil.[116] "What a sea of mischifes hath floued out of thys more than a Turkyshe tyranie!" cried Crowley.[117] He alluded to a landlord who had tripled his rents and then curtly replied to the charge of oppressing his peasants: "That wyth hys own he myghte alwayes do as he lyste."[118] Some landlords allowed their houses to fall into such disrepair that tenants were forced to leave, thereby rendering widows, the elderly, and children homeless.[119]

The Commonwealthmen roundly condemned what seems to have been the fairly common practice in town and country of lease mongering: the buying up of leases from poor tenants and then subletting the holdings to them at much higher rates, compelling them to meet the increases or be evicted.[120] Lease mongers were destined for hell warned Crowley: "But all men se you do aduance / Your selfe by pore mens hyderaunce."[121] Nine-tenths of London houses, according to Crowley, were leased not by the owners but by lease mongers, some of whom lived free of charge on their holdings, subletting the unoccupied portion.[122] Lever cited the case of an "honest landlord" a few miles from London who had leased land to "poor honest tenants" for two shillings four pence per acre. The leases were subsequently bought from the tenants by a lease monger, who evicted them and raised the rents to nine shillings or even nineteen shillings per acre.[123]

Forestalling and regrating referred to the practice of buying up particular commodities, often before they were actually produced, in order to monopolize the market and increase the profit.[124] Becon was provoked by "certain rich and greedy cormorants, those locusts and caterpillars of the commonweal," who "when they have plenty of grain, and see abundance thereof reign among the people . . . do not only sell their own corn to maintain the commodity of the poor, but also buy other men's grain, and hoard it up until they have made a great dearth."[125] When prices then rose in the midst of such scarcity the grain was sold at enormous profit. Lever noted an instance when corn was bought while still growing at eight pounds per acre and then sold for ten pounds; the final price was thirteen pounds to the person who conveyed the harvested corn to market.[126] Lever branded these middlemen and others like lease mongers "marchauntes of myschyefe" who came between "the barke and the tree," making all things dear. He called them "ydle vacaboundes" and "craftye couetous extorcioners" living and profiting parasitically off the sweat and toil of others. William Harrison, another cleric and a neighbor of Sir Thomas Smith in Essex, described a special kind of middleman, the "bodger" or "badger," the itinerant grain dealer.[127] Such dealers bought the commodity cheaply from the small producer to supply wealthy proprietors, who were either using their arable for grazing and needed the grain or hoarding the grain until the price rose because of scarcity. Such dubious methods, together with purveyance and the manipulation of variable standards of weights and measures, aroused Harrison's ire: "And thereby we may see how each one of us endeavoreth to fleece and eat up another."[128]

The Commonwealthmen rejected usury for violating the law of God and condemned it as outright theft.[129] Crowley, in the chapter "Of Usurers" in *Epigrams*, detailed an ingenious mode of extracting an exorbitant rate of interest for a hard-pressed victim.[130] The usurer employed £20 of capital from the sale of his own land to loan out for one month with good security and a bill of sale. If the loan was not repaid, no cause for delinquency was accepted. The interest charged (per month) was 1 penny per shilling, or for twelve months, 1 shilling interest per shilling loaned. In other words, on the £20 loaned on a monthly basis for twelve months, the annual interest charged was 100 percent or £20.

Fortescue had praised England in the previous century for being a veritable paradise, with the material life of the ordinary person far superior to that of his Continental counterpart.[131] By the time of Edward VI, Becon contended, "The state of England was never so miserable as it is at present,"[132] and Lever bemoaned the situation as one of "everye manne pullynge and halynge towardes them selues, one from another."[133] The realm consequently was not "onelye diuyded, but also rente, torne, and plucked cleane in pieces," and many were "in miseries without comfort, and in pouertie, and lacke help."[134] While Crowley feared that the victimization of the poor majority by the wealthy minority would condemn the average Englishman "to the lyke slauery tht the French men are in,"[135] the analysis in *Policies to Reduce This Realme of Englande* reflected a somewhat greater sophistication.[136] The anonymous author argued that even in impoverishment, the state of the humble Englishman was superior to that of his Continental equivalent. English beggars, he observed, did much better than French laborers and artisans and what sufficed for three French peasants would not maintain a single servant in England. His point seemed to be the important one of relative deprivation. The English were so accustomed to living well that a sudden fall in their income and standard of living, even though they were still better off than the French, produced discontent or civil unrest and might eventuate in rebellion and insurrection.

Causes and Culprits

The Commonwealthmen believed that the source of the serious troubles lay in human nature, the uninhibited covetousness, ambition, and pride that were coming to the fore in the England of their day.[137] Why this sudden wave of greed and egoism should so suddenly sweep the country, they did not explain. The focus on the central problem of human sin seems to have prevented their identifying the emergence of what C. B. Macpherson calls "possessive individualism," a development accompanying the basic structural changes taking place in English society, in short, the beginnings of capitalism in the form of Marx's primitive accumulation.[138] This transformation in human behavior, fracturing the customary way of life, could not yet be accommodated by their Christian creed. Despite their awareness of change, their social criticism and analysis resorted to the traditional Augustinian and later Protestant conception of the flawed human being.

Covetousness and its variants became key terms of their social diagnosis, just as they had been for More. They considered all humans tarnished by an insidious covetousness—lords, gentlemen, clergy, commoners, some more than others—and felt that all would assuredly be punished by God for their transgressions. Commenting on those involved on all sides in the southeastern and northern uprisings, gentlemen and commoners alike, Latimer insisted that "covetousness is the cause of rebellion" and referred to the "pestilent poison of ambition."[139] "Covetousness of money is the root of all evil," asserted Becon in agreement with Crowley, claiming that the "pride of these our days is Lucifer-like."[140] To mitigate this covetousness, he wrote:

> The magistrate ought not to take much of his subjects, nor to over-
> charge them with intolerable payments. . . . They that exercise
> themselves in merchandise, in buying and selling, in husbandry, in
> manual arts and handy occupations &c., ought so to travail in their
> mysteries, that all craft and subtility, all falsehood and dissimula-
> tion set apart, they may deal truly and faithfully with all men. . . .
> The gentlemen and landlords ought so to let out their farms, lands,
> tenements, lorships [sic], &c., for a reasonable price, that their ten-
> ants may be able to live under them.[141]

The "cruell wolfe of couetousnesse," Lever believed, drove many nobles,
clerics, and commoners away from Christ into the "seruyce of wycked
Mammon."[142] An overweening concern with the accumulation of worldly
goods, the corrupting standard by which all was valued, led Latimer to reflect on "belly-wisdom" and Becon to make a strident denunciation of
"belly-care."[143] If the former prosperity and harmony of England were to
be revived, the Commonwealthmen averred in one voice, covetousness
must be purged from the hearts of all by a universal moral regeneration
to make every individual an upright, loving Christian.

All humans might be tainted by the sin of covetousness, but a minority of the well-to-do were more guilty than the oppressed and impoverished majority. The Commonwealthmen were bolder even than More and
Starkey in their assignment of the responsibility for the plight of the
poor and the material burdens of their countrymen to the upper classes.
Latimer was at the forefront in challenging his fellow clerics to do their
Christian duty:

> Therefore, you preachers, out with your swords and strike at the
> root. Speak against covetousness, and cry out upon it. Stand not
> ticking and toying at the branches nor at the boughs, for then will
> new boughs and branches spring again of them; but strike at the
> root, and fear not these giants of England, these great men and
> men of power, these men that are oppressors of the poor; fear
> them not, but strike at the root of all evil, which is mischievous
> covetousness.[144]

Latimer's clarion call hailed others, who in forthright and combative language more scornful and comprehensive than the indictments of Dudley,
More, and Starkey, threw down the gauntlet to their peers and superiors.
Mincing no words, they directed their accusations against a broad spectrum of the covetous: lords and gentlemen, officeholders, clergy, and
greedy commoners, especially merchants, lawyers, and physicians.

Crowley led the way with caustic invective condemning self-seeking lords and gentlemen. They were "gredie cormeruantes," "gredye gulles," "ungentle gentlemen," "churles chickens," the "only cause" of the sedition of 1549; their enclosures were responsible for the "stealeyng, robbyng, & reueynge" of the lower orders.[145] He presented the case of the poor against wealthy enclosing gentlemen, and then in turn he recited their own brief against the poor: that they were too well-off, disobedient lawless levelers who would have all things held in common, open up pastures, destroy parks, and fix rents.[146] Crowley's judgment was that the poor may have got what they deserved in the 1549 disorders but that gentlemen had to shoulder an important part of the blame. Because of their enclosing, despite the royal proclamation prohibiting it, and because of their rack-renting and stripping the poor of their customary rights, they could not be absolved of the responsibility for the troubles of 1549. It was in their own self-interest not to continue in their ways: "Be warned therefore, & seke not to kepe the commones of England in Slauery, for that is next way to destroie your selves!"[147] Not to be outdone by Crowley's abuse of enclosing lords and gentlemen, Becon also attacked these "greedy wolves," "cumberous cormorants" and "ungentle gentlemen."[148] He assailed the nobility for their lack of nobility, for their hubris and licentious conduct,[149] bluntly stating that

> the cause of all this wretchedness and beggary in the commonweal are the greedy gentlemen, which are sheepmongers and graziers. While they study for their own private commodity, the commonweal is like to decay. . . . They which in time past were wont to be defenders of the poor, are now become the destroyers of the same. They by whom the commonweal sometime was preserved, are now become the caterpillars of the commonweal. . . . So they may be enriched, they care not who be impoverished. They are right brothers of Cain, which had rather slay his brother Abel, than he should have any part with him of worldly possessions.[150]

Later in *The Fortress of the Faithful* Becon distinguished between the "true gentleman" and those despoilers of the poor.[151] Instead of being "fathers of the country, maintainers of the poor, defenders of the widows and fatherless, succourers of the needy, comforters of the comfortless, and upholders of the commonweal" or the "pearls and jewels to a realm," these "caterpillars of the commonweal"—he employed the expression repeatedly—"poll, they pill, they wake, they rake, they sweat, they fret, they gripe, they nip, they face, they brase, they semble, they dissemble; yea, they move every stone, as they say, to maintain and set forth their unnoble nobility, not caring how they come by it, so they have it."[152] So

Becon inveighed against these false gentlemen, the pillagers of the realm.[153] Lever likewise contributed to the torrent of invective against covetous landlords (as well as officeholders and preachers): "wolfes in lambes skyns" and "deuyles in mans vysers."[154] His chief contention with lords and gentlemen (along with clerics and merchants) was that in their hunger after riches, they had allowed, by their failure to provide the necessary funds, grammar schools and universities to decay.[155]

Although the Commonwealthmen may have been overstating their case against venality in office, they were highly critical of public officials, a category that of course included lords and gentlemen. The buying and selling of offices was a prime concern, for the reformers knew that offices would not customarily be marketed unless the profits gained far exceeded the cost of purchase.[156] Officeholders were derelict in their obligation to maintain law and order; they exercised their powers not so much to defend the poor as to fleece them, exacting lucrative fees, tributes, tolls, and duties. Latimer set forth criteria for the good officeholder. He would be an individual of knowledge and an effective man of action, honest and trustworthy, God-fearing, with a hatred of covetousness, one who would not succumb to graft and venality.

While the Commonwealthmen were clerics (except Crowley at the time of his writing), they displayed little timidity in chastising other members of their order for laxity and avarice.[157] They were servants of mammon leading lives that were far too worldly and providing little in the way of spiritual guidance for their parishioners. Nor did they perform their appropriate educational functions in schools and universities. Clerics' advice to officeholders was little more than what they desired to hear; the reformers spoke of "pestilent prelates whyche by flattery poyson the hygh powers of authorytye."[158] Especially disturbing was the accumulation of benefices for profit, so many "dumme Dogges, choked with benefices," Lever opined.[159] Summarizing the protest of the others against their fellow churchmen, he added: "Do ye se howe by these seruantes of Mammon, enemyes of Chryste, gredy wolues in Lamb skynnes, the paryshes be spoyled, the people vntaughte, God vnknowen."[160]

Commoners too—merchants, lawyers, physicians—aroused the Commonwealthmen by their greed. Merchants were rebuked for using their capital to buy up landed property, enclosing and rack-renting to the disadvantage of the poor.[161] The critics noted the unprincipled avarice of some merchants, revealed by their unreasonable profits, sale of shoddy goods, and questionable business practices, not least of which was the use of fraudulent weights and measures. Lever singled out for complaint merchants' export of unwrought lead, wool, and leather, commodities that might have employed many Englishmen in gainful productive activity, and their import of frivolous luxury goods such as silks, sables, and feathers, items that could be of no benefit to the poor.[162] In his inimitable fashion Becon summed up the attitude of the Commonwealthmen: "What craft, deceit, subtility, and falsehood use merchants in buying and selling! How rejoice they when they have beguiled their christian brother!"[163]

Lawyers, likewise, did not escape the anger of the Commonwealthmen, who condemned their money-grubbing proclivities, prohibitive fees, and deliberate prolongation of litigation. "Thy callng is good and godly," Crowley put it in characteristic fashion, "If thou wouldste walke therein aryght; / But thou art so passing gredy, / That Gods feare is out of thy syght." A lawyer should, he instructs,

> Fyrst call vnto thy memorye
> For what cause the laws wer fyrst made;
> And then apply busily
> To the same end use thy trade.
> The lawes were made, vndoubtedly
> That al suche men are oppreste,
> Myght in the same fynde remedy,
> And leade their lyues in quiet reste.
> Doest thou then walke in thy callyng.[164]

Becon left no doubt as to his view of the many lawyers dedicated to mammon: "O gaping wolves! O ramping lions! O insatiable dogs! O crafty foxes!"[165] Like merchants and lawyers with an eye to profit, physicians were not innocent of contributing to the vexing situation in England.[166] In the spirit of aid to fellow humans, argued the critics, medical services should be available to the poor as well as to the rich.

The Commonwealthmen thus deplored the deteriorating social and economic conditions, largely blaming a minority of wealthy gentlemen, clergymen, and commoners for subordinating the common interest in their individualistic quest for profit and power and for abdicating all responsibility for the poor and unfortunate. Such egoistic behavior, according to Latimer, violated the "king's honor" (which in the opinion of some "standeth in the great multitude of people") by depriving them of employment and life's necessities.[167] Becon developed this theme in much the same way as Fortescue, Dudley, and Starkey by appealing to the self-interest of the ruler: "The richer and the wealthier that the commons are in the realm, the richer and wealthier is the prince of that realm, yea, and the stronger also is he, and the further from all jeopardy and danger."

Then he added: "But, contrariwise, the poorer and the baser that the commons are in any realm, the more feeble and less valiant is the prince against his enemies."[168]

Returning to the subject in *The Fortress of the Faithful*, after criticizing the exploitation of the people by "ungentle gentlemen," Becon quoted Solomon in Proverbs 14:28, a lesson that all should take seriously: "The increase and prosperity of the commons is the king's honor; but the decay of the people is the confusion of the prince."[169] This biblical text was apparently the ultimate authority for the precept that the interest of government was identical with the common interest, a principle espoused by Fortescue, Dudley, More, and Starkey, taken up by Latimer and Becon, and one that was to be an important element in Hobbes's argument for absolutism. Becon maintained that "they are not friendly to the king, by Salomon's saying, that impoverish the commons."[170] Next, reciting a long list of exploiters of the commons, Becon exclaimed "O unworthy act! O unseemly sight! O abomination! What is it to beggar the realm, to famish the king's subjects, to bring slavery into this realm, if this be not? Do they not suck the poor men's blood, that suffer them not to have whereof to live?"[171]

The Commonwealthmen, however, in spite of all their criticisms and protests, made it quite clear that their own loyalty to the crown was unswerving. They portrayed the king (along with the poor) as the unwitting victim of the acquisitive individualism of the wealthy and his government as the prime means of correcting the abuses and improving the conditions of the people through enlightened public policy. Their hostility to the insurrections of 1549 reveals their allegiance to the king. The rebels failed to consider their duty to God to obey the prince, Latimer contended, and in their prayers for victory actually prayed against themselves.[172] Despite the abysmal circumstances provoking discord, Becon certainly did not condone the uprisings. Yet he was deeply moved by them, crying, "Who, except, an enemy to all good order, sorrowfully sorroweth not?"[173] These critics clearly felt that in resorting to violence against established authority the rebels committed a grievous sin. Crowley, also deeply perturbed by civil disorder and sedition, devoted a chapter of *Epigrams* to "Commotioners," those "desyrouse to breake the publyke unitie."[174] The public body must be purged of such "rotten humours," if not by the sword, then "discrete counsell" must "fynde wayes to kyll / The powr of those rebelles, and let them of theyr wyll."[175] Sedition, however, could be prevented by efforts of government and the ruling classes to strengthen the "humours natural" of the commonwealth, to win the loyalty of the people through attention to their welfare. If greedy gentry valued their prosperity and security, Crowley warned, they should seriously take to heart the causes of sedition, for by failing to do so, they might lose all.[176]

Notwithstanding the dreadful conditions of the commons, the Commonwealthmen were unanimous in their vigorous disapproval of all rebellion. Paul's Epistle to the Romans, chapter 13, was the chief scriptural authority for their denunciation of civil disobedience and insistence on loyalty to the crown.[177] Because God appointed every ruler, good and bad alike, all subjects had an absolute moral duty to obey his commands. Servants should always defer to their masters and citizens to their magistrates. If, however, in any relationship between superior and inferior, the latter was ordered by the former to contravene the law of God, then disobedience was a moral duty, but disobedience was to be passive and the penalty for it accepted. Under no circumstances was active disobedience or resistance justifiable. No matter how wrong or unfair the command of a superior power appeared to those subject to it, no matter how oppressed they were, they were always to obey—with the exception noted—and never try to take law and justice into their own hands. Irresponsible rulers and public officials, rack-renting and enclosing landlords, and harsh masters would be punished by God, not by the downtrodden and exploited. Rebellion, as disobedience to God, was always sinful, and rebels would be punished by God. Rich and poor existed by divine ordination, and if the poor were made to suffer by the rich, the poor were being chastised by God for their own sins. Instead of resorting to violence and revolt, the oppressed were commanded to lead upright lives, turn to God in their distress, and bear their trials and tribulations with Christian fortitude.

From the perspective of the Commonwealthmen, covetousness was a universal malady. Not confined to the ruling classes alone, it was also a failing of the dispossessed, unemployed, and impoverished, who had to carry the cross of their sins, depending solely on God for succor. As Latimer saw the matter, "Covetousness is the cause of rebellion," not the covetousness of one party to a conflict despoiling the other, but the covetousness of all concerned, despoilers and despoiled alike.[178] Although the reformers' analyses of the seditious troubles admit that greedy gentlemen, clerics, and commoners have been more covetous than their hapless victims, the critics never accepted any excuse for usurping the functions of duly constituted authority. Addressing the rich, Crowley explained that the poor had received less than they deserved from their superiors and "if their offence wer laied in an equall balaunce with yours (as no doubt thei are in the sight [of] God) doubt not but you should sone be ashamed of youre parte. For what can you laye vnto their charge, but they haue had examples of the same in you? If you charge them wythe disobedience, you were firste disobedient."[179] Still more forthright was his later apportionment of the blame for the crime and sedition engulfing the commonwealth: "If the sturdy fall to stealeyng, robbyng, & reueynge, then are you the causers thereof, for you dygge in, enclose, and wytholde from them the earth out of the whych they should dygge and plowe theyr lyuenge."[180] None of the other Commonwealthmen was as bold as Crowley. Yet even a muted doubt was expressed by Lever: " . . . in Englande pore men have been rebels, and ryche men have not done their duetie. Both have done euyll to prouoke goddes vengeance, neyther doth repente to procure gods mercye."[181] He cautioned rulers against oppression as the means of preventing disorder: "And as the people can haue no remedye against euyll rulers by rebellyon, so can the rulers have no redresse of rebellious people by oppresyon."[182] His conclusion, nonetheless, was shared by the other Commonwealthmen. The only remedy for the disorders of the realm was rooting out covetousness in all, high and low, rich and poor, gentlemen and yeomen.[183]

Wishing to absolve themselves of any charge of radicalism, the Commonwealthmen hastened to deny a popular notion of the day that preachers were fomenters of rebellion. As early as 1530 Latimer wrote Henry VIII supporting the free publication of religious books, refuting the idea that it would promote insurrection.[184] Later, he reasoned that if covetousness was the cause of rebellion, preaching against covetousness could hardly be blamed for rebellion: " . . . our preaching is the cause of rebellion, much like as Christ was the cause of the destruction of Jerusalem."[185] True, he continued, the new Lutheran preaching was accompanied by an increase in civil disorders, but to have seen in one the cause of the other was just as ridiculous as the claim made in a story related by Sir Thomas More.[186] As one of the commissioners sent to Kent to investigate the sanding up of Sandwich harbor, More called on a local patriarch, the oldest in the audience at the hearing, for his opinion. The elderly man stated with conviction that the cause was the construction of Tenterden steeple, for not until it was built did the sanding occur. Becon did not excuse all preachers from blame for the troubles of 1549.[187] A few, those who were not properly ordained, perhaps Papists, might have been guilty. But by far the greatest number, true preachers to be differentiated from false preachers, just as there were true and false gentlemen, could only benefit the commonwealth by their exposure and criticism of covetousness and their pleas for obedience, humility, and patience.

A marked contrast to the attitude of the Commonwealthmen toward civil disobedience and resistance was the more sophisticated and searching examination of the problem by their contemporary, Bishop John Ponet, who may have influenced the later arguments of the French constitutionalists.[188] Indeed civil disobedience was the focus of Ponet's remarkable *Shorte Treatise*. Deprived of his see, probably involved in Wyatts' rebellion to depose Mary, and forced into exile with Crowley, Becon, and Lever, Ponet had every reason to develop a cogent case for active civil disobedience and tyrannicide. He began with two of the fundamental assumptions of the Commonwealthmen: that the ruler was ordained by God and subject to his law and that he was so appointed for the good of the people. Then, however, Ponet steered his own course in a radical and intellectually astute manner.[189]

Ponet's line of reasoning was briefly as follows. The authority of the ruler cannot be absolute because he is selected by God to defend the faith, maintain justice, and promote the material well-being of his subjects. His rule is limited therefore by the very purpose for which he is ordained by God. Only God, not his appointed ruler, has absolute power over men. Like the divinely ordained powers of fathers over children and masters over servants, rulers are solely the executors of the grant of power from God, subject to his laws; likewise, they are merely ministers of the laws of their realms. Rulers are subject to the positive law of their states, for they cannot rightfully disobey the laws they prescribe for others. Moreover, the powers of the ruler granted by God and executed in accord with his divine purpose are concerned only with the outward conduct of citizens, not with their internal, spiritual life. God alone has power both over the soul and body of man. If a ruler is negligent in the execution of his divinely delegated civil power over the bodies of citizens, God, of course, may intervene. Because rulers are men, and like all men prone to err, citizens have a duty to determine whether government violates the law of God and to disobey any ruler's commands that negate the end for which his office was divinely instituted. Both God and country or state are superior to the ruler and his government. Thus if the ruler acts either to defy God or harm the state, citizens have a duty to disobey. It is a matter of conscience for the individual citizen whether in disobeying the ruler for the reasons just given he should flee the country or remain and accept the penalties for disobedience. Rulers have no rights to the goods of their subjects as their own. Private property precedes the state, for it was ordained by God by the penalty—that is, labor—for sin. Any violation of a citizen's property is an infringement of the divine laws against theft and coveting a neighbor's possessions. The office of the ruler is held in "trust" and the ruler's authority is derived from God through the people. Rulers are therefore accountable to the people as God's trustees for their benefit, and rulers are subject to punishment for wrongdoing which may justifiably include deposition and possibly tyrannicide. Rulers are ordained by God for the people, not the people for rulers, who are only members of the body politic, albeit the chief members, and are not to be identified with the whole body. In the case of tyrannical rule, because the ruler is subject to civil law and its prohibitions against murder, theft, and adultery, he must be brought to civil judgment, just like any other citizen.

The people have several courses of action for dealing with a tyrant; the one they choose depends on the severity of tyranny and the institutions of the country. Nobility and councillors are responsible for calling a king to account, and Ponet viewed the office of constable in England as having been established for this very object. The people also have recourse to the chief minister of God for the excommunication of a tyrant. Execution of a tyrant should only be a last resort, when all other means of curbing his behavior had been exhausted. Ponet justified tyrannicide in such a situation on the grounds of the law of nature and history. By the law of nature the surgical removal of a defective member of the body which threatens the health of the whole is natural and right. From the perspective of history tyrannicide is legitimate because it has occurred through the ages and hence cannot be contrary to God's will.

The Good and Just Commonwealth

How then did the Commonwealthmen conceive of the rightful polity? They were traditionalists who accepted and endorsed the monarchy and the established structure of society. They had little to recommend in respect to concrete governmental policies or institutional change. They were religious crusaders, not political activists or revolutionaries, so they looked to moral regeneration of their countrymen as the primary means of arresting decay and improving the conditions of life; wise and prudent state action was to support this effort. Their ideal was a Christian cooperative commonwealth in which the individualistic pursuit of wealth and power at the expense of the common interest would be discouraged.

High among their priorities for a just society was the eradication of idleness and the encouragement of labor. Idleness would be eliminated so that every individual could labor conscientiously in his calling in a social hierarchy in which the rich and powerful served as God's "stewards" to care for the poor and unfortunate. Idleness—"that hydeouse serpent," in Forrest's characterization—was the foremost vice, the source of all evils.[190] In the words of Crowley: "Idlenes, therefore, maye ryghte well be named / The gate of all mischief that euer was framed."[191] Ponet insisted: "Idleness is a uice wherwith God is offended," the fount of stealing, killing, whoremongering, and other sins.[192] To curtail idleness the author of *Policies to Reduce This Realme of Englande* even recommended that the number of holidays, not counting Sundays, be reduced from thirty-five to twenty, thereby enriching the country to the amount of £600,000.[193] No one should be idle, Latimer intoned: "Every man should labour; yea, though he be a king, yet he must labor."[194] Because of Adam's fall it was man's burden to labor just as birds were ordained to fly.[195] The position of the Commonwealthmen was summed up by Crowley: "But with all myne herte I would wysh that no man wer suffered to eate but such as woulde laboure in thyr vocacion and callyng, accordynge to the rule that Paul gave to the Thessalonians."[196] In addition to Genesis 3:19—"In the sweat of thy face though shalt eat thy bread"—Paul's exhortation in 2 Thessalonians 3:10—"He that laboureth not, let him not eat"—was widely quoted by the Commonwealthmen as biblical authority for the injunction to labor and refrain from idleness.[197] For Christ and his followers were all dedicated laborers. Thus Latimer commented: "Our Saviour Christ, before he began preaching, lived of his occupation; he was a carpenter, and got his living with great labour. Therefore let no man disdain or think scorn to follow him in a mean living, a mean vocation, or a common calling and occupation."[198] Biblical characters who labored, from Cain the ploughman and Abel the shepherd to Paul the tentmaker, were listed at length by Becon.[199]

Labor included both mental and physical activity, neither in God's view superior to the other. No one, rich or poor, high or low, was exempt from strenuous labor in his divinely appointed calling, and each was to work—and be remunerated accordingly—not in his own interest alone but for the good of all. Nor should the individual aspire to rise above his calling or covet the vocation of another, for all were equal before God. Each was urged to be content with his lot in life. Diligent and persevering labor in a social hierarchy of differential tasks and rewards, each conscientiously striving for the common good, was the ideal to be sustained by the appropriate governmental measures. Lever explained the proper social division of labor in the cooperative endeavor joining all in the hierarchy of callings:

> . . . the magistrate by authorytye must dyspose the punyshmente of vyce, and the maynenaunce of vertue.
>
> The ryche man by liberalytye, must dyspose reliefe and comforte vnto the poor and nedye. The Marchaunt by byinge and sell-

ynge, and the craftes man by his occupacion, muste prouyde vnto the common wealthe of necessarye wares, sufficiente plentye. The landlorde by lettyng of fermes must dyspose vnto the tenants necessary lands, and houses of an indifferent rente. The housbandmen by tyllyng of the ground and kepyng of cattel, must dyspose vnto theyr landlordes, dew rentes, and vnto them selves and other, both corne, and other vytals. So euerye man by doynge of hys dutye muste dyspose vnto other that commodytye and benefyte, whiche is committed of god vnto theym to be dysposed vnto other, by the faythful and diligent doyng of thyr dutyes.[200]

In their concern over idleness and the importance of dutiful labor, the Commonwealthmen stressed that the existence of rich and poor and rulers and ruled was the divinely appointed way of things.[201] Crowley maintained that rulers existed not by nature but by God's ordinance for the good of the ruled.[202] Latimer justified the celestial wisdom of dividing the world between rich and poor in two ways.[203] If all were rich no one would do anything. In other words, there would be no one to perform the manual tasks and menial labor so vital for the life of all. Only if the poor existed, moreover, could the rich perform their Christian obligation of charity. Rich and poor (and rulers and ruled), the Commonwealthmen agreed, were morally equal, in Latimer's words: "The poorest ploughman is in Christ equal with the greatest prince that is."[204] Becon invoked the natural equality of all humans, no matter their wealth or rank, in a passage reminiscent of Dudley, criticizing the nobility who gloried in their lineage and despised others of humble origins: "O foolish, rude ignorant people! Why rather do they not consider that both rich and poor, noble and unnoble, high or base, do consist and are made of the same elements, subject unto like diseases, and bond to the same affects? Earth we all are and dust, and unto earth and dust shall we return."[205] Becon, with Latimer, affirmed that God favored neither rich nor poor.[206] Wealth was "indifferent," not in itself good or evil and hence not condemned by God. The use to which riches were put was of sole importance to our Maker. There was no obstacle to the rich man's entering heaven, provided he did not set his heart on acquisition and employed his wealth for worthy ends. He did not have to cast away his fortune in order to be saved. Conversely, poverty itself was no guarantee of salvation, nor was the poor man especially blessed or favored by God. The poor were urged to have faith, be content, accept and adhere to their callings, and labor without complaint or envy. Then they would be just as acceptable to God as the morally virtuous rich.

Those who were divinely selected to be rich and to rule had a sacred duty to employ their wealth and power for the welfare of the poor and the ruled. Brinklow called the rich "stuardes" accountable to God for the use of their land.[207] "Possessioners," Crowley's term for the wealthy, were to remember the divine source of their advantages and the purpose for which they were bestowed and consequently view themselves as "stuardes, and not Lords over theyr possessions."[208] The whole earth belonged to all men, but the rich were divinely appointed trustees for the distribution of its fruits. God would hold the rich accountable for the use of their wealth, for it was conferred on them in trust for the amelioration of the poor and unfortunate, not for their oppression and exploitation. If wealth was employed in this divinely intended way, any desire for common ownership cherished by those of lowly station would be pointless.

The rich as divinely ordained stewards was a continuing theme in the sermons and writings of the Commonwealthmen. The wealthy man for Latimer was "God's treasurer," not the owner of his riches, "but a steward over" them.[209] "Stewards of God and the dispensators of his treasures" was Becon's description of the wealthy, who should not spend their riches on frivolous and useless pastimes, but for their own necessaries and the benefit of the poor.[210] Rulers were also stewards, charged by God with the care and well-being of all citizens. Lever agreed that the rich were stewards and he called officeholders "sheppehardes of the fold, stewardes of the famylye of Chryste," each Christian commonwealth being "the house of hys [God's] famylye."[211] And finally when Ponet termed the king "Goddes stuarde," he no doubt had in mind his emphasis on government as a "trust" for the benefit and wealth of the governed, a point never so exactly put by the Commonwealthmen.[212]

One can only admire the Commonwealthmen for the courage and determination they displayed in their outspoken social protest. They were not acute social analysts and theorists recommending practical policies for rescuing England from the dangerous straits of poverty, unemployment, inflation, and civil discord. Instead, as we might expect from conscience-stricken men of God, they urged a moral and spiritual revolution that would end the unrestrained and individualistic quest for wealth, power, and prestige to which their countrymen had succumbed. Only thus could the realm be restored to cooperative endeavor and well-being and the existing order of hierarchy and privilege be salvaged. But rank and privilege carried weighty obligations toward the less fortunate, and the Commonwealthmen never flinched in strongly denouncing superiors for failing in their duty to inferiors. Only when each person, regardless of station, labored diligently in his calling in true Christian fellowship aimed at the common interest, they insisted, was there any possibility of regenerating the nation.

Yet in their detailed social criticism and heartfelt pleas for a return to Christian principles the Commonwealthmen displayed a rare perceptiveness about the realities of life. Although from their standpoint all men were tarnished by Adam's fall, they nevertheless concluded that humane, enlightened treatment of the many by the few would appreciably ease everyone's burden of sin. If the vast majority were freed from penury and the problems of bare survival, they would have both opportunity and incentive to live full and wholesome lives in peace and harmony. It was thus the pressing responsibility of those in power and authority to fashion and maintain a salubrious social environment. The dominant classes, and government, in particular, must recognize that their true advantage rested firmly on the improvement of the material circumstances of the people. The only alternative to prosperity in the commons was increasing crime and insurrection and the eventual disintegration of the commonwealth. From the mixed motives of Christian charity and prudence, therefore, relief of the economic hardships of the people emerged as the major goal of the state, thereby enabling men, despite their ingrained selfishness, to achieve a modicum of happiness in this perilous passage to the hereafter.

But the promise of renewal of human souls urged by the Commonwealthmen could scarcely compete with the immediate and far-reaching secular changes occurring in English society. If man was indeed as selfish as they believed, moral appeals could hardly divert such egoism and drive for personal aggrandizement. Social theory could only guide practical policies of amelioration by accepting man as he was, sinful or not, and making the best of it, or such was the approach of Sir Thomas Smith, neither a utopian like More nor an ethical crusader like Latimer. Nonetheless, the vision of the Commonwealthmen was a noble one, noble in that it was uncompromising in highlighting the social iniquities of the age, uncompromising in the unhesitating assignment of blame for the injustices, and uncompromising in the demands for social betterment. The Commonwealthmen were among the first critics inspired by the social message of Christ to demand their country's rejuvenation.

9   Sir Thomas Smith's New "Moral Philosophy"

Sir Thomas Smith (1513–1577) no doubt sympathized with some of the views of the Commonwealthmen and he is often linked with them.[1] He too was country bred and Cambridge educated. Unlike them, however, he was not a cleric but combined a keen intellect with extensive governmental service.[2] A shrewd and experienced man of affairs, his social and political outlook was more secular and rational than it was religious and moralistic, and his analysis of events and proposals for reform was both more incisive and more practical. He can be called the first political economist, indeed the founder of that science, and hence he is worthy of remembrance and close study.

Born in what is now Saffron Walden, Essex, the son of a farmer, Smith went up to Queen's College, Cambridge, where he remained a fellow, and gained a reputation as a brilliant classicist, accomplished orator, and influential teacher. "The flower of the University of Cambridge," one of his former students, the noted geographer Richard Eden, praised him.[3] Among other pupils were John Ponet, Roger Ascham, and John Aylmer. Through the intercession at court of Dr. William Butts of Gonville Hall, who had also befriended Latimer, Smith and John Cheke were awarded exhibitions for study abroad. In 1540 the first Regius chairs were established at Cambridge. Smith was appointed Professor of Civil Law and Cheke Professor of Greek. Because Smith knew little law he spent the next two years studying the subject in Orléans, Paris, and Padua before assuming his professorial duties. In 1543 he became vice-chancellor of the University and in 1547 provost of Eton and dean of Carlisle. Capable of reading six languages, he energetically studied mathematics, chemistry, and medicine as well as philosophy, law, and theology. A passion for architecture led him to design his country house, High Hill, near Saffron

Walden, one of the most distinguished examples of residential planning of the sixteenth century.

Smith entered Parliament after the death of Henry VIII and held his seat during the reigns of Edward VI, Mary, and Elizabeth. Principal secretary of state from 1547 to 1549 during Somerset's protectorate and knighted in 1548, he specialized in financial and economic policy, becoming an expert in the field. Although living in retirement under Mary, he received an annual pension of 100 pounds from her, apparently as a reward for financial advice given to the lord chancellor Stephen Gardiner. Under Elizabeth he served as ambassador to France from 1562 to 1566 and again in 1572, when his astute diplomacy was climaxed by the Treaty of Blois; he thus gained the favor of the sovereign, who had never cared for him, a feeling reciprocated by Smith. Increasingly intimate with Cecil, despite an early rupture, and a friend of Francis Walsingham and Thomas Wilson, Smith served as principal secretary until 1576, when a fatal illness, probably cancer of the throat, forced him to retire. He died the following year. Despite Strype's comment in 1698 that "by his great wisdom and moderation, though he sometimes fell, he fell softly, and fell to rise again with more glory," Smith's governmental career was not commensurate with his exceptional talents.[4] He lacked the vigor, the self-confident toughness, and the ability to manage men, so crucial to successful statesmanship. Not only did he lack powerful friends among the great but he also was too outspoken and arrogant in personal relationships to advance his public career.

Smith found time to write a variety of works, although only three were published during his lifetime: treatises on a new pronunciation of Greek and on English orthography appeared in 1542 and in 1571 he published a book promoting a cherished project for the colonialization of Ireland. In addition, in 1554 he probably produced an important economic memorandum, "For the Understanding of the Exchange"; he also composed verse and translated the *Psalms*. In 1561 Smith wrote a dialogue on the perils of Queen Elizabeth's spinsterhood, and in 1562 a monograph, "The Wages of a Roman Footsoldier," appeared.[5] The two works on which his fame now rests, *A Discourse of the Commonweal of This Realm of England* and *De republica Anglorum*, were published posthumously, in 1581 and 1583, respectively. Both were relatively short books, of approximately equal length, something over forty thousand words.

The *Discourse* was issued anonymously in 1581 by "W. S.," possibly Smith's nephew William Smith, and dedicated to Queen Elizabeth. The author apparently revised the manuscript (as well as that of *Republica*) in 1576, the year before his death. Circulated in manuscript before publication, the 1581 edition has been reprinted four times, together with four other editions, including Mary Dewar's recent version. Before Dewar's rewarding scholarship, the *Discourse* had usually been attributed to John Hales (d. 1571), a member of parliament and enclosure commissioner who is often included among the Commonwealthmen.[6] Dewar's case for Smith's authorship is most convincing and now widely accepted. Smith probably drafted the book at Eton College in the three months from July through September 1549; he had been forced to retire there by Somerset because of his steadfast opposition to the debasement of the currency. Perturbed by the disorders of the realm, Smith wrote to his colleague Cecil on 19 July 1549 of "the miserable estate, our commonwealth" and probably intended the manuscript (a remedy for Somerset's disastrous economic program) for Cecil's eyes alone.[7]

With the *Discourse* Smith founded the science of political economy. Nothing quite like the volume had appeared prior to Bodin in either English or Continental thought.[8] One can only conclude that Smith in the *Discourse* was a true pioneer, an evaluation admitted by historians of economic thought. A "remarkable" book was the verdict of Eli Heckscher, "the first work representing, on the whole, the outlook of a mature mercantilism."[9] In the opinion of George Unwin the *Discourse* was "the most advanced statement of economic thought in Tudor England."[10] A trifle less laudatory was Schumpeter's remark that "most of it was sound common sense" and that "in its implications, it approaches the status of analytic work."[11] More generous is Terence Hutchison's recent appraisal of Smith's outlook as a harbinger of the independent subject of economics, separated from philosophical and moral concerns.[12] Nevertheless, despite these favorable evaluations, the full measure of Smith's accomplishment remains to be taken.

Smith's second major work, *De republica Anglorum,* more widely read than the *Discourse,* presented a descriptive analysis of the English constitution, structure of government, and society. Written in Toulouse in the mid-sixties while Smith was ambassador to France and originally intended to introduce French readers to the English polity, the work was probably touched up by Smith in 1576, as was the *Discourse.* The *Republica* was published first in 1583, with fifteen later reprintings, four Latin editions, and late seventeenth-century Dutch and German translations of several chapters. Portions of the work devoted to English society seem to have been taken from William Harrison's *Description of England;* Smith probably read an early draft manuscript, perhaps receiving it from the author himself, a friend and neighbor in Essex. To the student of Tudor state and society *Republica* is indispensable, as Maitland says:

"No one would think of writing about the England of Elizabeth's day without paying heed to what was written about the matter by her learned and accomplished Secretary of State."[13]

Although I will ultimately concentrate on the *Discourse*, my examination of Smith begins with the *Republica*—written sixteen years later—because it provides the context of political and social ideas necessary for understanding the earlier work. Despite the time separating the two books and their different subjects (the one on economics, the other on the English constitution), they do not appear to be substantively at odds. A common characteristic of both volumes that cannot be overemphasized is their unmistakable secularism and rationalism. Religious and ethical considerations are at best peripheral. Far from being a dry legalistic work, the *Republica* displays a profound interest in the principles of political science and in political sociology—the social structure of political power. This approach is not surprising in light of Smith's explanation, written from Toulouse in 1565 to a friend: "I have written it moreover in the language of our own country, in a style midway between the historical and the philosophical; giving it the shape in which I imagined that Aristotle wrote of the many Greek commonwealths, books which are no longer extant."[14] From our standpoint the significant section is book 1, especially the first half dealing learnedly and perceptively with the nature and origins of the state and its varieties. The ideas in these pages tend to confirm, strengthen, and illuminate some of those of the *Discourse*. The second half of book 1 treats the English social formation—nobility, gentlemen, yeoman, and lesser commons—as it pertained to the exercise of political power. Only then (books 2 and 3) did Smith discuss formal constitutional, governmental, and legal arrangements. On all these subjects it seems improbable that Smith's views had fundamentally altered over the years, except by way of refinement. After all, well before writing the *Discourse* he had been immersed in the classics and history, studied law, lectured and tutored in the subject at Cambridge, and had become thoroughly acquainted with the corridors of power in London. The two works can therefore perhaps best be treated as complementing each other, forming a harmonious intellectual whole, book 1 of the *Republica* forming the context for the *Discourse*. I shall begin with the "politics" of Smith and within that setting explore his "economics." Together they may be said to constitute his "political economy."

Theory of the State in the *Republica*

Throughout the first book of the *Republica* Smith like Aristotle employed the comparative method and showed a keen appreciation of social change and the dynamics of human society.[15] He began by adopting the Aristotelian tripartite classification of commonwealths in terms of the differing natures of their governments: the rule of one, the few, the many—monarchy, aristocracy, democracy.[16] These are the three simple forms of commonwealth or constitutional types, each of which is subject to corruption and may degenerate into tyranny, oligarchy, and ochlocracy, or mob rule. In reality, Smith observed, commonwealths are mixtures of at least two of these simple modes of government but are identified by the form that tends to predominate.[17] By "common wealth" Smith meant the state in the institutional sense, as we shall shortly see, and he distinguished government from state as part to whole. Government is the institutional part of the state ruling all its members or citizens.

The government of every simple form of commonwealth is thought by its citizens to be just and lawful. The "just" in each is "the profite of the ruling and most strong part" or, in other words, the interest of government, whether it is that of one, the few, or the many.[18] On his identification of justice with ruling-class interest, Smith acknowledged his agreement with Thrasymachus in book 1 of Plato's *Republic*, who, he said, was not as misguided as the Platonic Socrates suggested, a refreshing instance of Smith's candor and analytic acumen.[19] He added, however, that if it is to be maintained that justice is always perceived by citizens of a specific state to be in the interest of the ruling class, then we must always mean the genuine interest or profit, not merely the appearance of interest or profit. On this point Smith seemed to accept the correction made by Socrates to Thrasymachus's original formulation and agreed to by the latter.

Smith next considered the corrupt forms—tyranny, oligarchy, ochlocracy—of the three simple states, although we have to wait until his treatment of king and tyrant to learn the basis of his differentiation of corrupt from uncorrupt types.[20] The uncorrupt forms (Smith only deals with monarchy) are those supported by the people, ruled in accordance with law and fairness, and aimed at the profit or interest of the people as much as at that of the ruling class or governing part.[21] How do we reconcile this view with his previous position that justice was always in the interest of the governing class, no matter its nature? Smith failed to raise the question, but he might have responded that the authentic interest in contrast to the mere appearance of the interest of the ruling class in each of the simple uncorrupted states was always to promote the interest of the governed. A tyrant, on the contrary, was solely concerned with his own narrow self-interest to the detriment of the common interest, a spurious interest as against a genuine interest; consequently he undermined his power and endangered his grip on government. Smith was probably familiar with Aristotle's reflections on the "good" and "bad" tyrant in book 5 of the *Politics*. The good tyrant, if he wished to survive and maintain his power, Aristotle concluded, would act no differently from the just and beneficent king. Smith therefore equated the authentic interest of government and the governing class of whatever kind with the common interest. Thus it is always to government's distinct advantage to safeguard and promote the interest of the governed. Smith's stance on this matter did not differ from that of Fortescue, Dudley, Starkey, and the Commonwealthmen. Becon offered the endorsement of biblical authority for the principle, whereas Smith relied on the secular wisdom of the ancients and the prudence of an officer of state.[22] Without citing him, Smith, moreover, seemed to agree with Cicero that justice and the true common interest were never in conflict. All viable states embodied justice to some degree.

Smith explicitly addressed the fundamental question of the just and rightful in a corrupt state.[23] Government of a corrupt state is evil and unjust, and the laws "as most like they be alwayes to maintain estate," that is, to uphold evil and unjust rule.[24] Is it just for a citizen to obey such a government and its laws, or is civil disobedience and resistance under a corrupt regime the just course of action? As we might imagine, the ever-cautious Smith hesitated to commit himself openly on this critical matter. He might have replied as did the Commonwealth preachers that our duty is always to obey the higher authorities unless we are commanded to violate God's law. In that case only passive obedience is licit. Or Smith might have agreed with his former pupil John Ponet that the evil laws of a corrupt state contravene the laws of God and of nature. The citizen is thereby relieved of all obligation to obey evil laws, in fact, he has the moral duty to disobey them and may, depending on circumstances, actively resist the government attempting to enforce them and resort to insurrection and tyrannicide if necessary.[25] Smith, however, never invoked the divine or natural law. Instead, he pointed out that in the past under tyrannical rule great men—citing Dion against Dionysus of Syrause, Thrasybulus against the Thirty Tyrants of Athens, and Brutus and Cassius against Tarquin the Proud—resisted and overthrew corrupt governments. Then, possibly thinking of the famous passage that the "end secures the means" of chapter 18 of Machiavelli's *Prince*, Smith commented that ordinary people judged such actions to be just or unjust according to whether their result was successful or unsuccessful.[26] But Smith, perhaps taking his cue from Machiavelli's *Discourses* or from Cicero's *De officiis*, suggested that "learned" men judged such actions by the intentions of the actors and "the estate of the time then present."[27] So, neither justifying nor condemning civil disobedience in a corrupt state on moral or religious grounds, Smith seemed to be purely pragmatic and utilitarian in handling the problem. His wary conclusion was similarly prudent: "Certaine it is that it is alwayes a doubtfull and hasardous matter to meddle with the chaunging of the lawes and governement, or to disobey the orders of the rule of government, which a man doth finde alreadie established."[28]

The message of much of Smith's circumlocution seems obvious enough. The government of any state, if it is to exist and be strong, must have the common interest as its first and foremost aim; that is, the government must seek security from foreign interference, maintain order, protect property, and ensure the material well-being of the citizens. To the extent that the government succeeds, it is just in the sense of giving to each his due and assuring fair treatment for all. Every enduring state is just up to a point; it must be just in order to survive. Unless a state protects and promotes the common interest, it will not last long, and before its demise it will become increasingly weak, the prey of more powerful states, incapable of ensuring law and order, and plagued by insurrection. The idea that justice in some minimal form is the foundation of all governments and states—even a gang of thieves—is at least as old as Cicero's speculations, although justice is distinguished from narrow self-interest. In the long term, a happy life defined as the predominance of lasting and constructive pleasures over pains depends on some modicum of justice: respect for life, possessions, promises, the truth, as well as mutual helpfulness and charity toward the unfortunate. Smith seemed to adhere to this view, which as we shall see was central to his *Discourse*, in that he concluded that pleasures and pains were those actually felt by people as constituted, not as they might be reshaped by some all-powerful and authoritative agency, religious or secular.[29] To his mind the chief purpose of the state was the common interest, conceived of as the happiness of the people, that is, the increase of their pleasures and the decrease of their pains. England in 1549, he might have argued, was no longer as just a state as it should have been because the common interest was weakened by the mad scramble of acquisitive, self-seeking individuals freed from secular and religious restraints, to the jeopardy of the greatest number. A secular and utilitarian conception of justice and the state and their relationship was the informing design of his edifice of social and economic ideas.

In neither *Discourse* nor *Republica* did Smith use *state* to designate commonwealth, as did Starkey and Ponet.[30] Nevertheless, the political vocabulary of the *Republica* was perhaps as important as theirs. Like his predecessors, he frequently used "kingdom," "realm," "country," and

"nation." "Common wealth," however, was the word he employed most
often to denote the state rather than the common interest. From the title
De republica Anglorum, it is clear that like More he identified commonwealth with *res publica.* At the end of the chapter in which he defined
"common wealth," he referred to it in terms of both *res publica* and *politeia,* the latter the Greek word for constitution in the broadest sense, for
civic body or state.[31] It was the title of Plato's dialogue, customarily translated *Republic.* The conventional "body politic," in Smith's version "politique bodie" or "bodie politique," was another of his expressions for commonwealth as state.[32] Unlike previous thinkers, Smith frequently used
"government" in the abstract, collective sense, defining it in effect as that
part of the state that ruled or exercised "the supreme and highest authoritie of commaundment . . . which doth controwle, correct all other members of the common wealth."[33]

Indeed, one could argue that Smith held an incipient idea of sovereignty in his view that parliament was the "most high and absolute
power of the realme of Englande."[34] By this he meant the king in parliament. Parliament was the "hole head and bodie of the realme of Englande."[35] Parliament incorporated the head—the king—and the body of
the commonwealth, that is, the nobility and commons. Head and body
thus represented in parliament constituted the supreme power, the source
of all lawmaking and taxation.[36] England then was a mixed monarchy.
Although Smith never applied the term in this context, he evidently accepted the existing arrangement as being far preferable to the absolutist
dominium regale so criticized by Fortescue. While nobility, commons,
and king shared in lawmaking and taxation, the king alone possessed the
prerogative powers of conducting foreign affairs, making war and peace,
regulating the coinage, and appointing chief officers and magistrates.[37]
Bodin's conception of sovereignty was not too distant from Smith's formulation.[38] But whereas the sovereign power for Bodin was subject to the
laws of God and nature and certain fundamental laws of the land, Smith
did not mention such moral limitations. His approach appears to have
been completely secular.[39]

Smith therefore distinguished government from the state (as did Bodin) and government became the defining characteristic of the state. He
occasionally identified "policy" with "government," for example, in the
full title: *De republica Anglorum: The Maner of Gouernement or Policie
of the Realme of England.*[40] His frequent use of "administration" with
the meaning of the management of public affairs and sometimes of government is interesting; this usage appeared previously in the Latin of
Fortescue's *De natura* but only became common in this latter sense from

the end of the seventeenth century.[41] Like Elyot, Smith differentiated "commons" from *populus,* or "people," the latter referring to "the whole body and the three estates of the common wealth."[42] He did not use "commynalty" in either *Discourse* or *Republica.*

Also important is Smith's use of "society" or "societie." With the exception of Fortescue and Starkey, both of whom employed the word in passing, Smith was the first of the writers examined to do so in a significant sense.[43] The definition of "common wealth" in the *Republica* begins by calling it "a society or common doing of a multitude of free men."[44] So it seems that "society" was his equivalent of the Greek *koinonia* and the Latin *societas,* any group of persons—household, village, cult, club, commercial combination, state—sharing something in common and having a similar objective. For Smith household or family was a "society" in this sense, as was the commonwealth and presumably the village.[45] More interesting was his use of "societie civill" and "civill societie" to describe cities, towns, nations, and kingdoms; this is possibly the first use of the expression in English and it is certainly the first among the authors surveyed.[46] Smith explicitly calls a "common wealth" a "societie civill."[47] The state then is a civil society, an association of men for a common purpose organized by means of government and law, thus distinguished from other human societies. "Civil society," so denoted, of course became a convention in the next century.[48] In sum, despite his failure to use the word *state,* as did Starkey and Ponet, Smith's political vocabulary, no less than theirs, contained the ingredients of the modern conception of the state. The evolution of terminology is perhaps reflective of the slow but unmistakable process of modern state formation then taking place in England.

Smith in book 1 of the *Republica* went beyond either Starkey or Ponet in his definition of the state and reference to its purpose. He secularized the state, assigning it no higher moral or religious end. The dual medieval idea of the state's aim—religious and secular—disappeared in Smith. The full force and novelty of his position can best be appreciated by comparing his definition of the state with those of five other authors: Cicero, Bodin, Elyot, Morison, and Starkey:

> Cicero: an assemblage of people in large numbers associated in an agreement in respect to justice and a partnership for the common interest.[49]

> Bodin, 1576: a rightful government of many families and that which is common to them under a sovereign power. . . . a commonwealth without sovereign power to unite all its several mem-

bers, whether families, colleges, or corporate bodies, is not a true commonwealth.[50]

Elyot, 1531: a body living, compact or made of sundry estates and degrees of men, which is disposed by the order of equity and governed by the rule of reason.[51]

Morison, 1536: a number of cities, towns, shires that all agree upon one law and one head, united and knit together by the observation of the laws.[52]

Starkey, 1530s: the gud ordur & pollycy by gud lawys stablyschyd & set, & by hedys & rularys put in effect by the wyche the hole body as by reson ys gouernyd & rulyd, to the intent that thys multytude of pepul & hole commynalty so helthy & so welthy havyng convenyent abundaunce of al thyngys necessary for the mayntenance therof, may wyth dew honowr reverence & love relygyously worschype god, as fountayn of al gudnes maker and governour of al thys world, every one also dowyng hys duty to other wyth brotherly love one lovyng a nother as membrys & partys of one body.[53]

Smith, 1565: a society or common doing of a multitude of free men collected together and united by common accord and covenauntes among themselves, for the conservation of themselves in peace as in warre.[54]

Smith again wrote of the state in terms of "common and mutual consent for their conservation."[55] Unlike the others (Morison excepted), he did not refer in his definition to justice, right, equity, the rule of reason, God, or morality. The defense and promotion of Christian worship and values seemed to have no part in his conception of the state, unlike the position of Starkey and the Commonwealthmen. States, however, that aimed at the authentic common interest of the citizens were more just than those whose goal was a spurious common interest, one that in actuality was the self-interest of the rulers.

Possibly the most rewarding contrast is with Elyot. Elyot tended to emphasize the organic nature of the state, which rested on the "estates and degrees" to which the people belonged rather than directly on individuals. Morison also saw not individuals but corporations such as "cities, towns, and shires" as the foundation of the state, as did Bodin. On the contrary, Smith seemed closer in spirit to Hobbes than to medieval corporativism, conceptualizing the state as a "society" or collection of individuals who as individuals agreed directly—not indirectly, as with Elyot and Morison, through orders to which individuals belonged—to unite for

their common interest by covenanting—giving their "common and mu-
tuall consent"—each with every other.[56] The basic units of Smith's state
were thus the unmediated consenting individuals acting for their own interests. These were persons who, he asserted in another context, knew
"howe to demeane and order their matters, best for the conservation of
themselves, and ech of their families, generally and particularly."[57] A
state or "politique body" was composed of the bodies of its citizens.[58] It
was in effect a mixture of these individuals, not a compound in which
their individuality disappeared in a new whole. This individualism expressed in the idea of the state as a collection of persons consenting by
mutual covenants sets Smith apart not only from Elyot and Morison but
also from Cicero, Bodin, and Starkey.

Smith nevertheless agreed with the last three that the object of the
union was the common interest. Before giving his definition, he stressed
that the goal of the simple uncorrupt commonwealth was the "common
profit" as distinct from the "private profit" of the rulers. And in his definition this "common profit" apparently meant "conservation of themselves in peace as well as in warre," a point twice repeated. "Common
profit" or common interest and "conservation" in the context signified
more than "bare Preservation" in Hobbes's words.[59] Smith's terms had to
do with the individual's quest for honor and gain, with his "ease" and
"pleasure," and with "quiet," social peace and security.[60] The preservation
of lives and possessions of citizens and their material well-being were the
referents of "common profit" and "conservation." The three decades or
more separating the pronouncements of Smith and Elyot might as well
have been three centuries in respect to the diversity of outlook reflected
by their definitions of the state. Smith would probably have seconded the
view of the anonymous author of *Policies to Reduce This Realme of Englande* (1548) who defined "the Floreshing estate of a realm" as one
which "consisteth cheifly in being strong against theirvasion of eneymies,
not molested with cyvile warres the people being wealthie, and not oppressed with famyn nor penury of victuelles."[61]

A final element of Smith's definition of the state warranting brief attention is his use of "free men," a term absent in the other definitions.
Free men, not bondmen or unfree men, agreed to institute the state for
the advancement of their common interest.[62] Somewhat later he identified "subjects and citizens of the common wealth" with "free men" and
explicitly excluded women (with the exception of those who inherited a
title such as queen), children, and bondmen "who can beare no rule nor
jurisdiction over freemen, as they who be taken but as instruments of the
goods and possessions of others."[63] Bondmen, according to his classifi-

cation, were "slaves, serfs, apprentices, and servaunts or serving men or women," the latter group consisting of "all servaunts, labourers, and other not maryed."[64] Except that these servants and laborers were hired for wages by the year and bound to their master during that period, they unlike apprentices were "full free men and women." Nevertheless, they were part of the household, economically dependent on their employer, instruments of a private interest, and therefore could not be full citizens of the state, unlike others of lowly status who in fact were free men and full citizens but without the right to vote. This last category of laborers, as distinct from bondmen, included free and independent day laborers, merchants and retailers without landed property, copyholders, and small artisans.[65] These, Smith wrote, existed "onelie to be ruled, not to rule other," although they could not be "altogether neglected" since in corporate towns they were eligible for jury duty and in the country served as church wardens and constables.[66] To be differentiated from these free laborers, bondmen (apart from apprentices) were probably resident domestic servants and "servants in husbandry" in rural areas.[67] Smith then, referring to "free men" in his definition and excluding bondmen, made explicit what the other thinkers undoubtedly agreed to but saw no need to articulate. He alone did so possibly because he wished to emphasize that the foundation of the state was the consent of mutually covenanting individuals as individuals, unmediated by the corporate orders to which they belonged.

Among the most obvious general characteristics of Smith's conception of the state in the *Republica* are therefore its secularism, rationalism, economism, and individualism, all qualities that, as we shall see, also mark his outlook in the *Discourse*. In a disarmingly matter-of-fact and secular fashion Smith in the *Republica* conceived of the state as an institutional complex aimed at advancing and securing the economic interests of the individuals composing it. One more noticeable feature of the work (already touched on) of relevance to his position in the *Discourse* must be considered, but as a matter for speculation, not definitive conclusion. This was his use of "societie civill" and "common wealth" for the state. Why unlike Starkey and Ponet did Smith fail to employ the word *state*? We know that the use of *state* by humanists of the time was not a rarity and that *l'état* and *lo stato* were already fairly common on the Continent.[68] We might have expected a learned professor of civil law and an experienced man of affairs like Smith to follow suit. He must have been familiar with the book of his former pupil John Ponet. Moreover, Smith's friend and colleague Thomas Wilson employed *state* institutionally in his dialogue on usury, published after the drafting of *Republica* but before the revision of 1576.[69]

If anyone was favorably placed to use *state*, it was Smith. That he relied in *Republica* on "common wealth" for *state*, defining it as a "society," may be suggestive. "Common wealth," as the word literally denotes, was the common economic interest or profit; and in the institutional sense of *state*, as Smith said in his definition, a commonwealth consisted of individuals sharing a common end, composing a society or fraternity designed to advance that economic interest. Smith may very well have observed that the use by his contemporaries of *state* designated a definite legalistic and jurisdictional whole. But, in contrast, he seemed to be primarily interested, in the *Discourse*, at any rate, in the interrelationships of the social division of labor that resulted in the production of common wealth or profit. The basic unit of production was the household, the archetypal "society," according to Smith in *Republica*, the origin of other kinds of societies.[70] Unlike the household, however, each of the other societies he mentioned—cities, towns, nations, and kingdoms—was not simply a society but a "societie civill," a society organized by government and law. He unambiguously equated "common wealth" or *state* with civil society. Was Smith's preference as well as the evident fondness of later English thinkers for *commonwealth, society,* and *civil society* over *state* possibly a result of their conclusion that the state was fundamentally an economic arena of profit-seeking individuals competing and cooperating for the production of wealth?[71] Did their vocabulary then reflect the gradual absorption of the English state by the economy? Did they choose these terms because the dominant propertied classes in parliament were fashioning a political community or civil society to which the state was increasingly subordinated, in roughly the same way that ancient Roman republican aristocrats thought of themselves "much less as administrators than possessors" of the state?[72] Although answers to these questions must be purely conjectural, an assessment of the *Discourse* helps to support such a line of argument. For there Smith was primarily concerned with a society of individuals making profits and incurring losses in the activities of production, distribution, and exchange, all within a framework of law and order imposed by the actors themselves (either directly or by proxy in parliament) through their government, in essence a civil society.

The *Discourse and Its Notion of Human Nature*

With the *Discourse of the Commonwealth of This Realm of England* Smith launched a remarkable and even revolutionary mode of analysis, that of political economy. Nothing like it in either substance or form had appeared before. In the *Discourse* he defined the common interest largely in economic terms and offered an economic conception of the state (as he does in the *Republica*) emphasizing worldly considerations, thus completing a tendency already observed in his Tudor predecessors. The *Discourse* was written in July–September 1549 during "some vacation from other business," apparently a reference to his rustication to Eton College.[73] The work was essentially a treatise on inflation, the so-called "dearth," its causes and remedies. Smith opened by explaining that he was responding to "the manifold complaints of men touching the decay of this Commonweal that we be in, moved more at this present than of long time past has been heard."[74] He proposed to do so by describing the "griefs"— mainly of an economic kind—that had produced these complaints, by identifying their causes, and by proposals for reform, allotting a dialogue or part of the work to each of the topics.[75]

Smith made it clear at the outset that he intended the book to be part of "Moral Philosophy" since it pertained to the "policy or good government of a Commonweal."[76] Later he explained that moral philosophy was devoted to the proper ethical guidance of individual and family and "how a city or realm or any other Commonweal should be well ordered and governed in time of peace and also war."[77] He saw the *Discourse* as a modest effort in the spirit of Plato's *Republic* to apply knowledge to the problems of government. In doing so Smith thus continued the traditional intellectual preoccupation with the question of counsel.[78] The aim of the *Discourse*, however, differs markedly from both the intention of Plato and the traditional understanding of moral philosophy. The ordering of state and society so as to create the proper conditions for the realization of the morally virtuous life was one of the commonly accepted goals of moral philosophy, certainly in keeping with the views of Plato, Aristotle, and St. Thomas Aquinas. An important part of moral philosophy during the Middle Ages and Renaissance was the popular mirror-of-princes literature, central to which was the theme of a well-ordered polity dependent on a morally upright and sagacious ruler whose education was of critical importance; an example is the moralizing of Erasmus in *The Education of the Christian Prince* (1516). In a way Smith shattered this paradigmatic mode of discourse. He may occasionally have paid lip service to moral concerns, but he made no reference to the education of the prince or the structure of his rule, focusing instead on how governmental policy could best handle deteriorating economic conditions. While "commonwealth" figured in the title, the term appears infrequently in the text.

Any idea of the state in the *Discourse* seems to have been absorbed by an elementary notion of the economy. Politics, indeed, appears to be all but reduced to economics and the manipulation of the economy by government for the advancement of the common interest defined by the people in their parliament. Smith in the *Discourse* was far more interested in the sphere of economic activity (to be called "civil society" in the distant future) than in the state in any legalistic, jurisdictional, or constitutional sense.

If Smith thus transformed the common meaning of moral philosophy, his employment of the dialogue form may also have indicated something of the novelty of the enterprise. His use of the dialogue for a technical subject—even for a compendium of economic advice—was not extraordinary. We only have to think of Machiavelli's *Art of War*, Christopher St. German's *Doctor and Student*, and Thomas Wilson's *Discourse upon Usury*. But a unique formal characteristic of Smith's dialogue was its dramatis personae, its five active participants: a knight, merchant, doctor of divinity, husbandman, and craftsman. Smith's conclave included a single learned individual and "members of every estate that . . . grieved nowadays" who in congenial debate would arrive at the truth of the matters under discussion.[79] For a distinguished Cambridge scholar, Essex landlord, and man of affairs to compose a dialogue on "moral philosophy" whose cast of five included two gentlemen and three practical men of the lower orders, all making positive contributions to the conversation, was uncommon. This approach seems to have little precedent in intellectual dialogues and perhaps reflects the radical character of the work. Smith himself posed as a mere *rapporteur* who "will declare unto you what communication a knight told me was between him and certain other persons of late about this matter," the troubles besetting England.[80] We have in effect the record of the meeting of a "dining society" of four stalwarts of the local community and an outsider in the person of the doctor, all spending an evening of lively discourse over venison pasty and claret. The knight, a landlord and justice of the peace, had spent the day with his fellow justices of the county testifying before a royal commission on enclosures. After the rigors of the meeting, he was taking refreshment with "an honest husbandman whom for his honesty and good discretion I loved very well."[81] Perhaps he was a tenant of the knight, obviously a middling farmer, possibly a yeoman. The scene may have been Saffron Walden, Essex, where Smith was born and near which he lived. They were joined by the merchant, "a man of good estimation and substance," and then by Doctor Pandotheus (to worship or stretch out to God), the only individual mentioned by name.[82] He was a highly respected theologian, probably a Cambridge don, who voiced Smith's own views, taking the leading role in the conversation, summarizing the points made, and drawing conclusions. The last participant was a master craftsman, a capper or manufacturer of caps, like the others a pillar of the community, "an honest man."[83] Possibly for the first time in English history, or for that matter in world history, we have in literary form a symposium of those whose vital economic interests were at stake in the ills of their country: representatives of the gentry and clergy and lower-class spokesmen for the mercantile, agricultural, and manufacturing sectors.

A final formal characteristic of the *Discourse* deserves comment. Although Smith was obviously at ease with the classics, he did not rely excessively on them and he was not overburdened by their authority. Except for passing references to Erasmus and *Utopia*, Smith cited no modern authors or works.[84] Plato, Aristotle, and Cicero were his most frequent ancient sources. He mentioned the "divine philosopher" Plato (along with Cicero) for perceiving that men were not born to themselves alone and praised him for the idea of the fusion of knowledge and political power symbolized by the philosopher-king; Smith also upheld Plato's notion that all men were covetous of money.[85] Aristotle, "the sharpest philosopher of wit that ever was," was named in four passages—the only instances—for his insight that coinage was devised simply as a convenient means of exchange.[86] Smith also credits "that wise and politic Senator" and "great clerk" Cicero with the view that a state is held together by reward and punishment and that no law can satisfy everyone but can at best work to the advantage of the most and to the disadvantage of the fewest.[87] Among the other ancients Smith cited incidentally were Columella, Vegetius, Vitruvius, Pythagoras, Solon, Pliny, Pomponius, Mela, Cato, and Polydorus.[88] Smith was clearly his own man. He adhered to literary convention by paying lip service to the ancients as seals of approval for certain points, but he was by no means substantively indebted to them. This admirable independence of mind may suggest an awareness of the new approach to moral philosophy he was inaugurating.

Smith's economic analysis and recommendations seem to rest squarely on his conception of man. Although he never systematically treated human nature, the few remarks on the subject in the *Discourse* supplemented by reference to the *Republica* leave the reader with few doubts about his viewpoint. At the beginning of the *Discourse*, citing Cicero (presumably *De officiis*) to the effect that men were not created for themselves alone but for the benefit of their country, parents, kin, friends, and neighbors, Smith concluded that of all living creatures human beings are most like God and have a natural potential for doing good.[89] But the astute and ever-practical Smith knew that in reality this potential was seldom realized. Tarnished by selfishness, he wrote in *Republica*, man is a frail vessel who cannot hold absolute and uncontrolled power "without swelling into too much pride and insolence."[90] Physically "the nature of man is never to stand still in one maner of estate, but to grow from the lesse to the more, and so to decay from the more againe to the lesse, till it come to the fatall end and destruction, with many turnes and turmoyles of sicknesse and recovering, seldom standing in perfect health."[91] Men were of such base nature that they must always war against themselves. Their chief aim in society and state was "honour and profitt."[92] In any undertaking, according to the *Discourse*, each seeks to enhance his advantage and increase his profit.[93] Buying cheap and selling dear apparently was a behavioral law of man's fallen nature.[94] All were naturally avaricious and would follow the path promising the greatest remuneration. None of this deviated from a conventional Christian outlook. By his fallen nature man was weak and selfish, ambitious, avaricious and lustful, an egoist with little concern for the good of others. These few scattered passages indicating Smith's basically Augustinian view of human nature would have been endorsed by the Commonwealthmen.

Despite his apparent acceptance of a common Christian position, Smith was saying much more. Since humans are fundamentally egoists who cannot be changed, they must accept that nature and instead of trying futilely to remold the imperfect human raw material use that very selfishness for the welfare of all. "Can we devise," Smith queried rhetorically, "that all covetousness may be taken from men."[95] "No, no more," he replied, "than we can make man to be without ire, without gladness, without fear, and without all affections. What then? We must take away from men the occasion of their covetousness in this part." (The latter is a reference to the avarice that induced enclosure and the conversion of arable to pasture for the production of livestock.) Since all are motivated to seek their own profit and since this human propensity cannot be eradicated, Smith argued, the monetary advantage of the cultivator of arable must be made equal to that of the enclosing graziers and sheepmasters.

Thus rather than attempting the remodeling of man, the lover of lucre, that very love must be manipulated so as to encourage farmers to return to the plow. Governmental policies and laws should aim at channeling the pursuit of narrow self-interest for the good of the whole state. Far from being an inherently destructive force, self-interest could be in Smith's view the dynamic of the economy if properly utilized by government to advance the common interest. Smith took pains to explain the principles to be followed by government in the matter:

> We must understand also that all things that should be done in a Commonweal be not to be forced, or to be constrained by the straight penalties of the law, but some so and some other by allure-ment and rewards rather. For what law can compel men to be indus-trious in travail and labor of his body or studious to learn any sci-ence or knowledge of the mind? To these things men may be well provoked, encouraged, and allured as if they that be industrious and painful be rewarded well for their pains and be suffered to take gains and wealth as reward for their labors. . . . Take these rewards from them and go about to compel them by laws thereto, what man will plow or dig the ground or exercise any manual art where is any pain? Or who will adventure overseas for any merchandise? Or use any faculty wherein any peril or danger should be, seeing his re-ward shall be no more than his that sits still?[96]

After this pronouncement, Smith cited a letter of Cicero to Atticus to the effect that the state is maintained by reward and pain.[97] Citizens should be moved to do good by reward and abstain from evil by pain.

Smith's intellectual posture, resulting perhaps from his own practical experience as administrator and public official and possibly from his read-ing of Machiavelli, was essentially utilitarian. Man, ever striving for hap-piness, seeks to enhance his pleasure and reduce his pain. Human plea-sure (and thus happiness), however, as conceived by Smith, depended primarily on the increase of profits and the decrease of monetary losses. He offered what amounts to a rudimentary model of economic man, an acquisitive individual who acts rationally in choosing the most efficient means of maximizing his profits and minimizing his losses. This kind of profit-orientated behavior not only drives the economy but also enables government to utilize it for the common interest. Anticipating Bernard Mandeville by a century and a half, Smith clearly recognized that "pri-vate vices" yield "public benefits" only when mediated by government.[98] Governmental policy and law from Smith's perspective could only be ef-fective instruments of social control when premised on this understand-ing of human nature. Advancing human pleasure and happiness by re-warding socially useful actions, the successful government would make it profitable and pleasurable for subjects to comply with the law and painful to resist. Laws, however, could not realistically be framed to inconveni-ence no one.[99] Their goal instead would have to be the profit and pleasure of the greatest number and the disadvantage and pain of the fewest. The guiding assumption of policymaking and lawmaking should therefore be the greatest happiness of the greatest number, achieved through the legal application of reward and punishment.

Smith, of course, did not express his views in this fully articulated, utilitarian manner, but such appears to be the direction he was taking, one that became the course of future political economy. If at least part of the economy functions like a mechanism, as he suggested, then its prime motive force is precisely those human passions aiming at pleasure, and hence happiness, through increasing profits and decreasing losses, by producing more and cutting costs, by buying cheap and selling dear in the market. A contemporary of the Commonwealthmen, Smith's perspective could not have been more different from their own, although they all began with similar assumptions about human nature. His outlook was far removed from their uncompromising denunciation of human greed and their call for religious and spiritual renewal. While they were doctors of the soul, Smith was a physician of the body politic and he accepted human nature for what it was. Smith's conclusion was that we must put up with the unregenerate nature of human egoism, which if history has any lessons is a universal constant. If, however, argued Smith, we are to survive in peace and prosperity, living the kind of civilized life we have constructed, in contrast to the misery and backwardness of most of the world, this is the only path, assigning to responsible, limited government the onerous and complex task of guiding us.

Notwithstanding his advocacy of economic individualism, Smith did not argue that uncontrolled pursuit of personal gain would automatically produce the common good. He was not an early advocate of the doctrine of the natural harmony of interests. That conception was discussed in the *Discourse*, only to be discarded. In an exchange between the knight and Pandotheus about the consequences of ill-considered enclosure, which brought with it the expropriation of peasant holdings and the loss of arable to pasture, the knight tendered the argument that enclosure was legitimate if it was profitable.[100] He reasoned that a commonwealth was little more than an atomistic collection of individuals and that what was profitable for one was profitable for all, to the advantage of the entire state. The individual should always strive to promote whatever commodity was produced. In the case of sheep production, the enterprise should be rendered as profitable as possible, for such behavior could only be to the common interest. Smith in the guise of Pandotheus admitted his agreement with much of this classic brief for the natural harmony of interests, which must have been one of its first appearances in the history of social discourse. But he made the qualification that the individuals composing society "may not purchase themselves profit by that which may be hurtful to others."[101] Again he repeated that what "is profitable to each man by himself, so it be not prejudicial to anyone else, is profitable to the whole Commonweal," and again he asserted that men should advance their own commodities as much as possible, providing it does not hinder others in promoting their commodities.[102] Had all men, for example, followed the lead of the enclosers and converted arable to pasture, the result would have been disastrous: "What should ensue but a mere solitude and utter desolation of the whole realm, furnished only with sheep and shepherds instead of good men?"[103]

The question raised by much of the discussion was who should determine whether the actions of the profit-oriented individual were harmful to others and who was to take the measures necessary to curtail such abuses? From subsequent remarks, it appears that Smith thought that men as pursuers of self-interest should be encouraged to seek their own advantage, but always within the limiting framework of the common interest.[104] Society might well be an arena of competing social atoms, but government could serve as arbiter of the common interest, as defined by the people in their parliament, intervening when necessary through prudent policies and laws to secure the welfare of the whole. Instead of the natural harmony of interests, Smith clearly favored an artificial harmony of interests, with government having the function of balancer, mediator, and guarantor of the long-term interests of the state; in other words, government had the task of managing egoistic individualism for the public welfare. The profit motive may have been the motor of society, but government was its regulator for the benefit of all. Smith might easily have reasoned this way at a time when a modern centralized and unified state was gradually being forged in England.

Smith's attitude toward human nature is further illustrated by his constant anxiety about insurrection, to which economic considerations had proved so central. Hoping to make the best in the nature of fallen man, he wished to capitalize on both its strengths and weaknesses for the sake of reforming and strengthening the state. The *Discourse* was begun in the summer of 1549 during the uprisings in the East and Southwest. These serious outbreaks must have weighed heavily on his mind as he was writing, for he returned time and again to the specter of civil disorder. The language attests to his worries. We encounter a constant stream of references to the disturbances and the possibility of their continuing if reforms were not undertaken: the "wild and unhappy uproars," "great tumult and disorder," "great stirs and commotions," "busyness and tumults," "great sedition and division."[105] Yet Smith never expressed the moral outrage of the Commonwealthmen for the predicament of the rebels, nor their stern and unrelenting admonitions to all parties to the turmoils. Rather, he took a matter-of-fact view of the troubles, working to show how they had been provoked and how they could best be prevented from recurring.

Smith was basically a social environmentalist who subscribed to the age-old doctrine of human malleability so dear to the ancients and to Renaissance thinkers like Machiavelli, Pico, Erasmus, Vives, More, and Starkey. All of us, according to the doctrine, were in varying degrees plastic creatures whose natures—at least up to a point—could be shaped by upbringing and education, by social, political, and legal institutions and arrangements. What, Smith essentially asked, did we expect other than seditious conflict and desperate protest given the dire straits of many commoners, their impoverishment, unemployment, and homelessness as a result of enclosure and the decline of manufactures in decaying towns and given the sectarian religious zeal that fueled all these discontents? Covetousness and pride might be the origin of the upheavals, but this was no time, he intimated, for righteous indignation and pleas for moral revival. The only antidote for the poisons of the commonwealth was material improvement in town and country and an end to religious controversy, all brought about by cool and prudent heads. Certainly the ruthless and repressive measures of the French were not to be emulated.[106] "God forbid that ever we had any such tyrants amongst us," protested Smith's farmer, thinking of the oppression of the French peasantry.[107] Pandotheus reminded him that the troops stationed throughout France, which did not enjoy England's insular position, were not solely for the maintenance of internal order but were also required for the security of the state against foreign encroachments. He said, nevertheless, that he "would not have a small sore cured by a greater grief, nor for avoiding of sedition popular, which happens very seldom and soon quenched, to bring in a continual yoke and charge both to the King and his people."[108] Smith did not mean to belittle the dangers of rebellion, only to emphasize that the medicine must suit the disease. The government needed to make every effort to reduce the likelihood of civil disorder through a rational assessment of the situation and rational policies of reforming the social environment.

A Concept of the Economy?

Smith's procedure in the second part of the *Discourse*, extending into the third, was to "discuss and search what should be the causes of the said common and universal dearth [inflation] of all things."[109] After rejecting various explanations of the inflation, Pandotheus concluded that the "chief cause of all this dearth of things and of the manifest impoverishment of this realm . . . is, the debasing or rather corrupting of our own coin and treasure"; later he repeated that the debasement of the coinage was the "chief and principal cause of this universal dearth."[110] Quoting Aristotle's axiom *sublata causa tollitur effectus* (the removal of the principal cause takes away the effect), Smith stressed the crucial practical consequences of his method.[111] If the prime cause of inflation could be discovered and precisely defined, then the effects could be corrected by removing that cause. In the search for the fundamental cause of inflation, he warned that "because there may be divers causes of one thing and yet but one principal cause that brings forth the thing to pass, let us seek out that cause, omitting all the mean causes which are driven forward by the original cause."[112]

Smith listed various common explanations for inflation: high prices charged by tenant farmers for their commodities, excessive rents set by the landlords, enclosure and conversion of arable to pasture, and alteration of the value of the coinage.[113] Smith admitted that while all these phenomena currently accompanied inflation in a period not of shortage but of plentiful supply of goods, the phenomena were not necessarily the cause of inflation. Smith cited the familiar story of the erection of Tenterden steeple as the cause of the sanding of the nearby harbor, a story whose source was said to be Thomas More and which Hugh Latimer used to absolve preachers from responsibility for the recent civil disorders.[114] The building of the steeple had nothing to do with the sanding of the harbor, he pointed out, although the two occurrences were coeval. The farmers' markup of food prices, he continued, was a result of the increase in rents, which landlords were compelled to charge because of the inflated cost of commodities. Landlords were thus forced to enclose land, reduce their labor costs, and enhance their profits by the conversion of arable to pasture. "Thus," Smith maintained, relying on the analogy of a clock, "one thing hangs upon another and sets forward one another but first of all is the chief cause of all this circular motion and impulsion."[115]

Smith's initial attempt to account for the "circular motion" or flow of economic phenomena in the 1549 draft was that the debasement of the coinage was the "first original cause" of the inflation.[116] He was forced, however, because of events after 1549, to qualify this explanation in his revision of the 1549 draft (probably completed in 1576, the year before his death) for posthumous publication in 1581.[117] The knight in the new version asked why inflation still remained even after the coinage had been restored to its original value.[118] To which Pandotheus replied that while the price spiral in the first instance was caused by the debasement of the coinage, "two special causes" were responsible for the continuation of inflation even after the renewal of the value of the coinage.[119] One was the rack-renting by landlords in response to the general increase in prices following debasement, compelling farmers to contribute to inflation by their high charges for food. A second "special cause" of the persistence of inflationary pressure, Smith contended, probably influenced by reading Bodin's *Response au paradoxe de monsieur de Malestroit* (1568), was the recent influx of gold and treasure from the New World.

Smith used several interesting analogies in the course of his economic argument about the causes of inflation. The most telling and certainly the most original of these analogies used to differentiate the primary cause from secondary ones is that drawn from mechanics: "as in a clock there may be many wheels yet the first wheel being stirred it drives the next, and that the third, and so forth until the last that moves the instrument that strikes the clock."[120]

Invoking the clock metaphor again a few pages later (with other analogies), Smith's specific aim was clearly to explain that "chiefest grief," inflation, by distinguishing the principal cause from secondary causes.[121] Only then, he believed, would he be able to suggest appropriate remedial measures. Nowhere else did he employ the analogy in his analysis of the other economic maladies "exhausting of the treasure of this realm," enclosure and use of arable for grazing, decay of towns and villages.[122] Smith resorted to the clock analogy to illuminate only one of the economic problems—the major one in his view—plaguing England. So he was not maintaining that all the complexities entailed by production, distribution, and exchange constituted a simple interrelated system operating like a gigantic clockwork mechanism, autonomous from the state and with its own laws of movement.[123] Nonetheless, when we recognize that Smith was only particularizing his rhetorical device, applying it solely to understanding inflation, the implications, if universalized—as later political economists were to do—were revolutionary. So what Smith actually said was not so important as the inferences that others might make based on the logic of his particular position. We can therefore argue that, in conjunction with other aspects of his thought, Smith opened the way for the discovery of the economy as an independent whole functioning with a circular flow.

Smith's clock analogy, likening a particular feature of English economic life to a mechanism of interdependent constituents with a prime mover whose motion was transferred to every other part, was clearly remarkable. Although the mechanical clock dated to the thirteenth century, only in the fifteenth century were portable clocks made possible by the invention of the coil spring.[124] By the sixteenth century domestic clocks, still fairly crude by modern standards, were relatively common, but too expensive for any but affluent households. Hans Holbein's pen drawing of 1526 "Sir Thomas More and the Family," a sketch for a painting now lost, showed that the More ménage possessed a clock.[125] Likewise Smith may have had a clock at home or in his study at Eton where he penned the *Discourse*. So perhaps his use of the clock metaphor to explain the circular movement of one aspect of the economy is not surprising. But no previous writer seems to have employed the analogy to describe any of the economic operations of society.[126] The frequency of its subsequent use in this manner is unclear, but two centuries after Smith, Sir James Steuart in his *Inquiry into the Principles of Political Oeconomy* (1767) compared the "modern economy" to a watch.[127]

The implications of Smith's use of the clock analogy are momentous. For he was beginning to articulate the view, which he himself never attained, that the diverse economic phenomena of a state operated as an integral whole, possessing at least for analytic purposes an autonomy from the rest of state and society. In this sense he could be said in his particularistic fashion to have pointed the direction to the discovery of the economy as distinct from the rest of society. The economy so conceived was an equilibrium of moving parts, each part transmitting motion originating in the prime mover to another part in a dynamic and circular process or flow of interaction and interdependence. If the motion of the prime mover became defective, at least by the logic of the analogy, the defect would be passed on to the other parts of the economic mechanism. The circular economic motion can be adjusted and corrected, but only by experts, or such is the implication of Smith's conception. Informed governmental policy devised by specialists can adjust the economic mechanism just as master craftsmen can repair a clock. Ignorant tampering with either mechanism will simply compound the malfunction.

Not only was Smith struggling to delineate the distinctive realm of the economy but he also sought to show that economic matters were not confined by the borders of a specific state. Once more he seems to have been among the first—the roots were in *The Libel of English Policy* and in the tracts of Clement Armstrong—to perceive that economic factors transcended the boundary of a state, interacting with economic phenomena of other states.[128] Smith seemed to be on the verge of saying that a national economy was an integral component of the international economy. Plato, Aristotle, and the scholastics fully recognized that the social division of labor was an important foundation of the state. Smith, however, realized that the social division of labor of one state could not be divorced from that of other states. According to the divine plan for mankind, he asserted, no country was capable of producing all the commodities required for its own use. What one country lacked, another was capable of producing; moreover, there was a year-by-year variation in the needs of one and the ability of others to supply those needs. Each nation therefore required the assistance of others in making up its deficiencies. Through mutual aid in the form of the exchange of goods, "love and society . . . grow amongst all men the more." Although "God is bountiful unto us and sends us many great commodities, yet we could not live without the commodities of others."[129] Again, he emphasized that no country could lead an inward, isolated economic existence and set its prices at will in disregard of prices elsewhere: "But since we must have need of other and they of us, we must frame our things not after our own fantasies but to follow the *common market of all the world,* and we may not set the price of things at our pleasure but follow the price of the *universal market of the world.*"[130]

Rejecting the ideal of economic autarky, part of the all-pervasive notion of self-sufficiency so beloved by the ancients, Smith offered a justification for the pursuit of international commerce. He envisaged national economic affairs as part of an international arena characterized by constant flux and transformation. Any change in production, the national market, the price mechanism, and the value of coinage could not be made unilaterally but had to operate within the totality of "the common market of all the world."[131] Reciprocal economic relationships involving all the complexities of international trade so imperative for advanced nations—indeed for Smith this was a sure sign of the high level of European civilization—meant that national economic policy could never be made in isolation. Such economic interdependence redounded to the good of all concerned, he suggested, since a rationally organized commerce among nations would draw them more closely together, tightening the mutual bonds of friendship. The implication was that mutual commercial relations would appreciably contribute to and strengthen international stability, order, and peace. Smith thus anticipated one of the hallmarks of eighteenth- and nineteenth-century political economy in which international trade was considered conducive to universal peace, giving rise to goodwill and a refinement of manners among nations.[132] In his opinion the common interest of the English could not in the final analysis be considered apart from the larger context of the common interest of the international community.

Smith's parallel between state and household or family in his discussion of economic matters may also be significant. This comparison did not contradict but rather complemented his conception of the economic interdependence of nations. While he never related the two ideas, his reason-

ing might have been that just as households were economically interdependent, so were states. Smith was not the first to compare the state to
household, nor was he the first to utilize the analogy for economic argumentation, but he seems to have been among the first to use it extensively
in this way to make a number of major points. He might have been familiar with the passage in Erasmus's *The Education of the Christian Prince*:
"The good prince ought to have the same attitude toward his subjects,
as a good *paterfamilias* toward his household—for what else is a kingdom but a great family? What is the king if not the father to a multitude?" Erasmus then concluded that like the head of a household the true
prince "considers the possessions of his subjects to represent his own
wealth. Them he holds bound over to him through love, so that they
have nothing to fear at all from the prince for either their lives or their
possessions."[133]

Smith used the household analogy to exemplify some basic economic
precepts. Although he never explicitly maintained that the state was like
a household, sometimes only comparing the proper action of the state to
that of a prudent farmer, his parallels between state and household are
nonetheless too noticeable to be discounted. Following Aristotle, Smith in
Republica saw the origins of the first state in the patriarchal household,
and in general he viewed the rule of the family as similar to the government of existing polities: the aristocratic regime of the parents and the
democracy prevailing among their children.[134] But in the *Discourse* he
implied that the state was the household in macrocosm by his comparisons of the economic life of each. First, he urged the English state not
to retain all commodities produced at home but to sell them abroad in
order to import needed goods, making sure to export more than was imported.[135] So the prudent farmer, dependent solely on revenue from his
husbandry, was not to buy more than he sold at market. Second, arguing
that coinage in a state is simply a medium of exchange allowing for an
easy and efficient method of receiving surpluses and hence creating the
power to purchase goods needed and in short supply, Smith pointed out
that a farmer could exchange his grain surplus for a commodity like
money, which unlike grain would not spoil and which could be used at
any time to supply the farmer's wants.[136] Third, a ruler should not discourage an increase in population just because many subjects were more
difficult to govern than a few.[137] No more should the master of the household reduce the number of his employees or sell his land because of the
trouble entailed in managing large numbers of workers or vast acreage. In
both cases the lesson was to employ as many people as possible in useful
activity instead of depriving them of jobs. Finally, Smith noted that in

commonwealth as well as household the more people set to work, the greater profits for their respective heads.[138] It is significant that in these examples Smith dealt with some of the most urgent economic problems of the age: balance of trade, coinage, population, and employment.

After Smith the household–state metaphor came to the fore in economic questions, culminating in the conception of "political economy." Writing in 1576 in his *Six Books of the Commonwealth*, Bodin also noted the origins of the state in the household, claiming that it was the archetype of successful government.[139] Both household and state sought to acquire goods to provide for the prosperity of their members, and in each prudent management depended on a single all-powerful ruler. The absolute sovereign was the manager of the public economy for the welfare of his subjects. From Bodin's analogy several salient economic conclusions follow. If the king headed a household writ large, the promotion of the public interest was essentially to his advantage. Therefore, the wise ruler would take suitable measures to encourage production, expand exports and reduce imports, just as the wise household head should increase revenues over expenditures. In keeping with this reasoning Gerrard de Malynes in 1601 declared that "a common wealth is nothing else but a household or family"; hence the prince like a shrewd householder should strive to secure a favorable balance of trade.[140] Somewhat later Antoine de Montchrétien, relying on the household–state metaphor, was the first to use "political economy" in the title of a book: *Traicté de l'oeconomie politique* (1615).[141] In so doing he was applying the Greek *oeconomia*, or science of household management, to the state, conceiving of it as the great household, the locus of economic production and exchange supervised by the royal paterfamilias. Even in later preclassical political economy the household–state analogy proved useful for illustrative purposes.[142] So by his conception of man and his rudimentary notions of the clockwork movement or circular flow of some economic activity, by the transnational character of many economic matters, together with the use of the household metaphor, Smith seemed to be indicating the direction that future political economists would take in isolating and defining the distinctive realm of the economy.

Economic Problems and Their Resolution

Smith's tone differed appreciably from that of the Commonwealthmen. Absent from his more pedestrian and less ornamented prose was their impassioned criticism of English conditions, their heartfelt sympathy for the poor, and their righteous indignation against greedy landlords and enclosers. Smith was never the wrathful moralizer, nor did he, like the

Commonwealthmen, shower bitter invective on what they took to be the chief culprits, censuring them for the pursuit of private gain at the expense of the common interest. Critical though Smith was of the clergy, he did not stigmatize them as "pestilent prelates" and "Dumme dogges" like Lever; and he never resorted to Becon's colorful imagery of avaricious lords and gentry as "cumberous cormorants" and "caterpillars of the commonweal."[143] Although Smith condemned rack-renting, he envisioned no "Turkyshe tyranie" in the making, as did Crowley. Always matter-of-fact and somewhat flat in tone, Smith was more tempered in his protests, less prone to exaggerated statement. His manner was more in keeping with the more concise and less emotional treatments of writers like Clement Armstrong. Smith was the first to admit that the fundamental cause of England's economic difficulties was the individualistic drive for money, power, and status and that vain pride and unremitting greed were becoming paramount. But he did not indulge in the emotionalism of the Commonwealthmen over this possessive individualism or call for its abolition by spiritual revival and moral rejuvenation.

Smith emerges as an early prototype of the modern social scientist. He was a dispassionate recorder of observable behavior and a searcher for its causes, his object being to design policies for the restoration of unity and order to the state. When he drafted the *Discourse* he was a lapsed public official, seeking, like Machiavelli with *The Prince*, a return to public office, conveying to a trusted friend and colleague, William Cecil, his estimate of the situation and recommendations for its correction. *Policy science*, a twentieth-century term, might be an accurate label for his project, just as it might describe Sir William Petty's *Treatise of Taxes and Contributions* (1662) and some subsequent works in political economy. Accepting and supporting the status quo, Smith neither proposed sweeping governmental reforms nor sought to inculpate specific social groups for the current problems. In his estimation the responsibility for the ills of England lay not so much with individuals as with impersonal social forces. Not so much that individuals were blameless, but all were in some sense victims, if unwitting ones, of these inexorable and impersonal forces. Or such was the logic of his reasoning.

Although a supporter of the status quo, Smith made few concessions to the traditionalism of the Commonwealthmen and previous English thinkers. Rather than castigating the growing economic individualism and acquisitiveness of the time, he wished to utilize and manage it for the well-being of the state. Displaying no particular nostalgia for the good old days, Smith looked to the future, theorizing that it could be shaped if government seized the initiative and acted in a positive, constructive, and rational way instead of merely responding to the vagaries of fortune. Never in the *Discourse* did Smith explicitly subscribe to the favored social ideal of a hierarchy of ranks and stations of differential duties and rights, each individual pursuing conscientiously his ordained calling.[144] While he took the question of labor and idleness very seriously, it did not become an *idée fixe*. His recognition of the plight of the poor never reflected the genuine and eloquent sympathy of the Commonwealthmen and their predecessors. He was as perturbed as they were by the alarming problem of civil disorder and insurrection, perceiving the connection between disorder and declining living conditions and poverty but never discussing crime, beggary, vagabondage, and demographic problems. Clearly aware of the contrast between the sumptuous lives of the wealthy minority and the hand-to-mouth existence of the lowly majority, his comment—to be compared to the angry protest of Lever—about the erection of the palatial buildings of the rich amid the hovels of the poor was only that their construction provided a much needed stimulus to employment.[145] A "new man" himself, he apparently did not object to the rise of the talented individual in quest of wealth, power, and prestige.[146] He neither mentioned nor justified the existence of rich and poor, nor did he exalt the former as God's "stewards" for the benefit of the latter. Like Dudley, Starkey, and Lever, however, Smith was highly critical of the state of higher education—and for much the same reasons. He recognized that without educational reform the future ruling classes would lack the learning required for wise counsel and judicious political leadership. Except for his criticism of enclosure, the conversion of arable to pasture, and rack-renting and engrossment, he never referred to the sharp business practices—lease mongering, forestalling and regrating, usury—which so angered the Commonwealthmen. I do not mean to imply that Smith was in some way morally deficient or unconcerned by the human factor in the crisis of English society, only that in his eyes the human costs resulted from the operation of impersonal economic forces, which became his primary focus of attention.

One could argue that Smith's relative restraint was a result of the late publication date of the *Discourse*, which appeared under Elizabeth when the worst of the economic crisis was over. But in fact the 1549 draft, barring the altered explanation of inflation, was not substantially altered. Smith's attitude did not change with the improvement of social and economic conditions. Perhaps his sober approach can be explained in another way. Until July 1549 and the breach with Somerset over the handling of economic problems, Smith was blessed by fortune with a rags-to-riches career. Despite a temporary lull in his public life, he was unquestionably a virtuoso who eventually attained new and higher honors and posts in the service of his country. Smith wrote from the standpoint of a public official who strived to accomplish as much as possible in a most imperfect world. No one could have been more attuned to politics as the art of the possible, for he had profited from the long experience of survival and advancement in an increasingly competitive and cutthroat milieu. In revolutionizing moral philosophy, he could not have been more sensitive to the reality that economics in the service of governmental policy should always begin with and return to the feasible. He was a secular analyst of social forces and their harmful effects, a proponent of constructive policies designed to curb them. A master social engineer, an individual of empirical temper, moderate, rational, and commonsensical in outlook, Smith in the *Discourse* hoped to check and reduce inflation, prevent the drainage of gold and silver from the realm, increase and diversify agricultural and manufacturing production, and neutralize ideological conflict, all for the prosperity and strength of the Tudor state.

Increasing prices had worried social commentators from the time of Dudley, but never as much as during the sharp inflationary spiral commencing in the early forties. Rapidly rising prices—the "dearth," as it was called—were a matter of the utmost urgency. Smith's presentation of the soaring cost of living, although not presented systematically, was far more detailed and comprehensive than the others', and insofar as we can understand his statistical evidence, much of his evidence may have been closer to the truth. While the rich use of quantifiable empirical data in the *Discourse* was unprecedented, its world of facts and figures still lacked the precision and rigor we now require for adequate assessment. In spite of the quantitative confusions, however, the overall impression generated by his economic analysis was a bleak one, justifying the deep concern of Smith and his contemporaries.

The mounting cost of living thus received careful attention. According to the 1549 draft of the *Discourse*, the price of food and other commodities was about one-third or more higher than seven years before, notwithstanding the plentiful supply of corn, grass, and cattle.[147] Elsewhere in the *Discourse* Smith reported that all goods were 50 percent dearer.[148] In the three or four years prior to 1549, he noted that corn was plentiful and cheap enough, one acre producing what had formerly required two acres, but cattle, beef, and mutton were still expensive.[149] A pig or goose at 4d. eight years ago now sold for 8d. Chickens then at a penny, capons at 3d. to 4d., hens at 2d., doubled in price as did mutton and beef.[150] These increases perhaps took place over a longer time span than his conjecture in the same passage and later that all things were dearer by one-half.[151]

To compound the statistical jumble, Smith also maintained that foreign imports—silks, wines, oil, wood, madder, iron, steel, wax, flax, linen cloth, paper, glass and glasses, pins, needles—were up one-third or more in price over seven years ago; English goods likewise cost one-third more, which was half again higher than before.[152] A yard of cloth costing 4s. 8d. ten years ago now sold for 8s.[153] A cap, formerly 14d., now cost 2s. 6d.; a pair of shoes originally 6d. had risen to 12d.[154] The rate for shoeing a horse had increased from 6d. or 8d. to 10d. or 12d.[155] Master craftsmen could afford to keep few apprentices, and journeymen found current wages completely insufficient to meet the rising living costs.[156] Even a 2d. increase in daily wages was of little help.[157] Laborers at 8d. per day and serving men at 40s. per annum could not survive.[158] A daily wage of 6d. would not go as far as 4d. had before.[159]

Smith was also concerned about the plight of the landed classes. Most of the farm land, he noted, was still rented at the old charges.[160] Many leases and copyholds had not expired, and even when they had, landlords seemed reluctant to raise rents; if rents increased, the change was not as high as 100 percent. While recipients of monastery land had raised their rents, the acreage involved amounted to less than half the total. Latimer's father at the beginning of the century probably paid about 6d. per acre at the minimum total rate given by his son of £3, which suggested that his holdings were probably in the neighborhood of 120 acres.[161] Smith's husbandman in the *Discourse* paid £6 13s. 4d. annual rent, or over twice as much as Latimer's father for holdings about one-quarter smaller, at a rate of 18d. per acre in 1549.[162] The wealthy as well as the lowly were often hard pressed by inflation. Smith informs us that a substantial landlord could not maintain an establishment suitable to his rank on £200 as he could on just over half the amount in 1535. Later he declared that the expenditure of £300 per year by a gentleman would not procure a better life now than £200 spent by his father before him.[163] In the revisions for the 1581 edition Smith wrote that after paying all costs, an individual worth £30 to £40 was at one time deemed rich, whereas by the late sixteenth century he was considered little better than a beggar.[164] It was only understandable that landlords, instead of allowing their incomes to be further depleted by the inflated prices of the commodities they purchased, were tempted by rack-renting and by the high profits and low costs afforded by enclosure and engrossment, the conversion of arable to pasture, and large-scale livestock production.

Smith's accumulation of statistics for inflation, despite their deficiencies, seems to confirm the findings of modern scholarship. By 1550 the average price of all grains was three and a half times higher than in 1500.

Cattle prices reached a new peak by mid-century. Between 1540 and 1550 the cost of food and woolen cloth very nearly doubled. For the same period many rents rose by over 50 percent.[165]

How did Smith propose to cure the malady of inflation? In 1549 he identified the "principal cause" of inflation as the debasement of the coinage. At that time he believed the pressure of inflation could be eased by restoring the value of the coinage. But when inflation persisted even after Elizabeth had taken this step, Smith found it necessary in his revision to amend the original explanation by the addition of two "special causes," rack-renting and the influx of treasure from the New World. But rack-renting could not be reduced "without the common consent of our landed men throughout the whole realm," an action which to Smith and his readers must have been highly unlikely.[166] On relieving the other special cause of inflation, Smith appeared just as pessimistic. Because other nations had also received treasure from the Americas, their prices had risen proportionately. Consequently, for England unilaterally to sell its commodities abroad at the old lower prices would have been economic suicide, a matter of selling cheap and buying dear in the international market.[167] Apparently, Smith had no practical solution to offer for the serious problem of inflation.

Associated with Smith's anxiety over inflation was his concern about the inordinate loss of English treasure to pay for imports. On this subject he made several concrete proposals for reform. Because of the original debasement of English coinage and the counterfeiting of English coins by foreigners, Continental exporters now demanded payment in gold or silver or in their own coin, effectively requiring England to sell cheap and buy dear, thus exhausting its treasure.[168] Because of these high prices for foreign imports, farmers in turn were forced to raise their prices, then landlords increased rents, enclosed, and engrossed, and so the process gained momentum. Smith made a number of recommendations to impede this inflationary impetus and to slow down the circular motion of the economic mechanism. His suggestions focused on preventing the perilous drain of English treasure and dampening the inflationary effect at home for such high payment overseas. To these ends he advocated restrictions on the import of useless luxury goods ("trifles") and foreign items manufactured from English raw materials and on the export of all unwrought commodities.[169] He believed these measures would stimulate home production, particularly in the manufacturing sector, create employment, and help resuscitate the blighted urban centers. Whether they would have had a deflationary effect, however, is open to question.

Smith's description of rural conditions was by now a familiar one. He believed that enclosure, engrossment, conversion of arable to pasture, and rack-renting had caused the dispossession of many small farmers, unemployment, poverty, lack of housing, depopulation, and the decay of villages. If enclosure increased in the next twenty years at the same rate as it had for an equal period in the past, the consequence Smith feared more than inflation was "the great desolation and weakening of the King's strength of this realm."[170] Enclosure, depriving many of land and livelihood, was a basic cause of civil disorder: "The people still increasing and their livings diminishing it must needs come to pass that a great part of the people shall be idle and lack livings, and hunger is a bitter thing to bear. Wherefore they must need, when they lack, murmer against them that have plenty and so stir these tumults."[171] The husbandman of the dialogue complained that enclosure and grazing in his neighborhood during the last seven years had meant that within six miles a dozen plows were laid down. Where forty persons were once provided with a living, now all was in the hands of one man and his shepherd.[172] The propertied, let alone the poor, had difficulty in making ends meet. No longer were many able to maintain large households with numerous servants, to keep a London residence, to put anything aside for a rainy day, or to do good works.[173] "Sheep are the cause of all these mischiefs" inflicted on both rich and poor, wrote Smith, "for they have driven husbandry out of the country by the which was increased before all kind of victuals. And now altogether sheep, sheep, sheep."[174]

In his analysis of rural problems Smith (like More) acknowledged, if only implicitly, the triadic organization of the social relations of agricultural production, at least in those rural areas with which he was familiar.[175] His recognition of the division beginning to typify portions of the English countryside—landlords, tenants, and laborers living respectively on rents, profits, and wages—is apparent from his general remarks and particularly clear in his comparison of the profits from grazing and tillage. More money, he calculated, could be made by a grazier with ten acres of pasture than by a cultivator with twenty acres of arable.[176] Tillage of ten acres of arable, however, brought more total gross profit to the farmer and his laborer than did grazing twenty acres of pasture. But the net profit of the farmer was always less than that of the grazier because the farmer had to pay out "great charge of servants and of labor."[177] In addition to the higher costs of production entailed by tillage, the farmer suffered from a further handicap. The grazier was free to sell his livestock at home or abroad without paying duties, wherever the price was the highest.[178] The farmer, in contrast, hindered by export duties on his corn, lost if the market price was low, and if it was high he still lost because the demand was less. The triadic organization of rural social relations can be seen in these examples by the grazier and farmer's dependence on profit, their renting of acreage from a landlord, and their hiring of wage laborers the one engaging a single shepherd and the other several tillers, to be paid from their profits.

While Smith only implicitly acknowledged the triad in the *Discourse*, he left no doubt as to its nature in the *Republica*. There, he described the yeoman as one who possessed a freehold worth forty shillings (or six pounds in the current money) and who was socially superior to laborers and artisans.[179] Yeomen, he said, are what Cato called "*aratores* and *optimos cives in republica*," farmers and the best citizens in the state; Aristotle labeled them men of the "middle class." The yeoman, besides his freehold, was usually a tenant renting acreage from a gentlemanly landlord. Yeomen

> commonly live welthilie, keepe good houses, do their businesse, and travaile to get riches: these be (for the most part) fermors to gentlemen, and with grasing, frequenting of markettes, and keeping servauntes, not idle servants as the gentleman doth, but such as get both their owne living and parte of their maisters: by these meanes doe come to such wealth, that they are able and daily doe buy the landes of unthriftie gentlemen, and after setting their sonnes to schooles, to the Universities, to the lawe of the Realme, or otherwise leaving them sufficient whereon they may live without labour, doe make their saide sonnes by these meanes gentlemen.[180]

The lowest of the three classes by which England "is governed, administred, and manied [maintained]," yeomen, although not eligible for election to parliament, had the franchise, sat on juries, and paid taxes.[181]

These statements in the *Discourse* and *Republica* constitute the fullest, clearest, and earliest testimony to the emergence of the triad. Enterprising tenants (yeomen and others) who rented land for cultivation and grazing from gentlemanly proprietors and who employed wage laborers were, along with some profit-motivated landlords, the dynamic element in English agriculture. They were among the pioneer agrarian capitalists, constantly striving to cut costs and increase the productivity of their holdings, thus maximizing their profits from the sale of commodities in the market. By mid-century, therefore, Smith had identified in the triad a mode of rural social relations increasingly characteristic of the corn and mixed corn and livestock areas in the southern downlands and eastern counties. By the reign of Henry VIII Joan Thirsk estimates that "the downland farmers were engaged in large-scale capitalist farming, which can only have been undertaken with large numbers of wage labourers." In the chalk country of Wiltshire Eric Kerridge conjectures that "by the early sixteenth century, most of the land was in the hands of capitalist farmers."[182]

Smith thought that the rural decay of England and the threat of popular uprisings could be ended not by the prohibition of enclosure, to which so many of the current ills were traceable, but by prudent governmental policies that attempted to resolve the crucial problem of overspecialization in livestock production and the decline of arable and diversified farming. Smith defended enclosure, as Starkey did, provided the process was moderate and rational, regulated by the state.[183] Pandotheus agreed with the knight's point that the wealthiest counties (Essex, Kent, Devon) were those with the most enclosures and that farming was better done on individual than on common holdings. So if arable was not converted into pasture as part of enclosure and if not done forcibly and violently but gradually with the approval of the commoners concerned, each receiving his share of the enclosed land, the result might be beneficial to all. The vital problem for Smith was not so much enclosure per se. It was how to restrain men—always prone to profit-seeking by their very nature—from converting arable to pasture for grazing, which in view of existing market conditions was obviously the most lucrative and sensible course of action. Considering the money-loving propensity of men, government had to make the best of human nature by measures discouraging the conversion of arable to pasture and the profit-seeking obsession with the production of livestock.

Governmental intervention would ensure that tillage was made as profitable as grazing. This regulation could be accomplished in several ways.[184] The farmer who relied on the cultivation of arable, the producer of corn, for instance, would be as free to sell his commodities at all times and in all places, both at home and abroad, as all other producers, for example, graziers. Wool must therefore be subject to the same export restrictions as corn and duties on raw wool must be increased. If necessary, grazing land was to be more heavily taxed than arable. Once the profit from arable was widely perceived to be as much as that from pasture and grazing, much of the enclosed land converted to pasture would be reconverted to arable and wasteland would be fully exploited for cultivation.[185] Little perhaps could be done to stop rack-renting, except through the unlikely possibility of an act of parliament approved by the landed classes. Engrossment, however, might be impeded by protecting the traditional dispersed holdings of small husbandmen.

Smith blamed the disintegration of urban life on the decline of the manufacturing sector. Once populous, thriving towns suffered from appalling unemployment and depopulation. He pointed to the physical deterioration of these former prosperous centers, to their delapidation and the drop in the quality of life. The single exception was London, which seemed to be flourishing more than ever before. In many towns numerous houses, walls, streets and highways, public buildings, and bridges had fallen into disrepair because of lack of funds for their maintenance.[186] Townsmen could no longer afford to hold their customary civic and social events, such as games, sports, and plays. Much of the population decrease, unemployment, and physical decay was a result of the decline of the crafts for which the towns were previously renowned and in which their artisans specialized.[187] Smith cited Coventry, famed for its production of blue thread, and Bristol for its ornamental lace. A fall in the export demand for the commodities of these towns and the mounting consumer desire for imported manufactures were for Smith the chief cause of the towns' wretched condition. The manufacture of woolen cloth, for which England had acquired such an international reputation, was especially hard hit by this development and by the graziers' temptation for easy profit by the export of raw wool.

Many of the civil disorders, said Smith's knight, reflecting popular opinion, had begun among the impoverished and unemployed clothiers: "For when our clothiers lack vent oversea, there is a great multitude of these clothiers idle, they then assemble in companies and murmur for lack of living and so pick one quarrel or other to stir the poor commons, that be as idle as they, to a commotion."[188] The same was true of farmers—Smith stressed through Pandotheus—who lacking a market for their corn overseas were "driven to be idle; and consequently, for lack of living, to assemble together and make their uproars."[189] He hastened to allow, however, that increased employment of clothiers might not end their tumults, for in France with its numerous employed craftsmen there were still "many great stirs and commotions." Yet the French government, unlike the English, appeared wise enough to support craftsmen because their commodities were an important source of revenue for the state.

Smith's recommendations for urban reform dealt almost exclusively with the revival of manufacturing.[190] His proposals assumed the mercantilistic principle that a favorable balance of trade must be achieved by an increase of exports over imports in order to bring into the country more gold and silver than was let out. Smith displayed no interest in occupations that neither conveyed money abroad nor brought it in, such as the callings of victualers, innkeepers, butchers, bakers, brewers, tailors, saddlers, masons, coopers. But he was particularly anxious about those tradesmen and merchants—mercers, grocers, vintners, haberdashers, milliners, apothecaries, fustian sellers, among others—who relied on the sale of imported goods, thus exhausting the treasure of the realm. Apart from silks, wines, and spices brought in from overseas, whose consumption at home might advisedly be reduced, the English had developed a self-destructive fancy for all manner of "trifles" from foreign lands: drinking and looking glasses, painted clothes, perfumed gloves, cards, balls, puppets, penhorns, inkhorns, pins, laces, buttons, clasps, brooches, toothpicks, cutlery, and paper and parchment. Many of these items were insubstantial and could be readily manufactured in England, Smith estimated, employing twenty thousand workers. Moreover, many of the imported trifles were made from exported English commodities. London's shops glittered with foreign wares often manufactured from English materials. Smith decreed that unwrought commodities like wool, hides, tin, and lead should not be exported. They should instead be worked at home into a variety of manufactured goods to be sold both at home and abroad.

By these measures the export of English treasure would be lessened, manufactures stimulated, employment increased, and the towns once more prosperous centers of industry and trade. Smith was thinking of numerous manufactures and occupations that might be revived: cloth; manufacture of which he called "our natural occupation," caps and hats, gloves, girdles, thread, purses, lace, glass and glasses, baskets, cutlery, needles and pins, and tools of all kinds as well as the occupations of tanning, turning, goldsmithing, blacksmithing, and forging. Government needed to encourage artisans skilled in these crafts and in making goods to be sold on the export market to settle and ply their trades in towns. In order to attract new craftsmen a town might offer them its freedom, even though they might not have served their apprenticeship there, and perhaps a rent-free house or some stock to be loaned from the common stock of the municipality. To further overcome urban decay, restore civic spirit and pride, and promote excellence in craftsmanship, Smith recommended that all commodities bear the seal of the town, a token of its endorsement.

Smith's special interest in the revival of English manufacturing and agriculture and my thesis that he was the founder of political economy are illuminated by the remarks of Joan Thirsk in the Ford Lectures of 1975. Thirsk maintained that long before Defoe's *Essay on Projects* (1692–1693) Smith was among the first to be preoccupied with "projects," thus foreshadowing the growing interest of late seventeenth-century political economists.[191] She defined a project as "a practical scheme for exploiting material things . . . capable of being realized through industry and ingenuity."[192] Smith, some of his contemporaries, and his successors—enterprising businessmen as well as theoreticians—increasingly devoted their energies to the question of producing in manufacturing and agriculture a growing variety of consumer goods, ranging, for example, from luxuries (silks, laces, carpets, tapestries, dyes) and "trifles" (looking and drinking glasses, brooches, cards, tennis balls, pins, needles) to necessities (oil, salt, pitch, tar, flax, rosin, steel and iron, tools).[193] Production of this kind would prevent the drain of English financial resources for the costly import of such commodities from abroad; this manufacture would also create sorely needed employment at home and open up a seemingly limitless spectrum of opportunities for investment and profit-making. Smith and William Cecil were evidently the leading projectors in governmental service.[194] Smith along with Nicholas Bacon, brother-in-law of Cecil and father of Francis, were members of the committee that prepared a legislative program for the promotion of woad production to replace the import of the blue dye at exorbitant prices.[195] Smith was also a moving spirit, publicist, and investor in an unsuccessful project for the economic exploitation of Ireland. His *Discourse* Thirsk terms "one of the most informative and early drafts of a programme for projects," and she also claims that the book "was, in part at least, a programme for the setting-up of new industries and introducing new crops."[196] So over a century before Defoe's dating of the "Age of Projects" as beginning in 1680, Smith blazed the trail to be taken by future inventive entrepreneurs and political economists.[197]

Ideological Problems: Diversity of Religious Opinion

Ideological differences revealed in sectarian conflict as well as deteriorating economic conditions in town and country fired protest and revolt, according to Smith, who concluded the *Discourse* with a lengthy treatment of the diversity of religious opinion.[198] He introduced the discussion with the knight's comment on the relationship between civil disorder and the unprecedented rise in England of great differences of religious opinion within communities and even within families: "For if we were never so poor and did nevertheless agree among ourselves, we should lick ourselves whole again in short space."[199]

Following his usual procedure, Smith first identified the cause and then suggested remedies. Pandotheus singled out two main causes of the growing religious differences and sectarian strife: the behavior of the clergy and that of the laity. Of the two he deemed the corruption of the clergy the principal cause and suggested that unless reform took place "the general schism and division in religion" would not be resolved.

From its privileged position the clergy had become increasingly greedy for material gain and worldly possessions; this acquisitiveness manifested itself primarily in the accumulation of benefices. Moreover, clergymen were lax about taking up permanent residence in their parishes and delinquent in the conscientious performance of their pastoral duties. In effect, they no longer were worthy examples of upright living, Christian spirituality, and moral leadership for the laity, who in their disillusion looked elsewhere for solace and guidance.[200] Because the corruption of the clergy was secular in nature, Smith believed the church could best be reformed by the intervention of the secular power, the state. In this respect Smith shared some of the anticlericalism of Dudley and Starkey.

Laymen, no longer able to look to the clergy for guidance in the difficulties of life, took it upon themselves to make decisions in religious and spiritual matters, Smith's second cause of the diversity of opinion. With neither long study nor great experience, young men rashly judged and hastily pronounced on the most complex theological questions, just as they seemed prone to do in other sciences, in law, grammar, logic, and rhetoric.[201] Having reached their conclusions and unable or unwilling to recognize their own errors or acknowledge the virtues of an opposing position or argument, they used all their power and authority to win over others to their position. Few realized that truth did not always reside on the side with the greatest power to enforce belief. Christianity thus suffered from multiplying schisms and contending sects. If all were dedicated to the discovery of truth, argued Smith, why should not the disputed questions and issues be debated in an atmosphere of freedom and toleration, none of the parties to the disagreements seeking to force their own beliefs on others by resort to violence? If such a course were followed, or such was his implication, perhaps the threat of sectarian strife so threatening to civil order and harmony would be removed. Theological controversies could best be settled, as they had in the past, by open, peaceful, and tolerant discussion in conferences called for that specific purpose, for example, in a synod or general council of the church.

Smith proposed two ways of reducing the intolerant climate of religious opinion and avoiding the sectarian conflict that contributed to civil disorder. First, government should reform the secular aspects of the church subject to corruption. Second, in exclusively spiritual matters the church should put its house in order through the convocation of a general council. Where secular and spiritual problems were intermixed, a combination of the two modes of reform would be effective.

Another method of reform, strongly suggested if never explicitly recommended, appears in Smith's remarks in part 1 of the *Discourse* on learning and the universities, which he as well as Dudley, Starkey, and Commonwealthmen like Lever thought were in a state of decline.[202] Clerics, after all, as well as laymen were educated in the universities, whose curricula, quality of instruction, and intellectual atmosphere should thus be of utmost concern to the nation. In part 3 Smith posed two questions of complaint about the clergy in comments that struck at the heart of the matter: "What better trial or examination is there now in the admitting of the priests and other ministers of the church? What more exact search is made by our bishops for worthy men to be admitted to the cure of souls?"[203] The thrust of the questions seemed to be that to an extent at least the corruption of the clergy resulted from their recruitment from persons of poor ability. Furthermore, as Smith made clear in part 1, the responsibility for this condition was the decline of the universities and the faulty education of the youth destined for the clergy or even for prominent roles in the secular life of the state.

In these reflections Pandotheus responded to a number of complaints by the capper. That worthy artisan was highly critical of what he took to be the idleness of the clergy and learned men, blaming them for the diversity of views generating the conflicts troubling the country: "not the least cause of these wild uproars of the people."[204] In his opinion it made little difference if there were no learned men in the kingdom, a judgment that seemed to be widespread.[205] To which charges Smith speedily replied, "Care not therefore good man capper, you shall have few enough of learned men within a while if this world hold on," and he then lectured his audience on the degeneration of the universities.[206] University students, he feared, were interested in little more than learning to read and write and acquiring a knowledge of Latin and other languages in order to get well-paying jobs at graduation. If the attitude prevailed, he maintained, "This realm within a short space will be made as empty of wise and politic men and consequently barbarous, and, at the last, thrall and subject to other nations whereof we were lords before."[207] Learning, he insisted, was a vital auxiliary of practical experience in all fields of human endeavor. It was necessary for the conduct of war to study Vegetius and to master arithmetic and geography or for successful seamanship to learn geography and astronomy. The farmer could profit from reading Columella and the architect should know Vitruvius. Prudent statecraft depended on the use of power guided by knowledge, as exemplified by Plato's philosopher-king, and effective governmental policy required a foundation in moral philosophy. Because students in Smith's time were motivated not by a love of learning but solely by the anticipation of future profitable employment, they turned to theology, law, and medicine and completely neglected the former prerequisites for professional training, the "seven liberal sciences": grammar, logic, rhetoric, arithmetic, geometry, music, and astronomy. Without a thorough grounding in these liberal sciences, students could not excel in their practical vocations. Indeed, the diversity of opinion and resulting conflict and strife, complained about by the capper, were a product of this failure to study the liberal sciences: "All beginners in every science be very quick and overhasty in giving their judgment of things . . . and then . . . they will see nothing that will sound contrary to the same but either they will construe it to their own fantasy or utterly deny it to be of any authority."[208] This explanation is basically similar to the one given in part 3 for the diversity of religious opinion among the laity.

Smith, like Lever, lamented the decline of the student population and was especially perturbed by the intolerant atmosphere in the colleges and the persecution of scholars for their views. He offered possibly the first vigorous protest against threats within the universities to academic freedom:

> Marry, have you not seen how many learned men have been put to trouble of late within these twelve or sixteen years and all for declaring their opinions in things that have risen in controversy? Have you not known when one opinion has been set forth and whosoever said against that were put to trouble, and shortly after when the contrary opinion was furthered and set forth were not the other that prospered before put to trouble for saying their mind against the latter opinion? . . . Who now, seeing instead of honor and preferment, dishonor and hindrance recompensed for a reward of learning, will other put his child to that science that may bring him no better fruit than this? Or what scholar shall have any courage to study to come to that end? And the rarity of scholars and solitude of the universities do declare this to be truer than any man with speech can declare.[209]

No one was better placed in his time to defend academic freedom than Smith, former Regius Professor and vice-chancellor. His view seemed to be that in England free disputation, not intolerance and persecution of heterodox belief, was the only way to handle religious diversity as a cause of civil disorder. Governmental action to address the problems of rural and urban decay and the concomitant reform of the clergy, he appeared to reason, would only partially solve the social and economic troubles of England. More clearly than Dudley, Starkey, or Lever, Smith recognized that in the future prudent governmental policy, wise political leadership, a revitalized clergy, and a peaceful and harmonious laity had to be grounded on the reform of the universities and the creation of a free and

tolerant climate of expression. Hardly could there be a more fitting cap-
stone to the secular edifice of the state theorized by Smith, who in some
ways was an apostle of modernity before his time.

In the ten pages of the *Discourse* allotted to universities Smith in
length and substance went well beyond the concern of Dudley, Starkey,
and Lever over educational decline and the need for reform. We might
even claim that he thus began an important tradition in English social
discourse. Despite their profound differences, Smith, Bacon, Hobbes, and
Locke were theorists of opinion who believed that social unity depended
on education (in the broad and narrow senses), not on the radical transformation of existing institutions and arrangements. Both Bacon and
Hobbes were enormously interested in the role of universities and in the
reconstitution of their curricula.[210] Locke was critical of the universities,
but he concentrated his literary efforts on the early education of youth,
producing the popular and influential *Some Thoughts Concerning Education* (1693).[211] In his various other works he can almost be said to have
developed Smith's insight that social conflict could best be decreased
through the establishment of religious toleration, freedom of association,
thought, and expression, all to be guaranteed by responsible, constitutional government. Whatever the explanation for the emphasis on education and opinion in early modern English thought, in the cases of Bacon,
Hobbes, and Locke, it was undoubtedly related to their social environmentalism, individualism, psychologism, and empiricism.[212] Smith's mode
of thinking shared some of these traits.

A Harbinger of Modernity?

How finally can Smith's importance as a social and political thinker be
best summarized? He gave the time-hallowed concept of "moral philosophy" a new meaning, thereby launching a novel mode of discourse, political economy. The way a commonwealth "should be well ordered and
governed"—Smith's definition of the principal aim of moral philosphy—
was conceived in a fresh and daring way. For at the heart of his idea of
moral philosophy was a secular, utilitarian, and economic conception of
the state. The state was an aggregate of mutually consenting individuals
united for the primary purpose of securing their economic prosperity and
promoting their economic interests. According to Smith, these interests,
registered by the individuals either in person or by proxy in their legislature, consisted essentially (although he did not say so specifically) of the
greatest pleasure of the greatest number and the least pain of the fewest.
He described individual pleasures and pains in this context as fundamentally economic in character: profits and losses. Smith's emphasis on the

material well-being of citizens and their economic motivation was joined to a central preoccupation with the arena of production, consumption, and exchange. He seemed to be one of the first thinkers to move in the direction of viewing the "economy" as an autonomous sphere of human activity, a mechanism arising from the social division of labor which possessed a dynamic and logic of its own and transcended national boundaries. Government's function was chiefly to regulate and strengthen economic life through rational policies that increased the profits of the greatest number, reduced the losses of the fewest, and prevented the economic behavior of any individual from harming the interests of others. That Smith should have placed such reliance on the monitoring functions and powers of government was probably connected with the gradual replacement of personalized and fragmented rule by institutionalized, centralized, and unified rule occurring in England. The individualistic pursuit of economic interests within the guiding framework imposed by government constituted "civil society," an expression briefly used by Smith and equated with the state and one that was to be important in the future.

Something of the intellectual significance of Smith's accomplishment is highlighted by reference to the views of his younger contemporary, Thomas Wilson (1525?–1581). They were friends, fellow Cantabrigians, humanists, active in government, economic specialists.[213] Wilson, after studying civil law in Italy, became a member of parliament, Master of Requests, ambassador to the Netherlands, and succeeded Smith as principal secretary of state. On the basis of his interests, especially in Portugal, and the publication of *A Discourse uppon Usury* Wilson also gained a reputation in economic matters. Both thought that something unprecedented was happening in English society in the form of acquisitive individualism and both believed that the development was traceable to natural human egoism.[214]

Here, however, Smith and Wilson parted company, representing contrasting outlooks. *A Discourse uppon Usury,* first drafted in 1569 and published in 1572, was a lengthy and learned critique in dialogue form not against all interest, but against "pure interest" that involved the promise to pay a fixed amount for the loan of a sum of money for a stated period of time. In case of default by the borrower, the lender could acquire the collateral initially agreed upon. Usury was simply money made from money. Essentially the problem with Wilson's argument was his failure to appreciate that most of English agriculture, manufacturing, and foreign commerce was being increasingly financed by the very credit arrangements he so scathingly condemned; his recommended law against usury if implemented would have all but destroyed the English economy.

It is unimaginable that the worldly-wise Smith, who never mentioned usury or interest in his two books or referred to any of the many business transactions involving the payment of "illegitimate" interest so meticulously cataloged by Wilson, could have possibly agreed with his friend.

The economic individualism so blandly accepted by Smith was for Wilson most virulently and destructively manifested in the spreading contagion of usury. He found the principal cause of unbridled profit-seeking in a tidal wave of covetousness that threatened to engulf society. He differed markedly from Smith in his moralizing and censorious attitude. Wilson angrily inveighed against "that ouglie, detestable, and hurtefull synne of usurie" and "the greedie cormoraunte wolfes in deede that ravyn up both beaste and man."[215] The wealthy "live most idely, without doing any thing els but making money of money."[216] He reviled the prevailing "hardnes of harte, so unmercifull dealinge, suche bribinge, suche oppression, suche bytinge, and such wringinge of oure poor brethren [as] was never in any worlde, as I think."[217] "For what is hee nowe a dayes," laments the merchant of the dialogue converted to Wilson's way of thinking by the doctor of civil law, "that is of anye estymacion, if he want wealth? Who maketh anye accompte of him, bee hee never so learned, never so vertuous, or never so worthy, that hath not the goods of this world?"[218] Far from the neutral language of Smith, these were the impassioned reflections and the invective of the Commonwealthmen who would remake errant man by spiritual renewal. Wilson began the dialogue by warning that "the ende of thys worlde is nyghe at hande" and then later asked how we should "temper thys unsaciable desyre and gredy covetousness?"[219] We should no longer tolerate the evil, but protest against it, he pronounced, cautioning the evil-doers of the justice to be meted out by God. Wilson ended by saying that even if perfection was not of this life, he would pray, and he enjoined all good people to do likewise, for men in all walks of life to mend their ways and for the kingdom of God to come soon among us.[220]

The difference in attitude of these two thinkers, who otherwise had so much in common, could not be more striking. While Wilson was the traditional humanistic moralist obsessed by profit-seeking individualism and the increasing covetousness of his age, Smith was willing to seize the bull by the horns. Instead of excoriating economic individualism, he embraced it, seeing in it a bright prospect for the future, a means of revitalizing England, provided it was harnessed and used constructively for the welfare of all. Wilson was more a romantic, in love with the sterner, heroic qualities of the past. Smith appeared to discard any romantic notions he might have harbored for the glorious days of yore. He exhibited instead a rationalistic, realistic, and calculating way of thinking. He wrote the *Discourse* from the standpoint of a public official whose task it was to strive for what was possible in a most imperfect world.

Taken together the *Discourse* and *Republica* reflect an outlook that might qualify Smith for the label "theorist of emergent capitalism." He was not the discerning economic analyst or technical innovator, for instance, that Petty and Locke were, but he manifested something of the spirit of capitalism. Smith's life and writings revealed that spirit in their individualism, secularism, rationalism, and economism. To use the glosses of Schumpeter and Weber on Marx's perception of capitalist development: this was the beginning of the unromantic and "anti-heroic" attitude that in the epoch to come contributed to a civilization dedicated to the progressive "disenchantment of the world." Such realism, perhaps more than anything else, was Smith's intellectual response to the basic structural changes occurring in England, a response that put in place a new moral philosophy and the foundations of political economy.

10   Conclusion

The early Tudor reformers were among the most fascinating and perceptive social and political thinkers of the beginning of the early modern period. Obviously they cannot be ranked with the greats from Plato and Aristotle to Hegel and Marx. Nor can they be legitimately placed with theorists of a second order like Cicero, Machiavelli, and Burke. Instead, they must be included in a third group of lesser but still important intellects, a classification hardly excusing their common neglect today. The reformers may not have been philosophical giants or accomplished system builders or the most acute of analysts; nonetheless, there are several compelling reasons for studying them and urging others to do likewise. These thinkers lived and wrote at a time in England when a modern state was being constructed out of the personalized rule of medieval kingship. Moreover, they were the world's first observers—albeit unwitting ones—of an incipient rural capitalism and some of its harsh social and economic consequences; in response they produced a pioneer literature of protest and criticism, outspoken in its condemnation of conditions and unhesitating in its assignment of responsibility. These social critics also seem to have been the first to engage in a realistic assessment—using the scanty empirical evidence available—of the problems of ordinary people in their everyday lives. They were not simply critics and protesters, however, but reformers calling for remedial action by governmental intervention.

The exceptional quality of a number of the Tudor reformers' ideas demands our close attention. It is a pity that most of these reformers have been all but forgotten by historians of social and political thought in their understandable haste to move from the medieval classics to those of the seventeenth century. By thus relegating the Tudor reformers to the dustbin of history, we run the risk of overlooking significant links between the medieval and the modern, and we miss a further opportunity of illuminating the relationship between social and political ideas and their historical context. Aside from their intrinsic merit, some of the reformers' ideas require close scrutiny because they foreshadow future developments in English theorizing. The unique mode of later English thought from Bacon to Locke (in contrast to Continental reflections) may be rooted in and bring to fruition various ideas of the reformers. Indeed, some of the basic elements of a distant liberalism may originate in the reformers' speculative endeavors. I illustrate these contentions by reference to three closely interrelated themes of this study: the conception of the state, the notion of social environmentalism, and the critique of individualism. A brief discussion of the three themes provides a convenient way of summarizing the originality of the reformers and justifying their remembrance.

The reformers' conception of the state encompassed their views on the nature of the best constitution, their political vocabulary, and their emphasis on economic goals. The dangers of absolute rule and the threat of tyranny were always worrisome matters for the reformers. Fortescue, More, Starkey, and Smith (as well as Ponet) thought that the surest guarantee against arbitrary, irresponsible domination was some form of mixed constitution that institutionally checked the power of the prince or the ruling class and the people. In contrast to French absolutism, the existing English governmental arrangement described by Fortescue was *dominium politicum et regale*, a mixture assigning lawmaking and taxing power neither to monarch nor to parliament alone but to the king in parliament. Fortescue's interpretation of the English constitution became a much lauded and influential convention. More's novel variant of the idea was the republican scheme of each of the Utopian city-states, designed to bridle the power of the people as well as of the ruling intellectual elite. Possibly influenced by his experience in Italy and his reading of Fortescue, More, and the Italian humanists, Starkey proposed a mixed constitution for England entailing the revival of the traditional office of constable as a counterpoise to the king and a dual system of councils to ensure the domination of the aristocracy and prevent any faction of it from usurping power. Arguing that the constitutions of all states were to some extent mixtures, Smith accepted (as did the Commonwealthmen) the existing English parliamentary monarchy, which granted important prerogative powers to the king, who, however, shared a legislative and taxing role with parliament. That assembly was thought to contain all the subjects of the realm either in person or by proxy: king, nobility, and commons. A mixed constitution like English parliamentary monarchy (or something similar), the clear choice of the reformers and the model for many thinkers to come, entailed a diffusion of central governmental power. The reformers' commitment to a constitutional mixture reflected their dread of tyranny, their emphasis on security of person and property, their attachment to social hierarchy, and their fear of democracy.

Turning to the reformers' political vocabulary, we can plot a steady movement in usage of *state* as personalized rule in Fortescue and Dudley to *state* as institutional totality in Starkey and Smith (and Ponet). While the Commonwealthmen added little to the political lexicon, Starkey (and Ponet) made something of a conceptual breakthrough in his occasional employment of the word *state*, probably for the first time in England, to denote more than status or condition. Vague as he was, Starkey appeared to be striving to identify *state* with the institutional whole or constitutional unity, which entity differed from the abstract collectivity of government on the one hand and from society on the other. Smith seemed to be doing something similar in his use of *common wealth*. Consequently, both Starkey and Smith (along with Ponet) were approaching the modern conception of the state worked out by Bodin, Grotius, Hobbes, and others. Perhaps the efforts of the reformers, inspired in part by reading Machiavelli and Cicero's *De officiis*, were an unconscious ideological response to a major development in sixteenth-century English history: the formation of a modern state with increasing institutionalized control and developing centralization and unification. Under the Tudors a state with a distinctive national, cultural, political, and constitutional identity was being shaped out of a medieval kingdom.

What was lacking in the reformers' reflections on the state—in addition to greater precision and systematic analysis—was a clear notion of sovereignty. Although Smith struggled to formulate such a concept, his attempt was possibly inhibited by his acceptance (like other reformers') of the mixed constitution, one of whose chief traits was divided sovereignty. At the same time we must note that the idea of the supreme power of the king in parliament—so basic to Smith's mixed constitution—was fundamentally power over individual citizens of the realm. Not for him as later for Bodin did the privileges and jurisdictions of corporate bodies within the commonwealth shield individuals from the exercise of such centralized power. But Smith apparently failed to delineate a more distinct concept of sovereignty for another reason. This was his equation of "common wealth" with "civil society" (here we encounter perhaps the first use of the latter expression). Why he employed the uncustomary "civil society," to become a well-worn convention in seventeenth-century England, is not at all obvious. He may quite unconsciously have intended to emphasize the realm of economic activity, to which the state in an important sense was subordinate, instead of its legalistic and jurisdictional character. In particular, he may have wished to stress that the commonwealth was a collection of individual private proprietors forming the political nation. At any rate, if the reformers, and especially Starkey and Smith, failed to achieve the modern conception of the state, their language indicated a change in thinking about the subject that was to bear fruit in the following years.

A significant characteristic of the reformers' conception of the state was the attention given to its economic ends. Roughly parallel with the shift in meaning of *state* from personalized rule to institutional whole was the increasing stress on the aim of economic security and well-being. Not that the traditional objectives of defender and judge were discounted, only that more attention was paid to the economic functions of the state. This emphasis is apparent as early as Fortescue and Dudley and later in the Commonwealthmen. More's *Utopia* was almost entirely given over to economic considerations and much of Starkey's *Dialogue* concentrated on them. It remained for Smith, however, to carry through the logic of the tendency. In his thinking the state was transformed in part into an economic mechanism with a dynamic of its own. The state, he apparently believed, was principally a secular contrivance for the satisfaction of human material needs.

The changing perception of the purpose of the state accompanied several other related alterations in the perspective of the reformers. They transformed the medieval notion that social and political institutions and arrangements should advance human happiness, which depended on the condition of both soul and body of the individual. The highest happiness in the here and now, according to the medieval view, required a healthy soul, one turned toward God and moral virtue, in a physically sound body. The reformers developed a distinction made previously between pleasures of the soul and pleasures of the body; in turn they distinguished between true and false pleasures. Only by cultivating the true pleasures of soul and body and avoiding the corresponding pains could genuine happiness be attained. An individual, of course, could achieve happiness by realizing the true pleasures of the soul alone, but the highest terrestrial happiness also necessitated fulfillment of the true bodily pleasures. These arose from physical well-being and personal security and were the necessary if not sufficient conditions of the highest happiness. For More the bodily health of Utopians—the sine qua non of their happiness—required the abolition of private property and a collectivistic ordering of society so that all might live in material comfort with sufficient food, shelter, and clothing. Starkey followed suit but with a far from collectivistic and a more worldly ideal.

Once the advancement of true bodily pleasures and the decrease of bodily pains in terms of material well-being became a major purpose of the state, the stage was set for further conceptual change. The distinction between true and false bodily pleasures was blurred and the enhancement of these homogeneous pleasures and the lessening of bodily pains began to be interpreted in terms of monetary profits and losses. This was basically the position of Smith. The task of the state was, therefore, to take measures to increase the profits and decrease the losses, not of the few but of the many. To anticipate a later utilitarian model, which perhaps does no great injustice to Smith's outlook, the primary aim of the state was the greatest happiness of the greatest number and the least pain of the fewest as they themselves judged their respective pleasures and pains, translated into economic profits and losses. In the process of this transmutation of happiness vis-á-vis the proper functions of the state a comparable change seemed to occur in the meaning of *common interest,* which now came close to being equated with the sum of the greatest profits and fewest losses by those incurring profits and losses, citizens in person or by representation in their legislature.

The reformers required the state to take all requisite steps to advance the common interest so conceived. They no longer viewed parliament essentially as a court applying the higher norms of custom and the moral dictates of God and nature to particular circumstances; instead they saw a lawmaking body, a legislature that promoted the common interest by fashioning new laws and changing or abrogating old laws. Government had the responsibility either directly or indirectly to the governed to construct positive, creative policies, informed by detailed knowledge of the current social and economic situation, and to embody them in laws to be implemented for the common interest. Commissions of inquiry and other fact-finding instruments were to be used for devising rational public policies and effective laws. Increasingly reformers thought that government should be given a prominent economic role and public policy a reforming and remedial function in the social sphere. The politics of the interventionist state was progressively transformed into political economy.

To what extent men of affairs appreciated and took to heart the coupling of the humanitarian and the prudential in the reflections of the reformers on the common interest is impossible to say. In highlighting and criticizing the many social and economic injustices of the realm, the reformers reiterated time and again that England could only be a strong and viable state, secure in the world and unified internally, if steps were taken to enhance the material lot of the people. Consequently, the interest of the rulers—government, public officials, and the dominant classes—was always to serve the common interest. Instead of exercising power willfully and irresponsibly for immediate gain and shortsighted self-aggrandizement, rulers should govern with their own long-term advantage ever in mind, realizing that it ultimately depended on happy, prosperous citizens living securely without serious economic difficulties. For the reformers the common interest was the firmest and most lasting foundation of the self-interest of rulers, a prudential counsel never to be disregarded. That the power and wealth of the ruler was no greater than the power and wealth of the ruled was a gem of political wisdom as old as Solomon and Aristotle. It was one that imbued Hobbes's prescriptions for the conservation of sovereign power, nevertheless one almost universally ignored by tyrants throughout history.

A second broad theme of this study, linked to the identification of the interest of government and governed, was the social environmentalism of the reformers.[1] This notion too in various forms was as old as social and political theorizing. Social environmentalism essentially entailed a belief in the malleability of human nature, an idea figuring in much of the thought of classical antiquity and central to the outlook of a number of Renaissance authors. If the individual's nature was partially plastic and if mentality and behavior were to a degree determined by family upbringing, example, schooling, associations, and circumstances of life, then it followed that the individual could to a point be shaped by manipulation of the social environment. For humans to be happy, virtuous, and cooperative, dedicated to the common good, their social context had to be made conducive to such goals. Social, political, and legal institutions and arrangements could be instrumental in shaping the raw stuff of humanity according to the ideal desired, either by gradual change and reform or by the radical restructuring of society. Delinquency, crime, rioting, and insurrection could be reduced if not prevented by rational reforms and adjustments of the social setting. Nurture, therefore, became a more important consideration than nature in the management of human beings.

Elements of this sort of doctrine permeated the thought of the reformers. Although they believed—according to their Augustinian or Lutheran convictions—in the basic flawed nature of man, at the same time they thought that the worst antisocial behavior could be diminished and contained through improvement of social conditions and proper education. Humans might be inherently selfish, but they could be influenced, especially in their youth. Anxious about impoverishment, unemployment, and social dislocation, the reformers raised the specter of crime and revolt which would result from government's failure to remedy the grievous situation. From their standpoint poverty definitely bred crime and sedition. So government and the ruling classes needed to shape a material environment allowing people to live in peace and prosperity, happy in the work of their calling and free from anxiety about survival. Remedial social and economic measures could not completely eliminate crime or prevent revolt because of human egoism, but the potential of subversive conduct would be considerably diminished.

The reformers were not solely concerned with bettering the material aspects of the social environment. They were also vitally interested in the quality of formal education and its crucial part in molding youth. Even if humans became set in their ways in later life, during their early years they were sufficiently pliable and susceptible to the influences of their surroundings to make their schooling indispensable to a durable, thriving state. The fashioning of opinion was a critical question for the reformers, who drew a distinction, usually only tacitly, between true and false opinion, between those beliefs supportive of a healthy state and those undermining it. And when recreating the social environment and the appropriate educational measures failed to reduce the antisocial behavior of powerholders, the apparatus of the mixed constitution (even in the case of More) was the ultimate safeguard against their egoism.

Because the improvement and governance of the state demanded knowledgeable and enlightened leadership, the education of youths who would be future clerics, public officials, and men of affairs was a priority for the reformers. With the exception of More, they did not advocate universal formal education, but they felt that careful training of lower-class youth was the key to producing an obedient, industrious, enterprising, and skilled labor force. The real concern of the reformers, however, was for the opinion-makers: the clergy and gentlemenly classes. By setting a personal example of selfless virtue and using their talents in caring for parishioners, the clergy could be the bastion of the regime.

The foundation of the education of the clergy and future notables of the commonwealth was the universities and schools. Thomas More carried his interest in education to an extreme. He accomplished the molding of true opinion and the extirpation of false, socially subversive beliefs in his radical experiment by universal education and rule by an exclusive intellectual elite. His meritocratic ideal may have prompted Starkey in a far more mundane way to recommend special schools for educating aristocratic youths in moral virtue and to urge the reform of universities. But even a hard-bitten politico like Dudley, awaiting execution in 1510, decried the decay of universities, mindful of their mission of molding the ruling class. Likewise the Commonwealthman and master of a Cambridge college Lever was deeply worried by the decline of schools and universities. It was Smith, however, former vice-chancellor of Cambridge, who commented most tellingly and substantially on the state of the universities. He was agitated by the growing materialistic values of students whom he criticized for being less attracted to true learning than to acquiring the skills necessary for a future livelihood. He obliquely suggested university reform by stressing the revitalization of the teaching of liberal arts and by discouraging the oppressive atmosphere of intolerance and dogmatism that threatened academic freedom. Similar anxieties about the degeneration of education and a recognition of its critical function in molding opinion and enhancing the social environment were to continue and increase in England, becoming a preoccupation of the virtuosi of the next century, Bacon, Hobbes, and Locke. Even Puritan radicals shared in the distress, pleading for the reform of the universities in their attacks on these institutions for being anti-Christian.[2]

Deteriorating social and economic conditions in England probably sensitized the reformers to an environmental doctrine that could be gleaned from a wealth of ancient, medieval, and humanistic sources. It may be significant that both Fortescue and Starkey invoked the concept of tabula rasa, later to become the touchstone of empiricism and social environmentalism. The notion that the mind of the individual at birth was a blank slate to be imprinted by subsequent experience is found in Plato, Aristotle, and the Stoics. Aristotle's classic formulation of the concept in *De anima*, repeated by St. Thomas Aquinas, must have been well known since the book was a best-seller in the sixteenth century and the title proved to be a favorite for original works like Vives's *De anima et vita* (1538). Possibly as important was the enthusiastic response to Cicero, whose *Academics* and *Tusculan Disputations* were widely acclaimed. Even the lesser known *Laws* went through half a dozen editions before midcentury. Although Cicero apparently never employed the expression *tabula rasa*, he expounded a view in these works, practically paraphrased by Starkey, which distinguished between true and false opinion. We act evilly, Cicero argued, not by nature but because of our corruption by evil customs and false opinions arising from improper upbringing and education. The correction of such corruption would enable us to recover our original purity and to act rationally and virtuously. The idea of the intimate relationship between opinion, will, and action and the formative role of the social environment in general and education in particular was fundamental to the outlook of some of the reformers. When combined with a more refined concept of tabula rasa, the idea became axiomatic to the social theorizing of the seventeenth-century English empiricists. The reformers, with their mainly tacit distinction between true and false opinion, emphasis on the importance of education, focus on the individual, and rejection of radical social engineering (More excepted), seem to have presaged the shape taken in the future by English social speculation.

The coexistence in the Tudor reformers' thought of an Augustinian or Lutheran concept of human nature and in varying degrees a doctrine of social environmentalism brings us to a third related theme of this study: the critique of individualism. Much of the angry protest of the reformers targeted what they assumed to be the unprecedented emergence of unrestrained selfishness, manifested by the egoistic drive of some members of every social order—clergy, nobility, and commons—for wealth, power, and prestige. Never before in England, they intimated, had there been so much uncurbed covetousness, such acquisitiveness and hubris, and such uninhibited impulse to put self-advancement before the public welfare. From More's memorable excoriation of the greed and conspicuous consumption of the aristocracy to Becon's castigation of "ungentle gentlemen" for being so many "caterpillars of the commonwealth," the criticisms were the same. Those guilty were the land-hungry gentlemen and tenants whose insatiable appetites to enclose, engross, and rack-rent deprived hapless smallholders of their livings and disgorged masses of penurious, unemployed, and homeless victims. In their desperate struggle for survival these unhappy people often turned to crime and even vented their discontent and insecurity in civil disturbances and revolt. The wrath of the reformers, however, was not simply showered on unscrupulous landholders. All who placed the pursuit of profit before the common good were subject to their ire: clerics, officials, merchants, lawyers, and physicians. Questionable business practices including forestalling, regrating, and usury were taken to task, as were parasitic middlemen engaged in the activities.

Ironically enough some of the Lutheran beliefs of the reformers may have indirectly sustained and reinforced the very individualism so bitterly denounced. Lutheran individualism rested on the tenet of the immediate direct relationship of the believer to God—each man his own priest. No longer was the reading of the Holy Word the monopoly of clerics. For the Bible in the vernacular was now available to all, an open book to the literate. Just as individualistic in its way was the Lutheran doctrine of calling. Each person was ordained by God with a calling or vocation and was expected to follow it conscientiously without envy of more exalted callings or contempt for those of a lesser kind. In God's sight all callings from the lowest to the highest were of equal moral value. The Lutheran world of callings was distinctly conservative, a hierarchy in which each person dutifully cleaved to a divinely appointed vocation in faith and good will, without aspirations of rising above it. The associated emphasis on labor also reveals the individualism of the doctrine. Each individual—the highest or the lowest—was expected to work strenuously, with the utmost industry and perseverance. Voluntary idleness of any sort was considered despicable and ungodly. Whether it was the gentleman spending his time in hunting or gaming or the manual worker frequenting taverns, idleness was the root of all sin. No one whose calling entailed either mental or physical labor could legitimately abdicate the responsibility for unrelenting exertion. Most of the reformers dwelt on the importance of this kind of dedicated, energetic, and individualistic labor. Lutheranism, however, was evidently not the only ideational source of the work ethic with its abhorrence of idleness, for Catholics like Dudley and especially More—a vehement opponent of Lutheranism—were among its most avid supporters. The roots were possibly in St. Augustine (not to neglect medieval monasticism), which might account for More's enthusiastic advocacy, if not Dudley's.[3]

The economic individualism so provoking the reformers became more pronounced as the century passed. These critics' works seemed to be testifying to the proliferation of what we would term "economic man." He was most typically engaged directly or indirectly, irrespective of his social status, in production for the market, cutting costs so as to yield the largest profits and fewest losses and when possible investing the profits in the expansion of the enterprise. Not all such profit-oriented individuals were directly involved in agricultural or manufacturing production. Many, responding to developments in production, were brokers or factors who extended their mediating activities as far as the market would bear. The economic man par excellence was in fact the capitalist, the principal actor of early capitalism whose appearance dates from at least the latter half of the previous century. Agrarian capitalism and the putting-out system of woolen manufacture, the initial manifestations of English capitalism in the era of the reformers, stimulated the beginnings of a metropolitan market centering on London which in the next centuries would spawn a complex distribution and financial network. The burgeoning "covetousness" so opposed by the reformers was the character of economic man, whose calculating and relentless pursuit of gain reflected something of the spirit of capitalism. To maintain that the reformers were the first observers of the prototypical capitalist is not to suggest that this was the only kind of economic behavior within their purview. By no means was every individual motivated by economic gain a capitalist. The bazaar mentality has ancient lineage. Much of the individualistic greed witnessed by the reformers must be ascribed to those treading the well-worn path of buying cheap and selling dear and seeking to profit quickly in a time of short supply, increasing demand, and rising prices. The reformers could not be expected to have discriminated between diverse modes of individualistic acquisitiveness; instead they perceived them all as examples of a single, unmitigated selfishness.

If the reformers agonized over the problem of economic individualism, the lone voice of acceptance was Smith's. Economic man, so vilified by the others, was to the realistic Smith a blessing in disguise. Refraining from the moralizing of the others, he accepted economic man for what he was, a decided instance of human egoism. Then Smith in his commonsensical way asked what was to be done? How was this surging economic egoism to be best handled for the good of the commonwealth? He clearly thought it a utopian folly to attempt the excision of original sin. On the contrary, Smith proposed making the best of fallen humans by harnessing their innate acquisitiveness for the welfare of all. Policies and laws could and should be framed to channel and manage this inherent selfishness for the common interest. Smith offered what amounted to a model of economic man and basically conceived of the state as a utilitarian mechanism for his control and manipulation. The core of effective public policy was economic. Indeed, the economy was central to the state. Smith thereby laid the foundations of the future science of political economy. His speculation about the conscription of economic individualism into the service of the state as well as his secularism and rationalism reflected something of the ethos of capitalism, perhaps entitling him to be called one of its earliest theorists. The bête noire of the reformers became the creative hub of much of subsequent social thought. The idea and ideal of possessive individualism at the heart of the future liberal outlook may in fact have been grounded in the Augustinian-Lutheran conception of man and some of its permutations in sixteenth-century England.

How can we explain this unique intellectual achievement of the English reformers, which reached a high point in the thought of Thomas Smith and had no parallel on the Continent? What was there about early Tudor England which set it apart from the rest of Western Europe, which may help account for the novelty of these social and political ideas? Tentative answers to these questions are significant not only in themselves but also because they help to illuminate the course taken by future English theorizing.

The most obvious natural characteristic of England then as well as now is its insularity. In an age of primitive technology, at least by twentieth-century standards, the country was relatively free from the constant dangers of foreign invasions and territorial disputes experienced by Continental powers. We are therefore not surprised that some English applied the realism of Italian Renaissance thinkers like Machiavelli to the analysis of internal social and economic difficulties rather than to problems of international politics, for instance, the conduct of foreign policy and war.

While isolation may help explain the novelty of the reformers' thought, perhaps more significant was the English structure of rule. From the Norman Conquest a highly centralized feudal monarchy had wielded power, whereas political fragmentation characterized much of Western Europe. By the sixteenth-century England had become a more unified state without the deep cultural and political divisions so typical of France and with a pivotal central representative assembly possessing full lawmaking and taxing jurisdiction for the whole realm. The state was in the hands of an aristocracy of wealthy landed proprietors who bore the principal financial burden of government from the rents of their enormous holdings. At the sixteenth century's end through the shrewd efforts of the Tudors, England had become a political nation with its own church under the crown and with a cultural, legal, and constitutional identity of its own. The Tudors had gone a long way in fashioning a centralized, unified institutional totality out of a personalized medieval monarchy, although the long and arduous process of modern state formation had by no means been completed. Small wonder then that the reformers turned to the central government, already in possession of the requisite power and authority, as the means of alleviating the economic and social distress of the people. It is likely that the unique nature of the English monarchy and its consolidation in the sixteenth century may have influenced the conceptualization of the state by the reformers.

Selected economic factors may also aid in understanding the configuration of ideas peculiar to the reformers. Economically, England about 1500 differed in several ways from her European neighbors. Foreign travelers as well as the English themselves commented on the great prosperity of the country: the bountiful food supply, the vast fields enclosed by hedgerows, the thriving market towns, and the riches of London, whose merchants sold an astonishing variety of goods. The high standard of living of the lower classes was invariably noted. They were better fed, housed, and clothed than their Continental counterparts. An awareness of the dramatic contrast between a booming England in 1500 and the depressed years of the following decades was undoubtedly one reason for the reformers' nostalgia for the past and perhaps for the acute feeling of deprivation that intensified their social protest. Chiefly responsible for the wealth of England in 1500 was wool production and the manufacture of woolen textiles; in both sectors rural capitalist enterprise was increasingly important. English woolens were famous throughout Europe and a flourishing export trade filled English coffers. A virtual monopoly over woolen exports exercised by the Merchants of the Staple in Calais and the Company of Merchant Adventurers in Antwerp may have indirectly stimulated the English fact-gathering propensity, already noticeable by 1500. Company records and inventories of customs duties on a single commodity, concentrated at several locations instead of dispersed among many, rendered a clearer and more accessible overview of foreign trade statistics, sharpening the quantitative focus.

Even from the time of the Norman Conquest the English commenced to show an interest—perhaps without parallel on the Continent—in collecting data on land and human resources (recall Domesday Book of 1085), basically for the purpose of taxation. The tendency was probably facilitated by political unity, governmental centralization, and the unusually extensive control of landed property by the nobility. Whatever the reasons, the inclination slowly grew, as evidenced by the fifteenth-century evaluations of England's economy: *The Libel of English Policy* and *The Comodytes of England*. After 1500, once the economy had begun to decline, these kinds of empirical and policy-oriented surveys proliferated in such compilations as Wolsey's musters, royal commission inquiries, municipal censuses of the poor (also on the Continent), the economic tracts of Clement Armstrong and others, and the fact-gathering of the reformers, notably Thomas Smith. Thereafter, from the early seventeenth century onward, the propensity for amassing economic and social information began to bloom; we encounter the treatises of Malynes, Misselden, and Mun, followed by William Petty's Down Survey of Ireland and his conception of "political arithmetic," Graunt's study of London mortality statistics, the "natural histories" of the Royal Society, and Gregory King's examination of English social structure.

Within this historical context then, what mélange of features specific to the reformers' age and culture may have shaped their social and political thought? In certain areas of the English countryside since the fifteenth century capitalism had been making its first appearance on the world scene. Continuing to advance and strengthen throughout the sixteenth century, capitalistic endeavor, however, was only a partial, if important cause of the increasing economic and social problems cataloged by the reformers. A complex of factors, including this incipient capitalism and demographic growth, was responsible for problematic economic developments since the halcyon days of the century's opening. England seems to have been the first of the major countries of Western Europe—France, Spain, the Netherlands, Italy, and Germany—to experience grave economic difficulties and so much human suffering at such an early date. We are seeing not so much a period of economic decline but rather the emergence of a new pattern of economic growth with all its social trials and tribulations, the rich becoming richer and the poor poorer, a novel development that aroused the reformers.

Intellectual and ideological factors of the early Tudor period also impressed the reformers' thinking with a distinctive stamp. The recent import into England of Lutheranism, with its creed of love, benevolence, charity, and its condemnation of covetousness, may have heightened an awareness of some of the social injustices afflicting the people, particularly when coupled with the inherited medieval ideal of a cooperative Christian polity. Another significant influence on all the reformers was Continental humanism, which arrived late in England and in some respects was the handmaid of early Lutheranism. The result was enthusiastic reading and discussion of the great thinkers of classical antiquity—Plato, Aristotle, Cicero—as humanism pervaded English intellectual life. All three of these ancient philosophers transmitted the principles of the mixed constitution and social environmentalism. Aristotle's comparative study of politics exposed the reformers to cultural differences and problems of social change and perhaps awakened them to the possibilities of a more exhaustive kind of economic analysis. The comments of Cicero on the nature of the state and government probably struck a vibrant chord in an age of Tudor nation-building. Humanism, perhaps above all, brought to England an acute sense of realism and a rational spirit of enquiry from which the reformers benefited in their grappling with current social questions. The seminal ideas and challenging outlook of Lutheranism and humanism reached an ever-widening audience because of the invention of printing in the mid-fifteenth century and the establishment of the first English press in 1476. Although English book production lagged behind Europe's, many religious writings together with the works of the ancients and humanists, some in translation, were published with increasing frequency. During a time of troubles the growing publication of printed books, pamphlets, and tracts broadened the circulation and exchange of ideas, encouraged the debate of urgent public issues among the literate classes, and generated a new social consciousness of the obligations of citizenship.

In our own challenging times it seems appropriate to ask what lessons can be learned from the early Tudor reformers? Today, when conservatism in many different guises dominates much of our thought and practice, we should remember that these early reformers, far from being starry-eyed radicals, were staunchly antidemocratic and conservative, seeking only to strengthen and streamline the status quo. Their down-to-earth and moderate goal was to reform, not revolutionize, existing society by ensuring the survival of all classes in a secure, harmonious, and flourishing material life. Whatever their intellectual shortcomings, the reformers sincerely believed that individuals thrived only in a prosperous society. Private interest depended ultimately on the common interest. Individuals could not look solely to themselves or to their own advantage, separate from the interests of others. The just was closely tied to the prudential in the reformers' emphasis on the priority of the common interest over short-sighted egoism and self-promotion.

As theorists of the common interest, the reformers also clearly recognized that only government representing the interests of all citizens had the capacity to act as arbiter and champion of the common interest. Since the material well-being and security of all citizens was the crux of the common interest for the reformers, they argued that government must assume the imaginative and constructive function of social architect. Such a role could not be relegated to individuals or groups within the state because, no matter how well-intentioned, they would inevitably look to their own interests to the detriment of the whole. The reformers, moreover, with a keen prudential sensibility, understood that unless economic and social conditions were improved by the remedial measures of government, the result would be a decrease of the power and authority of the state and an increase of crime and civil disorder. Government was therefore obliged, if only for its own survival, to fashion a social environment in which each person would be able to live as a human being in comfort and dignity. To succeed, the reforms of government had to be grounded in the meticulous and exhaustive inquiry into actual conditions, one in which the identification of social and economic problems was absolutely critical. Aside from their remarkable humanity and heartfelt compassion for the less fortunate, perhaps the reformers' most commendable quality was their conviction that people no longer needed to be the helpless victims of forces beyond their control. By recreating individuals and the social habitat through decisive, enlightened action, men could live as true human beings.

Notes

1: INTRODUCTION

1. The influential Fortescue, who died before Henry VII came to the throne, is included because in some ways he prefigured the approach of the reformers. Christopher St. German and John Ponet, important as they are in the history of political thought, have not been included, although some of their ideas, especially those of Ponet, are discussed in the following chapters. For a number of reasons, which will become apparent, neither thinker fits very well into my category of "reformer."

For short, illuminating treatments of most of these thinkers, see: J. W. Allen, *A History of Political Thought in the Sixteenth Century*, rev. ed. (London: Methuen, 1957; orig. published, 1928); Christopher Morris, *Political Thought in England: Tyndale to Hooker* (London: Oxford University Press, 1953); Quentin Skinner, *The Foundations of Modern Political Thought* (Cambridge: Cambridge University Press, 1978), vols. 1 and 2.

In addition to more specialized works on the individual thinkers cited throughout this study, the following are valuable: Franklin Le van Baumer, *The Early Tudor Theory of Kingship* (New Haven: Yale University Press, 1940); S. B. Chrimes, *English Constitutional Ideas in the Fifteenth Century* (Cambridge: Cambridge University Press, 1936); Arthur B. Ferguson, *The Articulate Citizen and the English Renaissance* (Durham, N.C.: Duke University Press, 1965); Whitney R. D. Jones, *The Tudor Commonwealth 1529–1559: A Study of the Impact of Mid-Tudor England upon Contemporary Concepts of the Nature and Duties of the Commonwealth* (London: University of London, Athlone Press, 1970); W. Gordon Zeeveld, *Foundations of Tudor Policy* (Cambridge, Mass.: Harvard University Press, 1948).

To avoid any misunderstanding, my definition of "political economy" should be clarified. Political economy is a systematic mode of social discourse focusing on the problem of the "wealth of nations." It is policy oriented and hence political, designed to make recommendations for governmental action in respect to economic matters. It is concerned with the functions of state and government, conceived of either positively or negatively, in contributing to the wealth of nations. The history of British political economy can be roughly divided chronologically between a "preclassical" phase, largely mercantilistic in outlook (Malynes, Misselden, Mun, Petty, Locke, Child, North, Barbon, Davenant), and a "classical" laissez-faire phase (Adam Smith, Malthus, Ricardo, James Mill, J. S. Mill).

2. The reader will note that here and elsewhere I state that Starkey and Smith (and others) "anticipated" (or some such wording in other contexts) a future position. In so doing I do not wish to suggest that I hold a teleological view of history. On the contrary, I believe that history is a continuous process of causally related occurrences, not a series of disconnected, discrete events. Past events may often be of a contingent, unpredictable nature, but this does not reduce history to pure contingency. The benefit of historical hindsight indicates that ideas and practices have temporal beginnings (which often are amenable to causal explanations), frequently "before their time," before they become commonplace and widely adopted. This is not to argue that such ideas and practices were predetermined to appear when they did and to proliferate, all driven by some kind of inexorable teleological dynamic.

3. Terence Hutchison, *Before Adam Smith: The Emergence of Political Economy, 1662–1776* (Oxford: Blackwell, 1988), 6–7, 21–22.

4. My position throughout this book is at variance with the provocative thesis of Alan Macfarlane, *The Origins of English Individualism: The Family, Property and Social Transition*, corrected ed. (Oxford: Blackwell, 1979), and his *The Culture of Capitalism* (Oxford: Blackwell, 1987). English capitalism (and individualism), according to Macfarlane, did not emerge in our period but was at least as old as the thirteenth century. For a detailed critique of Macfarlane's views on this matter, see Ellen Meiksins Wood, *The Pristine Culture of Capitalism: A Historical Essay on Old Regimes and Modern States* (London: Verso, 1991), chap. 8.

5. This is the cogently argued position of Mary Dewar. See her *Sir Thomas Smith: A Tudor Intellectual in Office* (London: University of London, Athlone Press, 1964), 53–55; "The Authorship of the *Discourse of the Commonweal*," *Economic History Review*, 2d ser., 19 (1966): 388–400, and the introduction to her edition of *A Discourse of the Commonweal of This Realm of England: Attributed to Sir Thomas Smith* (Charlottesville: University Press of Virginia, for the Folger Shakespeare Library, 1969), xviii–xxiv. Before Dewar's treatment of the subject, the *Discourse*, although sometimes assigned to Smith, was widely thought to be by John Hales, following Elizabeth Lamond, ed., *A Discourse of the Common Weal of This Realm of England* (Cambridge: Cambridge

University Press, 1893; reprinted, 1929 and 1954). For a dissent to Dewar's brief for Smith in favor of Lamond's view, see W. K. Jordan, *Edward VI: The Young King: The Protectorship of the Duke of Somerset* (London: Allen and Unwin, 1968), 395 and n. 4. Jordan concludes, however, by doubting whether the dispute can be satisfactorily resolved. In my opinion and apparently that of many scholars today, Dewar presents a strong and convincing case for Smith's authorship, and such will be the assumption throughout this book.

6. My attempt to justify this characterization of More's social and political thought in *Utopia*, which is not the usual view, can be found in chapter 6 of this book.

7. Fortescue, *De laudibus legum Anglie,* trans. and ed. S. B. Chrimes, general preface by H. D. Hazeltine (Cambridge: Cambridge University Press, 1942), 69.

8. More, *Utopia*, in vol. 4 of *The Complete Works of St. Thomas More,* ed. Edward Surtz and J. H. Hexter (New Haven: Yale University Press, 1965), 65–67.

9. Starkey, *A Dialogue between Pole and Lupset,* ed. T. F. Mayer, Camden Society Fourth Series, vol. 37 (London: Royal Historical Society, 1989), 36, 60–61. On Morison's view, see Zeeveld, *Foundations of Tudor Policy,* 217. Also on the favorable contrast of English with foreign conditions, see Jones, *Tudor Commonwealth,* 116–117.

10. W. K. Jordan, ed., *The Chronicle and Political Papers of King Edward VI* (London: Allen and Unwin, 1966), 161.

11. J. C. K. Cornwall, *Wealth and Society in Early Sixteenth-Century England* (London: Routledge and Kegan Paul, 1988), 180. He dates it to 1485, the first year of Henry VII's reign.

2: EARLY SIXTEENTH-CENTURY ENGLAND

1. On these matters my methodological differences from J. G. A. Pocock and Quentin Skinner and the scholars whom they have influenced should be obvious. While no one can dispute their signal contributions to the history of social and political thought, their methodology in my opinion is marred by pronounced idealism, linguistic reductionism, and failure to relate in detail social and political ideas to the relevant material context or to consider the interaction between the two. For Pocock, see *The Machiavellian Moment: Florentine Political Thought and the Atlantic Republican Tradition* (Princeton, N.J.: Princeton University Press, 1975), and *Virtue, Commerce, and History: Essays on Political Thought and History, Chiefly in the Eighteenth Century* (Cambridge: Cambridge University Press, 1985). For Skinner, in addition to his writings cited throughout this book, see "Meaning and Understanding in the History of Ideas," *History and Theory* 8 (1969): 3–53; "Social Meaning and the

Explanation of Social Action," in *Philosophy, Politics and Society*, 4th ser., ed. Peter Laslett, W. G. Runciman, and Quentin Skinner (Oxford: Blackwell, 1972), 136–157; "Some Problems in the Analysis of Political Thought and Action," *Political Theory* 2 (August 1974): 277–303; *Machiavelli* (Oxford: Oxford University Press, 1981). Since the publication of his masterful two-volume study *The Foundations of Modern Political Thought* (Cambridge: Cambridge University Press, 1978), Skinner's idealism, indebted to R. G. Collingwood, seems to have become even more pronounced. For some detailed criticism of Skinner's position see my *John Locke and Agrarian Capitalism* (Berkeley, Los Angeles, London: University of California Press, 1984), chap. 1.

In Pocock and especially Skinner, it is almost as if the economic, for instance, and the political belong to completely unconnected, autonomous realms—contrary to what we know of social reality—and political economy is often a cipher. A recent example by other authors is the useful collection of essays edited by J. H. Burns, with the assistance of Mark Goldie, *The Cambridge History of Political Thought 1450–1700* (Cambridge: Cambridge University Press, 1991). Apart from the failure to assess the impact of the beginnings of modern state formation on the shaping of the political ideas of the period, Burns's introduction and the subsequent essays do little by way of examining the possible link between the development of political ideas and the crucial changes occurring in agriculture, manufacture, commerce, population, and technology. There is no treatment of political economy, and he gives emergent capitalism little role in the unfolding of this drama of pure ideas.

2. See the works cited throughout this book.

3. Lawrence Stone, *The Past and the Present Revisited*, rev. ed. (London and New York: Routledge and Kegan Paul, 1987), 122.

Unless otherwise cited the facts and figures throughout this chapter are based on the following works, usually without specific acknowledgment: A. L. Beier, *Masterless Men: The Vagrancy Problem in England, 1560–1640* (London: Methuen, 1985); S. T. Bindoff, *Tudor England* (Harmondsworth, Middlesex: Penguin, 1950); Robert Brenner, *The Brenner Debate: Agrarian Class Structure and Economic Development in Pre-Industrial Europe*, ed. T. H. Aston and C. H. E. Philpin (Cambridge: Cambridge University Press, 1985); J. C. K. Cornwall, *Wealth and Society in Early Sixteenth-Century England* (London: Routledge and Kegan Paul, 1988); C. S. L. Davies, *Peace, Print and Protestantism 1450–1558* (London: Paladin, 1984); G. R. Elton, *England under the Tudors*, rev. ed. (London: Methuen, 1974); G. R. Elton, *The Tudor Revolution in Government: Administrative Changes in the Reign of Henry VIII* (Cambridge: Cambridge University Press, 1953); John Guy, *Tudor England* (Oxford: Clarendon Press, 1989); Eric Kerridge, *The Agricultural Revolution* (London:

Allen and Unwin, 1967); Eric Kerridge, *Trade and Banking in Early Modern England* (Manchester: University of Manchester Press, 1988); J. J. Scarisbrick, *Henry VIII* (London: Eyre and Spottiswoode, 1968); Paul Slack, *Poverty and Policy in Tudor and Stuart England* (London and New York: Longman, 1988); R. H. Tawney, *The Agrarian Problem in the Sixteenth Century* (London: Macmillan, 1911); Joan Thirsk, ed., *The Agrarian History of England*, vol. 4, *1500–1640* (Cambridge: Cambridge University Press, 1967); Penry Williams, *The Tudor Regime* (Oxford: Clarendon Press, 1979); Joyce Youings, *Sixteenth-Century England* (Harmondsworth, Middlesex: Penguin, 1984).

4. The description of Cromwell is that of Scarisbrick, *Henry VIII*, 303.

5. This section is derivative, indebted to the works of Davies and Williams, cited in n. 3 of this chapter, and especially to Elton's *Tudor Revolution* and Guy's *Tudor England*. Elton's thesis of the "Tudor revolution in government" has been subjected to much criticism and emendation by recent historians, a matter discussed by these other three scholars. For our purposes there seems to be no good reason to go beyond their conclusions.

6. Elton, *Tudor Revolution*, 426, concludes that in respect to "political and social structure, the sixteenth century produced something quite new in England—the self-contained sovereign state in which no power on earth could challenge the supremacy of statute made by the crown in parliament."

7. Cornwall, *Wealth and Society*, 210.

8. Fortescue, *De laudibus legum Anglie*, trans. and ed. S. B. Chrimes, general preface by H. D. Hazeltine (Cambridge: Cambridge University Press, 1942), 69.

9. This and the next paragraph rely on Kerridge, *Trade and Banking*.

10. On the fear of popular revolt during the period: Franklin Le van Baumer, *The Early Tudor Theory of Kingship* (New Haven: Yale University Press, 1940), 103–111; Whitney R. D. Jones, *The Tudor Commonwealth 1529–1559: A Study of the Impact of Mid-Tudor England upon Contemporary Concepts of Nature and Duties of the Commonwealth* (London: University of London, Athlone Press, 1970), 43–74. Jones writes of "an almost hysterical attitude towards rebellion" (p. 45) and of "the endemic nightmare" that economic difficulties might be productive of insurrection (p. 51).

For the civil unrest: Julian Cornwall, *Revolt of the Peasantry 1549* (London: Routledge and Kegan Paul, 1977); Anthony Fletcher, *Tudor Rebellions*, 3d ed. (London and New York: Longman, 1983); Anthony Fletcher and John Stevenson, eds., *Order and Disorder in Early Modern England* (Cambridge: Cambridge University Press, 1985); R. B. Manning, *Village Revolts: Social Protest and Popular Disturbances in England,*

1509–1640 (Oxford: Clarendon Press, 1988); Perez Zagorin, *Rebels and Rulers, 1500–1600* (Cambridge: Cambridge University Press, 1982), vol. 1, chap. 7.

11. Williams, *Tudor Regime*, 316–317; Scarisbrick, *Henry VIII*, 342.

12. Zagorin, *Rebels and Rulers*, 1:178: "The first and biggest agrarian insurrection of the sixteenth century was Kett's rebellion of 1549." He is comparing uprisings in England with those in France and Germany.

13. Guy, *Tudor England*, 208.

14. Useful treatments of early English humanism can be found in some of the works cited in n. 1 of this chapter, in n. 1 of chapter 1 of this book, and also in: J. H. Burns, ed., *Cambridge History*; Fritz Caspari, *Humanism and the Social Order in England* (Chicago: University of Chicago Press, 1954); Maria Dowling, *Humanism in the Age of Henry VIII* (London: Croom Helm, 1986); Alistair Fox, *Politics and Literature in the Reigns of Henry VII and Henry VIII* (Oxford: Blackwell, 1989); James Kelsey McConica, *English Humanists and Reformation Politics under Henry VIII and Edward VI* (Oxford: Clarendon Press, 1965); Quentin Skinner, "Political Philosophy," in *The Cambridge History of Renaissance Philosophy*, ed. C. B. Schmitt, Quentin Skinner, E. Kessler, J. Kraye (Cambridge: Cambridge University Press, 1988), esp. 442–452.

In this chapter I refer to several of the classical and Renaissance influences on the reformers, while in chapter 8 I will say something about the impact of Lutheranism and medieval scholasticism on the Commonwealthmen. For the general question of intellectual influences, see my comments at the beginning of this chapter.

15. Such is the verdict of John A. Gee, *The Life and Work of Thomas Lupset: With a Critical Text of the Original Treatises and the Letters* (New Haven: Yale University Press, 1928), 197.

16. On More's debt to Cicero, see esp.: Brendan Bradshaw, "Transalpine Humanism," in *Cambridge History*, ed. J. H. Burns, 113, 119, 122, 126–127; Quentin Skinner, "Political Philosophy"; Skinner, "Sir Thomas More's *Utopia* and the Language of Renaissance Humanism," in *The Language of Political Thought*, ed. Anthony Pagden (Cambridge: Cambridge University Press, 1987), 123–157. For the influence of Plato, particularly the *Laws*, see chapter 6 of this book.

17. Thomas F. Mayer, *Thomas Starkey and the Commonweal: Humanist Politics and Religion in the Reign of Henry VIII* (Cambridge: Cambridge University Press, 1989), 24, concludes that Cicero's *On Duties* "contains virtually the whole of Starkey's argument in his *Dialogue*."

18. See chapter 9 of this book and my article "Cicero and the Political Thought of the Early English Renaissance," *Modern Language Quarterly* 51 (June 1990): 185–207.

19. W. Gordan Zeeveld, *Foundations of Tudor Policy* (Cambridge, Mass.: Harvard University Press, 1948), 185–189. Smith's holdings of his

library in his country house, High Hill, Essex, 1 August 1566, are listed in John Strype, *The Life of the Learned Sir Thomas Smith*, new ed. (Oxford: Clarendon Press, 1820), 274–281. For an interesting treatment of English Machiavellianism, see Pocock, *The Machiavellian Moment*, chap. 10.

20. On this point, see Arthur B. Ferguson, *The Articulate Citizen and the English Renaissance* (Durham, N.C.: Duke University Press, 1965), 201.

21. The following is largely extracted from Lucien Febvre and Henri-Jean Martin, *The Coming of the Book: The Impact of Printing 1450–1800*, trans. David Gerard, ed. Geoffrey Nowell-Smith and David Wooton (London: Verso, 1984).

22. Fox, *Politics and Literature*, 3.

23. For reference to the early pamphlet literature, S. B. Chrimes, *English Constitutional Ideas in the Fifteenth Century* (Cambridge: Cambridge University Press, 1936), 305 and 333–334 n. 11.

24. Thomas (Fortescue), Lord Clermont, ed., *The Works of Sir John Fortescue* (London: Printed for Private Distribution, 1869), 1:523. This is a remark made by Fortescue, who was forced by Edward IV to repudiate the arguments in the three pamphlets. See 1:497–518 for the texts of the pamphlets.

25. Chrimes, *English Constitutional Ideas*, 305.

26. The remainder of this paragraph relies mainly on Ferguson, *Articulate Citizen*, 133–147.

3: TOWARD AN ECONOMIC CONCEPTION OF THE STATE

1. See Karl Polanyi, *The Great Transformation*, foreword by Robert M. MacIver (Boston: Beacon Press, 1957; orig. published, 1944), 46:

> The outstanding discovery of recent historical and anthropological research is that man's economy, as a rule, is submerged in his social relationships. He does not act so as to safeguard his individual interest in the possession of material goods; he acts so as to safeguard his social standing, his social claims, his social assets. He values material goods only insofar as they serve this end. Neither the process of production nor that of distribution is linked to specific economic interests attached to the possession of goods; but every single step in that process is geared to a number of social interests which eventually ensure that the required step be taken. These interests will be very different in a small hunting or fishing community from those in a vast despotic society, but in either case the economic system will be run on noneconomic motives.

This quotation is also contained in Polanyi, *Primitive, Archaic, and Modern Economies: Essays of Karl Polanyi*, ed. George Dalton (Boston: Beacon Press, 1971), 7.

2. S. B. Chrimes, *English Constitutional Ideas in the Fifteenth Century* (Cambridge: Cambridge University Press, 1936), 303–305, 332–333 nn. 6–9. On the importance of the idea of the "body politic" in early Tudor England: Whitney R. D. Jones, *The Tudor Commonwealth 1529–1559: A Study of the Impact of Mid-Tudor England upon Contemporary Concepts of the Nature and Duties of the Commonwealth* (London: University of London, Athlone Press, 1970), 13–18. He indicates that the medieval work of Christine de Pisan (1365–1430), *Le livre du corps de policie*, published in England in 1521 with the title *The Book Whiche is Called the Body of Polycye*, influenced members of the court. For a brief discussion of the book, see Jeannine Quillet, "Community, Counsel and Representation," in *Cambridge History of Medieval Political Thought c. 350–c. 1450*, ed. J. H. Burns (Cambridge: Cambridge University Press, 1988), 542–543. On p. 542 Quillet writes that Christine de Pisan "takes up, in an almost literal way, the symbolism of the social body that John of Salisbury had used in his *Polycraticus.*"

3. An excellent brief discussion of the emergence of the modern conception of the state is in Quentin Skinner, *The Foundations of Modern Political Thought* (Cambridge: Cambridge University Press, 1978), 2:353–358. Also see his essay, "The State," in *Political Innovation and Conceptual Change*, ed. Terence Ball, James Farr, Russell L. Hansen (Cambridge: Cambridge University Press, 1989), 90–131, and my *Cicero's Social and Political Thought* (Berkeley, Los Angeles, London: University of California Press, 1988), 123–125.

4. These and subsequent details are spelled out in chapter 9 of this book.

5. Smith, *De republica Anglorum*, ed. Mary Dewar (Cambridge: Cambridge University Press, 1982), 49, 78.

6. J. W. Allen, *A History of Political Thought in the Sixteenth Century*, rev. ed. (London: Methuen, 1957; orig. published, 1928), 151–152. Also see p. 134: "The idealists of the mid-century, therefore, tended to see in co-operation for economic purposes the immediate object of the social and political structure. But that tendency, too, is visible earlier; and as fully as Aquinas or St. Antonio of Florence, they found in religion the unifying and defining and animating purpose of society." Jones, *Tudor Commonwealth*, 214, who proceeds to quote Allen, comments: "While the concept of society derived from religious origins and assumptions, discussion of its functions was concerned very largely with economic issues."

7. Christopher Morris, *Political Thought in England: Tyndale to Hooker* (London: Oxford University Press, 1953), 1.

8. I am indebted to David McNally for this formulation.

9. Terence Hutchison, *Before Adam Smith: The Emergence of Political Economy, 1662–1776* (Oxford: Blackwell, 1988), 15–16; Eric Roll, *A*

History of Economic Thought, 4th ed. (London: Faber and Faber, 1973), 40–59; Joseph A. Schumpeter, *History of Economic Analysis,* ed. E. B. Schumpeter (New York: Oxford University Press, 1954), 162–164.

10. Erasmus wrote more on economic questions than any of the others. His chap. 4 is "On Tributes and Taxes." See *The Education of the Christian Prince,* trans. Lester K. Born (New York: Columbia University Press, 1936), 215–218. In addition to education Vives's book covers a vast range of topics, including the nature of politics and the state, but contains very little on economic questions.

11. C. W. Cole, *French Mercantilist Doctrines before Colbert* (New York: Octagon, 1969; orig. published, 1931), chap. 1.

12. On this and the following, Arthur B. Ferguson, *The Articulate Citizen and the English Renaissance* (Durham, N.C.: Duke University Press, 1965), xxiv–xv, 200–207.

13. Ibid., 201.

14. An abridged and edited version of *The Libel,* a poem, is in William Huse Dunham, Jr., and Stanley Pargellis, eds., *Complaint and Reform in England 1436–1714: Fifty Writings of the Time on Politics, Religion, Society, Economics, Architecture, Science, and Education* (New York: Oxford University Press, 1938), 3–30. The "libel" of the title is evidently from the Latin, *libellus,* little book. The text of *The Comodytes* is in Thomas (Fortescue), Lord Clermont, ed., *The Works of Sir John Fortescue* (London: Printed for Private Distribution, 1869), 1:545–554. Ferguson, *Articulate Citizen,* 99–106, discusses these and other early economic pamphlets.

15. Paul Slack, *Poverty and Policy in Tudor and Stuart England* (London and New York: Longman, 1988), 26–27, 61, 73, 122–123, 206, esp. for our period.

16. See J. C. K. Cornwall, *Wealth and Society in Early Sixteenth-Century England* (London: Routledge and Kegan Paul, 1988). The book is largely based on the data provided by the muster.

17. Jones, *Tudor Commonwealth,* 108–128, for an excellent discussion of the attitudes toward poverty.

18. A. L. Beier, *Masterless Men: The Vagrancy Problem in England, 1560–1640* (London: Methuen, 1985), xix, and 149 on More's *Utopia.*

19. A. E. J. Johnson, *Predecessors of Adam Smith: The Growth of British Economic Thought* (London: King; New York: Prentice-Hall, 1937), chaps. 13–14, suggests that this kind of outlook was a source, long before Adam Smith and the physiocrats (p. 282), of the distinction between "productive" and "unproductive" labor.

20. See chapter 9 of this book on this latter point and the following.

21. W. K. Jordan, ed., *The Chronicle and Political Papers of King Edward VI* (London: Allen and Unwin, 1966), 160. Jordan supplies a title for the discourse, "Discourse on the Reform of Abuses in Church and State,"

and the possible date of April 1551. Of the eight pages of text in the Jordan edition (pp. 159–167) only about a fifth concerns the ecclesiastical regimen, the rest being devoted to the temporal regimen.

22. This and the following characteristics of the thought of the reformers are treated in detail in the relevant chapters of this book.

23. For the medieval idea of counsel and the change to "constructive policy," Ferguson, *Articulate Citizen*, esp. 70–71, 280–281, 315–317.

24. Chrimes, *English Constitutional Ideas*, 192–193, 201–203. For Chrimes the notion of making new law lagged behind the late fifteenth-century English practice. St. German seems to have been the first to conceive of statutes' making new law.

4: FORERUNNER OF THE REFORMERS

1. All details about the life, works, and influence of Fortescue in these introductory remarks are taken from the prefaces and introductions of the indispensable editions of two of his works: *De laudibus legum Anglie*, trans. and ed. S. B. Chrimes, general preface by H. D. Hazeltine (Cambridge: Cambridge University Press, 1942), and *The Governance of England: Otherwise Called the Difference between an Absolute and a Limited Monarchy*, ed. Charles Plummer (Oxford: Clarendon Press, 1885). The first, containing interfaced Latin text and English translation, will be abbreviated in subsequent footnotes *L*, the second *G*. I have followed Chrime's translation in general, with occasional minor changes. For Fortescue's first book, *De natura legis naturae* (unpublished in his lifetime), abbreviated below *N*, I have relied on the Latin text and English translation in vol. 1, pp. 63–184 and 187–333, respectively, of *The Works of Sir John Fortescue*, ed. Thomas (Fortescue), Lord Clermont, 2 vols. (London: Printed for Private Distribution, 1869). The English translation of the Latin is by Chichester Fortescue.

For my purposes the most valuable commentaries on Fortescue's social and political ideas are J. H. Burns, "Fortescue and the Political Theory of *Dominium*," *The Historical Journal* 28 (1985): 777–797; Jean Dunbabin, "Government," *The Cambridge History of Medieval Political Thought c. 350–c. 1450*, ed. J. H. Burns (Cambridge: Cambridge University Press, 1988), 492–493, 507–508, 515–516; S. B. Chrimes, *English Constitutional Ideas in the Fifteenth Century* (Cambridge: Cambridge University Press, 1936), 300–341; Norman Doe, "Fifteenth-Century Concepts of Law: Fortescue and Pecock," *History of Political Thought* 10 (1989): 257–280. Arthur B. Ferguson, *The Articulate Citizen and the English Renaissance* (Durham, N.C.: Duke University Press, 1965), 111–129; Charles H. McIlwain, *The Growth of Political Thought in the West: From the Greeks to the End of the Middle Ages* (London: Macmillan, 1932), esp. 354–361; J. G. A. Pocock, *The Machiavellian Moment: Florentine Political Thought and the Atlantic Republican Tradition* (Princeton, N.J.: Princeton University Press, 1975), 9–22.

2. Franklin Le van Baumer, *The Early Tudor Theory of Kingship* (New Haven: Yale University Press, 1936), 8. *De natura* is divided into two parts. Part 1 stands alone as a treatise on the law of nature. Part 2 is concerned with the right of succession on the basis of conclusions reached in the first part. Fortescue's aim in writing was to argue for the Lancastrian Henry VI's claim to the throne against that of the Yorkist Edward IV.

3. Fortescue, apparently treated by participants on all sides of the seventeenth-century ideological debates as a medieval thinker, was used not so much for the substance of his ideas as a venerable imprint of authority. This was also certainly true of Bracton. See Cary J. Nederman, "Bracton on Kingship First Visited: The Idea of Sovereignty and Bractonian Political Thought," *Political Science* 40 (1988): 49–66.

4. *L, 3.*

5. *L, 3.*

6. Ferguson, *Articulate Citizen,* 112, 119.

7. Fortescue made no use in any of his works of previous English legal writers, such as Bracton, Fleta, or Britton, and with minor exceptions he made no direct connection between his ideas and theirs. See Chrimes, *English Constitutional Ideas,* 324–328.

8. Cary J. Nederman, "Aristotle as Authority: Alternative Aristotelian Sources of Late Mediaeval Political Theory," *History of European Ideas* 8 (1987): 39–41.

9. *N, 194.*

10. *N, 205.*

11. *L, 19.* See my article *"Tabula Rasa,* Social Environmentalism, and the English Paradigm," *Journal of the History of Ideas* 53 (1992): 647–668.

12. *N, 228–229.*

13. *N, 85, 170–172,* a total of eight instances.

14. *N,* city, 85, 150, 163; state, 132 (3 instances).

15. *N, 80, 81, 90, 97, 159, 164.*

16. *N, 88;* for *guberno, 79, 84, 86, 97.*

17. *N, 85, 139, 170–172.*

18. *L, 31.* The definition is from St. Augustine, *City of God,* XIX, 24, mistakenly cited by Fortescue as chapter 23. The Latin of Augustine as quoted by Fortescue is *Populus est cetus hominum iuris consensu et utilitatis sociatus.* It differs from Augustine's own Latin (Loeb Classical Library text), *Populus et coetus multitudinis rationalis, rerum quas deligit communione sociatus,* which is his rendition of Cicero's definition in *De re publica,* I, 39 (Loeb Classical Library text): *coetus multitudinis iuris consensu et utilitatis communione.* Fortescue's version seems to be somewhat closer to Cicero's original than Augustine's. On what follows about

Cicero see my *Cicero's Social and Political Thought* (Berkeley, Los Angeles, London: University of California Press, 1988), 125–128.

19. *L,* 31. *Corpus politicum* appears twice on this page, the only usage in the book. Also see *N,* 216.

20. *L,* 31–33.

21. *G,* 112.

22. See chapter 7 of this book for Starkey's elaboration of the "body politic" metaphor and its identification with "state" and chapter 9 for Smith's identification of *res publica,* "body politic," and "civil society" with "common wealth."

23. I do not intend to deal with the thorny problem of the possible intellectual sources. For a discussion of them, see Burns, "Fortescue and the Political Theory of *Dominium*"; Chrimes, *English Constitutional Ideas,* 314–317; McIlwain, *Growth of Political Thought,* 358–360.

24. Richard Tuck, *Natural Rights Theories: Their Origin and Development* (Cambridge: Cambridge University Press, 1979), chap. 1; also, Burns "Fortescue and the Political Theory of *Dominium*," esp. 796–797; Chrimes, *English Constitutional Ideas,* 307–308.

25. *N,* esp. 205–206, 213–218, 220–221, 306–310.

26. For what follows in the next two paragraphs the citations to *N* in n. 25 of this chapter are particularly relevant to the nature and "history" of the different kinds of *dominium.* The subject is also treated in *L,* 25–37 and *G,* 109–113. Also see Burns, "Fortescue and the Political Theory of *Dominium*"; Chrimes, *English Constitutional Ideas,* 304, 309–312.

27. *N,* 216, 218.

28. Jean Bodin, *Six Books of the Commonwealth,* I, vi; II, ii, iii; III, vii, viii; IV, i, ii. For Bodin, in agreement with Fortescue, Nimrod was the first ruler of a commonwealth. Bodin, however, does not mention Belus and identifies Ninus with Nimrod.

29. *L,* 29; *G,* 112.

30. See comment in Burns, "Fortescue and the Political Theory of *Dominium*," 788.

31. *N,* 205.

32. *L,* 25. English legislation, as conceived by Fortescue, is termed "a joint-stock enterprise" in Dunbabin, "Government," in Burns, ed., *Cambridge History of Medieval Political Thought,* 507. The king is obligated to obey the law so constituted by his coronation oath, *L,* 79.

33. *G,* 116.

34. McIlwain, *Growth of Political Thought,* 361–363; Chrimes, *English Constitutional Ideas,* 319–322. McIlwain is probably mistaken that Fortescue was reflecting a common medieval view.

35. For Chrimes's judgment in regard to Fortescue and the English constitution, see *English Constitutional Ideas,* 523.

36. N, 258. On the traditional view, Chrimes, *English Constitutional Ideas*, 14–15; Ferguson, *Articulate Citizen*, 125.

37. L, 11.

38. N, 243–245.

39. L, 13.

40. L, 31, 37, 41.

41. L, 25, 41, 87. Also N, 97, 162.

42. L, 25.

43. L, 33.

44. L, 37, 41.

45. L, 87.

46. N, 211–212, 291.

47. N, 193.

48. N, 211–212.

49. N, 291.

50. N, 211.

51. N, 291.

52. L, 25, 41, 87, 105.

53. L, 7, 9.

54. N, 304.

55. L, 105.

56. L, 27, 35, 81, 89–91.

57. L, 91.

58. *Works of Sir John Fortescue*, 1:552. Also see the somewhat earlier anonymous tract, *The Libel of English Policy*, in William Huse Dunham, Jr., and Stanley Pargellis, eds., *Complaint and Reform in England 1436–1714: Fifty Writings of the Time on Politics, Religion, Society, Economics, Architecture, Science, and Education* (New York: Oxford University Press, 1938), 3–30. The general impression given is one of a very prosperous nation, the main supplier of some vital raw commodities to the Continent, especially Flanders and Spain: "They may not live to maintain their degrees, / Without our English commodities, / Wool and tin; for the wool of England / Sustains the Flemish commons, I understand" (p. 6).

59. *A Relation, or Rather a True Account, of the Island of England; with Sundry Particulars of the Customs of These People, and of the Royal Revenues under King Henry the Seventh about the Year 1500*, trans. C. A. Sneyd (London: Camden Society, 1847), 28. Probably written by the secretary to Francesco Capello, Venetian envoy to the court of Henry VII.

60. Ibid., 42–43.

61. L, 81.

62. L, 81–83.

63. L, 83–85. Cf. G, 114–115: "But verely thai liven in the most ex-

treme pouertie and miserie, and yet dwellyn thai in on the most fertile reaume of the worlde."

64. *L*, 87. From Aristotle's *Rhetoric*, 1397a. See Nederman, "Aristotle as Authority."

65. *L*, 87–89. Cf. *G*, 115:

> But blessyd be God, this lande is rulid vndir a bettir lawe; and therefore the peple therof be not in such peynurie, nor therby hurt in thair persons, but thei bith welthe, and haue all thinges nescessarie to the sustenance of nature. Wherfore thai ben myghty, and able to resist the aduersaries of this reaume, and to beete ouer reaumes that do, or wolde do them wronge. Lo this is the fruyt of *Jus polliticum et regale*, vndre wich we liue.

66. *G*, 116.

67. *L*, 81. The title of chapter 3 of *G*, 113: "Here Bien Shewed The Fruytes of Jus Regale And The Fruyts of Jus Politicum Et Regale."

68. Aristotle, *Politics*, 1282a.

69. *L*, 43.

70. *L*, 71.

71. *L*, 73.

72. *L*, 57, 59–61, 67, 77.

73. *L*, 57, 61.

74. *L*, 59–61.

75. *L*, 61, 69.

76. *L*, 69, 71.

77. *L*, 67–71.

78. *L*, 69.

79. *L*, 71.

80. *L*, 71.

81. *L*, 71.

82. Fortescue's picture of the English agrarian scene is attested by the Italian visitor in *A Relation . . . of the Island of England*, 10:

> Agriculture is not practised in this island beyond what is required for the consumption of the people; because were they to plough and sow all the land that was capable of cultivation, they might sell a quantity of grain to the surrounding countries. This negligence is, however, atoned for, by an immense profusion of comestible animal, such as stags, goats, fallow-deer, hares, rabbits, pigs, and an infinity of oxen. . . . But above all, they have an enormous number of sheep, which yield them quantities of wool of the best quality.

83. Chrimes, *English Constitutional Ideas*, 332. He devotes a useful section (pp. 329–332) to a summary of Fortescue's administrative proposals in *G*.

84. Ferguson, *Articulate Citizen*, 125–126.

85. *G*, 117.

86. G, 119.

87. Chrimes emphasizes that Fortescue's distinction was in regard to expenses, not revenues. For the king the important difference would have been between "certain" and "casual" revenues. See his essay "The Reign of Henry VII," in S. B. Chrimes, C. D. Ross, and R. A. Griffiths, eds., *Fifteenth-Century England 1399–1509: Studies in Politics and Society* (Manchester: Manchester University Press, 1972), 79–80.

88. G, 155.

89. G, 155.

90. G, 137.

91. G, 137–138.

92. G, 137.

93. G, 141.

94. G, 140.

95. G, 141.

96. G, 139.

97. G, 148.

98. G, 148.

99. G, 149.

100. On this point see the valuable analysis of Doe, "Fifteenth-Century Concepts of Law."

5: FIRST OF THE REFORMERS

1. The text used throughout, cited *T*, is that of *The Tree of Commonwealth*, ed. D. M. Brodie (Cambridge: Cambridge University Press, 1948). The full manuscript title is *The Tree of Commonwealth: A Treatise Written by Edmund Dudley Minister to King Henry the VII whilst He Was in Prison, in the First Year of King Henry ye VIII*. Besides Brodie's introduction (pp. 1–17), useful discussions of Dudley's political ideas are Franklin Le van Baumer, *The Early Tudor Theory of Kingship* (New Haven: Yale University Press, 1940), 19–20, 208–209; Christopher Morris, *Political Thought in England: Tyndale to Hooker* (London: Oxford University Press, 1953), 15–17; Quentin Skinner, *The Foundation of Modern Political Thought* (Cambridge: Cambridge University Press, 1978), 2: 55–56.

Biographical details rely mainly on Brodie's introduction and the *Dictionary of National Biography*. Also see D. M. Brodie, "Edmund Dudley, Minister of Henry VII," *Transactions of the Royal Historical Society*, 4th ser., 15 (1932): 133–136; C. J. Harrison, "The Petition of Edmund Dudley," *English Historical Review* 87 (1972): 82–89.

2. Edward Hall, *The Union of the Two Noble and Illustre Famelies York and Lancaster*, ed. Ellis (1809), quoted in J. J. Scarisbrick, *Henry VIII* (London: Eyre and Spottiswoode, 1968), 11–12.

3. S. B. Chrimes, *Henry VII* (London: Eyre Methuen, 1972), 316–317.

4. Harrison, "The Petition of Edmund Dudley."

5. Richard Marius, *Thomas More: A Biography* (London: Dent, 1985), 53. More, a newly elected member in the parliament of 1504, of which Dudley was speaker, vigorously attacked a royal tax measure. Dudley, on his way to the block in 1510, supposedly reminded More of this past occasion, saying that if his opposition had become known to the crown, Henry VII would have ordered his execution.

6. *T*, 22, 23.

7. *T*, 22, 104.

8. Dudley evidently included both peers and gentry under *nobility*, the term he used throughout, that is, the greater and lesser nobility.

9. *T*, 91. The Jacquerie occurred in northern France a century and a half before. Why Dudley cited an example so remote in time is unclear.

10. *T*, 91.

11. *T*, 35, for the single reference to parliament in regard to a law against perjury.

12. *T*, 31–33.

13. Baumer, *Early Tudor Theory of Kingship*, 20.

14. *T*, 90–91.

15. *T*, 107.

16. Baumer, *Early Tudor Theory of Kingship*, 208; Morris, *Political Thought*, 15.

17. *T*, 31–32.

18. *T*, 34.

19. *T*, 39–40.

20. *T*, 44.

21. *T*, 40.

22. *T*, 48–49.

23. *T*, 51–53.

24. *T*, 92.

25. *T*, 61–67.

26. *T*, 68–69.

27. See Brodie's preface, *T*, vii and n. 37 of this chapter.

28. *T*, 31.

29. *T*, 31–32.

30. *T*, 21, 48 ("countrie"), 39 ("nacion"), 86 ("kingdom").

31. *T*, 25, 32, 101, 105, 107.

32. *T*, 22.

33. *T*, 39.

34. *T*, 37, 40.

35. For example, *T*, 34–37.

36. Cf. *T*, 107.

37. Brodie, preface, *T*, vii, maintains that Dudley meant "common-

wealth" in the special sense employed by a "remarkable group" of his contemporaries (including Frowyk) in Gray's Inn. They used the notion of "common reason" in the examination of legal principles and procedures, referring them to the "needs" of the "common weal" or "commonwealth," by which they denoted society, not state. Dudley, according to Brodie, used the word thus in his French Reading on Quo Warranto and in the title of his book. From what little Brodie says, I cannot judge the validity of her understanding of Dudley's usage. Her explanation, however, does not appear to be completely at odds with my own, since "society" implies common interests and values. My interpretation possibly has the virtue of placing Dudley's "commonwealth" more squarely within the context of common usage and making slightly more sense out of the initial description of the "tree" (pp. 31–32) and the treatise as a whole.

38. I stress that Dudley's observations on social groups are scattered throughout the book and intertwined with his metaphor, not presented, as here, in straightforward, coherent form.

39. *T*, 34–37.

40. *T*, 36.

41. *T*, 36.

42. *T*, 32.

43. *T*, 42–44.

44. *T*, 26.

45. *T*, 71–77.

46. *T*, 31.

47. *T*, 24.

48. *T*, 26, 62–66.

49. *T*, 39.

50. *T*, 41, 44.

51. *T*, 45.

52. Locke, *An Essay Concerning Human Understanding* (Nidditch ed.), IV, xx, 6.

53. *T*, 77–87.

54. *T*, 84.

55. *T*, 84.

56. *T*, 81–82.

57. *T*, 40–48.

58. *T*, 45–46.

59. *T*, 55.

60. *T*, 38–39.

61. *T*, 48–50.

62. *T*, 50.

63. *T*, 31, 50.

64. *T*, 31.

65. *T*, 46.
66. *T*, 40, 48, 55, 58, 67.
67. *T*, 55.
68. *T*, 67.
69. *T*, 67.
70. *T*, 46–47.
71. *T*, 58.
72. *T*, 47.
73. *T*, 87–92.
74. *T*, 87.
75. *T*, 88.
76. *T*, 91–92.
77. *T*, 92.

6: THE ENLIGHTENED CONSERVATIVE

1. Subsequent details of More's life rely chiefly on J. A. Guy, *The Public Career of Sir Thomas More* (New Haven, Yale University Press, 1980), and Richard Marius, *Thomas More: A Biography* (London: Dent, 1985). Also important for his life and intellectual outlook are R. W. Chambers, *Thomas More* (London: Cape, 1935), and Alistair Fox, *Thomas More: History and Providence* (Oxford: Blackwell, 1982). Indispensable to any examination of More and *Utopia* are the texts, notes, and lengthy introductions of vol. 4 of *The Complete Works of St. Thomas More*, ed. Edward Surtz and J. H. Hexter (New Haven: Yale University Press, 1965). The Latin text and English translation by Surtz in this volume have been used throughout, designated below by *U*. A short, readable treatment is Anthony Kenny, *Thomas More* (Oxford, Oxford University Press, 1983).

Very useful for the discussion of the social and political ideas of *Utopia*, in addition to the previous works and Hexter's introduction to vol. 4 of the *Complete Works* and his *More's Utopia: The Biography of an Idea* (Princeton, N.J.: Princeton University Press, 1952), are the following: J. W. Allen, *A History of Political Thought in the Sixteenth Century*, rev. ed. (London: Methuen, 1957; orig. published, 1928), 153–156; Russell Ames, *Citizen Thomas More and His Utopia* (Princeton, N.J.: Princeton University Press, 1949); Brendan Bradshaw, "More on Utopia," *The Historical Journal* 24 (1981): 1–27; Brendan Bradshaw, "Transalpine Humanism," *The Cambridge History of Political Thought 1450–1700*, ed. J. H. Burns with the assistance of Mark Goldie (Cambridge: Cambridge University Press, 1991), 95–131; W. E. Campbell, *More's Utopia and His Social Teaching* (London: Eyre and Spottiswoode, 1930); Fritz Caspari, *Humanism and the Social Order in England* (Chicago: University of Chicago Press, 1954); Martin Fleischer, *Radical Reform and Political Persuasion in the Life and Writings of Thomas More* (Geneva: Droz,

1972); Alistair Fox, *Politics and Literature in the Reigns of Henry VII and Henry VIII* (Oxford: Blackwell, 1989); Alistair Fox and John Guy, *Reassessing the Henrician Age: Humanism, Politics, and Reform, 1500–1550* (Oxford: Clarendon Press, 1986); Karl Kautsky, *Thomas More and His Utopia with a Historical Introduction*, trans. H. J. Stenning (London: A. and C. Black, 1927); George M. Logan, *The Meaning of More's "Utopia"* (Princeton, N.J.: Princeton University Press, 1983); T. F. Mayer, "Tournai and Tyranny: Imperial Kingship and Critical Humanism," *The Historical Journal* 34 (1991): 257–277; Christopher Morris, *Political Thought in England: Tyndale to Hooker* (London: Oxford University Press, 1953), 17–19, 127–131; Lyman Tower Sargent, "More's *Utopia*: An Interpretation of Its Social Theory," *History of Political Thought* 5 (1984): 195–210; Quentin Skinner, "More's *Utopia*," *Past and Present* 38 (1967): 153–168; Quentin Skinner, *The Foundations of Modern Political Thought* (Cambridge: Cambridge University Press, 1978), esp. 1:222–224, 255–262; Quentin Skinner, "Sir Thomas More's *Utopia* and the Language of Renaissance Humanism," in *The Languages of Political Theory in Early Modern Europe*, ed. Anthony Pagden (Cambridge: Cambridge University Press, 1987), 123–157.

2. Whitney R. D. Jones, *The Tudor Commonwealth 1529–1559: A Study of the Impact of Mid-Tudor England upon Contemporary Concepts of the Nature and Duties of the Commonwealth* (London: University of London, Athlone Press, 1970), 25–27. Pole highly esteemed More. See Francis A. Gasquet, *Cardinal Pole and His Early Friends* (London: Bell, 1927), 58–59. For More's relationship to Elyot, see Stanford E. Lehmberg, *Sir Thomas Elyot, Tudor Humanist* (Austin: University of Texas Press, 1960), 6–7, 14–17, 20–21; John M. Major, *Sir Thomas Elyot and Renaissance Humanism* (Lincoln: University of Nebraska Press, 1964), 89–109. Elyot wrote *The Boke Named the Governour* (1531) according to Major (p. 109) as a sort of anti-Utopia to defend traditional English society, and he repudiated More after his execution. On More and Lupset, see above, p. 26, and below, pp. 125, 276n.5.

3. Guy, *Public Career*, 104.

4. Ibid., 166.

5. William Morris, introduction to Kelmscott edition of *Utopia*, quoted in Campbell, *More's Utopia*, 50; see also Chambers's similar verdict in *Thomas More*, 359–372.

6. Hexter, introduction, *Complete Works of St. Thomas More*, vol. 4. "Humanist realism" is the expression used in Logan, *Meaning of More's "Utopia,"* 270.

7. The terms "idyll" and "ideal" are used in Bradshaw, "More on Utopia."

8. The translation is dedicated to Edward VI's principal secretary, Sir William Cecil, an old friend and schoolmate of Robynson's who appar-

ently was in the former's service at the time. See James K. McConica, *English Humanists and Reformation Politics under Henry VIII and Edward VI* (Oxford: Clarendon Press, 1965), 259. More seems to have preferred *Utopia* to remain untranslated during his lifetime for fear that its meaning might be misunderstood by a wider audience of non-Latin readers. See Campbell, *More's Utopia*, 24–25.

9. *U*, 237.

10. *U*, for example, 101.

11. *U*, 245.

12. Logan, *Meaning of More's "Utopia,"* 37–38.

13. Ibid., 59–61, 76–79, for stress on More's institutional approach.

14. Skinner, "Sir Thomas More's *Utopia*."

15. *U*, 245.

16. *U*, 245.

17. *U*, 245.

18. *U*, 105–107.

19. For Utopia as an ideal type, Bradshaw, "More on Utopia," 20–21, and "Transalpine Humanism," 122; Logan, *Meaning of More's "Utopia,"* 63–67.

20. On the "constructive policy" of More, see Arthur B. Ferguson, *The Articulate Citizen and the English Renaissance* (Durham, N.C.: Duke University Press, 1965), 176–177, 318–320. Also note Campbell, *More's Utopia*, 53–54.

21. For these possible reforms, *U*, 69–71, 95–97, 105.

22. On More's pragmatism, Bradshaw, "More on Utopia," 21–27.

23. *U*, 245.

24. *U*, 112, 134, 136, 246. *Patria* is used on p. 62.

25. *U*, 90, 92, 100, 106, 122.

26. *U*, 100, 104, 192.

27. *U*, 60, 64, 104, 124, 238, 240, 242.

28. *U*, 139.

29. *U*, 243–245.

30. *U*, 245.

31. *U*, 7, 243.

32. *U*, 105.

33. *U*, 105.

34. *U*, 239.

35. *U*, 105, 239.

36. On what follows in regard to distributive justice and the principles of proportionate and arithmetical equality, see Plato, *Laws*, 757a–d; Aristotle, *Nicomachean Ethics*, 1130b–1131b; Aristotle, *Politics*, 1280a–1282b, 1293a–1296b, 1301a–1302a, 1317b–1318a. I emphasize that More does not use these terms in the text.

37. *U*, 241.

38. *U*, 239–241.

39. *U*, 103.

40. *U*, 129–131.

41. *U*, 127.

42. *U*, 117, 149, 185.

43. *U*, 161–179.

44. Logan, *Meaning of More's "Utopia,"* 144. See his excellent detailed discussion, 144–186.

45. *U*, 175.

46. *U*, 173–175.

47. Logan, *Meaning of More's "Utopia,"* 186.

48. *U*, 179–181.

49. *U*, 61–71, for the main description of English conditions.

50. *U*, 61.

51. *U*, 63.

52. *U*, 57–58, 63, 67, 91–95, 131, 195, 239, 241.

53. *U*, 63, 67, 69. These are all subjects more fully discussed by the later reformers.

54. *U*, 65–67.

55. *U*, 67. In 1527 More himself was charged with being an enclosing landlord. He claimed in the court of exchequer that his lands in Fringford, Oxfordshire, had been reconverted to cultivation and a dwelling reconstructed. See John Guy, *Tudor England* (Oxford: Oxford University Press, 1988), 92–93.

56. *U*, 69.

57. *U*, 67.

58. *U*, 69.

59. Sir Thomas Smith, *De republica Anglorum*, ed. Mary Dewar (Cambridge: Cambridge University Press, 1982), 74.

60. Hugh Latimer, *Sermons*, ed. G. E. Corrie (Cambridge: Cambridge University Press, 1844), 1:101.

61. *U*, 67.

62. See Ann Kussmaul, *Servants in Husbandry in Early Modern England* (Cambridge: Cambridge University Press, 1981).

63. Peter Laslett, *The World We Have Lost, Further Explored*, 3d ed. (New York: Scribner's, 1984), 96; and *U*, 331, for Surtz's note.

64. Sir John Fortescue, *De laudibus legum Anglie*, trans. and ed. S. B. Chrimes, general preface by H. D. Hazeltine (Cambridge: Cambridge University Press, 1949), 67–69.

65. For the beginning of the triadic organization, see David McNally, *Political Economy and the Rise of Capitalism: A Reinterpretation* (Berkeley, Los Angeles, London: University of California Press, 1988), 7–8, 54–55, 63; and my *John Locke and Agrarian Capitalism* (Berkeley, Los Angeles, London: University of California Press, 1984), chaps. 2–3.

66. *U*, 69–71.
67. *U*, 95–97.
68. Kautsky, *Thomas More*, 233.
69. Ames, *Citizen Thomas More*, 6; also for an extended discussion of democracy in Utopia, 167–178. Unfortunately, Logan, *Meaning of More's "Utopia,"* never comes to grips with the problem of Utopian democracy. Although Caspari, *Humanism and Social Order*, 107, 112–113, 115–116, never discusses the role of women in Utopia, he perceives that its patriarchalism and rule of an intellectual elite severely restrict Utopian democracy. Likewise, Sargent, "More's Utopia," is one of the few commentators who emphasizes the authoritarianism of Utopia. Bradshaw, "Transalpine Humanism," 120, 130, 131, stresses the "populist dimension" of Utopia, that More through the institution of economic equality and social welfare measures was aiming at an "emancipated populace." He, however, skirts the question of Utopian democracy.
70. Surtz, introduction, *U*, clxix, and note on p. 398.
71. Ibid., clvii, clx.
72. The figures are derived from Surtz's notes, *U*, 410, 415.
73. *U*, 113.
74. *U*, 113, 147, 153.
75. Jean Bodin, *Les six livres de la république*, book 1, chap. 5, quoted in Robin Blackburn, *The Overthrow of Colonial Slavery: 1776–1848* (London: Verso, 1988), 40.
76. A "slave society" has been defined as one in which slaves constitute at least 18% to 20% or more of the population and dominate key sectors of the economy. See M. I. Finley, "Slavery," *The International Encyclopedia of the Social Sciences* (New York: Macmillan and The Free Press, 1968), 14:307–313; and Keith Hopkins, *Conquerors and Slaves* (Cambridge: Cambridge University Press, 1978), 99–102.
77. *U*, 185; also 221.
78. *U*, 193.
79. *U*, 125, 191.
80. Surtz's note, *U*, 474.
81. *U*, 115, 139–141, 147, 171.
82. *U*, 125–127.
83. *U*, 117, 135.
84. *U*, 225–227.
85. A point suggested in Ames, *Citizen Thomas More*, 170, and Logan, *Meaning of More's "Utopia,"* 170.
86. Kautsky, *Thomas More*, 234.
87. Ibid., 225: "the patriarchal family in his pages in almost classical form." Logan, *Meaning of More's "Utopia,"* 212: the Utopian family is "rigidly patriarchal." Both authors, however, tend to overlook how the

patriarchalism affects Utopian democracy as Caspari does not. See n. 69 above, this chapter.

88. *U*, 115, 135–137.
89. Laslett, *World We Have Lost*, 96–102.
90. *U*, 115, 135.
91. *U*, 195, 191.
92. *U*, 143–145.
93. *U*, 211.
94. *U*, 149, 193–195.
95. *U*, 129.
96. *U*, 191, 209–211.
97. *U*, 229.
98. *U*, 195. For a contrary interpretation, Ames, *Citizen Thomas More*, 174: "We cannot be sure that women have full political rights, including votes and the opportunity to hold office: More does not say that they have or have not. The atmosphere of the whole society suggests that his silence implies consent."
99. *U*, 137, 141.
100. *U*, 125, 127.
101. *U*, 123.
102. Surtz's note, *U*, 389.
103. *U*, 139.
104. *U*, 123.
105. *U*, 125.
106. Fortescue, *De laudibus*, 71.
107. *U*, 191, 195.
108. *U*, 191.
109. See above, p. 110.
110. Sargent, "More's *Utopia*," 202.
111. Campbell, *More's Utopia*, 123; also 118.
112. *U*, 131–133, for the fullest discussion of the intellectuals.
113. *U*, 133.
114. *U*, 159.
115. *U*, 175.
116. *U*, 129, 145, 159.
117. *U*, 229.
118. *U*, 229.
119. *U*, 229.
120. Fortescue, *De laudibus*, 19.
121. *U*, 151.
122. On Augustine's psychology of fallen man, see Herbert A. Deane, *The Political and Social Ideas of St. Augustine* (New York: Columbia University Press, 1963), chap. 2.

123. For Plato on the corruption of power, *Laws*, 691c–d, 713c–14a, 875a–d.

124. For a short discussion of the doctrine of the mixed constitution, see my *Cicero's Social and Political Thought* (Berkeley, Los Angeles, London: University of California Press, 1988), 159–162.

125. Mayer, "Tournai and Tyranny," 257. He stresses More's deep concern over the related problems of factionalism, intrigue, and tyranny and his view that "Utopian conciliar institutions (together with psychological means of controlling behavior) made sovereignty unnecessary" (p. 270). On *Richard III* and Utopia, also see Fox, *Politics and Literature*, chap. 7.

126. *U*, 105.

127. *U*, 125.

128. *U*, 193.

129. Campbell, *More's Utopia*, 124: "The whole method of government seemed to be devised as a check against the dangers of political individualism."

130. Surtz, introduction *U*, clxix, comments on the possible influence of Fortescue: "*Utopia* seems to enjoy a *dominium politicum et regale*, but the governorship is elective for life and not hereditary. Insofar as offices are elective and therefore all citizens have a share in the rule, Utopia is a democracy."

131. On Starkey and the Venetian model of government, see chapter 7 of this book.

132. On Plutarch's *Lycurgus* and the social and political institutions of Sparta and Utopia: Surtz, introduction, *U*, clx–clxi.

133. Plato's specific discussion of the Magnesian mixed constitution is in *Laws*, books 3–6.

134. Like More in *Utopia*, Plato in the *Laws* proposes "a radical transformation of society." See Ellen Meiksins Wood and Neal Wood, *Class Ideology and Ancient Political Theory: Socrates, Plato, and Aristotle in Social Context* (New York: Oxford University Press, 1978), 183–202.

135. *U*, 87–103, devoted to the Platonic question of knowledge and power.

7: A LIFE OF DIGNITY IN THE "TRUE COMMYN WELE"

1. The indispensable guide to the life and political thought of Starkey is Thomas F. Mayer, *Thomas Starkey and the Commonweal: Humanist Politics and Religion in the Reign of Henry VIII* (Cambridge: Cambridge University Press, 1989). Also see his "Faction and Ideology: Thomas Starkey's *Dialogue*," *The Historical Journal* 28 (1985): 1–25; "Thomas Starkey's Aristocratic Reform Programme," *History of Political Thought*

7 (1986): 439–461, and the introduction to his edition of Starkey, *A Dialogue between Pole and Lupset*, Camden Fourth Series, vol. 37 (London: Royal Historical Society, 1989). This is the text I have used and cited as *D.* Mayer's editorial symbols have been omitted in all quotations. Still of use is J. M. Cowper's text and introduction in *England in the Reign of King Henry the Eighth*, ed. S. J. Herrtage (London: Early English Text Society, N. Trübner, 1878). A modernized transcription has been edited by Kathleen M. Burton, *A Dialogue between Reginald Pole and Thomas Starkey* (London: Chatto and Windus, 1948).

Mayer, *Thomas Starkey*, also deals extensively with Starkey's religious thought, although much less so with his social ideas, on this score referring readers (p. 3 n. 1) to Arthur B. Ferguson, *The Articulate Citizen and the English Renaissance* (Durham, N.C.: Duke University Press, 1965). Ferguson has proved invaluable on Starkey (esp. pp. 171–176, 320–334, 370–380), as he has for other thinkers in this study. I have relied on the perceptive interpretations of Mayer and Ferguson, often without specific citation, but throughout I have attempted to steer my own course.

In addition, the following should be consulted: J. W. Allen, *A History of Political Thought in the Sixteenth Century*, rev. ed. (London: Methuen, 1957; orig. published, 1928), 142–153; A. R. Buck, "Rhetoric and Real Property in Tudor England: Thomas Starkey's *Dialogue between Pole and Lupset*," *Cardozo Studies in Law and Literature* 4 (1992): 27–43; G. R. Elton, "Reform by Statute: Thomas Starkey's *Dialogue* and Thomas Cromwell's Policy," *Proceedings of the British Academy* 54 (1968): 165–188, his *Policy and Police: The Enforcement of the Reformation in the Age of Thomas Cromwell* (Cambridge: Cambridge University Press, 1972), 190–194, and his *Reform and Renewal: Thomas Cromwell and the Common Weal* (Cambridge: Cambridge University Press, 1973), chap. 3; Christopher Morris, *Political Thought in England: Tyndale to Hooker* (London: Oxford University Press, 1953), esp. 40–41; Quentin Skinner, *The Foundations of Modern Political Thought* (Cambridge: Cambridge University Press, 1978), 1:222–225; 2:100–105, 235–236, 356–357; Neal Wood, "Cicero and the Political Thought of the Early English Renaissance," *Modern Language Quarterly* 51 (1990): 185–207; W. Gordon Zeeveld, *Foundations of Tudor Policy* (Cambridge, Mass.: Harvard University Press, 1948), esp. chap. 6.

2. The judgment is that of Mayer, "Faction and Ideology," 1.

3. On Pole see Wilhelm Schenk, *Reginald Pole, Cardinal of England* (London: Longmans, Green, 1950), and Francis A. Gasquet, *Cardinal Pole and His Early Friends* (London: Bell, 1927).

4. For Lupset, see John A. Gee, *The Life and Works of Thomas Lupset: With a Critical Text of the Original Treatises and the Letters* (New Haven: Yale University Press, 1928).

5. Ibid., 179. Gee maintains that the second edition was published without More's permission and contained many typographical errors.

6. Ibid., 91.

7. Lupset's mother and the countess of Salisbury, Pole's mother, were close friends, according to Gee, *The Life and Works of Thomas Lupset,* 161.

8. Mayer, "Faction and Ideology," esp. 1, 17–18, 24–25; Mayer, *Thomas Starkey,* passim. Gee, *Life and Works of Thomas Lupset,* 153, thinks that Lupset was possibly commissioned by Henry to persuade Pole to assume an active political role.

9. Mayer, *Thomas Starkey,* 4.

10. Mayer throughout *Thomas Starkey* treats these sources and many others in meticulous and illuminating detail.

11. The two parts of *D* are pp. 1–95 and 95–143.

12. *D,* 18.

13. Starkey's social and political views in *D* appear more moderate than Lupset's. On the evidence of his writings, Lupset upholds religious orthodoxy and the status quo, dreads disorder, and emphasizes obedience to all authority. See Gee, *Life and Works of Thomas Lupset,* 180–181. For Lupset's conservative outlook in *An Exhorticion to Young Men,* see in particular the single lengthy passage in Gee, 256–257.

14. *D,* 19, 22, for example.

15. Clement Armstrong, *A Treatise Concerninge the Staple and the Commodities of This Realm* and *Howe to Reforme the Realme in Settyng Them to Werke and to Restore Tillage,* in R. H. Tawney and Eileen Power, eds., *Tudor Economic Documents: Being Select Documents Illustrating the Economic and Social History of Tudor England* (London: Longmans, Green, 1924), 3:105, 114, 116. On Armstrong, see S. T. Bindoff, "Clement Armstrong and His Treatises of the Commonweal," *Economic History Review,* ser. 1, 14 (1944): 64–73. Bindoff dates both works to about 1535, in the two- to three-year period from 1533. Also see Elton, *Reform and Renewal,* 5, 26, 63, 69–70, 100, 106, 112–113, 160; Ferguson, *Articulate Citizen,* 153–154, 236–239, 347–348. Never one of Cromwell's advisors, Armstrong was a London businessman, the close friend of John Rastell, Protestant son-in-law of More and father of William Rastell, who is remembered for the publication in 1557 of the folio edition of his uncle's English works.

Christopher St. German, *Doctor and Student,* ed. T. F. T. Plucknett and J. L. Barton (London: Selden Society, 1974), "First Dialogue," 26–27, 44–47. The "First Dialogue," originally published in Latin in 1523, was followed by two reprintings in 1528 and the author's English translation in 1532. The "Second Dialogue," written in English, appeared in 1530. In this and subsequent footnotes the first figure in each set of page references to the "First Dialogue" is to the Latin and the second to St. German's English translation.

On his life and thought, in addition to the introduction (pp. xi–lxvii) by Plucknett and Barton to their edition of *Doctor and Student*, see: Franklin Le van Baumer, "Christopher St. German: The Political Philosophy of a Tudor Lawyer," *American Historical Review* 42 (1937): 631–651, and his *The Early Tudor Theory of Kingship* (New Haven: Yale University Press, 1940), 59–60, 65–68, 70–71, 73–74, 134, 140–142, 150–151, 181–182; S. B. Chrimes, *English Constitutional Ideas in the Fifteenth Century* (Cambridge: Cambridge University Press, 1936), 204–214; Elton, *Reform and Renewal*, 74–76; Pearl Hogrefe, "The Life of Christopher St. German," *Review of English Studies* 13 (1937): 398–404; Richard Marius, *Thomas More: A Biography* (London: Dent, 1985), 377–378, 380–382, 434–438, 445; Morris, *Political Thought in England*, 50–51, 55, 85; Skinner, *Foundations of Modern Political Thought*, 2:56–58.

A learned London lawyer of the Middle Temple and Master of Requests, St. German was a follower of Fortescue and founder of English legal philosophy. His *Doctor and Student* was an influential textbook until well into the eighteenth century. Consulted by Thomas Cromwell, St. German was a prolific publicist who supported the Act of Separation and became embroiled in a famous dispute with More over the question of ecclesiastical jurisdiction. The Latin editions of *Doctor and Student* of 1523 and 1528 were published by John Rastell, son-in-law of More and friend of Clement Armstrong.

16. *Doctor and Student*, "First Dialogue," 73–74, 110–111.

17. Sir Thomas Elyot, *The Book Named the Governor*, ed. S. E. Lehmberg (London and New York: Dent, Everymans Library, 1962), 1–2.

18. Elyot's definition of the "public weal" or state, *The Governor*, 1, to be discussed in chapter 9 of this book in connection with Sir Thomas Smith, is "a body living, compact or made of sundry estates and degrees of men, which is disposed by the order of equity and governed by the rule and moderation of reason."

19. *D*, 16, 21, 47, 71.

20. *D*, 18.

21. The earliest example cited in the *Oxford English Dictionary*. Starkey's usage is commented on by H. C. Dowdall, "The Word 'State,'" *The Law Quarterly Review* 39 (1923): 120, and by Skinner, *Foundations of Modern Political Thought*, 2:356–357.

22. *D*, 22, 24, 40, 68.

23. *D*, 119.

24. *D*, 67, 122, 120.

25. *D*, 33. Italics supplied. Mayer, *Thomas Starkey*, 124–126, feels that in this passage "state" means form or condition of government in-

stead of institutional totality. My view, however, is closer to that of Skinner, *Foundations of Modern Political Thought*, 2:356–357. This passage, read with the other on the same page and the one cited in n. 26 below together with my following argument, suggests that Starkey was thinking of more than condition. At any rate, and here no doubt Mayer would not disagree, Starkey appears to have been moving in the direction of *state* as institutional whole and away from *state* as personalized rule.

26. *D*, 120. Italics supplied.

27. *D*, for example, 33, 34, 38, 48, 68, 96, 122.

28. St. German, *Doctor and Student*, "Second Dialogue," 258; Elyot, *The Governor*, 6–7.

29. *D*, 33, 121.

30. Dudley, *The Tree of Commonwealth*, ed. D. M. Brodie (Cambridge: Cambridge University Press, 1948), 55, 67, 91, 96; Henry Brinklow, *Complaynt of Roderyck Mors*, ed. J. M. Cowper (London: Early English Text Society, N. Trübner, 1874), 73.

31. Elyot, *The Governor*, 2.

32. *The Libel of English Policy*, in William Huse Dunham, Jr., and Stanley Pargellis, eds., *Complaint and Reform in England 1436–1714: Fifty Writings of the Time on Politics, Religion, Society, Economics, Architecture, Science, and Education* (New York: Oxford University Press, 1938), 18.

33. Quoted in Tawney and Power, eds., *Tudor Economic Documents*, 1:13.

34. Mayer, *Thomas Starkey*, 116–118. Chap. 4 of Mayer's book is a much more thorough analysis on some points of Starkey's vocabulary than can be attempted here.

35. Ibid., 121.

36. Ibid., 129–130. Starkey is exceedingly confusing on this score, for example, *D*, 52, 53, 56, 60, 63, 64, 74, 75, 86, 87, 99, 103, 118, 121, 125, 127, 128, 129, 130, 131, 142–143. From his basic distinction between head and members of the body politic, it would follow that "nobility" includes gentry, although in places he appears to distinguish between them: 60, 64, 74–75, 87, 127. See references to primogeniture and n. 72 of this chapter.

37. Cf. use of "body politic" in example cited in *Oxford English Dictionary*: 1532–1533, Act 24 Henry VIII, xii, "This Realm of England is an Empire . . . governed by one Supreme Head and King unto whom a Body politick, compact of all Sorts and Degrees of People . . . been bounden and owen to bear a natural and humble Obedience."

38. *D*, 31.

39. *D*, 31.

40. *D*, 57–58.

41. *D*, 57.

42. For Starkey's only use (3 times) of "socyety," D, 6–7.

43. D, 60, 61.

44. D, 34.

45. D, 31, 34.

46. D, 14.

47. D, 34. Italics supplied.

48. D, 38. Italics supplied.

49. D, 137. Italics supplied.

50. D, 38.

51. D, 137.

52. For discussion and some references to the dignity of man, D, 5–10, 12, 35, 36, 38, 42, 53, 55, 104, 137.

53. D, 9.

54. For instance, on felicity, D, 26, 28–31, 41–42, 44, 108.

55. D, 13.

56. D, 13, 22, 43–44.

57. D, 105.

58. D, 111; also see below, p. 145.

59. D, 19–20; Sir John Fortescue, *De laudibus legum Anglie*, trans. and ed. S. B. Chrimes, general preface by H. D. Hazeltine (Cambridge: Cambridge University Press, 1942), 19; Sir Thomas More, *Utopia*, in vol. 4 of *The Complete Works of St. Thomas More*, ed. Edward Surtz and J. H. Hexter (New Haven: Yale University Press, 1965), 229. On Starkey's use of *tabula rasa*, see Ferguson, *Articulate Citizen*, 175–176. In citing the authority of Aristotle, Starkey was probably thinking of the classic passage in *De anima*, 430a, also referred to by St. Thomas, *Summa Theologica*, I, Q. 79, Art. 2. *De anima* was a sixteenth-century European bestseller. On this and the following see my article, "*Tabula Rasa*, Social Environmentalism, and the 'English Paradigm,'" *Journal of the History of Ideas* 53 (1992): 647–668.

60. D, 11, 12–13, 22, 45. Much of this seems to parallel Cicero's position, perhaps of Stoic derivation, in another sixteenth-century favorite, *Tusculan Disputations*, 2.53; 3.13; 4.65, 4:82–83; 5.39. Also Cicero, *Laws*, 1.28–30, 1:33.

61. D, 22.

62. D, 24.

63. D, 34.

64. D, 114, 117, 131.

65. D, 71.

66. D, 104.

67. Armstrong, *Howe to Reforme the Realme*, in Tawney and Power, eds., *Tudor Economic Documents*, 3:111–112.

68. D, 37.

69. D, 24.

70. On primogeniture and entail, D, 73–76, 129–131.

71. D, 74.

72. D, 75. Buck, "Rhetoric and Real Property," 35, maintains that Starkey "was arguing that the nobility should be set apart—even from the gentry." Primogeniture and entail, as he recommended them, would assure the domination of the nobility, thus separated from the gentry and the lower orders.

73. D, 21–24.

74. D, 24.

75. D, 24.

76. D, 25.

77. D, 26.

78. D, 27–30. Cf. Lupset, *An Exhortacion to Young Men*, in Gee, *Life and Works of Thomas Lupset*, 233–262. Lupset distinguished the "goods" of soul, body, and the world: goodness, health, and wealth. Health is necessary for the soul's sake and goodness, the highest end; wealth is for the body's sake. The work was published posthumously in 1535.

79. D, 30–45.

80. D, 31–33.

81. D, 33–45.

82. D, 46.

83. D, 46.

84. D, 47.

85. D, 48–51, for England's depleted population.

86. D, 51.

87. D, 99.

88. D, 99–100.

89. D, 100.

90. On idleness, D, 52–54.

91. D, 57–58.

92. D, 58.

93. D, 52.

94. D, 53. Clement Armstrong was even more emphatic than Starkey. Physical labor of commoners, "the holl welth of the body of the realm," was absolutely essential to the state. See Armstrong, *A Treatise*, in Tawney and Power, eds., *Tudor Economic Documents*, 3:105.

95. D, 53.

96. D, 54–55.

97. For the various remedies for idleness, D, 100–104, 130–131.

98. D, 103, 136. Lupset, 136, called them "conservaterys of the commyn wele." See the comment in Ferguson, *Articulate Citizen*, 331.

99. D, 55–58.

100. D, 105–106.

101. On poverty and prosperity, D, 59.

102. *D,* 59.

103. Compared to the prosperity of the kingdom at the ascension of Henry VIII in 1509, Clement Armstrong observed: "It is now dekeyed and made feble, week and power, by reason that the labours and lyvyng of all common people, members in the body of his realme, hath been destroyed, causing necessite and scarsite of mete and drinke, clothing and money." *Howe to Reforme the Realme,* in Tawney and Power, eds., *Tudor Economic Documents,* 3:115.

104. *D,* 60.

105. *D,* 65–66, for the comments on enclosure.

106. The popular treatment by John Fitzherbert, *The Book of Husbandry,* initially appearing in 1523, unique of its kind in Europe, probably offered the first published technical argument for enclosure. His later *Surveyenge* (1539) also recommended enclosure. Thomas Tusser's *Five Hundred Pointes of Good Husbandrie* (1573) stressed (chap. 52) the superiority of enclosed to unenclosed land.

107. For most of the recommendations for economic reforms, *D,* 114–118.

108. *D,* 106–107.

109. On the question of gentlemen being obligated to live in the cities, see the interesting remarks of C. S. Lewis, *English Literature in the Sixteenth Century, Excluding Drama* (Oxford: Clarendon Press, 1954), 285. Lewis relates Starkey's obsession with urban life to his humanism and classical influences. Mayer, *Thomas Starkey,* 23, pins it down by suggesting Cicero.

110. Armstrong, *A Treatise,* in Tawney and Power, eds., *Tudor Economic Documents,* vol. 3:109–110.

111. For a brief comparison of the economic reforms proposed by Starkey and Armstrong, see Elton, *Reform and Renewal,* 100.

112. *Letter to Henry VIII,* in Herrtage, ed., *England in the Reign of King Henry the Eighth,* liii, lv.

113. Elton, *Reform and Renewal,* 53.

114. *Letter to Henry VIII,* liv, lvi–lvii.

115. Ibid., lviii–lix.

116. *D,* esp., 67–68, 108–109, 129–134.

117. *D,* 67.

118. *D,* 69.

119. *D,* 69–70, 112.

120. *D,* 108–109.

121. *D,* 110–111.

122. *D,* 111. Mayer, *Thomas Starkey,* 113, says that on deposing a tyrant, Starkey "argued only in the abstract." Starkey like More was seriously concerned with the problem of tyranny (of the one, the few, and the many) and saw in the mixed constitution a prime means of prevent-

ing it. See chapter 6 of this book and Mayer, "Tournai and Tyranny: Imperial Kingship and Humanism," *The Historical Journal* 34, no. 2 (1991): 257–277.

123. *D,* 70–71, 110–113, 119–123, in general for Starkey's governmental reforms. Also see Mayer, *Thomas Starkey,* chap. 4.

124. *D,* 119, 120, 123.

125. *D,* 120.

126. *D,* 121–122. Starkey originally seems to have intended the office of constable for Pole. See Mayer, "Faction and Ideology," 19, and *Thomas Starkey,* 104–105, 154–155.

127. *D,* 121.

128. A point stressed by Mayer, *Thomas Starkey,* 133, as he also does in connection with the king's council.

129. *D,* 69, for Starkey's only reference, and that made in passing, to parliament's lawmaking function.

130. *D,* 122.

131. Mayer, *Thomas Starkey,* 137.

132. Ibid., 57–61, 147–153, for a discussion of Starkey in relation to Contarini, Giannotti, and Aristotle.

133. *D,* 136.

134. *D,* 129.

135. *D,* 72–75, 130–131.

136. *D,* 55, 79, 127–128.

137. William Langland, *Piers the Ploughman,* trans. J. F. Goodridge, rev. ed. (Harmondsworth, Middlesex: Penguin, 1966), 31, also 92.

138. *D,* 79.

139. *D,* 127–128.

140. *D,* 128, a proposal emphasized by Mayer, *Thomas Starkey,* 129.

141. *D,* 131–132, 137.

142. *D,* 124–131.

143. *D,* 86.

144. *D,* 86–87.

145. Dudley, *Tree of Commonwealth,* 45.

146. Elyot, *The Governour,* quoted in Maria Dowling, *Humanism in the Age of Henry VIII* (London: Croom Helm, 1968), 179.

147. Dowling, *Humanism,* 183, so judges the book.

148. *D,* 125–126.

149. *D,* 107.

150. *D,* 128–130.

151. Fortescue, *De laudibus,* 19; St German, *Doctor and Student,* "Second Dialogue," 282.

152. *D,* 138–139.

153. On Starkey's criticism of papal power in relation to the English church, see *D,* esp. 82–85, 132–133.

154. *D*, 132. For Starkey and Jean Gerson's conciliarism: Mayer, *Thomas Starkey*, 82–85.

155. *D*, 52, 55.

156. *D*, 87.

157. *D*, 85, 88.

158. For these remedies, see *D*, esp. 82, 85, 89–93, 133–135.

159. *D*, 89–91.

160. On the universities and the clergy, *D*, 135.

161. Dudley, *Tree of Commonwealth*, 26, 45, 62–66.

162. *D*, 135.

163. On Starkey and Sadoleto, see Mayer, "Faction and Ideology," 7–8, and his *Thomas Starkey*, 90, 93, 94, 171–173, 178–179, 280–281. Starkey, who studied law in the early 1530s in Avignon, only about fifteen miles from Carpentras, knew and admired Sadoleto.

164. *D*, 139–140. Mayer, *Thomas Starkey*, 92.

165. Ferguson, *Articulate Citizen*, 330.

166. See Wood, "*Tabula Rasa*."

167. Langland, *Piers the Ploughman*, 28.

8: SOCIAL PROTEST AND CHRISTIAN RENEWAL

1. Hugh Latimer, *Sermons*, ed. G. E. Corrie (Cambridge: Cambridge University Press, 1844), 1:29–30.

2. Ibid., 1:30.

3. Henry Brinklow, *Complaynt of Roderyck Mors, sometyme a gray fryre, unto the parliament house of England his natural cuntry: For the redress of certen wicked lawes, evel customs, a[n]d cruel decreys (about A.D. 1542), and The Lamentacyon of a Christen against the Cytye of London, made by Roderigo Mors (A.D. 1545)*, ed. J. M. Cowper (London: Trübner, for the Early English Text Society, 1874), 15–16.

4. Ibid., for biographical details, J. M. Cowper's introduction, v–xxxii and notes by Col. J. L. Chester, 121–125. Brief references to Brinklow and his ideas are in J. W. Allen, *A History of Political Thought in the Sixteenth Century*, rev. ed. (London: Methuen, 1957; orig. published, 1928), 210–211; Quentin Skinner, *The Foundations of Modern Political Thought* (Cambridge: Cambridge University Press, 1978), 1:224, 226.

5. In Col. Chester's notes, 124 (see nn. 3–4 for this chapter).

6. *Complaynt*, 1–76; *Lamentacyon*, 77–120.

7. *Complaynt*, 6.

8. *Complaynt*, 73.

9. *Complaynt*, 75.

10. *Complaynt*, 5.

11. *Complaynt*, 6.

12. *Complaynt*, 59.

13. *Complaynt,* 5.

14. *Complaynt,* 7–8.

15. *Complaynt,* 8.

16. *Complaynt,* 12–13.

17. *Complaynt,* esp. 9–12, 16–17, 37–38, 49.

18. *Complaynt,* 9.

19. *Complaynt,* 17–19.

20. *Complaynt,* 49.

21. *Complaynt,* 10.

22. *Complaynt,* 19.

23. *Complaynt,* 12.

24. *Complaynt,* 11–12.

25. *Complaynt,* 17. On the rich as God's stewards, see below in this chapter, pp. 186, 189.

26. *Complaynt,* 49.

27. *Complaynt,* 10.

28. *Complaynt,* 17.

29. *Complaynt,* 48.

30. *Complaynt,* 50–53.

31. *Complaynt,* 29–32, 38–41, 44–48, 53–73.

32. *Complaynt,* 29–32.

33. *Complaynt,* 14.

34. *Complaynt,* 23.

35. *Complaynt,* 25.

36. *Complaynt,* 27–29.

37. *Complaynt,* 41.

38. *Complaynt,* 44–48.

39. *Complaynt,* 49–50.

40. *Complaynt,* 42–43.

41. *Lamentacyon,* 90.

42. *Lamentacyon,* 77–91.

43. *Lamentacyon,* 92 ff.

44. *Lamentacyon,* 115–116.

45. I emphasize that this is a representative sample, not a comprehensive list of all those who could be called Commonwealthmen. I do not discuss the bishops John Hooper and Nicholas Ridley, for example. Nor do I treat John Hales in view of the research of Mary Dewar showing that in all probability the book commonly attributed to him, *A Discourse of the Commonweal of This Realm of England,* was the work of Sir Thomas Smith. See note 5 in chapter 1 of this book. Throughout the following discussion I will use John Ponet, sometimes at some length, by way of comparison to the Commonwealthmen. He seems to have been sympathetic to many of their ideas, although he is not ordinarily considered one of them.

Unless otherwise indicated, I have relied for information about the lives of the Commonwealthmen on the *Dictionary of National Biography* and Christina Hallowell Garrett, *The Marian Exiles: A Study in the Origins of Elizabethan Puritanism* (Cambridge: Cambridge University Press, 1938), esp. her "Biographical Census," 67–349.

On the ideas of the Commonwealthmen: Allen, *History of Political Thought*, 138–142; S. T. Bindoff, *Tudor England* (Harmondsworth, Middlesex: Penguin, 1950), 129–135; Whitney R. D. Jones, *The Tudor Commonwealth 1529–1559: A Study of the Impact of Mid-Tudor England upon Contemporary Concepts of the Nature and Duties of the Commonwealth* (London: University of London, Athlone Press, 1970), 32–42; W. K. Jordan, *Edward VI: The Young King: The Protectorship of the Duke of Somerset* (London: Allen and Unwin, 1968), 416–438; W. K. Jordan, *Edward VI: The Threshold of Power: The Dominance of the Duke of Northumberland* (London: Allen and Unwin, 1970), 278–292; Skinner, *Foundations*, 1:224–228.

46. J. Scarisbrick, *Henry VIII* (London: Eyre and Spottiswoode, 1968), 525.

47. For Latimer, see Allan G. Chester, *Hugh Latimer, Apostle to the English* (Philadelphia: University of Pennsylvania Press, 1954), and Harold S. Darby, *Hugh Latimer* (London: Epworth Press, 1953).

48. Apparently neither Latimer nor More liked each other, according to Chester, *Hugh Latimer*, 99.

49. Quoted in ibid., 172.

50. Quoted in Darby, *Hugh Latimer*, 247.

51. On Becon, see Derrick Sherwin Bailey, *Thomas Becon and the Reformation of the Church in England* (Edinburgh and London: Oliver and Boyd, 1952).

52. Thomas Becon, *The Catechism of Thomas Becon . . . with Other Pieces Written by Him in the Reign of King Edward the Sixth*, ed. John Ayre, for the Parker Society (Cambridge: Cambridge University Press, 1844), 424. For our purposes this is the most useful collection of Becon's many works. Two others, however, are of interest, both edited by John Ayre for the Parker Society: *The Early Works of Thomas Becon, S. T. P., Being the Treatises Published by Him in the Reign of King Henry VIII* (Cambridge: Cambridge University Press, 1843), and *Prayers and Other Pieces of Thomas Becon, S. T. P.* (Cambridge: Cambridge University Press, 1844).

53. Bailey, *Thomas Becon*, xiv.

54. Garrett, *Marian Exiles*, 53.

55. Ibid., 16.

56. Ibid., 15, 19.

57. Ibid., 59.

58. Latimer, *Sermons*, 1:101.

59. For example, Becon, *Catechism*, 587–593; *Early Works*, 253. Also see: Brinklow, *Complaynt*, 10, 75; the anonymous *Policies to Reduce This Realme of Englande vnto a Prosperus Wealthe and Estate* (1548), in R. H. Tawney and Eileen Power, eds., *Tudor Economic Documents: Being Select Documents Illustrating the Economic and Social History of Tudor England* (London: Longmans, Green, 1924), 3:328–329.

60. Julian Cornwall, *Revolt of the Peasantry 1549* (London: Routledge and Kegan Paul, 1977), 25.

61. R. H. Tawney, *The Agrarian Problem of the Sixteenth Century* (London: Macmillan, 1911), 13.

62. Crowley, *The Select Works*, ed. J. M. Cowper (London: Kegan Paul, Trench, Trübner, for the Early English Text Society, 1872), 21, 22, 39, 73, 131, 149, 163. Although this is the sole collection of Crowley's works, readers should also consult *The Fable of Philargyrie the Great Gigant* (London: Emery Walker, 1931). This is an anonymous, unpaginated volume of 64 pages (including the title page) printed by Crowley's press in 1551. It seems clear that he was the author. For Brinklow, *Complaynt*, 5, 10, 59, 73.

63. On Latimer's use, see, for example, *Sermons*, 1:299; 2:26, 27, 33. Becon, *Catechism*, 115, 116, 308, 432, 434, 593, 594, 598, 601, 602, 616. Thomas Lever, *Sermons*, ed. Edward Arber (London: Constable, 1895), 28, 29, 33, 67, 72, 74, 75, 104, 110, 142.

64. Becon, *Catechism*, 599. Lever, *Sermons*, 72.

65. Lever, *Sermons*, 67, 75.

66. Lever, *Sermons*, 126, 127, 141, 142. Brinklow's only use is in *Complaynt*, 73.

67. Lever, *Sermons*, 109.

68. Crowley, *Select Works*, 86.

69. Becon, *Catechism*, 435.

70. John Ponet, *A Shorte Treatise of Politike Pouuer, and of the true obedience which subiectes owe to kynges and other ciuile gouernours, with an exhortacion to all naturall Englishe men . . .* (1556). Probably first published either in Strasbourg or possibly Zurich, it is reproduced with separate pagination (pp. 1–183) at the end of Winthrop S. Hudson, *John Ponet (1516?–1556), Advocate of Limited Monarchy* (Chicago: University of Chicago Press, 1942). On Ponet, in addition to Hudson, see: Allen, *History of Political Thought*, 118–120; Christopher Morris, *Political Thought in England: Tyndale to Hooker* (London: Oxford University Press, 1953), 146–152; Skinner, *Foundations*, 2:221–230, 234–235, 238–241, 357; Neal Wood, "Cicero and the Political Thought of the Early English Renaissance," *Modern Language Quarterly* 51 (1990): 185–207; W. Gordon Zeeveld, *Foundations of Tudor Policy* (Cambridge, Mass.: Harvard University Press, 1948), 241–261, 270.

71. Garrett, *Marian Exiles*, 253: "Of John Ponet the man, there is lit-

tle good to be said: he was quarrelsome, avaricious, unscrupulous and a coward." This estimate is much more severe than Hudson's.

72. Ponet, *Shorte Treatise*, 8, 9, 22, 26, 27, 59, 98, 105, 110, 111, 145, 154. Occasionally the meaning is ambiguous, as when he referred to "mixed state" (pp. 9, 26). Did he mean *state* as condition or in the institutional sense? For Starkey's use of *state*, see chapter 7 of this book. On Ponet's conception of *state*, see Skinner, *Foundations*, 2:357, and Wood, "Cicero."

73. Ponet, *Shorte Treatise*, 2, 11, 25, 99, 100, 105, 125, 141, 145, 154.

74. Ponet, *Shorte Treatise*, 8.

75. Ponet, *Shorte Treatise*, 9, although as indicated in n. 72 above *state* in this sense might mean condition.

76. Ponet, *Shorte Treatise*, 9, 26. See nn. 72 and 75 above.

77. Ponet, *Shorte Treatise*, 61.

78. Ponet, *Shorte Treatise*, 98.

79. Ponet, *Shorte Treatise*, for example, 3, 47, 48, 50, 51, 54.

80. Ponet, *Shorte Treatise*, 108. For other examples of the body-politic metaphor, 11, 22, 25, 47, 61, 69, 105, 152, 153, 162–163.

81. Ponet, *Shorte Treatise*, esp. 11 and 152.

82. Latimer, *Sermons*, 1:99–100.

83. Latimer, *Sermons*, 1:215.

84. Becon, *Catechism*, 303, in his book, *A New Catechism*, addressed to his children; and 511, in an abbreviated version of the former, *The Principles of Christian Religion*, dedicated to young Thomas Cecil, son of Sir William Cecil and Cheke's daughter.

85. Becon, *Early Works*, 256; *Prayers*, 21.

86. Becon, *Catechism*, 616, in *The Fortress of the Faithful*, dedicated to Sir John Robsart, father of the ill-fated bride of Sir Edmund Dudley's grandson (Elizabeth's earl of Leicester), and ancestor of Sir Robert Walpole.

87. Ponet, *Shorte Treatise*, 40, 50.

88. Ponet, *Shorte Treatise*, 9, 26, 54, 78, 99.

89. Ponet, *Shorte Treatise*, 98.

90. Ponet, *Shorte Treatise*, 18, 54, 117.

91. Clement Armstrong, *A Treatise Concerninge the Staple*, in Tawney and Power, eds., *Tudor Economic Documents*, 3:105.

92. Tawney and Power, eds., *Tudor Economic Documents*, 3:313. Italics are the anonymous author's.

93. Thomas Smith, *De republica Anglorum*, ed. Mary Dewar (Cambridge: Cambridge University Press, 1982), 57.

94. Crowley, *Select Works*, 11.

95. Becon, *Catechism*, 593; also *Early Works*, 253; *Prayers*, 5.

96. Becon, *Catechism*, 593.

97. Tawney and Power, eds., *Tudor Economic Documents*, 3:313–314.

98. Sir William Forrest, "Pleasaunt Poesye of Princely Practice," in *England in the Reign of King Henry the Eighth*, ed. S. J. Herrtage (London: Trübner, for Early English Text Society, 1878), xcv.

99. Crowley, *Select Works*, 20. Latimer, *Sermons*, 1:279–280.

100. Becon, *Catechism*, 430.

101. Lever, *Sermons*, 77.

102. Becon, *Catechism*, 434.

103. Lever, *Sermons*, 123–124.

104. Lever, *Sermons*, 121, 123.

105. Tawney and Power, eds., *Tudor Economic Documents*, 3:327.

106. Crowley, *Select Works*, 112.

107. Crowley, *Select Works*, 144. Latimer, *Sermons*, 1:248. Lever, *Sermons*, 40.

108. Lever, *Sermons*, 39.

109. Becon, *Catechism*, 432.

110. Becon, *Catechism*, 434, 599; *Early Works*, 126; *Prayers*, 12.

111. Crowley, *Select Works*, 161. Becon, *Catechism*, 432; *Early Works*, 453.

112. Crowley, *Select Works*, 46–47, 165. Latimer, *Sermons*, 1:102.

113. Latimer, *Sermons*, 1:249.

114. Becon, *Catechism*, 115; *Early Works*, 253. For Latimer's autobiographical passage, see above and his *Sermons*, 1:101.

115. Crowley, *Select Works*, 41–42, 46–47, 87–88, 133, 165–166. Latimer, *Sermons*, 1:98–99. Becon, *Catechism*, 108, 590, 599. Lever, *Sermons*, 77. Also Forrest, "Pleasaunt Poesye," xcv.

116. Latimer, *Sermons*, 1:98–99. Becon, *Catechism*, 108.

117. Crowley, *Select Works*, 166.

118. Crowley, *Select Works*, 46–47.

119. Lever, *Sermons*, 77.

120. Crowley, *Select Works*, 40–41, 123, 166–167. Lever, *Sermons*, 129–130.

121. Crowley, *Select Works*, 41.

122. Crowley, *Select Works*, 167.

123. Lever, *Sermons*, 129.

124. Crowley, *Select Works*, 33–34. Latimer, *Sermons*, 1:279. Becon, *Catechism*, 108; *Early Works*, 253. Lever, *Sermons*, 128–129. Also Forrest, "Pleasaunt Poesye," lxxxvii.

125. Becon, *Early Works*, 253.

126. Lever, *Sermons*, 128–129.

127. William Harrison, *The Description of England*, ed. G. Edelen (Ithaca, N.Y.: Cornell University Press, for the Folger Shakespeare Library, 1968), 248–252, for detailed examples.

128. Ibid., 252.

129. Latimer, *Sermons*, 1:410. Becon, *Catechism*, 106. Lever, *Sermons*,

44. On usury also see Crowley, *Select Works*, 49–51; Latimer, *Sermons*, 1:213, 401, 404.

130. Crowley, *Select Works*, 49–51.

131. Sir John Fortescue, *De laudibus legum Anglie*, trans. and ed. S. B. Chrimes, general preface by H. D. Hazeltine (Cambridge: Cambridge University Press, 1942), 87–88; and chapter 4 of this book.

132. Becon, *Catechism*, 435.

133. Lever, *Sermons*, 23.

134. Lever, *Sermons*, 63.

135. Crowley, *Select Works*, 133.

136. Tawney and Power, eds., *Tudor Economic Documents*, 3:328–329.

137. Especially, for example, on covetousness, ambition, and pride: Crowley, *Select Works*, 64, 65, 82–83, 86, 91, 132, 161, 167; *Fable of Philargyrie*, passim. Latimer, *Sermons*, 1:247, 249; 2:26–27, 33, 214; "Letter to Henry VIII," in *Sermons*, 2:303–304. Becon, *Catechism*, 114, 431–434, 436, 587–591, 593, 602, 617–618; *Early Works*, 41, 126–127, 198–205, 222–223, 453–455; *Prayers*, 59–60. Lever, *Sermons*, 37, 89, 103–104, 107, 110–114, 119, 126–131, 140–143.

138. C. B. Macpherson, *The Political Theory of Possessive Individualism: Hobbes to Locke* (Oxford: Clarendon Press, 1962).

139. Latimer, *Sermons*, 1:249; 2:33.

140. Becon, *Catechism*, 114, 593; *Prayers*, 59. Crowley, *Select Works*, 161.

141. Becon, *Catechism*, 114–115.

142. Lever, *Sermons*, 89, 103–104.

143. Latimer, "Letter of Henry VIII," *Sermons*, 2:303–304. Becon, *Catechism*, 602.

144. Latimer, *Sermons*, 1:227.

145. Crowley, *Select Works*, 132, 142, 143, 146, 164.

146. Crowley, *Select Works*, 132–133, 142–143.

147. Crowley, *Select Works*, 144, 149.

148. Becon, *Catechism*, 432, 600.

149. Becon, *Catechism*, 436.

150. Becon, *Catechism*, 434.

151. Becon, *Catechism*, 598–599. Cf. with Ponet, *Shorte Treatise*, 109–110.

152. Becon, *Catechism*, 599. For his use of "caterpillars of the commonweal," see above, p. 174; *Early Works*, 126; *Prayers*, 12.

153. Becon, *Catechism*, 599–603.

154. Lever, *Sermons*, 68.

155. Lever, *Sermons*, 119–124.

156. Crowley, *Select Works*, 98. Latimer, *Sermons*, 2:26–28. Becon, *Catechism*, 107. Lever, *Sermons*, 64, 68, 89, 107, 110–114.

157. Crowley, *Select Works*, 27–28, 124, 139–140, 153–156. Latimer,

Sermons, 2:24, 28. Becon, *Catechism,* 107, 431–432, 587–591; *Early Works,* 255–256; *Prayers,* 21–22. Lever, *Sermons,* 64, 67, 68, 89, 110–119.

158. Lever, *Sermons,* 116.

159. Lever, *Sermons,* 115. For Becon, *Prayers,* 21–22, they are not only "dumb dogs" but also "unshamefaced dogs" and "idle lubbers."

160. Lever, *Sermons,* 119.

161. Crowley, *Select Works,* 41–42. Becon, *Early Works,* 253; *Prayers,* 25. Latimer, *Sermons,* 1:270–271. Lever, *Sermons,* 29.

162. Lever, *Sermons,* 131.

163. Becon, *Early Works,* 253.

164. Crowley, *Select Works,* 82–83.

165. Becon, *Early Works,* 253, also 360; *Prayers,* 25.

166. Crowley, *Select Works,* 79, 80, 81. Latimer, *Sermons,* 1:98–99.

167. Latimer, *Sermons,* 1:99–100.

168. Becon, *Catechism,* 308. See chapters 4, 5, and 7 of this book for the views of Fortescue, Dudley, and Starkey.

169. Becon, *Catechism,* 601.

170. Becon, *Catechism,* 601.

171. Becon, *Catechism,* 601.

172. Latimer, *Sermons,* 1:371.

173. Becon, *Catechism,* 593; *Early Works,* 211–222, 286–287.

174. Crowley, *Select Works,* 21.

175. Crowley, *Select Works,* 22.

176. Crowley, *Select Works,* 149.

177. For their views on civil obedience and insurrection: Crowley, *Select Works,* 68–69, 118, 133, 135–138, 141–145, 149, 164. Latimer, *Sermons,* 1:249, 298–300, 371, 373–374, 512. Becon, *Catechism,* 90, 311, 328, 601, 617–618; *Early Works,* 211–222, 286–287; *Prayers,* 26, 42–43. Lever, *Sermons,* 24–26, 34–37.

178. Latimer, *Sermons,* 1:249.

179. Crowley, *Select Works,* 143–144.

180. Crowley, *Select Works,* 164.

181. Lever, *Sermons,* 26.

182. Lever, *Sermons,* 35.

183. Lever, *Sermons,* 37.

184. Latimer, "Letter to Henry VIII," *Sermons,* 2:302–308.

185. Latimer, *Sermons,* 1:249.

186. Latimer, *Sermons,* 1:250–251. Latimer related the story ironically, since More, he suggested, prohibited the publication of one of Bilney's religious books on the very grounds that he himself was opposing.

187. Becon, *Catechism,* 596.

188. According to Garrett, *Marian Exiles,* 257, and Hudson, *John*

Ponet, 196, Hotman was in Strasbourg at the time Ponet was writing, apparently knew him, and may have read the *Shorte Treatise*.

189. The subsequent summary of Ponet's complex argument to which much of the book is devoted scarcely does justice to it. See *Shorte Treatise*, esp. 7–8, 10, 12–13, 21, 26–28, 33–34, 39–40, 42–44, 50–55, 60–61, 69–70, 74–76, 78, 81–89, 95–96, 98–101, 105–126, 158–165. Also see my article, "Cicero." Zeeveld, *Foundations of Tudor Policy*, 241–261, argues that Starkey was a great influence on Ponet, indeed his "philosophical antecedent" (p. 261). Zeeveld maintains that Ponet knew the *Dialogue* through Morison (p. 243), also in exile in Strasbourg, and that he was reading it in 1555 (p. 260). Thomas F. Mayer, "Faction and Ideology: Thomas Starkey's *Dialogue*," *The Historical Journal* 28 (1985): 24–25, in general is doubtful that Ponet or anyone else ever saw the *Dialogue*, and in particular that the idea of the constable, attributed by both Hudson and Zeeveld to Starkey's influence, was in fact derived by Ponet from him. See chapter 7 of this book.

190. Forrest, "Pleasaunt Poesy," xc. Crowley, *Select Works*, 37–38. Latimer, *Sermons*, 1:210, 211. Becon, *Catechism*, 101; *Early Works*, 444–446; *Prayers*, 60–61. Lever, *Sermons*, 87, 106.

191. Crowley, *Select Works*, 38.

192. Ponet, *Shorte Treatise*, 5.

193. Tawney and Power, eds., *Tudor Economic Documents*, 3:323.

194. Latimer, *Sermons*, 1:215.

195. Forrest, "Pleasaunt Poesy," xci. Ponet, *Shorte Treatise*, 79.

196. Crowley, *Select Works*, 156.

197. Crowley, *Select Works*, 156. Latimer, *Sermons*, 2:38–40. Becon, *Catechism*, 615. Lever, *Sermons*, 31. Also Ponet, *Shorte Treatise*, 79.

198. Latimer, *Sermons*, 1:214.

199. Becon, *Catechism*, 616; *Early Works*, 444–446; *Prayers*, 60–61.

200. Lever, *Sermons*, 106. This is more briefly what Becon said in *Catechism*, 114–115, and also *Early Works*, 2, 173; *Prayers*, 12, 25, 36–38. Latimer, *Sermons*, 2:35–38.

201. Crowley, *Select Works*, 157, 163–164. Latimer, *Sermons*, 1:399. Becon, *Catechism*, 111, 387–388, 398, 538, 588, 601. Lever, *Sermons*, 33.

202. Crowley, *Select Works*, 163.

203. Latimer, *Sermons*, 1:399.

204. Latimer, *Sermons*, 1:249.

205. Becon, *Catechism*, 436. For Dudley, see chapter 5 of this book.

206. Latimer, *Sermons*, 1:376; 2:201–202, 214. Becon, *Catechism*, 111–112, 387–388, 398.

207. Brinklow, *Complaynt*, 17. See above, p. 158.

208. Crowley, *Select Works*, 153, 157, 164.

209. Latimer, *Sermons*, 1:399.

210. Becon, *Catechism*, 538, 588.

211. Lever, *Sermons*, 107, 110.

212. Ponet, *Shorte Treatise*, 95. On his conception of government as a trust, 1, 13, 18, 107.

9: SIR THOMAS SMITH'S NEW "MORAL PHILOSOPHY"

1. On Smith: Mary Dewar, *Sir Thomas Smith: A Tudor Intellectual in Office* (London: University of London, Athlone Press, 1964); Mary Dewar, "The Memorandum *For the Understanding of the Exchange*: Its Authorship and Dating," *Economic History Review*, 2d ser., 17 (1965): 476–487; Mary Dewar, "The Authorship of the *Discourse of the Commonweal*," *Economic History Review*, 2d ser., 19 (1966): 388–400; and the introductions to her editions of Smith's two major works: *A Discourse of the Commonweal of This Realm of England: Attributed to Sir Thomas Smith* (Charlottesville: University Press of Virginia, for the Folger Shakespeare Library, 1969), and *De republica Anglorum* (Cambridge: Cambridge University Press, 1982). These are the texts used below, cited *D* and *R*, respectively.

Also of value are Arthur B. Ferguson, *The Articulate Citizen and the English Renaissance* (Durham, N.C.: Duke University Press, 1965), 279–314, 355–362, 385–396; E. A. J. Johnson, *Predecessors of Adam Smith: The Growth of British Economic Thought* (London: King, 1937; New York: Prentice Hall, 1937), chap. 2; Whitney R. D. Jones, *The Tudor Commonwealth 1529–1559: A Study of the Impact of Mid-Tudor England upon Contemporary Concepts of the Nature and Duties of the Commonwealth* (London: University of London, Athlone Press, 1970), 105–106, 141–142, 197–201; David McNally, *Political Economy and the Rise of Capitalism: A Reinterpretation* (Berkeley, Los Angeles, London: University of California Press, 1988), 25–28, 194–195; Joan Thirsk, *Economic Policy and Projects: The Development of a Consumer Society in Early Modern England* (Oxford: Clarendon Press, 1978), 13–15, 16, 18, 24, 27, 29, 33, 47, 55, 67, 78, 127. Also see my essay (derived in part from this chapter): "Foundations of Political Economy: The New Moral Philosophy of Sir Thomas Smith," in *Political Thought and the Tudor Commonwealth: Deep Structure, Discourse and Disguise*, ed. Paul A. Fideler and J. F. Mayer (London: Routledge, 1992), chap. 6.

2. Contrary to a common view, Smith was never ordained a priest, although he was the recipient of a benefice and became dean of Carlisle. See Dewar, *Sir Thomas Smith*, 29–30, 44.

3. Quoted in Dewar's introduction, *D*, xx.

4. John Strype, *The Life of the Learned Sir Thomas Smith*, new ed. (Oxford: Clarendon Press, 1820), iv–v.

5. Dewar, "The Memorandum," persuasively argues that "For the Un-

derstanding of the Exchange" was written not by Sir Francis Gresham but by Smith. This important and influential document dealt with the questions of recoinage, the exchange rate, the foreign debt, and the carrying trade.

In "The Wages of the Roman Footsoldier" Smith engaged in extensive and systematic calculation of the current English equivalent of the value of Roman money.

6. Dewar, esp. "The Authorship." See n. 5 of chapter 1 of this book.

7. Quoted in Dewar's introduction, *D*, xxiv.

8. On English and Continental economic thinking before the mid-sixteenth century, see chapter 3 of this book.

9. Eli F. Heckscher, *Mercantilism*, trans. M. Shapiro (London: Allen and Unwin, 1934), 2:227. Heckscher and Schumpeter were writing before Mary Dewar attributed the authorship of *D* to Smith. Of economic historians Heckscher seems to be the most appreciative of *D*, for example, 2:20, 46 ff., 131, 227 ff., 278–279, 293, 301, 310, 313–314.

10. Quoted in Dewar's introduction, *D*, xvi. In the context of the Commonwealthman, Bindoff (quoted in Dewar's introduction, p. xiv) describes the *Discourse* as "the movement's literary monument."

11. Schumpeter, *History of Economic Analysis*, ed. E. B. Schumpeter (New York: Oxford University Press, 1954), 166.

12. Hutchison, *Before Adam Smith: The Emergence of Political Economy, 1662–1776* (Oxford: Blackwell, 1988), 20–21.

13. Quoted in Dewar's introduction, *D*, xxii.

14. Quoted in Dewar's introduction, *R*, 1.

15. *R*, 51; Ferguson, *Articulate Citizen*, 395.

16. *R*, 49.

17. *R*, 52.

18. *R*, 50.

19. Plato, *Republic*, 338c–e, 340c–e.

20. *R*, 53.

21. *R*, 53.

22. Thomas Becon, *The Catechism of Thomas Becon*, ed. John Ayre, for the Parker Society (Cambridge: Cambridge University Press, 1844), 601. See chapter 8 of this book.

23. *R*, 51–52.

24. *R*, 52.

25. On the attitudes concerning civil disobedience of the Commonwealthmen and Ponet, see chapter 8 of this book.

26. According to Strype, *The Life of the Learned Sir Thomas Smith*, 276–277, Smith's library, 1 August 1566, in the gallery of his country house, High Hill, Essex, contained Machiavelli's *The Prince, Discourses*, and *Florentine History*.

27. *R*, 52. Cicero, *De officiis*, III, 19–32; Machiavelli, *Discourses*, I, ix.

28. *R,* 52.

29. *R,* 61.

30. Smith used "estate" to refer to the condition of the realm, *R,* 50, 51, 52. On Starkey's and Ponet's vocabulary, see chapters 7 and 8 of this book.

31. *R,* 58.

32. *R,* 51, 52, 62, 63, 88.

33. *R,* 49; for other examples of the use of "governement," 51, 52, 54, 58, 59, 88, 144.

34. *R,* 78. On the question of Smith and sovereignty, see Ferguson, *Articulate Citizen,* 386–387.

35. *R,* 88. Parliament "representeth and hath the power of the whole realme both the head and the bodie. For everie Englishman is entended to bee there present, either in person or by procuration and attornies . . . from the Prince . . . to the lowest person of Englande. And the consent of the Parliament is taken to be everie mans consent" (p. 79).

36. *R,* 88. For detailed powers of parliament:

> . . . abrogateth olde laws, maketh newe, giveth orders for thinges past, and for thinges hereafter to be followed, changeth rightes, and possessions of private men, legittimateth bastards, establisheth formes of religion, altereth weightes and measures, giveth formes of succession to the crowne, defineth of doubtfull rightes, whereof is no lawe alreadie made, appointeth subsidies, tailes, taxes, and impositions, giveth most free pardons and absolutions, re-storeth in blood and name as the highest court, condemneth or absolveth them whom the Prince will put to that triall (p. 78).

37. *R,* 85–88.

38. Bodin, *Six Books of the Commonwealth* (1576), book 1, chaps. 1, 8. Smith, of course, was writing a decade earlier.

39. "Secular," in this and other contexts relating to Smith's concept of the state, means the absence of concern with religious and moral matters. Judging from what he said in the *Discourse* and *Republica,* Smith conceived of the state as having to do with worldly affairs—defense, security of person and property, economic well-being. From both the economic and constitutional standpoints, he did not refer to God (except in passing), natural law, or the church in respect either to the origins, purpose, institutions, policies, or actions of the state. Of course, he might have assumed such considerations, but on the basis of these two books, it would be an unwarranted assumption to conclude that he did. Smith's secularization of the state in the above sense would have been consistent with what appeared to be his fundamental Lutheran or Augustinian religious persuasion.

40. Also *D,* 12.

41. *R,* 54, 55, 56, 58, 62, 144. On Fortescue see chapter 4 of this book.

42. *R,* 54. On Elyot see chapter 7 of this book.

43. *R*, 57, 58, 59, 60. On Fortescue and Starkey see chapters 4 and 7 of this book.

44. *R*, 57.

45. Smith used "society" three times to denote the family (*R*, 58) and implied that a village is a society (p. 59).

46. *R*, 57, 59, 60.

47. *R*, 57.

48. The first major English thinker after Smith to use "civil society" seems to have been Richard Hooker, *Of the Laws of Ecclesiastical Polity* (1593), I, x, 3, 4, 12; I, xvi, 7. Hobbes used "civil society" frequently in *De cive*, much less so in *Leviathan*, where he favored "commonwealth." He likewise occasionally employed "state" in both works. "Commonwealth" was the clear choice of James Harrington in *Oceana* (1656). Locke, *Second Treatise of Government*, chap. 10, identified "commonwealth" with *civitas* or the state, as did Hobbes, *Leviathan* (Penguin), chap. 17, p. 227. "State" seldom appeared in the *Second Treatise*, Locke using "commonwealth" interchangeably with "civil society" or "political society." It may possibly be significant that Rousseau constantly employed *l'état* and *société* in the *Social Contract*, not "civil society." One of his rare uses of the latter began the second part of the *Second Discourse*.

49. Cicero, *De re publica*, 1, 39 (Loeb Classical Library translation).

50. Jean Bodin, *Six Books of the Commonwealth*, book I, chaps. 1, 2 (Tooley trans.)

51. Sir Thomas Elyot, *The Book Named the Governor*, ed. S. E. Lehmberg (London and New York: Dent, Everymans Library, 1962), 1.

52. Richard Morison, *A Remedy for Sedition* (1536), quoted in G. R. Elton, *Policy and Police: The Enforcement of the Reformation in the Age of Thomas Cromwell* (Cambridge: Cambridge University Press, 1972), 202.

53. Thomas Starkey, *A Dialogue between Pole and Lupset*, ed. T. F. Mayer, Camden Fourth Series, vol. 37 (London: Royal Historical Society, 1989), 34. Mayer's editorial symbols have been omitted.

54. *R*, 57.

55. *R*, 59, also 61.

56. Cf. Hobbes, *Leviathan* (Penguin), chap. 18, pp. 228–229:

> A *Commonwealth* is said to be *Instituted*, when a *Multitude* of men do Agree, and *Covenant, everyone, with every one*, that to whatsoever *Man*, or *Assembly of Men*, shall be given by the major part, the *Right to Present* the Person of them all . . . to the end, to live peaceably amongst themselves, and be protected against other men.

57. *R*, 61.

58. *R*, 51.

59. Hobbes, *Leviathan* (Penguin), chap. 30, p. 376: "But by Safety

here, is not meant a bare Preservation, but also other Contentments of life, which every man by lawfull Industry, without danger, or hurt to the Commonwealth, shall acquire to himselfe."

60. *R*, 62, 63.

61. R. H. Tawney and Eileen Power, eds., *Tudor Economic Documents: Being Select Documents Illustrating the Economic and Social History of Tudor England* (London: Longmans, Green, 1924), 3:313.

62. Cf. John Locke's use of "free men" in his account of the institution of political society in *Second Treatise*, chap. 8.

63. *R*, 64.

64. *R*, 141. Book 3, chap. 8, pp. 135–142, is entitled "Of Bondage and Bondmen."

65. *R*, 76.

66. *R*, 76–77.

67. See Ann Kussmaul, *Servants in Husbandry in Early Modern England* (Cambridge: Cambridge University Press, 1981).

68. The conclusion of Skinner, *The Foundations of Modern Political Thought* (Cambridge: Cambridge University Press, 1978), 2:349–358. He refers to both Starkey and Ponet. Also see his essay "The State," *Political Innovation and Conceptual Change*, ed. Terence Ball, James Farr, Russell L. Hansen (Cambridge: Cambridge University Press, 1989), 90–131.

69. Thomas Wilson, *A Discourse uppon Usurye: By waye of dialogue and oracions, for the better vanitye and more delite of all those that shall reade thys treatise*, with historical introduction by R. H. Tawney (New York: Harcourt Brace, 1925). Wilson's dialogue is found on pp. 173–384 of this edition. Examples of his use of *state* in the institutional sense: 204–205, 222, 270–271, 311, 329, 375, 385.

70. *R*, 58–60.

71. See n. 48 of this chapter.

72. Mathias Gelzer, *The Roman Nobility*, trans. Robin Seager (Oxford: Blackwell, 1969), 137.

73. *D*, 11.

74. *D*, 11.

75. *D*, 13.

76. *D*, 12.

77. *D*, 29.

78. *D*, 29–30. Compare with More and Starkey.

79. *D*, 12.

80. *D*, 13.

81. *D*, 15.

82. *D*, 15, 16.

83. *D*, 16.

84. *D*, 75, 105. This second obvious reference to More is in the section (pp. 104–116) of the 1549 draft omitted in the 1581 edition.

85. *D*, 16, 29, 31, 107, 118, and perhaps the reference on 114 to the tale of Gyges ring, possibly derived from the *Republic*, 359d–360d.

86. *D*, 106, also 71, 72, 105.

87. *D*, 16, 59, 116, 134.

88. *D*, 28, 29, 31, 59, 75, 91, 134, 141.

89. *D*, 16–17.

90. *R*, 54. Smith referred to Plato, perhaps thinking of the *Laws*, 691c–d.

91. *R*, 51.

92. *R*, 62.

93. See in general, *D*, 54, 55, 58–60, 118, 119.

94. For example, *D*, 47–48.

95. *D*, 118.

96. *D*, 58–59.

97. *D*, 59–60.

98. M. M. Goldsmith, *Private Vices, Public Benefits: Bernard Mandeville's Social and Political Thought* (Cambridge: Cambridge University Press, 1985), 114–115.

99. *D*, 116.

100. *D*, 51–53.

101. *D*, 51.

102. *D*, 52.

103. *D*, 53.

104. *D*, 54–61.

105. *D*, 49, 50, 89, 92, 126.

106. *D*, 92–104.

107. *D*, 93.

108. *D*, 94.

109. *D*, 38.

110. *D*, 69, 101.

111. *D*, 95.

112. *D*, 96.

113. *D*, 97.

114. *D*, 98. Hugh Latimer, *Sermons*, ed. G. E. Corrie (Cambridge: Cambridge University Press, 1844), 1:250–251. Latimer cited More as the source. See chapter 8 of this book.

115. *D*, 98.

116. *D*, 101.

117. Smith replaced pp. 102–116 of the 1549 draft with a new section for the version that was published posthumously in 1581, pp. 143–146 in Dewar's appendix A of *D*.

118. *D*, 143.

119. *D*, 144–145.

120. *D*, 96.

121. *D*, 96, 98. The "chiefest grief," 95.

122. *D*, 95–96.

123. Cf. Ferguson, *Articulate Citizen*, 385:

> In its economic aspects, at least, the commonwealth has become for Smith a mechanism of forces, impersonal and amoral in character, subject to analysis and manipulation by intelligent policy. It was still not a developing thing. . . . But Smith is beginning to see economic life as a machine functioning according to laws of its own, natural laws that propel society toward ends of wealth and power rather than of stability.

124. On clocks in medieval and early modern Europe: Daniel J. Boorstin, *The Discoverers* (New York: Random House, 1983), 36–53, 64–72; Carlo M. Cipolla, ed., *The Fontana Economic History of Europe* (London: Collins/Fontana, 1972), 1:87–88, 2:282–283; Lynn White, Jr., *Medieval Technology and Social Change* (Oxford: Clarendon Press, 1962), 120–128.

125. For the drawing see David Piper, ed., *The Genius of British Painting* (London: Book Club Associates, 1975), 68. The new clocks contributed to an acute awareness of time and an abhorrence of idleness, in Thomas More, for example. See Richard Marius, *Thomas More: A Biography* (London: Dent, 1985), 12, 165, 224–225, 229.

126. But the clock analogy, first applied by Nicole Oresme (1330?–1382) to the workings of the universe constructed by the divine clockmaker, became commonplace in this regard in the early modern period. See Boorstin, *The Discoverers*, 71–72.

127. On the clock analogy and Steuart, see Albert O. Hirschman, *The Passions and the Interests: Political Arguments for Capitalism before Its Triumph* (Princeton, N.J.: Princeton University Press, 1981), 86–87.

128. Ferguson, *Articulate Citizen*, 308–309.

129. *D*, 62.

130. *D*, 86. Italics supplied.

131. *D*, 86, also 99.

132. This seems to be essentially at odds with Smith's mercantilism.

133. Erasmus, *The Education of a Christian Prince*, trans. Lester K. Born (New York: Columbia University Press, 1936), 170–171.

134. *R*, 58–60.

135. *D*, 63.

136. *D*, 73.

137. *D*, 87–88.

138. *D*, 89.

139. Jean Bodin, *Six Books of the Commonwealth*, book 1, chap. 2.

140. Gerrard de Malynes, *A Treatise of the Canker of England's Commonwealth* (1601), in Tawney and Power, eds., *Tudor Economic Documents*, 3:386.

141. See Ellen Meiksins Wood, "The State and Popular Sovereignty in French Political Thought: A Genealogy of Rousseau's 'General Will,'" *History of Political Thought* 4 (1983): 298–300; MacNally, *Political Economy*, 68–72.

142. For example, see John Locke, *Some Considerations of the Consequences of the Lowering of Interest, and Raising the Value of Money* (1692), in *The Works of John Locke*, 9th ed. (London: 1794), 4:19–20, 72.

143. For these remarks see chapter 8 of this book.

144. Smith, however, subscribed to the English hierarchical society, based on family and property, he described in *Republica*.

145. *D*, 83–84. Smith planned and built a fine house for himself in Essex. He complained (p. 84) about the furnishing and decoration of such buildings with imported materials, which entailed a further drain of English treasure abroad.

146. On this point, see Jones, *Tudor Commonwealth*, 105–106.

147. *D*, 18–19.

148. *D*, 40.

149. *D*, 53.

150. *D*, 39.

151. Also see *D*, 40.

152. *D*, 33.

153. *D*, 33.

154. *D*, 34–35.

155. *D*, 35.

156. *D*, 17–18.

157. *D*, 17.

158. *D*, 35.

159. *D*, 81.

160. *D*, 39–40.

161. See chapter 8 of this book, p. 167.

162. *D*, 42.

163. *D*, 21–22, 80.

164. *D*, 145.

165. For example, Joyce Youings, *Sixteenth-Century England* (Harmondsworth, Middlesex: Penguin, 1984), 143–144, and also the data in chapter 2 of this book.

166. *D*, 145.

167. *D*, 145–146.

168. *D*, 77–79.

169. *D*, 87.

170. *D*, 49.

171. *D*, 49–50.

172. *D*, 17.

173. *D*, 20–21.

174. *D*, 22.
175. On More and the triad, see chapter 6 of this book.
176. *D*, 118–119.
177. *D*, 119.
178. *D*, 54–56, 60–61.
179. *R*, 74–76.
180. *R*, 74.
181. *R*, 77.
182. Joan Thirsk, ed., *The Agrarian History of England*, vol. 4:1550–1640 (Cambridge: Cambridge University Press, 1967), 65; Eric Kerridge, "Agriculture, c. 1500–1793," in *V. C. H. Wiltshire*, vol. 4 (London, 1959), 57 ff., quoted in Robert Brenner, "The Agrarian Roots of European Capitalism," *Past and Present* 97 (1982): 95.
183. *D*, 50. See chapter 7 of this book for Starkey's defense of enclosure. Starkey and Smith must have been among the first to offer non-technical arguments for enclosure.
184. *D*, 54–56.
185. Also see *D*, 91.
186. *D*, 17–18, 121.
187. *D*, 123–124.
188. *D*, 87.
189. *D*, 89.
190. On the following, see *D*, 63–64, 87, 90–91, 123–126.
191. Thirsk, *Economic Policy and Projects*, 9.
192. Ibid., 1.
193. For some of Smith's references and recommendations for their production, *D*, 18, 62–66, 77–78, 87–88, 90–91, 121–126.
194. Thirsk, *Economic Policy and Projects*, 33.
195. Ibid., 29.
196. Ibid., 13, 24.
197. Ibid., 9.
198. *D*, 126–136.
199. *D*, 126–127.
200. *D*, 129.
201. *D*, 134–135.
202. *D*, 23–33, for the early discussion of learning and the universities.
203. *D*, 128.
204. *D*, 23.
205. *D*, 31.
206. *D*, 23.
207. *D*, 24, also 31.
208. *D*, 30–31.
209. *D*, 32–33.

210. Bacon, *The Advancement of Learning*, ed. G. W. Kitchen (London: Dent, Everymans Library, 1915), 61–69, and F. H. Anderson, *The Philosophy of Francis Bacon* (Chicago: University of Chicago Press, 1948), 17–22, 48–49, 294–297. Hobbes, *Leviathan*, (Penguin), 86–87, 383–386, 728; *Behemoth*, ed. Ferdinand Tönnies, introduction by M. M. Goldsmith, 2d ed. (London: Frank Cass, 1969), 23, 39–42, 56, 58–59, 147–148.

211. Although Locke did not explicitly call the universities into question in his writings, the frequent criticisms in the *Essay* of scholasticism, its abuse of language and wrangling over obscure and trivial points, were no doubt directed against the current university curricula. See *An Essay Concerning Human Understanding*, I, ii, 4, 27; III, iv, 9; III, x, 2, 6, 7, 9, 10; IV, iii, 30; IV, vi, 8; IV, vii, 11; IV, xvii, 4, 8.

212. See my essay "*Tabula Rasa*, Social Environmentalism, and the 'English Paradigm,'" *Journal of the History of Ideas* 53 (1992): 647–668.

213. For Wilson's life: Tawney's introduction to the *Discourse uppon Usury*, and *Dictionary of National Biography*. On Smith and Wilson: Dewar, *Sir Thomas Smith*, esp. 125, 134–135.

214. Again mention must be made of Alan Macfarlane's two books (cited in n. 4, chapter 1 of this book) in which he argues that in contrast to other Europeans, the English from the thirteenth century were thoroughgoing individualists who valued private property, individual liberty, and capitalist profit-seeking. If this was in fact the case, it is puzzling that only much later, beginning with the thought of the sixteenth century (for instance, Dudley, More, Starkey, Brinklow, the Commonwealthmen, Smith, Ponet, Wilson), did economic individualism first seem to present itself as a serious social problem. Economic individualism may not have been an entirely new phenomenon, but in our period it appears to have become so pervasive and intensive as to warrant agonizing concern by many socially conscious critics.

215. *Discourse uppon Usury*, 177, 182.

216. Ibid., 258.

217. Ibid., 353.

218. Ibid., 379.

219. Ibid., 177, 314.

220. Ibid., 384.

10: CONCLUSION

1. Much of what follows in the next few paragraphs is based on my article "*Tabula Rasa*, Social Environmentalism, and the 'English Paradigm,'" *Journal of the History of Ideas* 53 (1992): 647–668.

2. The radical Puritan attacks on the universities are discussed in Christopher Hill, *Antichrist in Seventeenth-Century England*, rev. ed. (London: Verso, 1990), 137–142.

3. Ernst Troeltsch, *The Social Teaching of the Christian Churches,* trans. Olive Wyon, introductory note by Charles Gore (London: Allen and Unwin; New York: Macmillan, 1931), 1:118–120, 2:554–555. See in particular the suggestive comments on St. Augustine in George Ovitt, Jr., *The Restoration of Perfection: Labor and Technology in Medieval Culture* (New Brunswick, N.J., and London: Rutgers University Press, 1987), 52–54, 98–200.

Index